Mixed Blessings

Laws, Religions, and Women's Rights in the Asia-Pacific Region

STUDIES IN RELIGION, SECULAR BELIEFS AND HUMAN RIGHTS

VOLUME 1

Mixed Blessings

Laws, Religions, and Women's Rights in the Asia-Pacific Region

Edited by
Amanda Whiting
and
Carolyn Evans

MARTINUS NIJHOFF PUBLISHERS
LEIDEN • BOSTON
2006

A C.I.P. record for this book is available from the Library of Congress.

ISSN: 1871-7829
ISBN-13: 978-90-04-15141-3
ISBN-10: 90-04-15141-9

PRINTED IN THE NETHERLANDS

For my grandparents, Alice and Colin Websdale
CME

For my daughter, Miriam
AJW

CONTENTS

CHAPTER SEVEN

CHAPTER EIGHT

CHAPTER NINE

ACKNOWLEDGMENTS

This book deals with a topic that is of great significance and it has taken several years to develop and complete. During that time we have been grateful for the assistance and support of a number of people.

The first of these is our outstanding research assistant Kathleen Kelly whose work was exemplary. We are also grateful to Professor Tim Lindsay for his encouragement and advice and for making funding available through the Asian Law Centre to assist with work on the book and to the Faculty of Law, University of Melbourne for its financial support. Chris Holt gave us wise advice in the early stages of the project, and we thank him for this.

In the initial stages of the project we were given direction and support by a number of generous academics in this field including Patricia Martinez, Juliet Sheen, Lori Beaman, Marion Maddox, Alice Tay, Jim Richardson, Virginia Hooker, Veronica Taylor, and Evalyn Ursua.

We are grateful to all at Martinus Nijhoff for their prompt and professional handling of the production of the book and in particular to Lindy Melman and Leonieke Aalders. We also acknowledge Angela Costi for her fine work on the index.

Finally, we are grateful to our families: Brendan, Gabriel and Miriam (for Amanda) and Stephen, Caitlin and Michael (for Carolyn) for their on-going support and love.

ABOUT THE AUTHORS

Margaret Bedggood

Margaret Bedggood is an Honorary Professor of Law at the School of Law, University of Waikato, Hamilton, Aotearoa/New Zealand, where she was the Dean from 1994 to 1999. She has a Masters degree in classics from the Universities of Auckland and London and a degree in law from the University of Otago, and has taught classics and law in a number of institutions and jurisdictions. She has published in the areas of labour law, torts, and human rights and her current research interests include the interface between human rights and religion and the implementation of human rights norms, especially economic, social and cultural rights in the domestic jurisdiction. She has a long standing interest in social justice issues and she was from 1989 to 1994 the Chief Commissioner of the Aotearoa/New Zealand Human Rights Commission. She was a member of the governing body of Amnesty International from 1999–2005 and of the Third Order of the Society of St. Francis in the Anglican Church.

Anne Black

Ann Black is a lecturer in law at the TC Beirne School of Law, The University of Queensland, Australia. She is on the Board of Management and a research fellow of the Center for Public, International and Comparative Law. Along with Jennifer Corrin Care she co-edits *LawAsia Journal*. She has undergraduate degrees in Arts, Social Work and Law (Hons), a Masters degree in Law from the University of Queensland and a Doctorate in Legal Science. Her SJD thesis was titled "Dispute resolution in Brunei Darussalam: the blending of acquired ideas with tradition". She teaches undergraduate and postgraduate courses on the legal systems of Asia, Islamic law, comparative law and criminal law, and her research is in these same areas of law. Recent publications include the chapter on Brunei Darussalam in *Legal Systems of the World: a Political, Social and Cultural Encyclopedia* (ABC-CLIO: 2002) and *Constitutions of the World* (Facts-on-File: 2005). She has published articles on law and dispute resolution in Brunei including "Survival or Extinction? Animistic Dispute Resolution in the Sultanate of Brunei," *Willamette Journal of International Law and Dispute Resolution* 13(2004): 1–25 and "ADR in Brunei Darussalam: the blending of imported and traditional processes," *Bond Law Review* 13 no. 2 (2001): 305–334.

Jennifer Corrin Care

Jennifer Corrin Care is Executive Director, Comparative Law, of the Centre for Public, International and Comparative Law, in the TC Beirne School of Law at The University of Queensland, Australia. She was formerly an Associate Professor in the School of Law at the University of the South Pacific, having joined the Faculty after nine years in her own legal firm in Solomon Islands. She is also admitted in Fiji Islands, England and Wales, and Queensland. With Anne Black she co-edits *LawAsia Journal*. She is the author of many journal articles and chapters on the laws and legal systems of the Pacific, and also of *Civil Procedure and Courts in the South Pacific* (London: Cavendish, 2004) and *Contract Law in the South Pacific* (London: Cavendish, 2001), and co-author of *Introduction to South Pacific Law* (London: Cavendish, 1999) and *Proving Customary Law in the Common Law Courts of the South Pacific* (London: British Institute of International and Comparative Law, 2002).

Carolyn Evans

Carolyn Evans is Deputy Director of the Centre for Comparative Constitutional Studies, in the Faculty of Law, The University of Melbourne, Australia. She has undergraduate degrees in Arts and Law from that university and a doctorate in law from the University of Oxford, where she studied as a Rhodes Scholar. She has taught at both Oxford and Melbourne. She is the author of *Freedom of Religion under the European Convention on Human Rights* (Oxford: Oxford University Press, 2001) and the co-editor of *Religion and International Law* (Leiden: Martinus Nijhoff, 1999). She has published articles and chapters in the areas of religious freedom and general international law. Her current research interests are in the areas of the intersection of religion and law (including issues of religious freedom) and the role of legislatures in the protection of human rights. She has given presentations on religious freedom issues in Australia, the United Kingdom, the United States, the Peoples' Republic of China and Russia.

Lucinda Peach

Lucinda Joy Peach is an associate professor in the Department of Philosophy and Religion at American University in Washington, DC. She received her PhD from the Department of Religious Studies at Indiana University (1995) and also holds a JD degree from New York University School of Law (1982). She is the author of *Legislating Morality: Religious Identity and Moral Pluralism* (New York: Oxford University Press, 2002), and the editor of *Women and World Religions* (Upper Saddle River, NJ: Prentice Hall, 2002) and *Women in Culture:*

A Women's Studies Anthology (Oxford: Blackwell Publishers, 1998), as well as co-editor (with April Morgan and Colette Mazucelli) of *Ethics and Global Affairs: An Active Learning Sourcebook* (New York: Kumarian Press, 2004). Her areas of research include the trafficking of women for the sex trade, the relationship between law, religion and ethics, gender and religion (especially women and Buddhism), women's human rights, and, most recently, corporate social responsibility for human rights.

Susan Harris Rimmer

Susan Harris Rimmer is a human rights lawyer who currently provides advice to Australian Federal Parliamentarians as part of the Parliamentary Library. She has worked as a Resettlement/Legal Officer for the UNHCR Regional Office in Canberra, as a refugee advocate with the National Council of Churches in Australia, and as the Human Rights Policy Officer at the Australian Council for International Development (ACFID). She is currently a Doctor of Juridical Science (SJD) candidate at ANU, having completed Honours in Arts and Law at the University of Queensland and received a University Medal in 1995. She has worked as a volunteer at the International Criminal Tribunal for the Former Yugoslavia in The Hague and in a Somali refugee camp in Kenya for UNHCR. Ms Harris Rimmer convened ACFID's East Timor Working Group for several years, consisting of Australian development agencies working in East Timor, and spent the month of January 2002 working with the East Timor NGO Forum in Dili. She was also involved with a judicial training project with the Indonesia ad hoc Human Rights Court for Australian Legal Resources International. She is a National Committee member of Australian Lawyers for Human Rights. She has written a chapter on the prosecution of sexual violence in East Timor for Sharon Pickering and Caroline Lambert, eds., *Global Issues, Women and Justice* (Sydney: Institute of Criminology, 2004) and is the author of several articles and numerous parliamentary submissions on the topics of refugee law, anti-racism, genocide, gender and international criminal law, and human rights and development.

Kathryn Robinson

Kathryn Robinson has published extensively on gender relations in Indonesia, most recently co-editing (with Sharon Bessell) *Women in Indonesia: Gender, Equity and Development* (Singapore: ISEAS, 2002). She has written on migration, state gender policy, and reproductive health. Her major research area is South Sulawesi, on topics ranging from traditional architecture and religious belief to mining. Her books on South Sulawesi include: *Stepchildren of Progress: The Political Economy of Development in an Indonesian Mining Town* (New

York: SUNY Press, 1986) and six edited collections on society and culture, jointly with Mukhlis Paini. The most recent of these is *Tapak Tapak Waktu* (Penerbit Inninawa/Australia Indonesia Institute, 2004). She has worked in Australian and Indonesian universities for 20 years and is currently Senior Fellow in Anthropology in the Research School of Pacific and Asian Studies, Australian National University. Her current research includes a study of local livelihoods in Southeast Sulawesi, research on internet mediated transnational marriages, and an investigation of the impact of Islam on gender relations in the Indonesian archipelago.

Li-ann Thio

Dr. Li-ann Thio, BA (Hons)(Oxford), LLM (Harvard), PhD (Cambridge) is Associate Professor, Law Faculty, National University of Singapore where she teaches public international law, human rights, and constitutional law. She is co-author of *Constitutional Law in Malaysia and Singapore* (Singapore/Malaysia/Hong Kong: Butterworths, 1997) and author of *Managing Babel: The International Legal Protection of Minorities in the Twentieth Century* (Leiden: Brill, 2005). She has published broadly in the fields of public law and international law, with a focus on human rights issues in Southeast Asia and international minority rights. She is Editor and Advisory Board member respectively of the *Singapore Yearbook of International Law* and *New Zealand Yearbook of International Law* and Singapore Correspondent for Blaustein & Flanzâ's *Constitutions of the Countries of the World* and the *International Journal of Constitutional Law*. Her publications include: International Law and Secession in the Asia-Pacific Region in *Secession: International Law Perspectives*, ed. Marcelo Kohen (Cambridge: Cambridge University Press, 2006); "Developing a Peace and Security Approach Towards Minorities Issues," *International and Comparative Law Quarterly* 53 (2003): 115–150; "The Right to Political Participation in Singapore," *Singapore Journal of International and Comparative Law* 6 (2002): 181–243; "The Secular Trumps the Sacred: Constitutional Issues Arising from *Colin Chan v PP*," in *Library of Social Change in Asia-Pacific* ed. Garry Rodan (London: Ashgate Press, 2001); "Implementing Human Rights in ASEAN Countries: Promises to Keep and Miles to Go before I Sleep," *Yale Human Rights and Development Law Journal* 2(1999): 1–86; and "Battling Balkanization: Regional Approaches Towards Minority Protection Beyond Europe," *Harvard International Law Journal* 43 no. 2(2002): 409–468.

Amanda Whiting

Amanda Whiting is a Lecturer in Law at The University of Melbourne and Associate Director, Malaysia, Asian Law Centre, also at The University of

Melbourne, Australia. She has taught both history and law at that University. She is Co-editor of the *Australian Journal of Asian Law* and author of "Situating Suhakam: Human Rights Debates and Malaysia's National Human Rights Commission," *Stanford Journal of International Law* 39 no.1 (2003): 59–98 and "'Some Women can shift it well enough:' a legal context for understanding the women petitioners of the seventeenth-century English Revolution," *Australian Feminist Law Journal* 21 (December) 2004: 77–100. Her current research interests include women and Islam in Southeast Asia; national and regional human rights institutions, values and practices in Southeast Asia; indigenous land claims in Malaysia; and the use of defamation to stifle public debate in Southeast Asia.

Leah Whiu

Leah Whiu is of the Ngapuhi and Ngatihine peoples of Aotearoa/New Zealand and she is a Senior Lecturer, School of Law, University of Waikato. She has a BSc from the University of Auckland and a LLB and LLM from the University of Waikato. Her research interests focus on the intersection of gender, race and sexuality, human rights, biculturalism and indigenous issues. Her recent publications include "Waikato Law School's Bicultural Vision—Anei te huarahi hei wero i a tatou katoa: This is a challenge confronting us all," *Waikato Law Review* 9 (2001): 265–292 and "Māori Women's Weavings of Law, Justice and Difference," *Balayi: Culture, Law and Colonialism* (2001). She assisted the New Zealand Ministry of Māori Development with the review of the Māori Land Act; was a member of the Human Rights Review Tribunal (1999-2004); and has been appointed to the National Advisory Council to the New Zealand Human Rights Commission to provide assistance and advice in the development of New Zealand's National Action Plan for Human Rights. She frequently addressed academic and public conferences on these issues.

Jean G. Zorn

Jean Zorn is a Professor of Law at the Florida International University College of Law. She has a BA from the University of California, Berkeley; her MA and JD are from the University of Wisconsin. Dr Zorn's research interests lie primarily in the areas of the customary and comparative law of the South Pacific. She has travelled regularly to the Pacific for many years, primarily to further her research on customary law and the relationship of custom to the formal legal system. She first served in the Pacific as a lecturer in law at the University of Papua New Guinea Law Faculty, where she originated the Pacific area's first course in customary law. When Papua New Guinea gained its independence, she served on the then newly formed Law

Reform Commission, which had as its statutory aim the re-integration of custom into the state legal system. She has also taught at the University of the South Pacific Law School, and consulted with various Pacific institutions on the role of customary law in the formal legal system, court administration, and commercial and consumer protection laws. She is the author or editor of numerous books and articles on Pacific law, most of them in the areas of constitutional development, process and procedure, land law, and women and law. Her recent articles on women and law include "Custom Then and Now: The Pacific Family" and "Issues in Contemporary Customary Law: Women and the Law," both in T. Newton and A. Jowitt (eds.) *Law, Society and Change* (Suva: Institute of Pacific Studies, 2002); "Women, Custom and International Law in the Pacific," *University of the South Pacific School of Law Occasional No. 5* (Port Vila, 2000); "Women's Rights Are Human Rights — International Law and the Culture of Domestic Violence," in *To Have and To Hit*, ed. Dorothy Ayers Counts, Judith K. Brown and Jacquelyn C. Campbell, 2d ed (Urbana and Chicago: University of Illinois Press, 1999).

CHAPTER ONE

SITUATING THE ISSUES, FRAMING THE ANALYSIS

Carolyn Evans and Amanda Whiting

Objectives and Scope

The essays in this volume explore some of the diverse and contradictory ways that the lives of women in the Asia-Pacific region are shaped by two powerful regimes—'religion' and 'law'—and by the interactions between them. They show that for women, laws (customary, colonial, post-independence, and international) and religions (indigenous or introduced, Buddhism, Christianity, Islam, and Confucianism) have been a 'mixed blessing'. These diverse legal systems and religious doctrines and institutions have variously denied women authority and the capacity to participate fully in the public organization of social, political, and religious life; they have furthermore constructed gender and familial relations in ways that subordinate women. Yet they have also offered promises of women's empowerment, and provided rules and procedures, norms, values, and interpretations of sacred traditions to deliver those emancipatory promises.

Over the last decade or so, many stimulating works have been published in several disciplines that address questions about women in Asia;[1] women, colonialism

[1] As the literature is indeed vast, and in order to avoid invidious omissions, this and the next seven notes cite only indicative scholarship. For scholarship on women in Asia, see the book of that name: Louise Edwards and Mina Roces, ed., *Women in Asia: Tradition, Modernity and Globalization* (St Leonards: Allen & Unwin, 2000). See also: Krishna Sen and Maila Stivens, ed., *Gender and Power in Affluent Asia* (London: Routledge, 1998) and Lonore Manderson and Linda Rae Bennett, ed., *Violence Against Women in Asian Societies* (London: RoutledgeCurzon, 2003). Select scholarship about particular countries includes: Kalpana Ram, *Mukkuvar Women: Gender, Hegemony and Capitalist Transformation in a South Indian Fishing Community* (North Sydney: Allen & Unwin, 1991); Maila Stivins, *Matriliny and Modernity: Sexual Politics and Social Change in Rural Malaysia* (Sydney: Allen & Unwin, 1996); Martha Nussbaum, "India: Implementing Sex Equality Through Law," *Chicago Journal of International Law* 2 (2001): 35–58; Andrea Whittaker, *Abortion, Sin and the State in Thailand* (London: Routledge, 2004).

and nationalism;[2] women and religious fundamentalism[3] (with its increasingly prominent sub-category of women and Islamic fundamentalism[4]); women's rights in international law;[5] and religion and law;[6] as well as combinations of these issues and themes.[7] Provocatively and productively, there is also a large literature on Third World feminisim(s).[8] Yet we perceive a need for a collection

---

[2] Kumari Jayawardena, *Feminism and Nationalism in the Third World* (London: Zed Books, 1986); Deniz Kandiyoti, ed., *Women, Islam and the State* (London, Macmillan, 1991); Valentine M Moghadam, ed., *Gender and National Identity: Women and Politics in Muslim Societies* (London: Zed Books, 1994); M. Jacqui Alexander and Chandra Talpade Mohanty, ed., *Feminist Genealogies, Colonial Legacies, Democratic Futures* (New York: Routledge, 1997); Radhika Mohanram, *Black Body: Women, Colonialism and Space* (St Leonards: Allen & Unwin, 1999).

[3] Courtney W. Howland, ed., *Religious Fundamentalisms and the Human Rights of Women* (New York: St Martin's Press, 1999); Patricia Jeffrey and Amrita Basu, ed., *Appropriating Gender: Women's Activism and Politicized Religion in South Asia* (London: Routledge:1998).

[4] Norani Othman, ed., *Shari'a Law and the Modern Nation-State: A Malaysian Symposium* (Kuala Lumpur: Sisters in Islam, 1994); Nahya Haider, "Islamic Legal Reform: The Case of Pakistan and Family Law," *Yale Journal of Law and Feminism* 12 (2000): 287–341. See also Moghadam, *Gender and National Identity*; and Kandiyoti, *Women, Islam and the State*.

[5] Rebecca J. Cook, ed., *Human Rights of Women: National and International Perspectives* (Philadelphia: University of Pennsylvania Press, 1994); Hilary Charlesworth, "Feminist Methods in International Law," *American Journal of International Law* 93 (1999): 379–393; Hilary Charlesworth and Christine Chinkin, *The Boundaries of International Law: A Feminist Analysis* (Manchester: Manchester University Press, 2000); Kelly D. Askin and Dorean M. Koenig, ed., *Women and International Human Rights Law* 3 vols (Ardsley, New York: Transnational, 1999); Courtney W. Howland, "The Challenge of Religious Fundamentalism to the Liberty and Equality Rights of Women: An Analysis under the United Nations Charter," *Columbia Journal of Transnational Law* 35 (1997): 271–377; Julie Peters and Andrea Wolper, ed., *Women's Rights, Human Rights: International Feminist Perspectives* (New York: Routledge, 1995); Sally Engle Merry, "Constructing a Global Law: Violence against Women and the Human Rights System," *Law and Social Inquiry* 28 (2003): 941–977.

[6] Rex Adhar, *Law and Religion* (Aldershot: Ashgate, 2000) and Andrew Lewis and Richard O'Dair, *Law and Religion* (Oxford: Oxford University Press, 2001); Mark W. Janis and Carolyn Evans, ed., *Religion and International Law* (The Hague: Martinus Nijhoff Publishers, 1999) Tayyab Mahmud, "Freedom of Religion and Religious Minorities in Pakistan: A Study of Judicial Practice," *Fordham International Law Journal* 19 (1995): 40–100.

[7] Of course many of the works cited in the above notes address several of these questions or themes, as is evident simply from their titles. But see additionally, Joseph A. Camilleri, ed., *Religion and Culture in Asia Pacific: Violence or Healing* (Melbourne: Pax Christi, 2001); Sally Engle Merry, "Rights, Religion, and Community: Approaches to Violence Against Women in the Context of Globalization," *Law and Society Review* 35 (2001): 39–88. Donna Sullivan, "Gender Equality and Religious Freedom: Toward a Framework for Conflict Resolution," *New York University Journal of International Law and Policy* 24 (1992): 795–856; Aihwa Ong and Michael Gates Peletz, ed., *Bewitching Women, Pious Men: Gender and Body Politics in Southeast Asia* (Berkeley: University of California Press, 1995); Jacqueline Aquino Siapno, *Gender, Islam, Nationalism and the State in Aceh: The Paradox of Power, Cooptation and Resistance* (London: Routledge, 2002); Jane H. Bayes and Nayereh Tohidi, ed., *Globalization, Gender and Religion: The Politics of Women's Rights in Catholic and Muslim Contexts* (New York: Palgrave, 2001).

[8] Chandra Talpade Mohanty, "Under Western Eyes: Feminist Scholarship and Colonial Discourses," *Feminist Review* 30 (1988): 64–88 and *Feminism Without Borders: Decolonizing Theory, Practicing Solidarity* (Durham: North Carolina University Press, 20030; Isabelle R. Gunning,

which attends to the specificities of women's location within national structures in the Asia-Pacific region as these state legal regimes intersect with, or are inflected by, religious values and institutions. In particular, we recognize a need for a collection which makes space for a sustained consideration of Pacific as well as 'Asian' nations and cultures, and which interprets religion broadly, bringing together in one volume studies of Buddhism, Christianity, Islam, and indigenous spiritual practices as they are constructed by, and intersect with, the state.

For this volume we invited authors to contribute a chapter devoted to a single state, to introduce the history and current framework of the national legal system, to explain the place of religion in the state, and then, using precise and detailed case studies or examples, to explore how these sometimes competing, sometimes colluding regimes constructed women, and how women interpreted this positioning and sought to resituate themselves. 'Asking the woman question'—to adopt Katharine Bartlett's deceptively simple feminist legal methodology[9]—inevitably has a destabilising effect upon established boundaries (disciplinary as well as national or jurisdictional) and this in turn is productive of fresh insights.

In Chapter 2, Lucinda Peach writes of sex workers and women seeking ordination as Buddhist nuns in Thailand, a developing nation that does not institutionalize the separation of state and religion, and has only recently entrenched rights guarantees in its constitutional framework. She explains how strong state support for the male Buddhist Order of monks (the Sangha) reinforces patriarchal Thai interpretations of Buddhism that denigrate female sexuality, making it impossible for women legally to achieve ordination as Buddhist nuns in Thailand. At the same time, she explains how strong state support for international tourism to Thailand (which is encouraged by multilateral financial organizations) has enabled female sex workers to increase their earning power. By applying this money to the support of their families, these women are able to earn merit in Buddhist terms, thus paradoxically lessening the disparagement of their disorderly female sexuality.

In the next four chapters the continuing influence of the Christian denominations, first as agents of colonization, then as instruments in post-colonial nation-building, comes under scrutiny. In her study in Chapter 3 of the judicial pronouncements in contemporary Papua New Guinea about men who

---

"Arrogant Perception, World-Traveling, and Multicultural Feminism: The Case of Female Genital Surgeries," *Columbia Human Rights Law Review* 23 (1992): 189–248; Uma Narayan, *Dislocating Cultures: Identities, Traditions and Third-World Feminism* (New York: Routledge, 1997).

[9] Katharine T. Bartlett, "Feminist Legal Methods," *Harvard Law Review* 103 (1990): 829–888. See also Margaret Davies, *Asking the Law Question: The Dissolution of Legal Theory*, 2nd ed. (Sydney: Lawbook Company, 2002).

kill women they claim are witches, Jean Zorn shows how the post-independence state, with its constitutional commitment to both a Christian polity and respect for indigenous traditions, cannot adequately recognize and protect indigenous customs and spirituality, nor can it deliver promises to protect and enhance women's rights. Similarly, Jennifer Corrin Care shows in Chapter 4 that in Solomon Islands—where, as elsewhere in the Pacific, Christianity is 'indigenized'[10]—patriarchal interpretations of both customary law and Christian scriptures can operate to women's detriment. At the same time, courts have sometimes been willing to interpret custom and post-independence laws in ways that are positive for women, and women have been using and enhancing their own positions of authority and influence within church-based associations to work towards a post-conflict society that is more respectful of them. Margaret Bedggood and Leah Whiu show in Chapter 5 that the history of the Christian churches in Aotearoa/New Zealand was directly involved in the destruction of many aspects of Māori society at the same time that it perpetuated unequal gender roles in Pākehā (settler) society. Bedggood shows how Christian organizations have campaigned for law reform, for example to remove oppressive working conditions for women and for women's suffrage, but now resist the extension of the state's sex discrimination regime to their own institutions. Whiu writes painfully of the inability of the law's regime of formal equality to comprehend indigenous Māori customary law and spirituality. According to Susan Harris Rimmer in Chapter 6, women in occupied and now independent Timor Lorosa'e have received 'mixed signals' from the Roman Catholic Church. When the sexual violence they suffer is caused by occupying Indonesian troops, they are hailed as heroines whose suffering requires full justice; when it is perpetrated within the family, they are expected to suffer in silence.

In Chapters 7 and 8 Kathryn Robinson and Ann Black examine how the intersections of Islam and national law affect women in Indonesia and Brunei, respectively. As in the constitutions of PNG and Solomon Islands, religion is enshrined in the Indonesian constitution. Under the state doctrine of *pancasila*, belief in a single God is unquestioned and a precondition for full national identity and participation. However, in Indonesia, unlike Brunei, there is no special place for Islam and it is not the national religion (although it is the religion of the majority). By tracing women's endeavours to reform family law in colonial, independent, and now post-*reformasi* Indonesia, Robinson shows how state law adopts and adapts aspects of Islam, and how women's groups struggle to

[10] See Bronwyn Douglas, "Why Religion, Race and Gender Matter in Pacific Politics," *Development Bulletin* 59 (2002): 11.

insert their emancipatory readings of Islamic law and tradition into the state's agenda. The robust civil society evident in Indonesia is absent from authoritarian Brunei, where women consequently have far fewer ways to participate (formally or informally) in the state's vigorous Islamization programme, with its attendant refashioning of family law and gender relations.

In the final chapter, Li-ann Thio investigates the religious laws and policies of the secular, soft-authoritarian state of Singapore. She shows how the government's desire to preserve religious harmony is linked to its need to manage communal relations, and how this in turn means that, in relation to the Muslim minority community, the government pays most heed to the patriarchal views of conservative male religious leaders. At the same time, the state is jealous of its position as a developed nation, and well aware that an educated female workforce enjoying adequate family-friendly work policies has been crucial to the attainment of that status. Hence, in its somewhat bizarre attempt to introduce neo-Confucianism as a state-sponsored secular 'religion', the government has been obliged to dilute the explicitly patriarchal aspects of traditional Confucianism in order to customize it for meritocratic Singaporean society.

The diverse experiences of women within each of these states cannot of course be conflated, as differences of class and status, employment and education, geographical location (urban or rural), ethnicity and so forth mean that women experience the convergence of law and religion in each state in different ways, just as the category of 'woman' is assembled differently under these different regimes.[11] Similarly, differences between state jurisdictions or religious communities are such that, beyond the level of bland generalization, it is as meaningless to speak of an 'Asia-Pacific' identity or way of doing things as it is to make assertions about 'women'.[12]

And yet, it is clear that there are common tensions between women's rights and religious authority, and women's rights and oppressive legal systems. These tensions, moreover, are reflected in struggles at the level of international

[11] Regarding the construction of 'Woman' in Western (and Anglophone) history, see Denise Riley, *Am I That Name? Feminism and the Category of "Woman"* (Minneapolis, University of Minnesota Press, 1988); for a consideration of the constructedness of 'Woman' in a Chinese context, see Tani Barlow, "Theorizing Woman: *Funü, Guojia, Jiating* (Chinese Women, Chinese State, Chinese Family)," in *Scattered Hegemonies: Postmodernity and Transnational Feminist Practices*, ed. Inderpal Grewal and Caren Kaplan (Minneapolis: University of Minnesota Press, 1994), 173–196.

[12] For a thoughtful review essay exploring some of the debates about the existence of a Southeast Asian "region", see Grant Evans, "Between the Global and the Local There Are Regions, Culture Areas, and National States: A Review Article," *Journal of Southeast Asian Studies* 33 (2002): 147–162. Regarding "Asia" as a legal category, see Veronica Taylor, "Beyond Legal Orientalism," in *Asian Law Through Australian Eyes*, ed. Veronica Taylor (Sydney: LBC, 1997), 47–62.

law and policy.[13] In an increasingly integrated world, international debates and the standards that emerge from them are of relevance in the domestic sphere. While the Asia-Pacific region participates less in international regimes dealing with human rights than other regions, nevertheless within this region international standards and human rights discourse do have an impact.[14] At the level of state recognition, for example, several governments have established national human rights institutions, and many of these were set up as a result of the program of action following on from the 1993 UN World Conference on Human Rights.[15] At the level of non-governmental and civil society advocacy, organizations like International Women's Rights Action Watch Asia-Pacific, a trans-national women's association which monitors the implementation of the UN Convention on the Elimination of All Forms of Discrimination Against Women (CEDAW), have made integration of international standards with domestic regimes central to their mission.[16]

Accordingly, in this introductory Chapter we look next to some international legal instruments: those dealing with women's rights, and also those concerning religious freedom—the latter being a right that is often used as a justification for continuing legal and religious practices that marginalize, silence and oppress women. By exploring the tension in international law between religion—often conflated with or reduced to 'culture'–and women's rights, we provide one context in which to view similar tensions as they occur at the domestic level.

---

[13] See generally, Michele Brandt and Jeffrey A. Kaplan, "The Tension between Women's Rights and Religious Rights: Reservations to CEDAW by Egypt, Bangladesh and Tunisia," *Journal of Law and Religion* 12 (1995): 105–142; Bahia Tahzib-Lie, "Applying a Gender Perspective in the Area of the Right to Freedom of Religion or Belief," *Brigham Young University Law Review* (2000): 967–988.

[14] Merry, "Constructing a Global Law", 968 argues that international human rights instruments, even non-binding declarations, do matter for a variety of political and economic reasons, and because they "offer the elites of many nations opportunities to circulate in the global space of modernity".

[15] See the discussion in Carolyn Evans, "Human Rights Commissions and Religious Conflict in the Asia-Pacific Region," *International and Comparative Law Quarterly* 53 (July 2004): 713; and Amanda Whiting, "Situating Suhakam: Human Rights Debates and Malaysia's National Human Rights Commission," *Stanford Journal of International Law* 39(1) (2003): 72–4.

[16] International Women's Rights Action Watch Asia Pacific (www.iwraw-ap.org) was formed in Malaysia in 1993. For recent examples of its work, see: Shanthi Dairiam, "The Status of CEDAW Implementation in ASEAN Countries and Selected Muslim Countries", a paper presented at the Roundtable Discussion on Rights and Obligations under CEDAW, 17 March 2003, Kuala Lumpur, Malaysia, organized by the Human Rights Commission of Malaysia (SUHAKAM); and Shanthi Dairiam, 'Impact of the Convention at the Domestic Level' paper delivered at the Conference "CEDAW at 25: Are We Moving Forward?" October 13 2004, United Nations Headquarters, New York,

The International Frame of Reference

General Human Rights Approaches

The international approach to human rights issues is generally thought to have begun in the period immediately after the Second World War and, in particular, with the establishment of the United Nations. While the Charter of the United Nations itself does not contain a comprehensive bill of rights, the preamble to the Charter declares that the "peoples of the United Nations" established the United Nations in part to "reaffirm faith in fundamental human rights, in the dignity and worth of the human person, in the equal rights of men and women." One of the purposes of the United Nations enunciated in article 1(3) is promoting and encouraging "respect for human rights and for fundamental freedoms for all without distinction as to race, sex, language or religion." Members of the United Nations pledge themselves to achieving "universal respect for, and observance of, human rights and fundamental freedoms for all without distinction as to race, sex, language, or religion."[17] While the details of the rights are not spelt out, the principle of non-discrimination in the application of rights is, and it is clear that what rights there are belong to all people regardless, inter alia, of their sex or religion.[18]

While the Charter outlined a commitment to rights in broadly expressed principle, it was left to the Universal Declaration of Human Rights (UDHR) to begin the process of detailing those rights.[19] The UDHR is a resolution of the General Assembly and thus not binding in the same way as a treaty, although it is strongly arguable that its provisions have become binding as customary international law.[20] A number of its provisions are of relevance to both women's rights and religious freedom. Article 2 sets out the general rule of non-discrimination on bases that include sex and religion.[21] The only other

---

[17] Charter of the United Nations, arts 55 and 56.

[18] For an overview of the history of the inclusion of rights in the Charter see Mary Ann Glendon, *A World Made New: Eleanor Roosevelt and the Universal Declaration of Human Rights* (New York: Random House, 2001), 3–20.

[19] *Universal Declaration of Human Rights*, G.A. Res. 217, 3(1) UN GAOR Res 71, U.N. Doc. A/811 (1948) (hereafter UDHR). For an interesting discussion of the drafting process of the Declaration and the important role played by a number of women, particularly Eleanor Roosevelt, in its drafting, see Glendon, *World Made New*.

[20] For an overview of this debate see Oscar Schachter, *International Law in Theory and Practice* (Boston: Martinus Nijhoff Publishers, 1991), chap. 15.

[21] UDHR, art. 2: "Everyone is entitled to all the rights and freedoms set forth in this Declaration, without distinction of any kind, such as race, colour, sex, language, religion, political or other opinion, national or social origin, property, birth or other status." Note that some of these additional criteria may play an important role in women's lives and that religion can be closely intertwined with other criteria mentioned here such as colour, social origin and status such as caste identification.

articles that specifically mention women are those dealing with family life. Article 16 sets out the freedom of "men and women of full age" to marry and found a family. It also says that men and women are "entitled to equal rights as to marriage, during marriage and at its dissolution" and that marriage will only be entered into with the "free and full consent of the spouses." The final sub-section of article 16 contains the contentious provision that the "family is the natural and fundamental group unit of society and is entitled to protection by society and by the State." A similarly double-edged provision is set out in article 25(2), which states that "Motherhood and childhood are entitled to special care and assistance."

Apart from the non-discrimination clause, these provisions that focus on the role of women as wives and mothers are the only ones that specifically mention women. There is a strong element of protectionism in the provisions, particularly when they tie motherhood and childhood together as requiring similar, paternalistic oversight. Article 16(3), which emphasises the 'natural and fundamental' nature of the family, is also problematic for women whose exclusion from the 'public realm' and oppression in the 'private realm'—however these boundaries are drawn[22]—is often tied to the perceived need to 'protect' the family unit.[23] The model of the family as the natural social unit and motherhood as a special state in which women need protection resonates with the conception of social organisation and the proper role of women that is propounded by many of the religions examined in this book.

The provision protecting religious freedom in the UDHR is less internally contradictory than the provisions about women's rights, although the terms in which religious freedom was to be recognized was a serious source of contention

---

[22] In using the familiar Western feminist terminology of 'public' and 'private' realms we do not ignore the criticism that such distinctions may have more salience in the West (to the extent that they are even correctly identified there) and therefore that they may have little applicability or resonance elsewhere. See, for example, Adrian Howe, "White Western Feminism meets International Law: Challenges/Complicity, Erasure/Encounters," *Australian Feminist Law Journal* 4 (1994): esp. 86 where this approach is castigated as "methodological universalism". And for trenchant criticisms of its applicability in the Western history, see for example: Carole Pateman, "Feminist Critiques of the Public/Private Dichotomy," in *Public and Private in Social Life*, ed. S. I. Benn and G. F. Gauss (London: Croom Helm; New York: St Martin's Press, 1983), 281–303; Anne Phillips, *Engendering Democracy* (Cambridge: Polity Press, 1991), esp. chap 4; and Amanda Vickery, "Golden Age to Separate Spheres? A Review of the Categories and Chronology of English Women's History," *The Historical Journal* 36 (1993): 383–414; Leonore Davidoff, "Regarding Some 'Old Husbands' Tales': Public and Private in Feminist History," in *Feminism, the Public and the Private*, ed. Joan Landes (Oxford: Oxford University Press, 1998), 164–94. It seems to us, however, that these distinctions are in fact being inscribed in these international instruments, or at the least that they are not precluded.

[23] Jo Lynn Southard, "Protection of Women's Human Rights Under the Convention on the Elimination of All Forms of Discrimination Against Women," *Pace International Law Review* 8 (1996): 12–15, 56–7.

in the debates over the UDHR.[24] Article 18 reads, "Everyone has the right to freedom of thought, conscience and religion; this right includes freedom to change his religion or belief, and freedom, either alone or in community with others and in public or private, to manifest his religion or belief in teaching, practice, worship and observance."[25] Clearly, in situations where the right to profess and practice a particular religion is restricted or effectively made impossible (for example, the persecution of the Ahmadis in Pakistan[26] or the state-sponsored pressure upon indigenous peoples in Malaysia and Brunei to convert to Islam[27]) then women as well as men do not enjoy freedom of religion. However for many women, the lack of freedom is experienced within religion, as when their capacity to participate fully or equally in the organisation and governance of their religious community is denied; or when the authority to interpret the sacred texts and practices of their faith in a way that is liberating for, and not oppressive of, women is withheld from them. These questions are taken up in this volume.

The rights in the UDHR are subject to a single limitations clause that states that "in the exercise of his rights and freedoms, everyone shall be subject only to such limitations as are determined by law solely for the purpose of securing due recognition and respect for the rights and freedoms of others and of meeting the just requirements of morality, public order and the general welfare in

[24] See, Bahiyyih G. Tahzib, *Freedom of Religion and Belief: Ensuring Effective International Protection* (Leiden: Martinus Nijhoff, 1996), 73–8. For a recent consideration of the divergent positions of some Muslim majority nations during debates on article 18, see Mahmud, "Freedom of Religion and Religious Minorities in Pakistan," 86.

[25] There is also both direct and indirect reference to religion in the right to education, where it is said that education shall promote "understanding, tolerance and friendship among all nations, racial or religious groups": UDHR art. 26(2). Less directly, clause three of article 26 also says that parents "have a prior right to choose the kind of education that shall be given to their children." While this last right does not specifically refer to religion, it is clear from the way in which this right developed in later human rights instruments that part of the purpose of this provision is to ensure that parents had the right to raise their children according to their own religious or philosophical beliefs. See for example *International Covenant on Civil and Political Rights*, G.A. Res. 2200A, 21 U.N. GAOR, U.N. Doc. A/6316 (1966) (hereafter, ICCPR), article 18(4) and article 5 of the *Declaration on the Elimination of All Forms of Intolerance and Discrimination Based on Religion or Belief*, G.A. Res. 36/55, U.N. GOAR Supp. (No. 51) 171, UN Doc. A/36/684 (1981). Clearly, this right can be a cause of tension with women's rights when religious education demands a different type of education for girls and boys, or includes religious teaching that justifies the oppression of women.

[26] Mahmud, "Freedom of Religion and Religious Minorities in Pakistan".

[27] Regarding the situation in Malaysia, see Robert Knox Dentan et al, *Malaysia and the "Original People": a Case Study in the Impact of Development on Indigenous Peoples* (Boston: Allyn and Bacon, 1997). A recent news report is Claudia Theophilus "Orang Asli cry foul over 'forced' conversion," *Malaysiakini.com*, February 3, 2005, http://www.malaysiakini.com/. The situation in Brunei is discussed in Anne Black's chapter in this volume.

a democratic society."[28] Thus, even at this early stage, it was recognised that most rights are not absolute and, more specifically, that it was sometimes necessary for rights to be limited in order to ensure the rights and freedoms of others. One area in which this has proved problematic, as illustrated in this book, is that of conflicts between women's rights and freedom of religious practices.[29]

Law, it should be noted, also plays a role in the limitations clause. In order to be justified, a limitation must be made "by law". While there are some very good rule-of-law justifications for this requirement the role played by law in the limitations clause is the classic liberal perception of law as a neutral, apolitical force that can mediate fairly between competing claims. Yet, as Madhavi Sunder has argued so compellingly,[30] and as the chapters in this book demonstrate, the neutrality of law is an assumption that cannot be maintained. Rather, law is deeply political and legal systems can and do align themselves to a particular side in a conflict of rights. In a number of the legal systems explored in this book, for example, the positive law of the state recognises and accommodates elements of religious law, particularly in areas such as marriage and custody of children, which are often detrimental to women's rights. The law often also recognizes and thus legitimates the voices only of a conservative, male leadership of a religion, ignoring contests over governance, teaching and principle in the religious group itself.[31] Law thus cannot be conceived of accurately as a neutral force in the conflict of rights anticipated by the UDHR.

Some decades after the UDHR was adopted by the General Assembly, the international community developed a series of binding treaties to elaborate these rights. The two most prominent of these are the International Covenant on Civil and Political Rights (ICCPR)[32] and the International Covenant on Economic, Social and Cultural Rights (ICESCR).[33] The specific references to women in these Covenants includes articles on non-discrimination on the basis of sex[34] and similar provisions to the UDHR in relation to the family being the "natural and fundamental group unit of society", the requirement of free consent

---

[28] UDHR art. 29(2). Article 29 also forbids the exercise of rights and freedoms contrary to the "purposes and principles" of the United Nations, which include the purpose of achieving rights for all regardless of sex.

[29] See also, Sullivan, *Gender Equality*, 822; Courtey W. Howland, ed., *Religious Fundamentalisms and the Human Rights of Women* (New York: St Martin's Press, 1999).

[30] Madhavi Sunder, "Piercing the Veil," *Yale Law Journal* 112 (2003): 1399–1472.

[31] This proposition is demonstrated forcefully by "Piercing the Veil" (2003) especially at 1425–1432; see also Sunder's earlier article "Cultural Dissent," *Stanford Law Review* 54 (2001): 495–568.

[32] ICCPR (above, note 25).

[33] *International Covenant on Economic, Social and Cultural Rights*, G.A. Res 2200A, U.N. Doc. A/6316 (1966) (hereafter, ICESCR).

[34] ICESCR, art. 2, ICCPR art. 3

before marriage, and the right to "special protection for mother" although by this stage that protection only extends to "a reasonable period before and after childbirth."[35] The ICESCR also includes reference to women's equality in relation to work-rights.[36] The ICCPR contains a provision for the protection of religious freedom in similar, although more detailed terms than the provision in the ICCPR.[37] Both Conventions, along with the UDHR, when not speaking specifically of women, use the masculine pronoun throughout, subtly distancing women from the more general rights contained in these treaties.[38]

Women's Rights and Religious Freedom in International Law

Both women's rights and religious freedom were supposed to be further developed in separate treaties that gave greater detail to those rights, but this has only been achieved for women's rights. The Convention on the Elimination of All Forms of Discrimination Against Women (CEDAW) was adopted by the General Assembly in 1979 and came into force in 1981.[39] The Convention included the establishment of a Committee to oversee the rights set out in the Convention,[40] and later that Committee was given power to hear complaints from individuals of States that ratified an Optional Protocol.[41] By contrast, despite decades of effort, no treaty dealing specifically with religious freedom has been concluded. In 1981, the General Assembly passed a Declaration on the Elimination of All Forms of Discrimination Based on Religion or Belief, but a declaration is not binding and does not have the legal force of a convention.[42] The United Nations has now also established a Special Rapporteur on Religion or Belief, but that official has more limited power than does the CEDAW Committee.[43] At a purely institutional or formal level, therefore, it

---

[35] ICESCR, art. 10, ICCPR art. 10. These are some of the few rights found in both Conventions.

[36] ICESCR art. 7(a)(i)

[37] ICCPR art. 18.

[38] Hilary Charlesworth, "What are 'Women's International Human Rights'?" in Cook, *Human Rights of Women*, 46, 68.

[39] *Convention on the Elimination of All Forms of Discrimination Against Women*, G.A. Res. 34/180, 34 UN GOAR, Supp. (No. 46), UN Doc A/34/46 (1979) (hereafter, CEDAW).

[40] CEDAW Part V. See also Elizabeth Evatt, "Finding a Voice for Women's Rights: The Early Days of CEDAW," *George Washington International Law Review* 34 (2002): 518–46.

[41] CEDAW, Optional Protocol.

[42] *Declaration on the Elimination of All Forms of Intolerance and Discrimination Based on Religion or Belief*, G.A. Res. 36/55, U.N. GOAR Supp. (No. 51) 171, UN Doc. A/36/684 (1981).

[43] For a discussion of the role and powers of the Special Rapporteur, including an analysis of the way in which he deals with conflicts between religious practices and women's rights, see Carolyn Evans, "The Special Rapporteur on Freedom of Religion or Belief," in *The Challenge of Religious Discrimination at the Dawn of the New Millennium*, ed, Nazila Ghanea (The Hague, Martinus Nijhoff: 2004), 33.

would appear that the rights of women are given stronger protection than is the right to engage in religious practices.

In terms of content also, CEDAW is stronger and less ambiguous than the Declaration on Religion or Belief. Although it has been criticized as focussing on masculinist equality standards[44] and lacks reference to certain important issues such as violence against women[45] and sexual rights, CEDAW does cover a wide variety of issues of relevance for women. Unlike the general international instruments that focus on women primarily as wives and mothers, CEDAW protects the rights of women in the workplace (art. 11), in education (art. 10), in public and political life (arts 7–8), health care (art. 12) and economic rights (art. 13) as well as dealing with issues such as marriage and childcare (arts 11(2), 16 and 17). In recognition of the role that legal systems often play in perpetuating discrimination against women, article 15 contains a general right of equality before the law between men and women, as well as a series of specific areas of law in which discrimination is not permitted. CEDAW certainly does not assume that the law is a neutral mediator of conflicting rights, but recognizes its potential to be involved in the continuing oppression, or emancipation, of women.

CEDAW deals only indirectly with the question of religion. The term religion or its derivations are not used throughout the treaty and there is no explicit recognition that religion traditionally has been a source and justification of many forms of discrimination against women—a phenomenon that is well-documented in the chapters in this book. CEDAW does, however, refer to culture and tradition as needing redefinition is order to promote women's equality and this reference should be taken as including religion[46] (although the fact that religion is not explicitly mentioned demonstrates the caution surrounding religious issues in the international sphere). In the Preamble, the parties to CEDAW note their awareness that "a change in the traditional role of men as well as the role of women in society and in the family is needed to achieve full equality between men and women." Even more forcefully, article 2, which deals with discrimination, places a legal obligation on States to "take all appropriate measures, including legislation, to modify or abolish existing law, regulations, *customs and practices* which constitute discrimination against women."[47] Further, article 5(a) requires parties to "modify social and cultural

[44] Dianne Otto, "Holding Up Half the Sky, But For Whose Benefit?: A Critical Analysis of the Fourth World Conference on Women," *Australian Feminist Law Journal* 6 (1996): 12–20; Southard, "Protection of Women's Human Rights Under the Convention", 4–11.

[45] The Committee does deal with domestic violence regularly, however. See Merry, "Constructing a Global Law," 952; Evatt, "Finding a Voice for Women's Rights," 546–551.

[46] Abdullahi Ahmed An-Na'im, "State Responsibility under International Human Rights Law to Change Religious and Customary Laws" in Cook, *Human Rights of Women*, 168.

[47] CEDAW art. 2(f), emphasis added.

patterns of conduct of men and women, with a view to achieving the elimination of prejudices and customary and all other practices which are based on the idea of the inferiority or the superiority of either of the sexes or stereotyped roles for men and women."

In contrast, the Declaration on Religion or Belief is a far more modest instrument, hedged about with limitations, exceptions and a concern for the potentially damaging effects of religion.[48] The Declaration acknowledges the harm that can be caused by religion when used as a means of "foreign interference in the affairs of other States" or in a manner inconsistent with the Charter.[49] Religious freedom is protected under the Declaration, but must not be exercised in a manner that coerces others and it may be subject to limitations necessary to "protect public safety, order, health or morals or the fundamental rights and freedoms of others" (art. 1). While parents and legal guardians have the right to bring up their children and have them educated "in accordance with their religion or belief ", "practices of a religion or belief in which a child is brought up must not be injurious to his physical or mental health or to his full development" (art. 5). Thus, unlike CEDAW, which contains no limitation clause, the Declaration gives significant scope to justified limitations on religious practices. In the limited case-law dealing with limitations on religious freedom (most of which emanates from a similar provision in the European Convention on Human Rights[50]) international courts have been ready to find limitations on religious freedom is justified in a wide range of circumstances, including concern for women's rights.[51]

Yet, despite developments in the international sphere that suggest far greater support for women's rights than for religious freedom, the chapters in this book demonstrate the many situations where religious practices and traditions are evoked by states to justify unequal and oppressive treatment of women and where the legal system refuses to recognise the full range of women's rights enunciated in CEDAW. What reasons explain this apparent disjunction between the dictates of international law and the lived reality of women in the Asia-Pacific region? Part of the reason for this can be found in the weak enforcement mechanisms used by CEDAW. The Convention only obliges parties to make regular reports on women's rights in their country. Such reports are often late, or fail to be produced at all, and in some cases are

---

[48] Donna J. Sullivan, "Advancing the Freedom of Religion or Belief Through the UN Declaration on the Elimination of Religious Intolerance and Discrimination," *American Journal of International Law* 82 (1988): 487–520.

[49] Declaration, preamble.

[50] See Carolyn Evans, *Freedom of Religion Under the European Convention on Human Rights* (Oxford: Oxford University Press, 2001), chap. 7.

[51] Eg. *Dahlab v. Switzerland* (dec.), App. No. 42393/98, Eur. Ct. H.R. 429 (2001–V).

of very poor quality.[52] The only penalty that the CEDAW Committee can impose for failing in either reporting obligations or in upholding the substantive commitments in the Convention is criticism, and this is often muted.[53] Even the new procedure of the Optional Protocol permitting individual complaints and inquiries into systematic violations of women's rights does not allow for any effective sanction or even result in a binding determination of the individual claim.[54] Nor is ratification of CEDAW universal, although it has increased significantly over the last few years.[55] While all of the States covered in this book other than Brunei are parties to CEDAW, a number are relative new-comers to the treaty.[56] Furthermore, religion can be an excuse for promoting non-ratification of CEDAW. Such arguments have been made in the United States, for example, where the consequences of ratifying CEDAW has been claimed to be "a violation of the rights of all Americans to worship, voice religious opinions, and teach their religion to their children. With the passage of this Convention, it is very conceivable that such teaching could be called harmful to society and forbidden by the government."[57] The refusal of the United States to ratify CEDAW may well undermine its effectiveness and prestige.

Despite now having a fairly high level of ratification, the conflicts between religious practices and teachings and the provisions of CEDAW have continued to undermine the effectiveness of CEDAW. One manifestation of this tension is the high level of reservations to CEDAW's provisions. A reservation is a means by which a State takes on most of the obligations under a treaty, but reserves the right to not adhere to (or not to fully adhere to) certain provisions.[58] A very large number of reservations have been made to this Convention, and some of them clearly demonstrate the tension between religious beliefs and women's

---

[52] Anne F. Bayefsky, "The CEDAW Convention: Its Contribution Today," *American Society of International Law Proceedings* 94 (2000): 199, noted in 2000 that there are more than 200 overdue reports to the Committee and that there was a two-year backlog of reports that had been submitted by States but not considered by the Committee. There have been some improvements to the system since then, but there are still serious inadequacies in terms of resources put into the Committee by the United Nations.

[53] Merry, "Constructing a Global Law," 954–8

[54] Kerri L. Ritz, "Soft Enforcement: Inadequacies of Optional Protocol as a Remedy for the Convention on the Elimination of All Forms of Discrimination Against Women," *Suffolk Transnational Law Review* 25 (2001): 191–216.

[55] Ritz, above, 203, notes that many of the worst violators of women's rights simply refuse to ratify CEDAW. At the time that she wrote the article, she noted Afghanistan as one of the worst offenders and one of those who refused to ratify in part for religious reasons.

[56] A full list of State parties can be found at http://untreaty/un.or/ENGLISH/bible/englishinternetbible/partI/chapterIV/treaty10.asp.

[57] Denesha Reid, Concerned Women for America, "Remarks by Denesha Reid," *American Society of International Law Proceedings* 94 (2000): 200–1.

[58] *Vienna Convention on the Law of Treaties,* May 23, 1969, U.N. Doc. A/conf.39/27, art. 1(d) a reservation is a 'unilateral statement, however phrased or named, made by a State, when signing, ratifying, accepting, approving or acceding to a treaty, whereby it purports to exclude or to modify the legal effect of certain provisions of the treaty in application to that State.'

rights.[59] There has been a particularly noticeable issue in relation to the ratification of CEDAW by predominantly Muslim States, where twelve States have reserved some or all provisions of CEDAW insofar as they conflict with Islamic law.[60] Malaysia, for example, has declared that it has ratified CEDAW "subject to the understanding that the provisions of the Convention do not conflict with the provisions of Islamic *syari'ah* law and the Federal Constitution of Malaysia."[61] Perhaps it is equally interesting to note that most non-Muslim States have not felt the need to make reservations regarding the discriminatory practices that are still engaged in by religious groups, unless the legal system recognises religious law or courts in certain areas.[62] For example, Australia has made reservations regarding the obligation in article 11(2) to provide paid maternity leave or comparable social benefits, but it does not feel the need to admit that religious organizations are not required by federal and state anti-discrimination law to admit women to positions of authority on the same basis as men.[63]

Another manifestation of the tension between women's rights and religious practices has been the use of culture and religion in State reports to justify failure to achieve the goals set out in CEDAW. Culture and religion are regularly portrayed to the Committee as monolithic and unchangeable, a characterization rejected by academic disciplines that make 'culture' and 'religion' their study, such as the discipline of contemporary anthropology,[64] as well as by

---

[59] Jennifer Riddle, "Making CEDAW Universal: A Critique of CEDAW's Reservation Regime under Art. 28 and the Effectiveness of the Reporting Process," *George Washington International Law Review* 34 (2002): 625–28.

[60] Brandt and Kaplan, "Tensions Between Women's Rights and Religious Rights." See the reservations of Bahrain, Bangladesh, Egypt, Iraq, Kuwait, Libya, Maldives, Mauritania, Morocco, Pakistan, Saudi Arabia, and Syria.

[61] http://untreaty/un.or/ENGLISH/bible/englishinternetbible/partI/chapterIV/treaty10.asp. Malaysia's original reservation then included a long list of particular provisions of CEDAW that it did not consider itself bound by, but withdrew many of these reservations in 1998.

[62] India, Lesotho, Singapore and Israel made reservations relevant to religious personal law and courts and Niger made reservations in regard to changing customs and practices.

[63] This is despite the fact that sections 36 and 37 of the *Sex Discrimination Act* 1984 (Australia) set out explicit exception from many of the non-discrimination principles in the Act to religious bodies and schools. On the ethical obligation of feminist researchers to note reservations by Western states rather than only those of Muslim states, see Howe, "White Western Feminism meets International Law," 87.

[64] This is the main thesis of Merry, "Constructing a Global Law". Regarding the debates in anthropology about 'culture', see Alfred Louis Kroeber and Clyde Kluckhohn, *Culture: A Critical Review of Concepts and Definitions* (New York: Vintage Books, 1963); Adam Kuper, "Culture, Identity and the Project of a Cosmopolitan Anthropology" *Man* 29 (3) (1994): 537–54 and *Culture: The Anthropologists' Account* (Cambridge, Mass.: Harvard University Press, 1999); and the recent review essay by Lars Rodseth, "Giving Up the Geist: Power, History and the Culture Concept in the Long Boasian Tradition," *Critique of Anthropology* 25(1) (2005): 5–11. For an analysis of the concept in contemporary Malaysia, see Joel S. Kahn, "Class, Ethnicity and Diversity: Some Remarks on Malay Culture in Malaysia," in *Fragmented Vision: Culture and Politics in Contemporary Malaysia*, ed. Joel S. Kahn and Francis Loh Kok Wah (Sydney: Asian Studies Association of Australia in Association with Allen & Unwin, 1992), 158–177.

women's organizations such as the Malaysian-based Sisters in Islam (SIS), which counters patriarchal and authoritarian interpretations of Islam with historicized readings of the sacred texts in order to show how patriarchal traditions are, quite literally, *man* made.[65] While such culturalist justifications are generally rejected by the CEDAW Committee as incompatible with the structure and substance of the convention (which requires government action to change cultural practices), the persistence of this form of justification demonstrates that the formal primacy of women's rights over cultural practices in CEDAW is not well accepted in many States. Dianne Otto, a scholar of international women's rights, notes that one of the predominant discourses about women in international law is that of "authoritarian states and religious fundamentalists arguing that the standards of female humanity are self-evident, as expressed by cultural or religious norms, and therefore not a matter for international judgment or scrutiny."[66] She goes on to examine the way in which "right-wing North American fundamentalist Protestants, the Holy See and Muslim extremists" banded together at the Beijing World Conference on Women to ensure that sexual orientation was not included in the final Beijing Declaration.[67] Indeed, paradoxically, the greater limitations placed on religious freedom than women's rights in international law arguably implies recognition of the real world power of religions and the relative powerlessness of women in many societies. There is no need for legal limitations on women's rights, because of the reality of women's powerlessness. Conversely, the very real power exercised by religions makes States more concerned to ensure that the rights of religious groups can be constrained.

Thus, when it comes to developing specific international law responses to particular issues (and even more so when international law principles are to be translated into domestic law and policy) the power of religious groups often proves superior in practice to that of women's groups. In areas such as

---

[65] Amina Wadud, *Qur'an and Woman: Rereading the Sacred Text from a Woman's Perspective* (Oxford, Oxford University Press, 1999); Norani Othman ed., *Shari'a Law and the Modern Nation-State* (Kuala Lumpur: SIS Publishing, 1994). A wealth of material can be read from the SIS Internet site: http://www.muslimtents.com/sistersinislam/.

[66] Dianne Otto, "Sexualities and Solidarities; Some Thoughts on Coalitional Strategies in the Context of International Law," *Australian Gay and Lesbian Law Journal*, 8 (1999): 28. This coalition also played a central role in the debate over whether reproductive rights and health should be included in the agenda. See Otto, "Holding Up Half the Sky", 16. She notes that when some progress was made in Bejing in regard to recognizing certain rights regarding sexuality and reproduction those provisions were subject to many reservations, including a general reservation to the whole health section made by the Holy See.

[67] Otto, "Sexualities and Solidarities," 29. See also Sullivan, "Gender Equality and Religious Freedom," 796 who claims that "The most comprehensive challenges mounted by states to the international norms guaranteeing women's rights, and their application, have been couched as defenses of religious liberty."

women's control of their own reproduction and sexuality, religious voices have proved a strong part of the debate. The Holy See is entitled to a place as a State in United Nations negotiations, and the governments of many Christian, Muslim and Buddhist countries are strongly influenced by religious teachings and principles. Women's groups, by contrast, are relegated to NGO status and have to work at lobbying governments that are overwhelmingly male-dominated and often closely linked with a particular religious group.[68] This is not to suggest that religious groups are monolithic on these issues—indeed transformative movements within religions have the potential to play an important role for women who are both deeply religious and committed to women's empowerment,[69] as we discuss below. But too often international law and international conferences treat religion as if it is a closed system with no room for internal debate and dissent. States tend to listen to and be influenced by conservative and patriarchal religious leaders rather than more liberal, marginal elements within religious groups.[70] Women's rights are thus constructed in international law as being in opposition to unchanging and unchangeable religious practices and hierarchies, rather than in recognition of the complexities of lived experience for women who contest religion, 'tradition' or 'culture' and patriarchal legal systems.[71]

The international human rights law regime, however, is only one frame of reference. As Abdullahai An-Na'im has argued, "it is useful to have the [international] framework and the specific provisions of the existing standards as a point of reference—that is to say, as something to debate or disagree with or

---

[68] Indeed, even within the United Nations, women are under-represented, particularly in more senior and influential positions. See Charlesworth and Chinkin, *Boundaries of International Law*. Despite this, the CEDAW Committee has been criticized for the absence of men. See Southard, 24.

[69] See Harold Coward, "Religious Responses to the Populatiôn Sustainability Problematic: Implications for Law," *Environmental Law* 27 (1997): 1169 for a discussion of how religious-based approaches to population control and women's empowerment has the potential to be far more effective than one based solely on individualistic liberalism. See generally: Jane H Bayes and Nayereh Tohidi, ed., *Globalization, Gender and Religion: The Politics of Women's Rights in Catholic and Muslim Contexts* (New York: Palgrave, 2001); Elizabeth Schüssler Fiorenza, "Public Discourse, Religion, and Wo/men's Struggles for Justice" *DePaul Law Review* 51 (2002): 1077–1102.

[70] An-Na'im, "State Responsibility under International Human Rights Law," 169: "No government can afford to disregard the politically articulated wishes or positions of powerful groups or segments of its population who might want to maintain religious and customary laws." This is true, he argues, of even the most despotic governments.

[71] Sunder, "Piercing the Veil," 1434–1442. Moreover, as L. Amede Obiora trenchantly observed: "When feminists are skeptical toward culture and its constituent elements, when they advocate the protection of women's interests within universalistic norms and standards of human rights, how can it be ensured that what they prescribe as norms and rights for the world at large are not at core reducible to customs of the West?": "Feminism, Globalization and Culture: After Bejing" *Indiana Journal of Global Legal Studies* 4 (1997): 358.

modify—in an effort to perfect the concept and better to articulate standards of genuinely universal human rights".[72] Certainly, the Singaporean women's organisations discussed by Li-ann Thio and the Indonesian women activists examined by Kathryn Robinson appeal to CEDAW as a meaningful source of authority; similarly, the Thai constitutional and human rights reforms discussed by Lucinda Peach and the New Zealand anti-discrimination provisions examined by Margaret Bedggood are direct state responses to international law obligations. Nevertheless, one of the things that surprised us the most as we read successive drafts of these chapters was how little reference the authors and the women they wrote about made to CEDAW or to other international instruments. The remainder of this introductory chapter, then, presents the competing frames of reference that are often of more direct relevance or immediate applicability to the women discussed in the chapters of this book, and it discusses some of the themes that emerge from them and methods adopted to understand them.

Issues, Themes and Methods

Each of the chapters in this collection examines the way that the positive law of the state creates a space for religion and regulates gender relations. Most of these states (Thailand, PNG, Solomon Islands, New Zealand, East Timor, Indonesia) explicitly provide for gender equality; others make no such explicit promises, but nonetheless oversee policies that give de facto recognition to gender equality (Singapore), or else have pursued development policies that encourage high rates of female participation in post-compulsory education and the paid workforce (Brunei). With the exception of Brunei, the constitutions of these states also explicitly guarantee religious freedom and respect for cultural diversity. Hence, one recurring theme of this collection is the extent to which states are able to deliver these promises to women, and how the second set of guarantees regarding religious freedom, toleration, and cultural pluralism often conflicts with the first set of promises regarding women's rights. This quandary confronts feminists and anti-colonialists as well: to reiterate the almost anguished lament of Jean Zorn, "we have never found a way to merge successfully our belief in custom with our belief in equality".

Feminist research on anti-colonialism and nationalism has shown how nationalist movements often enlist women in the struggle, representing women's plight or female virtues as emblems of the nation, and pledging a place for them

[72] Abdullahai Ahmed An-Na'im "Introduction" in *Human Rights in Cross-Cultural Perspectives: A Quest for Consensus,* ed. Abdullahai Ahmed An-Na'im (Philadelphia: University of Pennsylvania Press, 1991), 5.

in the new public life of the independent state.[73] Thio's discussion of the People's Action Party in Singapore, and Harris Rimmer's analysis of the current situation in East Timor demonstrate this clearly. As Valentine Moghadam has written, "women frequently become the sign or marker of political goals and of cultural identity during processes of revolution and state-building, and when power is being contested or reproduced." Thus, she writes, women are "linked to modernization and progress" or to "cultural rejuvenation and religious orthodoxy".[74] We can see their link to "divergent modernities"—in Maila Stivens apt phrase[75]—in the way that state-sponsored tourist propaganda, referred to by Peach and Thio, represent Thai and Singaporean women as progressive *and* pliant ('feminine') icons of the nation. Similarly, the chapters by Black and Robinson explore how revisions of the laws regulating marriage and divorce have been and remain central to contests in Brunei and Indonesia over national identity and government modernization agendas, just as in Thailand resistance to female ordination within the male dominated Buddhist Sangha is central claims about the purity of the Thai Buddhist tradition and the state's stake in those claims. The chapters on Brunei and Indonesia also show, as in a different way does the analyses of East Timor by Harris Rimmer, how the specific location of cultural rejuvenation and national development within religious orthodoxy has the effect of politicizing both religion and gender relations in a way offers both opportunities and dangers for women's human rights.

The tensions between law, with its emancipatory promises, on the one hand, and religion, 'tradition' or 'culture' on the other, can be traced in part to the legacy of the Western colonial powers (who directly governed every state discussed in this book except Thailand) and their creation of a separate regime of 'personal laws'.[76] The colonizing English position is typified in this 1869 decision, in which the judge concluded that the law of England:

> is subject in its application to the various alien races established here, to such modifications as are necessary to prevent it from operating unjustly or oppressively on

---

[73] E.g., Alexander and Mohanty, "Introduction: Genealogies, Legacies, Movements" in Alexander and Mohanty, *Feminist Genealogies*, xiii–xlii.

[74] Moghadam, "Introduction and Overview: Gender Dynamics of nationalism, Revolution and Islamization" in *Gender and National Identity*, 2.

[75] Maila Stivens, "Theorizing Gender, Power and Modernity" in Sen and Stivens, *Gender and Power in Afflluent Asia,* 10; see further Mina Roces and Louise Edwards, "Contesting Gender Narratives, 1970–2000" in Edwards and Roces, *Women in Asia,* 1–15.

[76] See generally M. B. Hooker, *A Concise Legal History of Southeast Asia* (Oxford: Oxford University Press, 1978); M. B. Hooker, *Adat Law in Modern Indonesia* (Kuala Lumpur: Oxford University Press, 1978); M. B. Hooker, *Adat Laws in Modern Malaya: Land Tenure, Traditional Government and Religion* (Kuala Lumpur: Oxford University Press, 1972); M. B. Hooker, *Legal Pluralism: An Introduction to Colonial and Neo-Colonial Laws* (Oxford: Clarendon Press, 1975); M. B. Hooker, *The Personal Laws of Malaysia* (Kuala Lumpur: Oxford University Press, 1976); M. B. Hooker, ed., *Laws of South-east Asia,* 2 vols (Singapore: Butterworths, 1986–88).

> them. Thus in a question of marriage or divorce, it would be impossible to apply our law to Mohammedans, Hindus and Buddhists, without the most absurd and intolerable consequences, and it is therefore held inapplicable to them[77]

In the logic of this decision we can see the logic of Enlightenment rationality. For this judge, it was self evident that the primary site of intimate gender relation—laws relating to marriage and divorce, custody of children and division of property—should be matters for the 'races' and their religions and customs. This colonial attitude to 'personal laws' can be traced, as Madhavi Sunder has compellingly argued, to the Enlightenment bifurcation of rationality and sentiment and the accompanying idea that religion is a private matter of interior and personal belief, to be tolerated (because this ensures civil peace), its dangerous passions controlled "by carefully tucking them away in the private sphere".[78] Sunder's conceptualization of religion as law's "Other" is helpful here. She argues that law "views religion as natural, irrational, incontestable, and imposed", the "Other" of the rational public sphere governed by legality, and so, she continues:

> failing to recognize cultural and religious communities as contested and subject to change, legal norms such as "freedom of religion", the "right to culture" and the guarantee of "self-determination" defer to the claims of patriarchal, religious elites, buttressing their power over the claims of modernizers.[79]

If the Enlightenment legal tradition of the West in general, and its more specific application via colonialism to legal regimes of the post-colonial states of the Asia-Pacific in particular, is one frame of reference for women, then religion is another. As Kathryn Robinson writes, in Indonesia, Islam has often been proffered as an alternative source of authority to the state. One question that she explores is: whose version of Islam? Who speaks for Islam? Whose voice is paramount? The same question is posed about each of the religions or spiritual traditions discussed in this book.

The chapters in this volume consider how the traditions upon which many of these states build, maintain and seek to reconstruct religious institutions and culture practices have been manufactured from incomplete sources, without sufficient attention to what woman have to say about their faith or community.[80] Thio

---

[77] *Chou Choon Neoh v. Spottiswoode* (1869) 1 Ky 216 per Maxwell C.J. In relation to the Dutch colonial position in the Dutch East Indies, see the comprehensive discussion by Charles Coppel, "The Indonesian Chinese as 'Foreign Orientals' in the Netherlands Indies" in *Indonesia: Law and Society*, ed. Tim Lindsey (Sydney: Federation Press, 1999), 33–41.

[78] Sunder, "Piercing the Veil," 1418.

[79] Ibid., 1402–3.

[80] Regarding the political and social construction of 'tradition' see the influential work of Eric Hobsbawm and Terrence Ranger, *The Invention of Tradition* (Cambridge: Cambridge University Press, 1983). There are many insightful studies of the manufacture of Asian traditions, for example the work of Maila Stivens in relation to Malaysia, *Matriliny and Modernity*, and of Uma Narayan in relation to India, *Dislocating Cultures: Identities, Traditions and Third-World Feminism* (New York: Routledge, 1997).

describes how the Singapore government's corporatized approach to religion enables it to deal only with the religious leaders it has already decided to recognise as legitimate. Unsurprisingly, dissentient female voices are not heeded unless it suits the government to do so. Similarly, the chapters about PNG, Solomon Islands and New Zealand show how colonial administrators and then post-independence states paid more attention to patriarchal interpretations of indigenous cultural practices and spirituality than to interpretations which gave women status or authority. Harris Rimmer's chapter explores how women are struggling to be heard, and to receive justice, in post-conflict East Timor; Peach analyses the way the Thai state recognises only the male Sangha and how interpretations of Buddhist texts that are hostile to women and female sexuality have more currency; and Black's study of the Islamization policies of Brunei describes how they are pursued with no formalised or democratic way to acknowledge women's voices or views.

Yet there are such voices, and, as this collection demonstrates, they are persistent (like the Indonesian women activists demonstrating outside the 'polygamy awards') and insistent, if sometimes quietly so (like the Solomon Islands organisation Women for Peace, which takes a 'motherly approach' to its role in conflict resolution and reconstruction). These "cultural dissenters", as Sunder calls them,[81] counter exclusionary, patriarchal and misogynistic interpretations of religious and cultural texts and practices (made by adherents as well as external observers) with interpretations that offer women more pathways for meaningful and dignified participation in the public and private life of their faith and community. A striking aspect of this activity is the extent to which it draws upon transnational scholarship and activism for support and inspiration. Thus Thai women seeking ordination turn to the international organization Sakyadhita ("Daughters of the Buddha") which facilitates inter-denominational ordination; members of the Roman Catholic Church hierarchy in East Timor—a transnational organisation if ever there was one—cite international human rights law in support of an amnesty settlement that delivers real justice to female victims of sexual violence; Justice Brunton in PNG refers to Western feminist scholarship on witchcraft to buttress his decision that witch-hunting is "a form of terror that holds women in their place"; and the Malaysian organisation, Sisters in Islam, is an inspirational and practical resource for Muslim women in Indonesia, Brunei and Singapore who read the Qur'an as a source of social justice and spiritual equality.[82] Sunder heralds this kind of activity as the "new enlightenment"[83] and Frances Adeney

---

[81] Sunder, "Cultural Dissent," 495ff.

[82] See further, Zainah Anwar, "The Struggle for Women's Rights within a Religious Framework: The Experience of Sisters in Islam," *Kultur* 2 no. 2 (2002): 103–115.

[83] Sunder, "Piercing the Veil," passim but esp. 1410–15.

welcomes it as the "third wave of the global women's movement that centers on spirituality."[84]

In her critique of Western feminist writing about Third-World women coupled with her alternative agenda for a research based upon a "noncolonizing feminist solidarity across borders", Mohanty enjoins feminist scholars to examine the lives of the "most marginalized communities of women" because "if we pay attention to and think from the space of some of the most disenfranchised communities of women in the world, we are most likely to envision a just and democratic society capable of treating all its citizens fairly".[85] In this book, Peach's examination of sex workers and renunciants in Thailand, Zorn's assessment of the way colonial and post-colonial Papua New Guinea law treats women alleged to be witches and the men accused of killing them, Whiu's analysis of the constructions of indigenous Māori women by white settler (Pākehā) law and society in Aotearoa/New Zealand, and Harris Rimmer's study of victims of gendered violence in East Timor, perform this task. In each of these chapters, the author uses the particularities of these marginalized groups of women to interrogate the national institutions of law and religion, demonstrating in each case the justice deficits for women that would not have been visible from a simple reading of the rights guarantees of state constitutions, or the statistically measured achievements of development programs. Thus, where more benign and generalizing examinations of the successes of development under current Thai law and policy quite correctly regard "improvements on the status of Thai women" as "phenomenal",[86] Peach argues that "the status of nuns, like that of prostitutes, is a poor one in contemporary Thailand," and Black and Thio look past the development statistics indicating high income, workforce participation and tertiary education for women in Brunei and Singapore, to question the state's achievements from the perspectives of indigenous women and of Muslim Indian women facing domestic violence. Similarly, Harris Rimmer looks beyond the reconciliation rhetoric of the East Timorese president to the 'grim realities' for female victims of sexual violence inflicted by occupying troops or domestic partners, and Zorn and Whiu demonstrate that state promises of gender equality and respect for 'custom' or 'tradition' fail to engage with the actual predicaments of the most disenfranchised groups of women in PNG and Aotearoa/New Zealand.

---

[84] Frances S. Adeney, *Christian Women in Indonesia: A Narrative Study of Gender and Religion* (Syracuse: Syracuse University Press, 2002), 3.

[85] Chandra Talpade Mohanty, *Feminism Without Borders: Decolonizing Theory, Practicing Solidarity* (Durham: Duke University Press, 2003), 224, 231.

[86] Roces and Edwards, 'Contesting Gender Narratives," 9, commenting upon chap. 12 by Bhassorn Limanonda, "Exploring Women's status in contemporary Thailand."

The studies in this volume are offered, then, as an exercise in "transnational feminist practice"[87] and feminist solidarity. We conclude with an observation on the approach of the chapter which most explicitly performs solidarity, or what Isabelle Gunning has famously called "world-travelling".[88] In their joint chapter about Aotearoa/New Zealand, Bedggood and Whiu carefully delineate their own situatedness as Pākehā and Māori, and they disavow the ability to speak for or on behalf of each other's communities. Yet, they take on the ethical responsibility of writing within the same chapter, and of jointly writing the introduction and conclusion. Their separately written chapters chart narratives of exclusion, violence, pain and regret; their joint conclusion, written in a spirit of solidarity with each other's community reaches out also to acknowledge other Aotearoa/New Zealand communities excluded from their self-consciously bicultural narratives,[89] and to express hope for more respectful future engagement based upon recognition of difference and commonalities.

[87] See further Inderpal Grewal and Caren Kaplan, "Introduction: Transnational Feminist Practices and Questions of Postmodernity," in Grewal and Kaplan, *Scattered Hegemonies*, 1–36, esp. 17–18.

[88] Gunning, "Arrogant Perception," 189ff. This approach is also endorsed by Radhika Coomaraswamy, "Different but Free: Cultural Relativism and Women's Rights as Human Rights," in *Religious Fundamentalisms and the Human Rights of Women*, ed. Courtney W Howland (New York: St Martin's Press, 1999), 79–90.

[89] See further Radhika Mohanram, *Black Body: Women, Colonialism and Space* (St Leonards: Allen and Unwin, 1999).

CHAPTER TWO

SEX OR SANGHA? NON-NORMATIVE GENDER ROLES FOR WOMEN IN THAI LAW AND RELIGION

Lucinda Peach

Introduction

Both 'religion' and 'law' are powerful discourses that shape people's understandings of their world, the place of sex and gender, and themselves as gendered beings. This chapter on Thailand examines an apparent paradox in the legal and religious status of prostitutes and nuns (*mae chi* and *bhikkhuni*) in contemporary Thailand. The ideal gender roles for women in Thai society are those of wife and mother. Thus, wives and mothers represent 'good women' in relation to prostitutes. Given this dichotomization of female gender roles, as well as the centrality of Buddhism to Thai culture and society, one might anticipate that nuns would be even more highly regarded, especially when compared with prostitutes. Certainly, this is the case in Western gender ideology, where the 'Madonna/whore complex' dichotomizes the virginal and chaste woman as the ideal and casts the sexually promiscuous one as at least bad and immoral, if not completely sinful. Surprisingly, however, this is not the case in Thailand.

In actual practice, while both monastic and sex worker roles for women are regarded negatively, nuns are even more maligned than prostitutes. In discussing this seeming paradox, I show how both law and religion in Thai society have mutually reinforced the normative roles of wife and mother, while according to prostitution a somewhat more elevated status than that ascribed to female monasticism. The position of prostitutes and nuns in Thai law and religion suggests a deep ambivalence about these roles for women, an ambivalence that I contend existed prior to, but has been both modified and exacerbated by, economic globalization. I further argue that the contemporary status of these two non-normative female roles, especially in relation to one another, is derived more from the gender ideology surrounding production and reproduction in Thailand—and to the closer proximity of prostitution than monasticism to the idealized roles of wife and mother—than from the perceived moral goodness of either.

This chapter proceeds as follows. I first give a brief overview of how religion and law have influenced women's status in Thailand and promoted the roles of wife and mother as the normative ideal for all women. Next I examine the sex trade and the Sangha (the official monastic establishment which in

Thailand, until now, has been exclusively male) to illustrate how Thai law and religion facilitate the discriminatory treatment of women who transgress their normative female roles by becoming prostitutes or nuns. I conclude by discussing some of the factors that have resulted in a 'reverse Madonna /whore complex' in Thailand.

In undertaking this study, I hope to avoid the "imperializing gaze" that Leslie Jeffrey identifies as having influenced much scholarship on Thailand, a gaze which depends upon reified notions "rather than upon examining how power informs the way in which such notions are constructed."[1] Although I am not Thai and so do not write from an insider perspective as having experience of being a woman in Thai society, nevertheless this chapter is written with an attitude of respect and empathy for the women in Thailand who are struggling with the consequences of having taken on non-normative sex roles, whether voluntarily or otherwise. The description and analysis here are based on opportunities to conduct fieldwork in the summer of 1998, upon the voices of Thai women available in English language sources, and upon a number of published studies on various aspects of Thai women's lives.

Women's Religious and Legal Status in Thailand

While the relative social status of Thai women has improved considerably throughout history (as has the status of women in many parts of the world), Thai women, in general terms, are not considered to be the equals of men in either lay or monastic life. This is evidenced by their unequal opportunities for education, work, professional and career development, monastic ordination and other aspects of religious and secular leadership, as well as by popular portrayals of women in the mass media. Both religion and law have been significant influences in shaping the status of, and roles available to, Thai women throughout history.

Women's Religious Status

The center of Thai culture is Theravada Buddhism, the earliest and most orthodox of the three great traditions or 'vehicles' of Buddhism, which developed in India after the death of the Buddha in approximately 544 B.C.E. As a predominantly Buddhist nation (90 percent of Thais profess to be Buddhist), the Buddhist religion has been the central norm shaping Thailand's social institutions and legal order, as well as its national identity.[2] Thus, it is artificial to speak of religion as

---

[1] Leslie Ann Jeffrey, *Sex and Borders: Gender, National Identity, and Prostitution Policy in Thailand* (Honolulu: University of Hawaii Press, 2002), xxi, xviii.

separate and independent from law in Thai culture. As Penny van Esterik and other scholars have observed, "Theravada Buddhism provides many Thai with a way of viewing the world, a sense of reality, moral standards, and a shared language and metaphors for analyzing their existing life situation."[3] Vietnamese scholar Thanh-Dam Truong adds that Buddhism in Thailand "provides a world-view which shapes people's consciousness and legitimates existing forms of social relations."[4] Buddhism is thus also important for an understanding of gender, as it is a central attribute of Thai identity.[5]

Buddhist Views of Women

In particular, Buddhist scriptures have contributed to shaping Thai gender identity, especially through cultural valuations of women as both inferior to men and as the embodiments of sexuality.[6] For example, women are described in *The Saddharmasmrtyupasthana* as "ever the root of ruin, and of loss of substance." The text goes on to ask:

> when men are to be controlled by women how can they gain happiness? [. . .] A woman is the destruction of destructions in this world and the next; hence one must ever avoid women if he desires happiness for himself.[7]

---

[2] Jeffrey, *Sex and Borders*, xxiii; Donald Swearer, *The Buddhist World of Southeast Asia* (Albany, NY: State University of New York Press, 1995), 12; Thomas Kirsch, "Text and Context: Buddhist Sex Roles/Culture of Gender Revisited," *American Ethnologist* 12 (1985): 315; Frank Reynolds, "Dhamma in Dispute: The Interactions of Religion and Law in Thailand," *Law and Society Review* 28(3) (1994): 433–52, 454.

[3] Penny van Esterik, *Materializing Thailand* (Oxford: Berg Books, 2000), 66.

[4] Thanh-Dam Truong, *Sex, Money, And Morality: Prostitution And Tourism In Southeast Asia* (London: Zed Books, 1990), 12; also L. S. Dewaraja, "The Position of Women in Buddhism," *The Wheel* (Columbo, Sri Lanka: Buddhist Publication Society, 1981), no. 280, online at *DharmaNet* website, http://www.enabling.org/ia/vipassana/Archive/D/Dewaraja/womenInBudCountyDewaraja.html.

[5] Van Esterik, *Materializing Thailand*, 65, adds that Buddhism "has a profound impact not only because of its texts and rituals, but also because of the paradoxes emerging from the gaps between doctrine and everyday life. Gender is enmeshed in these paradoxical gaps."

[6] Theravada Buddhist texts are collected in the Pali Canon. This doctrinal foundation of Theravada Buddhism contains the Tipitaka ("three baskets") of early Buddhist teachings: the Vinaya, or rules of ethics, much of which is devoted to rules governing monastics; Sutta, or teachings, attributed to the historical Buddha; and Abhidharma, or philosophical analysis of the components of reality. The Pali Canon is a vast body of literature which adds up to several thousand printed pages in English translation, most of which has been published in English over the years. The complete body of classical Theravada texts is comprised of the Tipitaka and the post-canonical texts such as commentaries, chronicles, and so on. See the website of *Access to Insight: Readings in Theravada Buddhism*, http://www.accesstoinsight.org/index.html.

[7] Cecil Bendall and W.H.D. Rouse, trans., *The Siksasamuccaya* (Delhi: Motilal Banarsidass, 1971), 77, quoted in Alan Sponberg, "Attitudes toward Women and the Feminine in Early Buddhism," in *Buddhism, Sexuality, and Gender*, ed. Jose Cabezon (Albany, NY: State University of New York Press, 1992), 19.

The *Anguttara Nikaya* III attributes to the Buddha the following:

> Monks, I see no other single form so enticing, so desirable, so intoxicating, so binding, so distracting, such a hindrance to winning the unsurpassed peace from effort [. . .] as a woman's form. Monks, whosoever clings to a woman's form—Infatuated, greedy, fettered, enslaved, enthralled—for many a long day shall grieve, snared by the charms of a woman's form.
>
> Monks, a woman, even when going along, will stop to ensnare the heart of a man; whether standing, sitting or lying down, laughing, talking or singing, weeping, stricken or dying, a woman will stop to ensnare the heart of a man. [. . .] Verily, one may say of womanhood: it is wholly a snare of [the Tempter], Mara.[8]

Women are also described in the Pali Canon itself as "easily losing their temper, being jealous, narrow-minded, of small intellect and without the capacity to participate in government, hold big responsibilities or travel to engage in foreign trade", and as "an enemy to the path of purity, and as unable to become a Buddha."[9]

However, what Alan Sponberg labels the "most blatantly misogynistic texts of the Pali literature"[10] are found in the stories of the *Jataka*. These are an (originally) pre-Buddhist collection of popular animal tales and hero legends[11] which have been highly influential in Thai Buddhist society for centuries.[12] The *Jatakas* include images and descriptions of women as:

> like robbers with braided locks, like a poisoned drink, like merchants that sing their own praises, crooked like a deer's horn, evil-tongued like snakes, like a pit that was covered over, like hell which was difficult to fill, like an ogress hard to satisfy, like the all-ravenous Yama, like all-devouring flame, like all-sweeping river, like wind blowing where it desires, undiscriminating like Mount Meru, and perpetually fruiting like a poison tree.[13]

---

[8] F. L. Woodward and M. E. Hare, trans., *Anguttara Nikaya (Gradual Sayings)* (London, Pali Text Society, 1932–36) I: 2ff, II: 224, quoted in Sponberg, "Attitudes toward Women," 20.

[9] Woodward and Hare *Anguttara Nikaya* II, 80, XX, 164; C. A. F. Rhys Davids, Suriya Sumangla Thera and F. L. Woodward, trans., *Samyutta Nikaya (Kindred Sayings)* (London: Pali Text Society, 1917–1930), I: 37, quoted in Suwanna Satha-Anand, "Looking to Buddhism to Turn Back Prostitution in Thailand," in *The East Asian Challenge for Human Rights*, ed. Joanne Bauer and Daniel Bell (New York: Cambridge University Press, 1999), 206.

[10] Sponberg, "Attitudes toward Women," 35 n. 29.

[11] Ibid.

[12] The precise origins of the *Jatakas* are lost to history, but it is thought that they were originally pre-Buddhist folk tales that were compiled in the third century BCE and were regarded as moral stories in the *Vinaya* (the section of the Pali Canon devoted to ethics). According to Buddhist scholar Gunapala Dharmasiri, the *Jatakas* have affected and shaped the lives of Buddhist villagers for centuries to a much greater extent than other highly original doctrinal texts, and they continue to influence religious culture in Buddhist countries significantly. See Kornvipa Boonsue, *Buddhism and Gender Bias: An Analysis of a Jataka Tale*, Paper No. 3, Working Paper Series: Thai Studies Project (York University, Toronto: 1989), 29.

[13] Bimala Churn Law, *Women in Buddhist Literature* (Varanasi, India: Indological Book House, 1981), 27, citing *Five Jatakas: Containing A Fairy Tale, a Comical Story, and Three Fables In the Original Pali Text*, trans. Viggo Fausbol (Copenhagen: C.A. Reitzel, 1861), *Jataka* V.

In addition, women are described as having lust or greed which consumes the rich man "like fuel caste in a blazing fire,"[14] and as assuming different poses to lure weak-minded men and cause them to fall prey to woman's sinful snare, and then ruining the men's character, wealth, and success.[15] Various *Jataka* stories further describe women as being unfaithful to their husbands,[16] as having a sensual, worldly nature and never having enough of "intercourse, adornment, and child-bearing,"[17] and as never tiring of sex, as "it is the nature of [their] birth."[18] In particular, women are depicted in Buddhist literature as sexual temptresses who deliberately attempt to sidetrack otherwise chaste and virtuous men away from the spiritual path.

Scholars have suggested that such images of women, which appear in many early Buddhist texts, indicate that monks considered women's sexuality as a threat to their pursuit of the spiritual path and to the stability of the monastic order as a whole.[19] This perspective finds ample support in Buddhist scriptures. For example, in one of the *Theragatha,* Kala threatens to leave his marital home, explaining that "Who'd want to live in Nala? Here women use their bodies to trap ascetics who only want to live by the Dharma."[20] Similarly, in the *Therigatha* (the songs or poems of the *Theri*, or women elders, many of

[14] Ibid., *Jataka* V, 452.

[15] Ibid., *Jataka* III, 40.

[16] E. B. Cowell, trans., *The Jataka or Stories of the Buddha's Former Births* (London: Pali Text Society, 1895–1907), I: 1293; II: 134.

[17] Ibid., *Jataka* III, 342.

[18] Ibid., *Jataka*, I, 440.

[19] Karen Andrews, "Women in Theravada Buddhism," Berkeley, CA: Institute of Buddhist Studies, http://www.enabling.org/ia/vipassana/Archive/A/Andrews/women TheraBud Andrews.html; Sponberg, "Attitudes toward Women," 20; Ria Kloppenberg, "Female Stereotypes in Early Buddhism: the Women of the Therigatha," in *Female Stereotypes in Religious Traditions*, ed. Ria Kloppenberg and Wouter Hanegraaff (Leiden: E.J. Brill, 1995), 152; Hiroko Kawanami, "Can Women Be Celibate: Sexuality and Abstinence in Theravada Buddhism," in *Celibacy, Culture, and Society: The Anthropology of Sexual Abstinence*, ed. Elisa Sobo and Sandra Bell (Madison, WI: University of Wisconsin Press, 2001), 141; Chatsumarn Kabilsingh, *Thai Women in Buddhism* (Berkeley, CA: Parallex Press, 1991), 25–29; Karen Lang, "Lord Death's Snare: Gender-Related Imagery in the Theragatha and the Therigatha," *Journal of Feminist Studies in Religion* 2 no. 1 (1986): 64; Diana Paul, *Women in Buddhism: Images of the Feminine in Mahayana Tradition* 2nd edn (Berkeley, CA: University of California Press, 1985), 303; Nancy Falk, "An Image of Woman In Old Buddhist Literature: The Daughters of Mara," in *Women and Religion*, ed. Judith Plaskow and Joan Arnold Romero (Missoula, MO: Scholars' Press, 1974), 108.

[20] Susan Murcott, *The First Buddhist Women: Translations and Commentaries on the Therigatha* (Berkeley, CA: Parallax Press, 1991), 108–11, 122; see also Caroline A. F. Rhys-Davids and K. R. Norman, trans., *Poems of the Early Buddhist Nuns* (Oxford: Pali Text Society, 1989), 108–14, 205–206.

whom were the first generation students of Shakyamuni Buddha[21]), Vimala, now a nun, describes her former life as a beautiful courtesan in the following words:

> Young
> intoxicated by my own
> lovely skin,
> my figure,
> my gorgeous looks,
> and famous too,
> I despised other women.
>
> Dressed to kill
> At the whorehouse door,
> I was a hunter
> and spread my snare for fools.
>
> And when I stripped for them
> I was the woman of their dreams;
> I laughed as I teased them.[22]

Understanding the female as symbolic of the world of sensuality is a common theme throughout the Buddhist world, beginning with the story of the Buddha's renunciation from lay life, and his rejection of his new wife Yasodhara and newborn son Rahula.[23] The Buddha's struggle under the Bodhi tree for enlightenment years later involves rejecting the sensual enticements of Mara's 'daughters' who have been sent to seduce him away from his spiritual goal. Women's identity is depicted in Buddhist scriptures as embodied and social, embedded in relationships with others, and dependent on things of this 'world'—the world of *samsara* or suffering. These texts emphasize that women are attached to the material world of the senses and emotions, in contrast to men, who are more able to practice detachment, and, consequently, pursue

---

[21] *The Therigatha* was passed on orally for six centuries prior to being written in Pali in Sri Lanka in the first century B.C.E. See Murcott, *First Buddhist Women*, 3. It appears in the *Khuddaka Nikaya*, which is the fifth part of the *Sutta-Pitaka*, or the "sutra basket" of the *Tripitaka*. Some of the *Theris'* stories are also recorded elsewhere in the Pali Canon. Two translations of the *Therigatha* appear in Rhys-Davids and Norman, *Poems*; see Murcott, *First Buddhist Women;* Law, *Women in Buddhist Literature,* 25–34; Horner, *Women Under Primitive Buddhism*, 86–94, 184–93.

[22] Murcott, *First Buddhist Women*, 126; also Rhys-Davids and Norman, *Poems,* 41, 178.

[23] Murcott, *First Buddhist Women*, 92, notes that early Buddhist art parallels this scriptural portrayal of women as seductress: "women are invariably depicted sensuously. They are large-breasted and wide-hipped; their stance and gestures are inviting."

the spiritual path.[24] Even today, writes one Thai Buddhist woman, "many monks misinterpret that women are enemies to their spiritual liberation, so they feel they have to stay away from them."[25]

In popular Buddhist understandings, to be born a woman is itself the result of previous bad *karma* (Pali: *kamma*: the result of actions in previous lives and previous moments in this life).[26] According to an old Thai belief, for example, a man who committed adultery would be reborn for 500 lifetimes as a woman, and another 500 as a transvestite, before working off the bad *karma* to be reborn as a man again.[27] It is widely believed that a woman can only achieve enlightenment after having been reborn as a male.[28] A vivid illustration of how deeply Thai women have taken this to heart is the inscription which the Queen Mother had placed on a monastery she founded during the commemoration event in 1399 BE: "I pray that I may be reborn as a male in a future existence."[29]

However, in order to obtain such a favorable rebirth, females must enhance their store of merit (virtue required to acquire good *karma* for this and future lives, basically understood as acts of generosity). Merit can be "made," not only for the actor, but also for others through "dedicating" it for their benefit. Traditional Thai Buddhist values of respect and honor for parents motivate children to make merit in order to satisfy their indebtedness to their parents.

A tenet of popular Thai Buddhism is that males can favorably improve their *karma* and make merit for their parents through entering the Sangha, even temporarily. This tenet is so strong that it supports the belief that "after a family sells their daughter into prostitution, they can clear their *karma* if their

[24] See, e.g., Alexandra R. Kapur-Fic, *Thailand: Buddhism, Society, and Women* (New Delhi, India: Abhinav Publications, 1998), 454; Sponberg, "Attitudes toward Women," 20; Lang, "Lord Death's Snare," 64; Paul, *Women in Buddhism*, 303; Falk, "An Image of Woman," 108.

[25] Ouyporn Khuankaew, "Thai Buddhism and Patriarchy," (undated), online at *American Buddha Website*, http://www.american-buddha.com/thai.buddh.patriarchy.htm #THAI%20 BUDDHISM%20AND%20PATRIARCHY, 5.

[26] Kapur-Fic, *Thailand*, 419–20; Dewaraja, "Position of Women in Buddhism," 3; Kabilsingh, *Women in Thai Buddhism*, 31; Satha-Anand, "Looking to Buddhism," 197–98.

[27] Sarutta, "Women's Status in Thai Society," *Thaiways* 19 no. 11 (September 10, 2002), online at *Anurak Thailand Tourism Website, 3* http://www.thaiwaysmagazine.com/thai_article/m 1911_thai_women_status/.

[28] Narumon Hinshiranan, "The Case of Buddhist Nuns in Thailand," Sakyadhita Newsletter (Summer 1993), 11, http://sakyadhita.org/NewsLetters/4-1.htm; Sponberg, "Attitudes toward Women," 24; Thomas Kirsch, "Economy, Polity, and Religion in Thailand," in *Change and Persistence in Buddhist Society*, ed. Thomas Kirsch and William Skinner (Ithaca, NY: Cornell University Press, 1975), 172–96.

[29] Dewaraja, "Position of Women in Buddhism," 4.

son ordains as a monk—even if only for 3 days."[30] Indeed, most young men become monastics on a temporary 'novice' or 'apprentice' basis, usually for only a few months rather than permanently.[31]

The exclusion of women from the official Sangha (described more fully below) thereby also excludes them from this important means of making merit and so contributes to the denigration of women in Buddhist cultures by providing 'evidence' of their spiritual inferiority.[32] Instead, women's accumulation of merit is related to their roles as daughters, wives, and mothers. As Alexandra Kapur-Fic observes, "in these capacities they are far more involved than men in performing the acts of routine merit making," which include practicing generosity by giving *dana* (donations—usually money, food and other provisions) to temples and individual monks, who then act as "fields of merit" for donors. As mothers, women also may raise sons who will enter the order: this is regarded as the greatest merit women can make.[33] In all these ways, women are dependent upon men for making merit.

Furthermore, after having satisfied their filial obligation by temporarily ordaining as a monk (which they typically do prior to marriage), sons are released from their familial obligations. On the other hand, daughters, especially the youngest in a family, feel a continuing responsibility to take care of their parents, especially when they get old. They can satisfy this obligation by earning money to provide for them.[34] Given the gender discrimination in employment in Thailand, one of the most effective means for Thai women to make a relatively good sum of money is through sex work. At the same time, because (men's) participation in the Sangha is socially highly respected, whereas (women's) engagement in sex work is not, the institutions of trafficking and merit-making synergistically serve to perpetuate the male domination of society.

---

[30] Bhikkhuni Dr. Lee, "Getting Clear: Revealing the Myths in Theravada Buddhism," *Seeds of Peace* 17 no. 2 (2001): 2.

[31] Khuankaew, "Thai Buddhism and Patriarchy,"1; United Nations Development Fund for Women, East and South East Asia (UNIFEM), *2000 Gender and Development in Thailand*: Section B—"Socio Economic Status of Women", Part 2, "Women's Economic Conditions," http://www.unifem-eseasia.org /resources/others /gendev/sectionb2.htm, B. 4 (cultural conditions).

[32] Nancy Eberhardt, "Introduction," in *Gender, Power, and the Construction of the Moral Order: Studies from the Thai Peripher,* ed. Nancy Eberhardt (Madison, WI: Center for Southeast Asian Studies, 1988), 78; Kirsch, "Text and Context," 304.

[33] Kapur-Fic, *Thailand,* 436–37. Conversely, a woman's inability to bear a son is viewed as the result of bad karma (p. 437–38); Isaline Blew Horner, *Women under Primitive Buddhism* (Amsterdam: Philo Press, 1930), 86–94, 184–93, 87.

[34] Khuankaew, "Thai Buddhism and Patriarchy," 1; Monique Beadle, "The Sangha and the Sex Industry" (August 26, 2003), online at *Institute for Global Engagement Website,* http://www.globalengage.org/issues/2003/08/sangha.htm, 1–5, 2; UNIFEM, *2000 Gender and Development in Thailand*: Section B, Part 2; Kirsch, "Text and Context," 308; Siriporn Skrobanek, Nattaya Boonpakdi, and Chutima Janthakeero, *The Traffic in Women: Human Realities of the International Sex Trade* (New York: Zed Books, 1997), 23, 69, 73–76, 79, 101.

Normative Views of Thai Women

Traditionally, Thai women (as women in Asia and much of the world more generally) have been expected to be wives and mothers. Thailand shares with other Southeast Asian Buddhist countries the prevailing belief that women fulfill their spiritual obligations through their domestic duties as wives and mothers, and are not required to make additional efforts. This ideology makes it quite difficult for many women to renounce lay lives or the traditional and still-normative gender role expectations that they will be wives and mothers.

This ideal image of a woman as a devoted, faithful, and obedient wife and mother dates back to the early Buddhist scriptures included in the Pali Canon.[35] Early Buddhist *Suttas* quote the Buddha's views on the ideal wife, the qualities a wife must possess to go to heaven (a higher realm, not enlightenment) and his descriptions of "good wives" as "always devoted and dutiful to their husbands," as sacrificing their personal comfort, and as "always ready to undergo all sorts of misery in order to wait upon their beloved husbands."[36]

In addition to the Pali Canon, images of women in Thailand have been shaped by extra-canonical texts, especially the *Jataka Stories*. According to Thai philosopher Suwanna Satha-Anand, "it is beyond controversy that of all the *Jatakas*, the *Vessantara* tale has been the most popular in Siam throughout history" and "has arguably served as the most important narrative of Thai cultural life."[37] In this story, Queen Madsi represents the ideal woman because she sacrifices everything, including her children, to benefit her husband's religious goal. She acquiesces in her husband's extreme generosity of giving away his children at the request of a greedy old man whose (much younger) wife threatens to leave him unless he does so, and turns her sorrow at the loss of her children into joy at her husband's goodness and virtue.[38] This narrative sends a powerful message to Thai women that their goal in life is to be devoted and selfless wives.

Popular print and electronic media today continue to celebrate women's roles as wives and mothers, while portraying alternatives in a disparaging light. For example, a 2002 issue of *Thaiways* magazine, issued by Anurak Thailand Tourism, states that contrary to the stereotype that Thai women

---

[35] Murcott, *First Buddhist Women*, 92, speculates that "(p)erhaps because this was the most common life-path for women, there is a comparatively large amount of information in the Pali Buddhist literature about married women. See also Satha-Anand, "Looking to Buddhism," 198 and Kawanami, "Can Women Be Celibate?" 137–56, 138–41. However, Kawanami argues that the image of the mother in early Buddhism is an ambivalent one, since she is seen as deeply attached to her family, which is associated with being mired in samsara, this cyclical existence of interminable suffering.

[36] *Samyutta Nikaya* I: 37, cited in Law, *Women in Buddhist Literature*, 35; Isaline Blew Horner, *The Book of Discipline*, vol I (London: Oxford University Press Warehouse, 1938), 140; Murcott, *First Buddhist Women*, 92.

[37] Satha-Anand, "Looking to Buddhism," 205, 208.

[38] Ibid., 208.

have "good manners, love to take care of their families and are followers of their husbands," many Thai women today "are more self-confident in the working world." By adding that "at the same time [they] do not neglect their expected duties of taking care of their families and doing household chores," as well as that "many Thai women still maintain their sweet manners, love to please their families, and try to live up to their expected role as a good mother,"[39] this widely-available magazine itself helps to perpetuate the stereotype that Thai women *are* still wives and mothers fundamentally and foremost.

However, whereas the roles of wife and mother in many societies (and prominently in Western societies) have not included obligations as wage earners or economic contributors to the household income, these responsibilities have been an important aspect of Thai women's traditional roles. This may stem in part from the historical necessity that women had to maintain the households as well as the fieldwork.[40] It may also be influenced by Buddhism, which has limited the occupations that women could pursue by excluding them from highly respected roles as members of the Sangha while not valuing the accumulation of wealth (a principle that may be changing in contemporary Thai society, as discussed below).[41]

In this era of economic globalization, Thai women's labor has become increasingly important as women now represent over 48 percent of the Thai work force.[42] About 68–70 percent of all females aged 13 and older participate in the work force, one of the highest figures in Asia.[43] As I discuss below, this dimension of Thai women's roles is an important factor in determining the relatively higher status of prostitutes than of nuns.

Non-normative Roles for Thai Women

Few alternative roles to those of wife and mother have been made available to Thai women over the centuries.[44] However, two of the non-normative roles that many Thai women have occupied have been those of prostitute or sex worker

---

[39] Sarutta, "Women's Status in Thai Society."

[40] UNIFEM, *2000 Gender and Development in Thailand*: Section B, Part 2; Satha-Anand, "Looking to Buddhism," 200, Kabilsingh, *Thai Women in Buddhism*, 18; *Sarutta*, "Women's Status in Thai Society," 2.

[41] See Kapur-Fic, *Thailand*, 438.

[42] UNIFEM, *2000 Gender and Development in Thailand*: Section B, Part 2; Jeffrey, *Sex and Borders*, 31; Busakorn Suriyasarn, "Historical Perspective," *Roles and Status of Thai Women* (1993), 7, online at http://www.busakorn.com/women/ThaiWomenRoles-Status.htm.

[43] UNIFEM, *2000 Gender and Development in Thailand*: Section B, Part 2, B. 4 ("Cultural Conditions"), 1; Joshua Kurlantzick, "Women and Controversy Ride Together on Lady Bus," *Christian Science Monitor* (June 22, 2000): 1; Economic and Social Commission for Asia and the Pacific (ESCAP), *Women in Thailand: A Country Profile*, Statistical Profiles no. 5 (New York: United Nations, 1996), 5.

[44] There have been a few notable exceptions, such as women warriors in Thai legend. Van Esterik, *Materializing Thailand*, 44 (describing a number of Thai women warriors in the images of women in Thai history, including Queen Suriyothai, the subject of a 2003 film by Martin Scorsese).

and nun (*mae chi*). Although women's ordination into the Buddhist Sangha was never officially recognized in Thailand, there have nevertheless been female Buddhist monastics since about the time that Buddhism was introduced to Thailand, sometime around the twelfth- or thirteenth century C.E.[45] They are not 'fully ordained' in the sense of having taken the over 300 vows specified in the *Vinaya* to become a *bhikkhuni*, and thus are not considered to be of equivalent status to the male monks (*bhikkhus*) in the eyes of the male Sangha, the government, or the public. Rather, they take the eight or ten precepts specified for laypersons (which laity usually take only on special occasions rather than on a daily basis) and thus are called *mae chi* or '10 precept women.'

Prostitutes have also existed in Thailand for many centuries, although often in earlier times in more specialized roles as courtesans or "temporary wives" rather than as the commercial sex workers they are today.[46] One might conjecture that, with Buddhism being so pervasive in Thai culture and society, and given the support provided to the male Sangha by both the state and laity, Thai women who chose roles as nuns would be highly respected, especially in comparison with women who become prostitutes. Surprisingly, perhaps, this is not the case, as the discussion below demonstrates.

Women's Legal Status

Unlike Western nations, such as the USA, Thailand does not recognize a strict separation between religion ('Church') and government ('State'). Rather, Thailand has maintained a close, mutually supportive and interdependent relationship between government and Sangha for many centuries.[47] In addition, Thai law (like the legal systems of many nations) has traditionally formalized discrimination against women, legitimating male dominance over women in marriage, divorce, and allocation of marital property, thus formalizing the disadvantaged status of both prostitutes and nuns in Thai society.[48]

---

[45] According to Kornvipa Boonsue, it is not clear how and exactly when Theravada Buddhism came to Thailand, although there are several theories: Boonsue, *Buddhism and Gender Bias*, 18–19.

[46] Kapur-Fic, *Thailand*, 454; Jeffrey, *Sex and Borders*, 5–14. I continue to use the term 'prostitute' rather than 'commercial sex worker' here, however, in order to signify the derogatory and female-gendered connotations that have surrounded the term.

[47] See, e.g., Swearer, *The Buddhist World of Southeast Asia*, 12; Reynolds, "Dhamma in Dispute," 454; Charles Keyes, "Mother or Mistress but Never a Monk: Buddhist Notions of Female Gender in Rural Thailand," *American Ethnologist* 11, no. 2 (1984): 223–41.

[48] Generally: Satha-Anand, "Looking to Buddhism," 198–99; Kabilsingh, *Thai Women in Buddhism*, 15–19; ESCAP, *Women in Thailand: A Country Profile*, 3; Suriyasarn, "Historical Perspective;" Truong, *Sex, Money, And Morality*; Khin Thitsa, *Providence and Prostitution: Image and Reality for Women in Buddhist Thailand* (London: CHANGE International Reports, 1980), 5–7.

Polygamy was legal until 1935 and most high status men had several wives. The Three Seals Law of 1805 legalized prostitution, confirming the husband's legal right to treat his women and wives as private property, bestowing punishment on them as he saw fit (including execution) and entitling him to manage his wives' money and land brought into the marriage.[49] Assumptions about a man's rights over 'his women' re-emerge today in the parental sale of daughters into debt-bondage as prostitutes.[50] Legal reforms in later decades, such as the Abolition of Slavery Act (1874),[51] the Land Act (1901), and the Monogamy Act (1935), formally improved the status of Thai women.

The educational system was first opened to girls in 1901, and while female literacy rates have risen dramatically since that time, there is still a big gap between rural and urban populations. In addition, statistics show that women have a lower level of education than men, and only half of the female population completes elementary school. The number of illiterate women is still nearly twice that of men. Improvement in educational attainment has increased the percentage of women engaged in white-collar occupations, but women still account for a very small part of total employment in this area. For example, only one out of every thousand administrative, executive, or managerial positions is held by a woman. Women are still discriminated against throughout all range of occupations, from agriculture to government positions.[52]

Thai women gained the right to vote in 1932 and first participated directly in national politics in 1949. Although a significant improvement over the 1–2 percent figures prior to 1995, Thai women even today only represent 6 percent of members of Parliament, and hold only about 10 percent of local administrative positions.[53] Laws governing divorce and child custody and maintenance are still

---

[49] Sarutta, "Women's Status in Thai Society," 2; van Esterik, *Materializing Thailand*, 83; Satha-Anand, "Looking to Buddhism," 198–99; Kapur-Fic, *Thailand*, 460–61.

[50] van Esterik, *Materializing Thailand*, 83; Jeffrey, *Sex and Borders*, 5.

[51] Ironically, the abolition of slavery in 1905 contributed to large numbers of women becoming prostitutes as a means of making money, since it eliminated the ability women had earlier had to earn some money for their families by selling themselves into slavery: Jeffrey, *Sex and Borders*, 11; van Esterik, *Materializing Thailand*, 174.

[52] Songsan Udomsilp, "Declaring of Asian Human Rights Charter: Thai Men Have Responsibility in Promoting Women's Rights," *Asia Human Rights Commission Website*, http://www.ahrchk.net/hrsolid/mainfile/php/1998vol08no08/1622/; UNIFEM, *2000 Gender and Development in Thailand*, Section A, Part 1, Section B, Part 2.

[53] Joshua Kurlantzick, "Women and Controversy Ride Together on Lady Bus," 1; Chitraporn Vanaspong, "Thailand Has Made Progress in Law to Promote Women's Rights," Asian Women's Resource Exchange (AWORC) Website, http://www.aworc.org/bpfa/gov/ escap/26oct03.html (2000), 1–2; UNIFEM, *2000 Gender and Development in Thailand*, Section 1, Part 1, 2. In fact, the UN ESCAP and Thailand's Ministry of Social Development and Human Security held the first Thai National Summit of Women Mayors and Councillors in Bangkok on October 2–3, 2003, where participants considered a national action plan to promote representation of women in Thai local government. *UNESCAP e-News Bulletin* (October, 2003), http://www.unescap.org/unis/UN_ESCAP_News_Bulletin/Oct-03/Oct03.pdf; SKALI Editorial Staff, "First Thai National Summit of Women Mayors and Councillors Opens 2 October," (Sept. 26, 2003,), SKALI Website, http://www.skali.com/index.php?ch=1&pg=266&ac=240&ct=.

more favorable to men than to women, with four out of five divorced women left to raise children on their own, without alimony or child support from their former husbands—this at a time when the divorce rate is skyrocketing.[54] Sexual harassment in work places only was made illegal in the Labour Protection Law enacted in 1998.[55] Marital rape is still not recognized as a crime, although it was put on the national agenda in 2003.[56] Domestic violence has been a growing problem, especially since the Asian financial crisis in the late 1990s, although legal protections were written into the 1997 Constitution.[57]

In addition to gender, class and regional differences have also played an important role in determining women's legal and social status in Thailand. Not surprisingly, as in many other regions, urban women have had more opportunities for education, a range of adequately paying occupations, the ability to participate in political life, and so forth, and more elite women have had more opportunities than have women living in poverty.[58]

Part of the failure of existing laws to function effectively to protect women's rights may result from the lack of a developed individual rights tradition in Thai law.[59] Social relations in Thailand are governed more by status than by formal legal rights. Larger forces in Thai society and culture value harmony in social relationships, the avoidance of confrontation, and the resolution of disputes through mutual understanding rather than rule-oriented systems involving bureaucratic institutions such as courts. The legal system in place today was in large part constructed from Western European models in the mid-nineteenth century, and thus was based on Western rather than Thai experience. Not surprisingly, then, courts and formal legal systems are frequently avoided in favor of resolving disputes by informal means such as tolerance, community or moral pressure, or informal systems of dispute resolution.[60]

Furthermore, many Thai women conceive of themselves relationally rather than as individual rights-bearers, and this inhibits their taking recourse in the law. It is frequently observed that women in this region are socialized to be relational, socially-embedded and family oriented rather than independent,

---

[54] UNIFEM, *2000 Gender and Development in Thailand*, Section B, Part 3 (between 1960 and 1990, the number of divorces increased 12 times).

[55] See Vanaspong, "Thailand Has Made Progress in Law to Promote Women's Rights," 1.

[56] T. Wallapa, "Thailand: When Husbands Rape," *The Daily Star* (August 10, 2003), internet edition online at http://www.thedailystar.net/law/200308/02/fact.htm, 1.

[57] Ava Vivian Gonzales, "Home is Where the Hurt Is," *Women in Action*, 1 (2001), online at http://www.isiswomen.org/pub/wia/wia101/hurt.html, 1.

[58] See, generally, United Nations Division for the Advancement of Women, *1999 World Survey on the Role of Women in Development: Globalization, Gender, and Work* (New York: United Nations, 1999); Jeffrey, *Sex and Borders*, 148.

[59] See Satha-Anand, "Looking to Buddhism," 197–98, 211; Ted McDorman, "The Teaching of the Law of Thailand," *Dalhousie Law Journal* 11 (1987–88): 927.

[60] McDorman, "Teaching of the Law of Thailand," 921–24.

autonomous, self-determining individuals. Thai philosopher Suwanna Satha-Anand observes that "in most cases, women have still not evolved as an individual [sic]; they are embedded within social webs, mostly defined by their parents and male relatives, including their husbands."[61] In addition, as the authors of a study of sex tourism in Thailand speculate, it may be the case that "the denial of individual rights by authoritarian regimes may have encouraged the perspective that individuals are sexual commodities to be utilized for furthering the national economic good."[62]

Women's legal status in Thailand may be improving, although the signs are mixed. Thailand acceded to the UN Convention on the Elimination of All Forms of Discrimination Against Women (CEDAW)[63] in 1985, although initially with several reservations.[64] In addition, as a result of struggles for political reform and democracy, the new constitution promulgated in 1997 (like the two that preceded it) guarantees equal rights for men and women, and makes provision for equal protection of the laws and the impermissibility of unjust discrimination based on sex.[65] A National Human Rights Commission of Thailand (NHRC) established under the Constitution to monitor respect for these human rights has already been significantly limited in its jurisdiction

---

[61] Satha-Anand, "Looking to Buddhism," 206; Juree Vichit-Vadakan, "Women and the Family in Thailand in the Midst of Social Change," *Law & Society Review* 28 no. 3 (1994): 516; Rita Nakashima Brock and Susan Brooks Thistlethwaite, *Casting Stones: Prostitution and Liberation in Asia and the United States* (Minneapolis: Fortress Press, 1996), 193–94.

[62] Chris Ryan and C. Michael Hall, *Sex Tourism: Marginal People and Liminalities* (London: Routledge, 2001), 142.

[63] *Convention on the Elimination of All Forms of Discrimination Against Women*, G.A. Res. 34/180, 34 UN GOAR, Supp. (No. 46), UN Doc A/34/46 (1979) (hereafter, CEDAW).

[64] UNIFEM, *2000 Gender and Development in Thailand*, Section B, Part 3: "Government Policies on Women and Development," 1. Since acceding to CEDAW, the Thai Government has gradually dropped the number of reservations to two. This has meant that women now have access to all government positions, whereas previously they were barred from certain positions. Women now have an equal opportunity to enrol in all types of educational institutions, including all military academies; and may take their mother's name rather than their father's. In addition, regulations now "allow for" equal pay for work of equal value by men and women, and women are accorded a legal capacity identical to that of men in relation to administering their property. Of the two remaining reservations, removal of the reservation relating to marriage and family life (art. 6) has to await an amendment to Thai family law to allow women the choice to retain their family names and to have access to similar grounds for divorce as their husbands. The reservation regarding settlement of disputes by the International Court of Justice (art. 27) will remain, since Thailand maintains the right to sovereignty in all international conventions it has joined.

[65] Section 30 specifies that "(a)ll persons are equal under the law and shall enjoy equal protection under the law. Men and women shall enjoy equal rights." Section 80 further specifies that "(t)he State shall develop and promote . . . the equality between women and men." *Constitution of the Kingdom of Thailand*, online at http://www.krisdika.go.th/searchResult.jsp?head = 4.

by the government, so its effectiveness remains to be seen, especially regarding the protection and promotion of women's rights.[66]

Virada Somswadi, a Thai women's rights activist and Law and Women's Studies professor at Chiangmai University, suggests that one reason for the disparity between the law and reality may be that "Thailand's criminal laws and judicial system are by design exclusive of women's specific interests and socio-cultural conditions."[67] Ratchadaport Kaewsanit of Women and the Constitution Network further notes that women's groups have been struggling for 10 years to change Thai law with little success so far because "it challenges the perceived 'male prerogative' to control women's bodies," and because "men justify the use of force as punishment for women who don't perform their duties."[68]

In short, Chiangmai University's Foundation for Women, Law and Rural Development concludes that "the goal of equality is still far from being reached" for women in Thailand.[69] This is particularly evident in the status of women who have contradicted their prescribed roles as wives and mothers by becoming monastics or sex workers, as the following sections will reveal.

Case Studies: the Sex Trade and the Sangha

The Sex Trade

As Jeffrey describes, "the construction of the category 'prostitute' is one of the forces that shape the lives and experiences of women, and it does so by delineating the boundaries of proper and improper female behaviour and seeking to penalize and/or regulate those who fall into the latter category."[70] Both Thai legal and religious institutions have played a part in policing this boundary, especially as it relates to the normative ideal for women.

---

[66] National Human Rights Commission of Thailand Website, http://www.nhrc.or.th/about_e.html; Pasuk Phongpaichit and Chris Baker, "Thailand: Human Rights as People Politics," *NIASnytt, newsletter of the Nordic Institute of Asian Studies* (Copenhagen Denmark, February, 2001), online at http://pioneer.netserv.chula.ac.th/~ppasuk/humanrightsaspeoplepolitics.doc.

[67] Ava Vivian Gonzales, "Home is Where the Hurt Is," *Women in Action*, 2; Naurin Ahmad-Zaki, "A Question of Rights" *Women's Studies Centre, Heinrich Boll Foundation Regional Office for Southeast Asia in Thailand* (undated), 2, online at *Heinrich Boll Foundation Website*, http://www.hbfasia.org/thailand/wsc.htm.

[68] T. Wallapa, "Thailand: When Husbands Rape," 1.

[69] Foundation for Women, Law and Development (FWLD), "Rationale," *FWLD Website*, http://www.soc.cmu.ac.th/~wsc/forward_e.htm, 1.

[70] Jeffrey, *Sex and Borders*, xvi–xvii. Thus, the law is both determined by the dominant social discourse of what prostitutes are, as well as reproducing that discourse in determining how prostitutes are positioned in society. Ibid., xvii.

Commercial prostitution first appeared in Southeast Asia in the late 1600s. Although originating in the colonial period, the sex trade in Thailand began to take its modern form with the influx of U.S. armed servicemen coming to Thailand for "rest and recreation" ('R&R') from the Vietnam War. During the 1960s, the number of women working as prostitutes grew from approximately 20,000 to 170,000 persons.[71] The sex industry in Thailand has continued to thrive and grow since that era. Since accurate statistics on the numbers of Thai women currently working as prostitutes are extremely difficult to obtain, estimates of the number of persons working in the sex industry differ wildly.[72] Nonetheless, a recent study by Chulalongkorn University political science professor Nitet Tinnakul indicates that the number of people entering Thailand's sex trade rose by 50,000 in 2003, despite an improving economy and the government's war on poverty. The study says that some 2.8 million Thais, including women, men, and children, served as sex workers throughout the country from 1999 to 2002.[73] Regardless of exact numbers, however, it is clear that sex trafficking, sex tourism, and commercial sex industries in Thailand are big business, involving an estimated $15 billion per year.[74]

In addition to Thai women working in the sex industry in Thailand, thousands are trafficked overseas and thousands of women and girls from other countries are trafficked into Thailand.[75] The U.S. Department of State Trafficking in Persons

---

[71] See Jeffrey, *Sex and Borders*, 37.

[72] According to the Protection Project at Johns Hopkins University, for example, there are approximately 100,000 sex workers in Thailand at present, 70,000 of them women and another 26,000 under-age youths. Protection Project, "Thailand," in *A Human Rights Report on Trafficking of Persons, Especially Women and Children*" (March 2002), *Protection Project Website*, http://www.protectionproject.org/main1.htm, 536. Another source estimates from 200,000–300,000 to one million sex workers in Thailand. "Testimony of Gary Haugen, President International Justice Mission, Congressional Human Rights Caucus Members' Briefing, June 6, 2003" *Congressional Human Rights Caucus Website*, http://www.hous.gov/lantos/caucus/TestimonyHaugen060602.htm, 5.

A third estimate is even greater, citing between two and four million sex workers in Thailand. Bhikkhuni Dr. Lee, "Getting Clear: Revealing the Myths in Theravada Buddhism," 1.

[73] Agence France Presse, "More Thais Entering Sex Trade Despite Improving Economy" (January 6, 2004), distributed online via Commercial Sexual Exploitation News, CSENEWS@PETE.URI.EDU.

[74] Protection Project, "Thailand," on Protection Project Website, http://209.190.246.239/ver2/cr/Thailand.pdf , citing Matt Warren, "Khoung is 14 Years Old, Enslaved to a Thai Brothel With Nowhere to Run," *The Scotsman* (May 8, 2001), online at http://www.protectionproject.org/vt/2002/ne510.htm. also Women's Organizations of Burma and Women's Affairs Department, National Coalition Government of the Union of Burma, *Burma: The Current State of Women Conflict Area Specific: A Shadow Report to the 22nd Session of CEDAW*, January 16, 2000.

[75] One source claims that between 100,000–200,000 Thai women are in sex work in other countries, 50,000–70,000 of them brought into Japan under false pretenses. See Protection Project, "Thailand," in *A Human Rights Report on Trafficking of Persons, Especially Women and Children*" (March 2002), Protection Project Website, http://www.protectionproject.org/main1.htm, 536, also

(TIPS) report for 2004 states that although internal trafficking has reportedly declined in Thailand, the trafficking of foreign women into Thailand has increased. Burma has become the largest source of women and girls for the Thai sex trade, with Cambodia, China, and Laos other significant 'source countries.' In addition, Thai women are being trafficked for the sex trade to other destinations, especially Japan, Taiwan, the United States, Australia, and Western Europe.[76]

The Thai sex industry has been fueled by economic globalization, which in Thailand has led to export-led industrialization policies that have drained resources from the rural areas into the urban ones. The growth in the Thai sex industry was also facilitated by the World Bank, which advised the Thai government in 1980 to develop its tourism industry. The Thai government took advantage of the existing infrastructure of brothels, bars, massage parlors, and other sex establishments to entice an influx of foreign 'tourists,' many of whom come to Thailand for the sex industry alone.[77] By 1989, the majority of the visitors to Bangkok were male. It is important to note, however, that prostitution in Thailand cannot be accounted for solely on the basis of the U.S. military R & R businesses and international sex tourism, since the particularities of the Thai marriage system, which historically allowed polygamy, and a long-established tradition of local prostitution, have also been important factors.[78]

Over the past few decades, growing poverty in the north, coupled with women's responsibility to provide for their families, has led more and more

---

Editorial, "Debate at Last on Prostitution," 1, Therese Caouette and Yuriko Saito, *To Japan and Back: Thai Women Recount Their Experiences* (Geneva: International Organization for Migration, 1999), 13, 25.

An International Labor Organization (ILO) report estimates that 200,000 to 300,000 women are trafficked for prostitution *into* Thailand each year. Cindy Sui, "Trafficking of Women and Children on the Rise in East Asia: UNICEF," Agence France Presse, May 14, 2001. According to another report, up to 40,000 Burmese women work in Thai brothels, many of them trafficked across the border. Matt Warren, "Khoung is 14 Years Old." Similar numbers of Cambodian women are reported trafficked annually into Thailand for sex work. Protection Project, "Thailand," on Protection Project Website, http://209.190.246.239/ver2/cr/Thailand.pdf, citing Kay Johnson and Khieu Kola, "Can't Control Brothel-Going Officials, Says PM at Launch," *South China Morning Post*, March 7, 2000. The 1998 United Nations Children Fund (UNICEF) estimate is lower, citing about 16,000 foreign women in prostitution in Thailand, of whom a significant number are trafficked and about one-third are under 18.

[76] U.S. Department of State, *Trafficking in Persons Report* (Washington, DC: U.S. State Dept., June 2004), online at U.S. Department of State Website, http://www.state.gov/g/tip/rls/tiprpt/2004/33197pf.htm.

[77] See van Esterik, *Materializing Thailand*, 178; Catherine Hill, "Planning for Prostitution: An Analysis of Thailand's Sex Industry," in *Women's Lives and Public Polic*, ed. Meredeth Turshen and Briavel Holcomb (Westport, CT: Greenwood Press, 1991), 133–44; Khin Thitsa, *Providence and Prostitution*, 12–13.

[78] Beadle, "Sangha and the Sex Industry," 3; Jeffrey, *Sex and Borders*, 87; van Esterik, *Materializing Thailand*, 188.

rural women to seek work as prostitutes, mostly in Bangkok. This has "provided one of the few better paid opportunities for peasant women whose other choice would be work in the poisonous and exploitative factories," or performing demeaning domestic service work.[79] Lack of other employment opportunities has also encouraged many Thai families to sell their daughters into debt-bondage in order to help maintain the rest of the family.

The experiences of Thai prostitutes and women working as prostitutes in Thailand are documented in a number of studies. One study, of Thai women trafficked to Japan, involved interviews of 55 Thai women who were trafficked into Japan for sex work.[80] A number of government and NGO reports have detailed the conditions under which many women from Thailand and Burma, some still teenagers, are encouraged, coerced, or even sold by their families or teachers, into the burgeoning sex trade in Thailand.[81] Many of these women are often forced into a system of debt-bondage. The debt may have accrued because of a loan to family members or as a result of the travel expenses associated with being trafficked across national borders and provided with employment. The amount of the debt is often the equivalent of tens of thousands of U.S. dollars (a vast sum of money for most people in

---

[79] Jeffrey, *Sex and Borders*, xii–xiii, 78.

[80] Caouette and Saito, *To Japan and Back*. The study is significant in being one of the few English language documents that reveals the motivations, experiences, and voices of Thai women trafficked for sex, something that is unfortunately often lacking from analyses of trafficking conducted by governments and NGO's, as we will see later in this paper. Also, Kinsey Alden Dinan, "Trafficking in Women: From Thailand to Japan: The Role of Organized Crime and Governmental Reponse," *Harvard Asia Quarterly* (Summer 2002), 1–17, online at http://www.fas.harvard.edu/~asiactr/haq/200203/0203a001/htm; Kinsey Dinan, "OWED JUSTICE: Thai Women Trafficked into Debt Bondage in Japan" (New York: Human Rights Watch, 2001), online at Human Rights Watch Website, http://www.hrw.org/reports/2000/japan/0-ack.htm.

[81] For descriptions of the sex trafficking and sex tourism industries in Thailand, see, e.g., Coalition Against Trafficking in Women (CATW), "Facts on Trafficking and Prostitution: Burma/Myanmar"(2000), and "Facts on Trafficking and Prostitution: Thailand" (2000), online at CATW Website, http://www.catwinternational.org; Global Alliance Against Trafficking in Women (GAATW), "Trafficking in the Global Context" (June 2002), GAATW Website, http://www.thai.net/gaatw; Lin Leam Lim, *The Sex Sector: The Economic and Social Bases of Prostitution in Southeast Asia* (Geneva: International Labor Office, 1998); Simon Montlake, "In Thailand, a Struggle to Halt Human Trafficking," *Christian Science Monitor* (August 29, 2003), online at http://www.csmonitor.com/2003/0829/p09s02-woap.html; Bhikkuni Dr. Lee, "Getting Clear: Revealing the Myths in Theravada Buddhism," 2; U.S. Department of State, *Trafficking in Persons Report*; Human Rights Watch Women's Rights Project, *Human Rights Watch Global Report on Women's Human Rights* (New York: Human Rights Watch, 1995), 205–229; Satha-Anand, "Looking to Buddhism," 208; Skrobanek, Boonpakdi, and Janthakeero, *Traffic in Women*; Siriporn Skrobanek, "Exotic, Subservient and Trapped: Confronting Prostitution and Traffic in Women in Southeast Asia," in *Freedom From Violence: Women's Strategies From Around the World*, ed. Margaret Schuler (New York: UNIFEM, 1992), 121–137.

developing countries, especially given the often meager 'payment' the women receive for servicing clients, which is often the equivalent of only a few U.S. dollars).[82] The difficulty of repaying the debt bondage contract is enhanced when women are resold before they have finished paying off the original debt, and are forced to begin all over again in a new establishment.[83]

In addition, many women forced into sex work are virtually imprisoned, made to work in impoverished conditions, physically abused, underpaid, and deprived of basic rights to liberty, freedom to leave the brothels, or to receive needed medical treatment. They frequently have been arrested for violating laws against prostitution, often at the point when they are trying to escape. This is, of course, a double standard, since the 'clients' and pimps are not arrested. Often the women are returned to the brothels by law enforcement personnel (or, in the case of Burmese women, returned to the Myanmar government to risk prosecution for leaving the country without permission) or subjected to prolonged detention (frequently sexually and otherwise physically abused while in detention), or both.

In addition to these violations of their liberty, many of these women are even deprived of the conditions necessary to protect themselves from HIV, which had been spreading at pandemic speed throughout Thailand until a 100 percent condom use policy was finally vigorously promoted by the government in the late 1980s and early 1990s. Women continue to fall victim to AIDS at a faster rate than men, however, in part because husbands return home after extramarital sexual relations (behavior that is socially condoned or ignored) and infect their wives.[84] The risk of HIV transmission has encouraged sex trade procurers to seek younger and younger women, especially from the hill tribe regions, to insure their 'cleanliness' from AIDS, and even sometimes to satisfy the prevalent myth that having sex with a young virgin can cure AIDS and other sexually transmitted diseases.[85]

Since 1982, Thailand has earned more foreign currency from tourism than any other economic activity, and a significant percentage of this has been

---

[82] In the Thai Trafficking Study, the debt amount ranged between U.S. $10,000 and $35,000, averaging $25,000. Caouette and Saito, *To Japan and Back*, 48, 50.

[83] Some of the women in the Thai Trafficking Study reported that this happened to them in circumstances when the "mama" did not like them. Caouette and Saito, *To Japan and Back*, 51.

[84] From 1984 until 1998 women represented only 1/4 of AIDS patients, but today they constitute 1/3 of AIDS patients. UNIFEM East and South East Asia, *2000 Gender and Development in Thailand*, Section A: "Thai Women at a Glance," 1; Section B: "Socio-Economic Status of Women".

[85] UNIFEM East and South East Asia, "Country Facts—Thailand," *Women, Gender and HIV/AIDS in East and Southeast Asia*, online at *UNIFEM East and South East Asia Website*, http://www.unifem-eseasia.org/resources/others/genaids/genaidtoc.htm; Human Rights Watch *Women's Rights Project Report*, 205–229.

earned through sex tourism. By 1988, for example, fifteen percent of Thailand's income from the export of goods and services was from tourism, a significant percentage of which was sex tourism.[86] This has created an incentive for the Thai government to allow the sex trade to continue, even as it formally 'makes efforts' to comply with international standards.

As a Theravada Buddhist country, the ethics of the orthodox Buddhist religion play a significant role in people's attitudes regarding prostitution in Thailand.[87] First, as already described, the denigration of women in Buddhist teachings facilitates women's involvement in the sex trade by conveying attitudes that women fulfill their role expectations as sexual and inferior beings. Thus, women's inferior status serves to legitimate or even excuse their involvement in 'immoral' or karmically-negative activities like prostitution.[88] At the same time, legislative debate surrounding the 1996 Prostitution Act suggests that Buddhists were opposed to legalizing prostitution because it would inappropriately signal government approval.[89]

According to traditional Buddhist teachings, prostitution violates the prohibition of sexual misconduct, one of the basic five precepts taken by lay Buddhists as well as monks (along with not killing, stealing, lying, or drinking alcohol). However interpretations of this precept vary widely throughout the Buddhist world. The most clear-cut violation is adultery, which is considered to be wrong both because it is a form of greed, and because it harms others. Not surprisingly, "Buddhist discussions of the third precept mainly focus on various circumstances in which men can be seen as breaking it,"[90] as illustrated in the following verse from the *Sutta-nipata*: "Not to be contented with one's own wife but to be seen with prostitutes or the wives of others—this is a cause of one's downfall."[91] A second rationale for the precept contained in the *Samyutta Nikaya* is an androcentric 'Golden Rule,' that is, since you would not want anyone fooling around with your wife, do not fool around with anyone else's wife.[92] A more

---

[86] See United Nations Division for the Advancement of Women, *1999 World Survey*, 11; Lim, *The Sex Sector*; Jeffrey, *Sex and Borders*, 78.

[87] Mettanando Bhikkhu, "Thailand: Legalized Prostitution is Not Enough for Society," *Korea Herald* (October 8, 2003), sent by CSENEWS@PETE.URI.EDU on October 8, 2003, 1.

[88] Eberhardt, "Introduction;" Keyes, "Mother or Mistress But Never a Monk," 224.

[89] Jeffrey, *Sex and Borders*, 111.

[90] Harvey, *An Introduction to Buddhist Ethics* (Cambridge, UK: Cambridge University Press, 2000), 72.

[91] K. R. Norman, trans., *The Group of Discourses (Sutta-Nipata)* (London: Pali Text Society, 1984), vol. 1, 108, cited in Harvey, *An Introduction to Buddhist Ethics*, 72.

[92] C. A. F. Rhys Davids and F. L. Woodward, trans., *The Book of Kindred Sayings (Samyutta Nikaya)* (London: Pali Text Society, 1917–30), 354; T. W. and C. A. F. Rhys Davids, trans., *Dialogues of the Buddha (Digha Nikaya)* (London: Pali Text Society, 1899–1921) III, 108

contemporary interpretation by the Thai teacher Bhikkhu Bodhi is that married persons should only have intercourse with their spouses.[93]

None of these interpretations directly addresses the morality of prostitution per se (with the exception of circumstances that involve adultery). Nonetheless, the sexual misconduct referred to in the precept is more often thought of as referring to 'unskillful' rather than as 'sinful' conduct, since sex itself is not viewed as a sin (*bap*), only as a form of bodily attachment and craving which must be abandoned in order to attain liberation.[94]

Such religious views have contributed to still prevalent (although recently changing) perceptions of prostitution as "indecent and immoral," and prostitutes as "objects of pity, victims who need help."[95] Although prostitution is believed to accumulate negative karma by reinforcing craving and attachment to the sensual world of desire (which perpetuates bondage to this world of *samsara* or suffering), throughout Buddhist history it has not been considered a "sin" or violation of fundamental religious laws, as it has been in Christianity, Islam, or other religions.[96] In fact, Mettanando Bhikkhu suggests that "Westerners may be surprised that in Thailand, Buddhism has so little problem with prostitution—especially when the profession was legal. In Bangkok, some brothels stand side by side with temples."[97]

Second, Buddhist views of prostitution and impermanence mean that having worked as a prostitute does not leave any permanent or irrevocable mark on one's identity. In fact, Mettanando Bhikkhu speculates that perhaps the apparent lack of concern most Buddhists express about prostitution "is that the majority believe in karma, which views sex workers as paying back their karmic debt."[98] Lacking other options for merit making, women's work in the sex industry, if temporary, is viewed as justified and remedied based on understandings of karma.[99]

Some Thai Buddhists believe that the negative karmic impact of prostitution is counteracted by the merit women are able to make for themselves and

---

[93] Bhikkhu Bodhi, *The Noble Eightfold Path* (Kandy, Sri Lanka: Buddhist Publication Society, 1984), 63, cited in Harvey, *Introduction to Buddhist Ethics*, 72.

[94] See Kapur-Fic, *Thailand*, 454; van Esterik, *Materializing Thailand*, 87; Truong, *Sex, Money and Morality*, 136.

[95] Skrobanek, Boonpakdi, and Janthakeero, *Traffic in Women*, 18; Beadle, "The Sangha and the Sex Industry," 2.

[96] Brock and Thistlethwaite, *Casting Stones*, 62–63; Murcott, *First Buddhist Women*, 119–21; Keyes, "Mother or Mistress But Never a Monk," 236.

[97] Mettanando Bhikkhu, "Legalized Prostitution Is Not Enough for Society."

[98] Ibid.; see also Keyes, "Mother or Mistress But Never a Monk," at 236. This is a view that goes back to early Buddhism. Kapur-Fic, *Thailand*, 420.

[99] Satha-Anand, "Looking to Buddhism," 197–98; Kapur-Fic, *Thailand*, 420, citing Horner, *Women Under Primitive Buddhism*, 94; Brock and Thistlethwaite, *Casting Stones*, 196; Khin Thitsa, *Providence and Prostitution*, 23.

their families from their earnings. Thus, family members may willfully neglect to inquire how the money that their daughters send home has been earned, especially as it can be used to make merit by giving lavish donations to the local temple.[100] Thai Bhikkhuni Dr. Lee mentions the beliefs that "a prostitute can clear her *kamma* by donating money to the temple" and that "if a woman gives her body to a monk for sex, she can gain merit" as two of the most prominent "myths and mis-teachings" of Buddhism in Thailand.[101] Nonetheless, the study of trafficked women in Thailand conducted by the Thai NGO Foundation for Women in 1996 (hereafter the "Traffic in Women Study") points out that "by accepting such donations, these institutions lend some legitimacy to the way the money is earned."[102]

In any event, as van Esterik puts it, "Buddhism does not irrevocably damn prostitutes as evil beings."[103] Indeed, prostitutes themselves are not viewed negatively in Buddhist scriptures. Courtesans (or "*sobhini*"—meaning "praise" or "beautiful") are described (or describe themselves) in early Buddhist scriptures as beautiful, of high social status, and able to command huge fees from their "clients." Several stories of courtesans or prostitutes are featured in the *Therigatha*, including Ambapali, Padumavati, Khema, Vimala, and Addhakasi[104] as well as other early Buddhist tests, including Sama and Sulasa in the *Jataka Tales*, Salavati in the *Sutta Nipata Commentary*, and Sirima in the *Dhammapada Commentary*.[105] The *Therigatha* poem of Ambapali, for example, tells the story of a courtesan who donates a pleasure garden to the Sangha and renounces worldly life to become a nun once she realizes the transience of her beauty.[106] Khema is notable as having become fully enlightened before leaving lay life,[107] although at least four courtesans attained enlightenment at some point during the Buddha's lifetime in this account.[108]

---

[100] Kapur-Fic, *Thailand*, 457; Skrobanek, Boonpakdi, and Janthakeero, *Traffic in Women*, 69–78; Vichit-Vadakan, "Women and the Family in Thailand," 518.

[101] Bhikkhuni Dr. Lee, "Getting Clear: Revealing the Myths in Theravada Buddhism," 2.

[102] Skrobanek, Boonpakdi, and Janthakeero, *Traffic in Women*, 74.

[103] van Esterik, *Materializing Thailand*, 170.

[104] Addhakhasi's story also appears in the *Cullavagga*. Max Mueller, trans., *Vinaya Kullavagga*, in *Sacred Books of the East*, ed. T. W. Rhys-Davids and Herman Oldenberg (Oxford, England: Clarendon Press, 1885), 20 (reprinted Delhi: Motilal Banarsidass, 1969), 360. She is said to have been reborn as a prostitute for having once insulted a woman renunciant by calling her a prostitute.

[105] Kapur-Fic, *Thailand*, 451, 453; see Isaline Blew Horner, *Women Under Primitive Buddhism* (Amsterdam: Philo Press, 1930), 86–94, 184–93; Law, *Women in Buddhist Literature*, 25–34.

[106] See Rhys Davids and Norman, *Poems of Early Buddhist Nuns*, 201–02; Murcott, *First Buddhist Women*, 131–34; Horner, *Women under Primitive Buddhism*, 90.

[107] Sponberg, "Attitudes toward Women," 4.

[108] Horner, *Women under Primitive Buddhism*, 89.

Furthermore, none of the "*ganika*," prostitutes who served the general public, are criticized or viewed negatively in the texts. Although the Pali Canon describes the Buddha as viewing the frequenting of prostitutes as a vice, he never criticized prostitutes for their immoral acts, but instead gave them many opportunities to discuss their behavior with him.[109] The Patimokha Laws of the *Vinaya* can be interpreted as sanctioning prostitution by listing ten kinds of wives, including a *Dhanakita*, "a woman bought with money for the purpose of sexual pleasure,"and a *Muhuttiya*, "a temporary wife, a wife for the moment."[110]

Third, although the all-male Sangha today does not condone the sexual exploitation of women through trafficking and coerced prostitution, it has not formally opposed the practice either. As the Thai authors of a study on trafficking observe, even though "Buddhist monks should in principle be opposed to prostitution, there has been little evidence of their involvement in activities to change the attitudes of the people."[111] For example, the Abbot of Rim Mon monastery told researchers: "We must be reasonable. . . . Besides, what is wrong if the employers of the girls make merit at the local temple or visit the village?"[112]

In order to provide an opportunity for prostitutes to work out their bad karma by making merit, monks accept alms from them and do not expel them from the temples.[113] One commentator claims that "many a prostitute has been encouraged by her local Buddhist monk to simply live out her life as a prostitute with the greatest degree of moral fortitude possible and to contribute a portion of her earnings to the local temple—consequently, elaborate temples and stupas are being funded in part by the country's largest underground economy."[114] Such attitudes are not surprising, given that women's sex work generates revenues which help to support the male monastic establishment.

More generally, Thai Buddhist attitudes towards wealth contribute to the affirmation of capitalist expansion, which indirectly supports trafficking and sex tourism. As anthropologist Charles Keyes has observed, the Sangha has adopted "'strategies of compromise, ambiguity, and silence' . . . to be a 'passive enabler' of capitalist development. No critique of capitalistic development has come from the Buddhist establishment because most recent governments

[109] Mettanando Bhikkhu, "Legalized Prostitution is Not Enough For Society," 1; Kabilsingh, *Thai Women in Buddhism*, 81; Horner, *Women under Primitive Buddhism*, 86–94, 184–93; Law, *Women in Buddhist Literature,* 25–34.

[110] Murcott, *First Buddhist Women*, 96; also Keyes, "Mother or Mistress But Never a Monk," 224; Truong, *Sex, Money and Morality*, 136.

[111] Skrobanek, Boonpakdi, and Janthakeero, *Traffic in Women*, 77–78, Kapur-Fic, *Thailand,* 454–55; Kabilsingh, *Thai Women in Buddhism*, 80–81.

[112] Skrobanek, Boonpakdi, and Janthakeero, *Traffic in Women*, 78.

[113] See Kapur-Fic, *Thailand,* 420; Kabilsingh, *Thai Women in Buddhism*, 83.

[114] Beadle, "The Sangha and the Sex Industry," 3.

have exerted very tight control over the Sangha and because the religion has clearly benefited materially . . . from the new wealth in the society."[115]

In addition to this support from religion, Thai law has also contributed to perpetuating the disadvantaged status of prostitutes and prostitution in Thai society. Although the legality of prostitution has varied over Thai history, it was made illegal when the Prostitution Prohibition Act (PPA) was passed in 1960.[116] The PPA emphasized women's sexual behavior rather than the monetary exchange, and targeted prostitutes as the source of the problem. It prohibited the selling of sex but not its purchase, thereby making prostitutes vulnerable to arrest, fines and 'rehabilitation' at a confinement facility. As the Traffic in Women Study notes, under the PPA, prostitutes "are morally judged, but their customers usually escape censure."[117]

In the face of concern over its national image, in the mid-1990s the Thai government finally allowed changes in the prostitution law, including, for the first time, provisions for the punishment of clients, and, in particular, for the punishment of clients of child prostitutes. Yet, even under the Prostitution Prevention and Suppression Act passed in 1996, which decriminalized prostitution, prescribed harsh punishment for those having sex with children under 18 years old, and enhanced the penalties for brothel owners, traffickers, pimps and clients, sex workers are still subject to fines of up to 1,000 Baht (U.S. $50.00) for soliciting in a public place, 'behaving' like a prostitute, or causing a nuisance to the public.[118] Due to rampant corruption in law enforcement, moreover, it is still generally the sex workers themselves, rather than the traffickers, pimps or brothel owners, who are arrested, prosecuted, and treated as the criminals.[119]

---

[115] Charles Keyes, "Buddhist Economics and Buddhist Fundamentalism in Burma and Thailand," in *Remaking the World: Fundamentalist Impact*, ed. Martin Marty and Scott Appleby (Chicago: University of Chicago Press, 1993), 389.

[116] Prostitution Prohibition Act, B.E. 2503. Prostitution was legal during the reign of King Rama I (1868–1910), a time when Thailand was opening its markets to international trade. "Thailand," in *A Human Rights Report on Trafficking of Persons, Especially Women and Children* (March 2002), Protection Project Website, http://www.protectionproject.org/main1.htm, 541; Kabilsingh, *Thai Women in Buddhism*, 71–72; Skrobanek, Boonpakdi, and Janthakeero, *Traffic in Women*, 8, 29.

[117] Skrobanek, Boonpakdi, and Janthakeero, *Traffic in Women*, 69.

[118] B.E. 2539 (1996), passed October 22, 1996, and effective as of December 21, 1996, on line at http://www.krisdika.go.th:8080/law/text/lawpub/e14102539/text.htm, repealing the Prostitution Prohibition Act of 1960; also Elaine Pearson, "Human Traffic, Human Rights: Redefining Victim Protection," (London, England: Anti-Slavery International, 2002), online at *http://www.antislavery.org* see AFP English Wire Service, "Thailand: Debate on Legalizing Prostitution Set for Late November" (November 4, 2003), distributed online via CSENEWS@ PETE.URI.EDU (Wednesday, November 5, 2003), 1.

[119] Pearson, Elaine, "Human Traffic, Human Rights: Redefining Victim Protection," (London, England: Anti-Slavery International, 2002), online at http://www.antislavery.org, 175.

In addition, the Thai government has failed to enforce either the international obligations under anti-trafficking conventions it has signed, or its domestic laws regulating prostitution and sex trafficking.[120] It is apparent that what Jeffrey considers as "the failure of police to take action despite the blatant operation of the industry and the extremely light penalties handed down to operators" was due in part to official involvement.[121] In the 1980s, the Thai government made special arrangements with foreign governments to prevent trafficking, which effectively "curtailed women's self-determination and freedom of movement, making them, 'for their own good,' objects of state control."[122] Raids on brothels by law enforcement officers had resulted in arrests of prostitute women, but not of owners and procurers. As Jeffrey observes, "whenever stronger measures against prostitution were enforced, it usually resulted in harsher realities for prostitute women."[123]

Somewhat ironically, efforts of international NGOs and Thai women's groups to improve the legal status of prostitutes has further entrenched the normative gender ideal of women as wives and mothers.[124] The issue of whether to legalize prostitution in Thailand was under debate during the fall of 2003, with two days of public hearings inviting prostitutes to participate.[125] Those arguing against legalization say that it "would be destructive to the moral values of Thai society and to the integrity of family units, that it would facilitate creating life-long stigmatization for those girls who decide to change their lives, and leave the 'profession,'"[126] as well as tarnish the "good image of the country and the dignity of Thai women."[127] Those advocating decriminalization argued that it was more beneficial to the sex workers themselves than continuing to have it operate underground, thereby facilitating trafficking and other illicit means of exploiting sex workers.[128] There is suspicion on both

---

[120] The U.S. Department of State *Trafficking in Persons Reports* for both 2003 and 2004 ranked Thailand as a "Tier Two" country. This signifies that in the State Department's estimation, the Thai government does not fully comply with the Act's minimum standards for the elimination of trafficking, but is making "significant efforts" to bring itself into compliance.

[121] Jeffrey, *Sex and Borders*, 92; see U.S. Department of State, 2003 and 2004 *Trafficking in Persons Reports*.

[122] Jeffrey, *Sex and Borders*, 88.

[123] Ibid., 90.

[124] Ibid., 72, 74, 82–85.

[125] AFP English Wire Service, "Thailand: Debate on Legalizing Prostitution Set for Late November" (November 4, 2003), distributed on line via CSENEWS@PETE.URI.EDU (Wednesday, November 5, 2003), 1.

[126] Mettanando Bhikkhu, "Thailand: Legalized Prostitution is Not Enough for Society," 1–2.

[127] Editorial, "Debate at Last on Prostitution," *Thai Nation* October 1, 2003, 1, distributed online via CSENEWS@PETE.URI.EDU, October 1, 2003.

[128] Editorial, "Debate at Last on Prostitution," 1; Editorial, "Decent Nutters," *Thai Anxieity Website*, http://www.thaianxiety.com/news03d.asp.

sides that the government is more interested in the tax revenues it could achieve by legalizing the sex trade than in protecting the women and children working in (or trafficked into) the industry.[129]

At the same time, the growth of materialist and consumerist values in Thailand appears to have brought about some shift in the predominance of negative views of prostitutes, and created a space for women to earn some sense of status, success, and even popularity and respect in this role. In an ironic twist, just as in early Buddhism, some Thai parents in recent years have expressed a preference for daughters, in contravention of long established son preference in Thai (as in all patriarchal societies), because of the revenues that their daughters can earn as prostitutes.[130] For example, Kapur-Fic notes that "the money that women make from prostitution has changed women's status to the extent that families now rejoice at the birth of a daughter."[131] The Traffic in Women Study found that "now a family with several daughters is considered lucky" as well as that "parents have even come to respect their daughters."[132]

Indeed, several anecdotal examples suggest that prostitution is increasingly accepted in Thailand, even respected, although there are still strong sentiments in society opposing its legitimation. According to Kapur-Fic,

> prostitution is perceived as a business transaction [and i]t is possible to rationalize that there is nothing wrong with prostituting one's self, even if there is a loss of face, because money earned, as has already been observed, will compensate this by bestowing upon the person a sense of personal power. [. . .] [133] As long as this money is used to take care of parents in their old age, and to meet the needs of other close relatives, the woman is considered a good person because she is repaying for their kindness and consideration during early years of her life.[134]

In addition, prostitutes have told researchers with pride how they can please their parents and their communities by sending money home. However, it is evident that many of them are pressured into sex work, and that sometimes this is because their families want material goods.[135] The women in the Japanese Thai Trafficking Study consistently discussed their success or failure in relation to their

---

[129] For example, Michael Mathes, "Thailand to Consider Legalising Its Famous Sex Industry," Agence France-Presse, November 2, 2003, distributed online via CSENEWS@PETE.URI.EDU listserve, November 3, 2003.

[130] Horner, *Women Under Primitive Buddhism*, 20: "in one not inconsiderable section of the population girls were preferred to boys. It was said of the courtesans that, if they had children at all . . . 'they will bestow care on a daughter, but not on a son,' for it is through a daughter that their line of business is maintained," citing Henry Clark Warren, trans., *Dhammapada Commentary* (Cambridge, Mass., Harvard University Press, 1921, vs. 21–23).

[131] Kapur-Fic, *Thailand*, 457.

[132] Skrobanek, Boonpakdi and Janthakeero, *Traffic in Women*, 74.

[133] Kapur-Fic, *Thailand*, 457, 459–60.

[134] Ibid.

[135] Caouette and Saito, *To Japan and Back*, 71; Kapur-Fic, *Thailand*, 458; Skrobanek, Boonpakdi, and Janthakeero, *Traffic in Women*, 23, 69.

family's financial situation and their family's position in the village.[136] Based on such considerations, the Thai NGO's Trafficking in Women Study notes:

> In communities such as Rim Mon, where migration for prostitution is long established, the women believe that the community no longer considers prostitution to be immoral: 'Before, when only a few women went into prostitution, people may have looked down on prostitutes. But now many women join the sex trade. And they come back to the village with their car and jewellery. People no longer criticize them'.[137]

The authors conclude that "the acceptability of otherwise 'immoral' conduct is attributable to the superior claims of economics."[138]

In part, this shifting valuation of prostitution may be the result of globalization, which has brought to Thailand increasingly Western consumerist and materialist values which already threaten, and may someday replace, traditional Buddhist spiritual and non-materialistic ones.[139] The report from the Trafficking in Women Study speculates that the family relationship may now often be viewed as a commercial one as a result of such factors:

> If a woman goes away as a sex worker, whether voluntarily or under duress, and regularly sends money home, she is considered successful. If she fails to send home substantial sums, the family says she is a victim of the sex trade. ... Families are nearly always defensive about the work of their daughters.[140]

The preceding discussion reveals the complexities of the status of prostitutes in Thai society. Amid the many factors responsible for the vast sex industry and accompanying sex trafficking, however, it is evident that both law and religion have played significant roles. Law has maintained an ambivalent, even hypocritical stance which enables government to profit from women's sex work at the same time that it continues to criminalize it and stigmatize the women who work in the sex industry. Religion contributes to the marginal status of prostitutes through teachings which denigrate the state of women and identify them as (essentially)[141] sexual beings whose own bad karma resulted in their becoming prostitutes, but also provides the opportunity for them to make merit towards a better rebirth by contributing to their family's income and making *dana* to their local Buddhist temples.

---

[136] Caouette and Saito, *To Japan and Back*, 71.

[137] Skrobanek, Boonpakdi, and Janthakeero, *Traffic in Women*, 76.

[138] Ibid., 75, 101.

[139] Generally, see: Tavivat Puntarigvivat, "Toward a Buddhist Social Ethics: the Case of Thailand," *Cross Currents* 48 no. 3 (Fall 1998): 347–65, online at http://sino-sv3.sino.uni-heidelberg.de/FULLTEXT/JR-ADM/tavivat.htm; Sulak Sivaraksa, *Seeds of Peace: a Buddhist Vision for Renewing Society* (Berkeley, CA: Parallex Press, 1992).

[140] Skrobanek, Boonpakdi and Janthakeero, *Traffic in Women*, 73.

[141] I use a parenthetical here since Buddhist philosophy holds that there are in fact not essences or inherent existences in any phenomena, including individual selves.

In the next section, I describe the status of another marginalized role for women in Thai society, that of the monastic, and evaluate how religion and law have both obstructed spiritual roles for women, thereby indirectly encouraging roles as prostitutes.

The Sangha

In general, Buddhism has been a male dominated religious tradition throughout its history, and women have struggled just to be included. Indeed, one of the great ironies of the relationship between women and Buddhism is that women are far greater supporters of Buddhist institutions and practices than men have been. Indeed, it is accurate to say that women are, and have been throughout Buddhist history, the main supporters and social reproducers of the Sangha, both as almsgivers and by sustaining the infrastructure of monastic and religious institutions. Without their support, it would be extremely difficult for the Sangha to sustain itself.[142] Yet, despite (or indeed precisely because of) their disproportionately greater material and practical support of Buddhism, women seeking spiritual careers are not supported by Thai Buddhist institutions nor by lay society. In both cases, a very practical reason is women's centrality to the institution of the Thai family.[143]

Women were admitted to the Buddhist monastic institution or Sangha from the first days of the Buddhist religion. Sometime after Theravada Buddhism was nearly destroyed in the tenth century CE by Cholian invaders to Sri Lanka, the nuns' order died out in both Sri Lanka and India.[144] Thus, when Theravada Buddhism spread from Sri Lanka to Thailand, Cambodia, Laos, and Burma, it was already lacking a *bhikkhuni* order. Although a formal order of nuns was never established in Thailand, many Thai women have nevertheless renounced lay life and have taken vows known as "*mae chi*" to uphold some portion of the hundreds of vows contained in the *Vinaya*.[145]

---

[142] van Esterik, *Materializing Thailand*, 75; Kapur-Fic, *Thailand*, 436; Sponberg, "Attitudes toward Women," 3–4.

[143] Kapur-Fic, *Thailand*, 435.

[144] For general background on the history of Buddhist nuns, Kabilsingh, *Thai Women in Buddhism*, ch. 4; D. Amarashir Weeraratne, "Binar Poya and the Bhikkuni Order," *Daily News* (Wednesday Sept. 10, 2003), 1–5, online at http://www.dailynews.lk/2003/09/10/fea03.html; Karme Lekshe Tsomo, *Buddhist Women Across Cultures: Realizations* (Albany: State University of New York Press, 1999); Tsomo, ed., *Sakyadhita: Daughters of the Buddha* (Ithaca: Snow Lion Publications, 1988).

[145] The earliest reference to *mae chi* was in a letter written by a foreigner visiting Thailand in 1639, which recounts that the order of *mae chi* was established in Thailand 300 years earlier. Hinshiranan, "The Case of Buddhist Nuns in Thailand," 9; generally, Kabilsingh, *Thai Women in Buddhism*, chap. 4.

Mae chi renounce lay lifestyles, shave their heads, wear monastic robes, take vows of celibacy, and usually live in nunneries or segregated from the monks in housing located at the outskirts of the monastic compounds. The status of Buddhist nuns or *mae chi* in Thailand is significantly below that of their male counterparts, the monks or *bhikkhus*. In part, this is because of well-entrenched androcentrism within Thai monastic institutions, and the attitudes they have imparted to the laity. The Thai government has refused to recognize *mae chi* as monastics (as they have not taken the full set of Vinaya vows that the monks have) and denies them the right to vote in national elections as well as the financial support that it accords to the male Sangha, such as free health care and public transport. Thus, they are not viewed as propagators of the Dhamma and are not allowed to interpret Buddhist texts, officially teach Buddhism, or hold religious rituals. Frequently, *mae chi* receive no social or familial support, and live lives of near destitution as a result.[146]

By being relegated to an inferior status as *mae chis*, Thai nuns are not viewed as highly as 'fields of merit' as monks are, although there is no textual evidence for this differentiation.[147] Indeed, Thai nun advocate Ouyporn Khuankaew states that the status of Thai nuns "is the lowest of all women, because they do not belong to any category of women, either within the lay or monastic community."[148] And as Kabilsingh argues, because women cannot be ordained, "the image of women is so negative, that even the lowest of places seems fitting for them. Women believe they are born lower and that they are unclean. They have a very negative image of themselves."[149]

The public image of *mae chi* in Thailand today is that of "poor old ladies who want to practice Dhamma in the temples during their last days and help with the temples' chores in return for free abode and food. The younger nuns are viewed as the heart-broken who take temporary refuge in the white robes."[150] Most *mae chi* live on the outskirts of male monasteries, where they spend much of their time cleaning, cooking, and caring for the monks. In this situation, nuns are clearly relegated to a secondary status in relation to that of

---

[146] van Esterik, *Materializing Thailand*, 76; Tessa Bartholomeusz, "Southeast Asian Buddhism," in *Encyclopedia of Women and World Religion*, ed. Serenity Young (New York: Macmillan Reference: 1999), 124–28; Kabilsingh, *Thai Women in Buddhism*, 36–66.

[147] Monte Leach, "Helping the Daughters of Buddha: Interview with Dr. Chatsumarn Kabilsingh" (undated), *Access New Age Website*, http://www.accessnewage.com/articles/mystic/BUDHADTR.HTM, 1–2; van Esterik, *Materializing Thailand*, 76.

[148] Khuankaew, "Thai Buddhism and Patriarchy," 1.

[149] Interview with Chatsumarn Kabilsingh, "The Buddha was a Feminist," *Yasodhara* 18(1) (Oct.–Dec. 2002): 3, *Thaibhikkhunis Website*, http://www.thaibhikkhunis.org/eyasodhara_no73_4.html.

[150] Bangkok Post editorial staff, "Focus on Thailand: Spiritual Education Gives New Hope to Young Women," *Sakyadhita Newsletter*, 3 no. 2 (1992): 11, http://www.sakyadhita.org/NewsLetters/3-1.htm#Young (reprinted from *Bangkok Post* June 9, 1991).

the monks.[151] As Narumon Hinshiranan has stated: "Thai religious ideology does not grant power and prestige to women's spiritual status."[152]

Laity generally accord less respect and provide fewer resources to *mae chi* than to *bhikkhus*, in part because of the view prevalent throughout Buddhist countries that making *dana* to male monastics earns greater merit than making donations to females.[153] One Thai nun describes how Thai families view a son becoming a monk in comparison with the prospect of a daughter becoming a nun: "While monkhood is a merit-accumulating practice, nunhood is still socially looked down upon as a refuge for dead-end women. With the boys of the families gone, either to the temples or to schools, practical needs require the girls to help with the household chores or to work and send remittances home."[154] Again, the irony is that it is precisely because it is women who are the bigger supporters of the *bhikkhus* and temples that they may not be encouraged to pursue monastic roles.

Contrary to the many schools available to monks, there are very few educational opportunities for *mae chi*. In addition, since most nunneries emphasize a spiritual life cut off from the outside world, most monastic women seeking education must struggle on their own.[155] The lack of education then exacerbates the nuns' feelings of inability to do social work. This inability is compounded by the lack of financial resources.[156]

Efforts to establish a Bhikkhuni Sangha in 1928 failed, with the result that the nuns were arrested and jailed and the monks who ordained them were deported.[157] A modern movement to reestablish ordination for Buddhist women throughout the world, led in part by the Buddhist women's organization

---

[151] Interview with Kabilsingh, "The Buddha was a Feminist," 3; Ahmad-Zaki, "A Question of Rights," 2; Hinshiranan, "The Case of Buddhist Nuns in Thailand," 10; Van Esterik, *Materializing Thailand*, 76. In some monasteries, this hierarchy is explained as a mere social convention which was designed to facilitate efficient decision making in the community. Thanissaro Bhikkhu, "Upasika Kee Nanayon and the Social Dynamic of Theravadin Buddhist Practice," *Sakyadhita Newsletter*, 3 no. 2 (1992): 5, http://www.sakyadhita.org/NewsLetters/8-2.html.

[152] Hinshiranan, "The Case of Buddhist Nuns in Thailand," 15.

[153] Begging for alms and living only on the basis of what is provided by the generosity of others is part of the earliest Buddhist tradition, still practiced by most Southeast Asian monks, as well as by certain (non-Buddhist) ascetics in India.

[154] Bangkok Post editorial staff, "Focus on Thailand: Spiritual Education Gives New Hope to Young Women," *Sakyadhita Newsletter*, 3 no. 2 (1992): 10 http://www.sakyadhita.org/News Letters/3-1.htm#Young (reprinted from *Bangkok Post* June 9, 1991).

[155] Bangkok Post editorial staff, "Focus on Thailand," 10; van Esterik, *Materializing Thailand*, 76–77.

[156] Rattigorn Rattanburi, "The Life of a Maechee," *Seeds of Peace* 17 no. 2 (2001) online at http://www.siam21.org/sop/17-2maechee.html; Hinshiranan, "The Case of Buddhist Nuns in Thailand," 9.

[157] D. Amarasiri Weeraratne, "Bhikkuni Sasana in Thailand," *The Island* (November 5, 2003), 1–2, online at http://www.buddhistnews.tv/current/bhikkhui-th-051103.php; Kabilsingh, *Thai Women in Buddhism*, ch. 5 "Two Bhikkhuni Movements in Thailand," 45–54.

Sakyadhita ('Daughters of the Buddha'),[158] has been led in Thailand by women followers of Bhikhuni Vorami Kabilsingh, who in 1959 received ordination in the Mahayana tradition. (Mahayana ordination is not recognized as legitimate by the Thai Sangha which follows the Therevada tradition.) In 1996, Mahayana nuns from Taiwan (where the tradition of female ordination has been preserved) ordained eleven Sri Lankan women as full *bhikkhunis* at Sarnath in India; in 1998 another group of 22 nuns were ordained at Bodhgaya, also in India.[159] Despite the participation and/or recognition of Bhikkhuni ordinations by high ranking monks in Sri Lanka, another Theravadan Buddhist country,[160] the Thai Sangha has refused to recognize this method of ordination of *bhikkhuni*. Some monks have objected on the basis that if the transmission of ordination is broken, it cannot be restored. Others oppose the ordinations on the more specific ground that the recent ceremonies have involved Mahayana and not Theravada nuns (even though male orders have been reintroduced in several other Theravada Buddhist countries after having disappeared). It is evident, although not frequently made explicit, that monks benefit from the status quo, in which nuns remain subservient to them, both in terms of status as well as practicalities such as having nuns cook and clean and provide other services for them which would no longer be available were *mae chi* allowed to receive full ordination.[161]

Vorami's daughter Chatsumarn Kabilsingh—who left a career as a professor of philosophy and religion at Thammasat University in Bangkok and was herself ordained in Sri Lanka on February 28, 2003 when she took the ordained name of Dhammananda—took her case for the full ordination of women to the Thai Senate in 2003.[162] On November 3, 2003, the head of a

---

[158] Since Sakyadhita was originally founded by western Buddhist women, it has been subject to the criticism by some opponents as being fomented by western feminists who lack sensitivity and understanding of traditional gender roles in Buddhist cultures. *Sakyadhita: The International Association of Buddhist Women Website*, http://www.sakyadhita.org/.

[159] Coincidentally, women's ordination had been introduced into China by Sri Lankan monks and nuns: Kabilsingh, *Thai Women in Buddhism*, 36–38. This ordination ceremony was preceded by an ordination involving Sri Lankan bhikkhunis in Los Angeles in 1988 by the Venerable Bhikhu Proessor H. Ranansara Maha Thero. *Seeds of Peace* Editorial Staff, "Bhikkhuni Ordination: Good News From Sri Lanka," *Seeds of Peace Newsletter*, 17 no. 2 (1991): 1, online at http://www.siam21.org/sop/17-2good%20news%20from%20sri%20lanka.html; Editorial. 1998. "World Buddhists Affirm Equality Of Women: An Unprecedented Ordination Ceremony," online at *Buddha.net Website*, http://www.buddhanet.net/nuns_ord.htm.

[160] *Seeds of Peace* Editorial Staff, "Bhikkhuni Ordination: Good News From Sri Lanka;" Ajahn Punnadhammo, "Editorial: Women's Ordination," *Toronto Star* (August 2000), online at *Arrow River Website*, http://www.baynet.net/~arcc/torStar/nuns.html.

[161] van Esterik, *Materializing Thailand*, 77.

[162] For general background on Dhammananda and her petition, see Gemma Tulud Cruz, "Bhikkhunis: Ordaining Buddhist Women," *National Catholic Reporter: The Independent Newsweekly* 1 no. 7 (May 14, 2003), online at http://www.nationalcatholicreproter.org/globalpers/gp051403.htm; Interview, "Ordination of Buddhist Women," *The Religion Report:*

sub-committee of the Thai Parliament set up to investigate the possibility of establishing the Bhikkhuni Order in Thailand briefed the Parliament regarding the sub-committee's findings that the Bhikkhuni Order should indeed be reestablished and Dhammananda was recognized as its head.[163]

Dhammanananda's petition presents an interesting case, in part because it illustrates the lack of strict separation between 'Church and State' in Thailand. Nonetheless, the Sangha will have the final say on the proposal, notwithstanding the Senate's decision, so the issue has not yet been settled.[164] Regardless of its ultimate success, however, Dhammanananda's petition represents a radical challenge to Thai legal and religious framings of women's appropriate roles.

The petition also represents a contested move within the ranks of female monastics in Thailand, as some object on the ground that formalizing women's status within the Sangha would re-subject them to the control and authority of male monks, in accordance with ancient Buddhist rules called the Gurudharma or '8 special rules' that have institutionalized the dominance of male over female monastics since the Buddha first agreed to ordain women.[165] Such reasons also have kept most nuns from joining the Lay Nun Association of Thailand, an organization recently established by the government (and sponsored by the Queen and senior monks in the national hierarchy) to provide an organizational structure for all nuns in the country.[166]

Despite these hardships, monastic institutions for women have been one place where Thai Buddhist women have been able—to some extent—to develop a 'separate sphere' away from male control and regulation. Many women have felt liberated by renouncing lay life for a spiritual existence with "sisters" who shared their spiritual aspirations. Freed from the obligations of domestic and child-bearing and caring responsibilities, many Buddhist renunciants have written glowingly of their good fortune at having left lay life for a spiritual one.

Radio National, September 7, 2003, online at http://www.abc.net.au/rn/talks/8.30/relrpt/stories/s898138.htm; *Seeds of Peace* staff, "Feel the Beauty of the Lotus: An Interview with Dhammanananda," *Seeds of Peace* 17 no. 2 (2001), online at http://www.siam21.org/sop/17-2Interview%20with%20Dhammananda.html; Interview with Kabilsingh, "The Buddha was a Feminist," 3.

163 Weeraratne, "Bhikkuni Sasana in Thailand," 3, noting that, "(u)nder the old constitution in Thailand, she would have been jailed or deported. Under the new constitution with its democratic values, religious freedom and civil liberties, she is fairly safe and her Bhikkuni Order bids fair to thrive and prosper for the greater glory of the Buddha Sasana in the modern world!"

164 Simon Montlake, "Bastion of Buddhism Faces Gender Debate," *Christian Science Monitor* (April 17, 2003), online at http://www.csmonitor.com/2003/0417/p07s01-woap.html.

165 See Kabilsingh, *Thai Women in Buddhism*, 28–29; van Esterik, *Materializing Thailand*, 77.

166 Hinshiranan, "The Case of Buddhist Nuns in Thailand," 9; Thanissaro Bhikkhu, "Upasika Kee Nanayon," 6.

Kawanami argues that the celibate practice that accompanies female monastics (and lay spinsters) is "a means to become autonomous, defy the social construction of womanhood, and subvert the patriarchal social order," thus allowing "the Buddhist woman an ultimate opportunity for empowerment and liberation."[167]

While they may be given less respect and resources as 'unauthorized' renunciant women, lay nuns and female monastics now have the freedom to practice the *dharma* and organize their lives as they see fit. Some unofficial monastic or semi-monastic institutions for women have been emerging in Thailand in recent decades which are not effectively under the authority of a monastery but are independent institutions. In addition, some laywomen have become meditation masters, and some instruct both monks and laity, thereby bypassing the Sangha altogether.[168] Thus, contrary to those who have advocated the introduction of full Bhikkhuni ordination in Thailand as the means for empowering women in spiritual roles, others have taken an alternative, non-mainstream approach which may prove to be even more effective at subverting sexist and patriarchal norms in Thai society. Only time will tell.

Meanwhile, the status of nuns, like that of prostitutes, is a poor one in contemporary Thailand. Neither role for women is accorded the status and respect given to women occupying their normatively prescribed roles as wives and mothers. Some commentators have noted that the number of prostitutes is about the same as the number of monks in Thailand, and that if Thai women and girls were accorded the same spiritual and educational opportunities that their brothers have, they would not have to resort to prostitution in order to make a living and repay their filial obligation to their parents.[169] Nonetheless, as I will argue in the final section, the status of prostitutes is improving at a more obvious pace than that of nuns, in part because of considerations far removed from either morality or spirituality.

Summary and Conclusions: Thai Law and Religion—Beyond Gender Ideology?

As we have seen, both prostitutes and nuns transgress their normative gender roles as women and thus are easy targets for legal and religious regulation. However, this circumstance does not explain the relatively and increasingly higher status of prostitutes in comparison with nuns, when it would seem logical for the contrary to be the case. How can we best explain this seeming

[167] Kawanami, "Can Women Be Celibate," 153.
[168] van Esterik, *Materializing Thailand*, 78, 89.
[169] See, e.g., Khuankaew, "Thai Buddhism and Patriarchy," 2.

anomaly, this departure from the dichotomized 'Madonna/Whore complex' that is so prevalent in Western understandings of women's sexual roles? One key, I contend, lies in women's roles as economic producers and reproducers in Thailand.

Prostitutes violate the Thai gender ideology of 'good women' by 'squandering their sexuality' (for example, by engaging in sexual relations outside the confines of marriage or by engaging in sexual relations with more than one man).[170] They thereby transgress the normative ideal for women's roles in Thailand. From this perspective, nuns similarly squander their sexuality by becoming monastics who take on vows of celibacy and thereby completely repudiating family responsibilities, including sex and reproduction. However, in a number of respects, nuns are more transgressive of their normative roles than are prostitutes.

First, whereas women who become prostitutes often do so, and increasingly have done so in recent years, in order to be better able to fulfill their filial obligations as daughters by supporting their families financially, nuns usually renounce family (or at least the possibility of having children of their own), and in most cases leave home to live in monasteries. The families that prostitutes labor to support through sex work may be parents, siblings, husbands or children whom they have left behind by migrating or being trafficked to a distant location. In some cases, prostitutes are also said to be instrumental in maintaining intact the family of their clients, which might otherwise be destroyed through the husband's adulterous affair, taking a mistress or 'second wife,' and so forth.[171] Thus, where prostitutes remain involved in supporting their families, and thus fulfill their normative roles in this respect, nuns are expected to renounce lay life altogether, especially the bonds of marriage and family which perpetuate *samsaric* existence.

In addition, nuns transgress the norms for women's gender roles more radically than prostitutes by renouncing sexuality and reproduction altogether. Hiroko Kawanami, writing about celibacy of Theravada nuns, observes that "it is not uncommon for nuns, who have digressed from the designated cultural norm of wife and mother, to be treated with suspicion and mockery. They are at times even cast as women who have failed in their secular womanhood."[172] Thus, nuns are subject to even greater suspicion and consequent

[170] Jeffrey, *Sex and Borders*, xx.

[171] See, e.g., Mike Douglass and Glenda Roberts, eds., *Japan and Global Migration: Foreign Workers and the Advent of a Multicultural Society* (Routledge, 2000; University of Hawai'i Press, 2003), 99–100: "Pressure to stay married leads wives to endure husbands having sexual liaisons outside of the marriage. This 'inside marriage divorce' may not be the norm, but they are reported with sufficient frequency to suggest that for some portion of married couples, the practice is routine." Although this is written about Japanese society, it may apply equally to the Thai context, despite the rapidly rising rates of divorce there in recent years.

[172] Kawanami, "Can Women Be Celibate?" 143.

marginalization than are prostitutes for their even greater heretical abandonment of their normative roles as women.[173]

Perhaps even more importantly than whether or not they maintain a relationship with their families, what distinguishes prostitutes from nuns is their capacity for and/or engagement in wage labor. As wage earners, prostitutes fulfill an important aspect of women's traditional roles in Thailand. Research conducted in the 1970s indicated that rural Thai women were entering the sex trade as an 'entrepreneurial move' to support their families in a situation of increasing economic pressure. According to Jeffrey, "they did so because their accustomed position in that rural society allocated them a considerable responsibility for earning income to sustain the family."[174] The 1996 study on prostitution by the Foundation for Women reported that "in some families, women are now considered the head of the household and women have a greater share of the decision-making power."[175]

At its starkest, the contrast between nun and prostitute illustrates that the nun does not use her sexuality at all, thereby wasting it and at the same time evading patriarchal control of it; whereas the sex worker uses her sexuality to fulfill a socially approved gender role of wage-laborer, whose earnings, moreover, are applied to the benefit of her family, village or temple. Thus prostitutes' work aligns them more closely to normative women's roles than do the activities of most *mae chi*. Because their sexual activity is profit-making in a manner which benefits the family, village, government and society, and not only the prostitute herself, I posit that beneath the surface moral views condemning prostitution, women engaging in sex work are actually viewed more favorably than nuns in Thai society.

Although this valuation of the status of women occupying non-normative roles in contemporary Thai society can be understood as largely fueled by economic globalization and the rise of consumerist and materialist values, it should be noted that the relatively more favorable view of prostitutes has antecedents in the earliest eras of the Buddhist tradition. As already noted, the Buddhist scriptures do not view prostitutes negatively, but depict them as

---

[173] Thus, I believe that Jeffrey's analysis is somewhat off the mark, in claiming (*Sex and Borders*, xxii) that the prostitute "appears as a liminal figure in relation to the mother, and she marks the borderlands of female sexuality. She is the internal 'other' that threatens the purity of the nation. The rise of the prostitute, in this formulation, signals the loss of control over female sexuality and, therefore, is a harbinger of the disintegration of national culture and identity. Most threatening of all, the prostitute—seen as one who uses her own sexuality for profit—is a subversive figure."

[174] Ibid., 86; see also Skrobanek, Boonpakdi and Janthakeero, *Traffic in Women*, 72–73.

[175] Cited in Jeffreys, *Sex and Borders*, 132. However, Jeffrey also observes that "prostitute women's own interpretations of their lives as, for example, wage earners and family supporters are silenced by dominant interpretations that focus on their cultural symbolism," ibid., 153.

friends of the Buddha who are generous benefactresses to the Sangha.[176] Nuns, however, have been viewed negatively in Buddhist literature, especially in relation to male monastics, even through "the earliest Buddhists clearly held that one's sex, like one's caste or class (*varna*), presents no barrier to attaining the Buddhist goal of liberation from suffering. Women can, we are told by the tradition, pursue the path."[177]

Then, as now, the disparity between the status of women working as prostitutes and those renouncing lay life as nuns can be viewed as at least partly a function of the potential of the two roles to productively and/or materially benefit Sangha and society. Whereas a number of courtesans directly benefited the Sangha financially during the Buddha's time, nuns could not because they had renounced their worldly belongings. Even today, Kawanami speculates that one reason for the discouragement of women from monastic roles is that the nun's "presence on the ascetic path is in itself problematic because she encroaches upon the sacred territory of men and threatens their valued place in the spiritual hierarchy."[178] Sadly, it seems unlikely that the status of either Thai women prostitutes or monastics is likely to improve significantly in the foreseeable future. But as long as the current trend continues of materialist and consumerist values increase while spiritual ones decline, it is likely that women in Thailand will continue to be more revered for sex than salvation.

[176] See Horner, *Women Under Primitive Buddhism*, 91.
[177] Sponberg, "Attitudes toward Women," 8; Kawanami, "Can Women Be Celibate?" 142.
[178] Kawanami, "Can Women Be Celibate?" 142.

CHAPTER THREE

WOMEN AND WITCHCRAFT: POSITIVIST, PRELAPSARIAN, AND POST-MODERN JUDICIAL INTERPRETATIONS IN PNG

Jean G. Zorn

Introduction

This chapter focuses on the treatment in Papua New Guinea's (PNG) formal, state courts of persons alleged to have killed women who were identified—by their killers, at any rate—as witches. An odd topic, one might think, even in a book about religion, gender, and law. However, it will be apparent that this subject opens vistas onto conflicts over core values that characterize not only Papua New Guinean, but also many other post-colonial societies. At the time of Independence (in 1975), many people had hoped that the foreign laws and legal processes that had been imposed upon PNG's diverse legal cultures during the colonial period would give way to laws and legal instutitions more reflective of PNG culture and circumstances. One of the themes of this chapter is that, for the most part, this did not happen.

Another theme is the complexity of the relationships between religion and law, and the layers of complexity that are added when gender relations become part of the picture. This is especially so in colonial and post-colonial situations. As sources of ideology and values, traditional religion and the imposed legal system are posited as opposites, with religion ostensibly standing for emotion, mystery, and magic, and law exemplifying rationality and scientific understanding. In their dealings with gender relations, however, these supposedly dissimilar institutions can have very similar cultural and social effects. In PNG, as this chapter will demonstrate, the introduced legal system describes itself as implacably opposed to traditional religious practices, such as witch-killing, but unites with customary religion in supporting a social order that discriminates against women and that punishes women for getting 'above themselves'.

The inter-relationships of law, religion and gender politics in post-colonial PNG are encapsulated in three very different judicial decisions: two written by judges of PNG's trial court (the National Court) and one by the justices of its appellate court (the Supreme Court).[1] The three decisions illustrate three different

[1] *Acting Public Prosecutor v. Aumane*, unreported Supreme Court judgment, SC 190 (1980); *State v. Gesie*, unreported National Court judgment, N254 (1980); *State v. Aigal*, unreported National Court judgment, N891 (1990).

approaches that the law could take to witch-killing. The Supreme Court decision (which is actually five decisions, since each of the five justices on the appellate panel felt obliged to contribute his own thoughts) illustrates the typical approach to witch-killing in particular, and custom in general, taken by the colonial and post-colonial courts. The courts have refused to accept claims about evil witchcraft as an absolute excuse for killing the person designated as a witch—an excuse that would absolve the killer of all liability. The rationale is that since witches do not exist and witchcraft cannot occur, any belief in them is too irrational to be given credence. At the same time, courts have also refused to punish witch-killers to the full extent allowed by the law. The rationale here is that anybody who would kill a person, believing that person to be a witch, must be too backward, primitive, and uneducated to understand what the law requires.[2] The two trial court decisions illustrate the roads unfortunately not taken—at least not by the ruling majorities on the courts. In one, a trial court judge shows how custom could successfully be integrated into the common law.[3] In the other, a judge relies on his reading in the anthropology of witchcraft to reveal the way that the state courts' decisions in this area have unwittingly supported the subjugation of women.[4]

Before examining those decisions in depth, the chapter provides some introduction to PNG itself, to concepts of religion and witchcraft, and to the colonial and post-colonial courts.

Locating Papua New Guinea

Papua New Guinea, a nation of islands, is located in the South Pacific between Indonesia and Australia. It was a colony—first of Germany and England, then, for most of the colonial period, of Australia—for approximately one hundred years, from the late-nineteenth century until 1975.[5] Topographically, it is characterized by great diversity. The geography varies from tiny, tropical coral atolls to long, lush temperate valleys hidden high in rugged volcanic mountain ranges.[6] It is culturally diverse as well. Although its

---

[2] *Acting Public Prosecutor v. Aumane*, unreported Supreme Court judgment, SC 190 (1980).

[3] *State v. Gesie*, unreported National Court judgment, N254 (1980).

[4] *State v. Aigal*, unreported National Court judgment, N891 (1990).

[5] The best colonial histories include Brij Lal and Hank Nelson, eds. *Lines Across the Sea: Colonial Inheritance in the Post-Colonial Pacific* (Brisbane: Pacific History Assoc., 1995); and, Hank Nelson, *Taim bilong Masta: The Australian Involvement with Papua New Guinea* (Sydney: Australian Broadcasting Commission, 1990); Sione Latukefu, ed., *Papua New Guinea: A Century of Colonial Impact* (Boroko: National Research Institute and the University of Papua Jew Guinea, 1989).

[6] Donald Denoon and Catherine Snowden, eds., *A Time to Plant and a Time to Uproot* (Port Moresby: Institute of Papua New Guinea Studies, 1980).

population is primarily Melanesian, anthropologists have counted over 600 separate language and culture groups.[7] While some communities are coastal traders and fisherfolk, others are Highlands warriors who, prior to the colonial period, had never seen the sea.

There are, however, some important similarities across PNG's differing social groups.[8] Prior to the colonial period, all of PNG's communities were small (ranging from a few hundred to no more than a few thousand people) and egalitarian. Membership of communities was based almost entirely on kinship; one was born into, or married into, one's society and into one's place in that society. Most societies had no formal governmental structure, nor did they need one. Instead, social norms were maintained by a combination of kinship norms, societal pressure and religious beliefs. The very simple technology made for successful subsistence economies based on hunting, fishing and swidden horticulture,[9] but did not permit societies to maintain sufficient surplus to establish castes, classes or institutions based on socio-economic differentiation. The only marked differences were between in-groups and out-groups, and, within societies, between men and women.[10]

Since styles of religious belief and observance are artifacts of culture, it is not surprising that PNG's traditional religions also varied considerably from one small socio-cultural group to another.[11] The religions of some cultures were characterized by animism, some by beliefs in the continuing ghostly presence of

---

[7] The literature on the indigenous societies of Papua New Guinea is vast. For this chapter, I relied most heavily on Annette B. Weiner, *Women of Value, Men of Renown* (1976; reprint, Austin: University of Texas, 1987); Marilyn Strathern, ed., *Dealing with Inequality: Analysing Gender Relations in Melanesia and Beyond* (Cambridge: Cambridge University Press, 1987); Roy A. Rappaport, *Pigs for the Ancestors: Ritual in the Ecology of a New Guinea People* (New Haven: Yale University Press, 1984); Robert J. Gordon and Mervyn J. Meggitt, *Law and Order in the New Guinea Highlands* (Hanover: University of Vermont, 1985).

[8] Ron Crocombe and Robin Hide, "New Guinea: Unity in Diversity," in *Land Tenure in the Pacific*, ed. Ron Crocombe, 3rd ed. (Suva: University of the South Pacific, 1987), 324–354.

[9] In swithin horticulture, each household maintains gardens sufficient for the needs of the household. A garden is used for several years, until it ceases to be productive, and then is allowed to lay fallow for several years, and land cleared for another garden in its place. Because land is cleared by cutting down and then burning off the brush that has grown up whilst the land was lying fallow, this form of horticulture is also known as "slash and burn".

[10] Strathern, *Dealing with Inequality*; Paula Brown and G. Buchbinder, eds., *Man and Woman in the New Guinea Highlands* (Washington, D.C.: Amer. Anthropological Assoc., 1976); Rick Marksbury, ed., *The Business of Marriage: Transformations in Oceanic Matrimony* (Pittsburgh: University of Pittsburgh Press, 1993).

[11] Ethnographies of religious belief in Papua New Guinea include F. Barth, *Ritual and Knowledge among the Baktaman of New Guinea* (New Haven: Yale University Press, 1975); Peter Lawrence and Mervyn J. Meggitt, eds., *Gods, Ghosts and Men in Melanesia: Some Religions of Australian New Guinea and the New Hebrides* (Melbourne: Oxford University Press, 1965); Bronislaw Malinowski, *Magic, Science and Religion and Other Essays* (Boston: Beacon Press, 1948; London: Souvenir Press, 1974).

ancestors. In most cultures, humans and natural objects both were presumed capable of exercising magical powers; magic—both for good and for ill—was widely assumed to be a powerful force. In some cultures, anyone could learn how to use magic. However in other cultures, magic spells and abilities were held by individuals who passed their powers on to children, nieces and nephews, or other favored members of the next generation; in yet others, it was assumed that only sorcerers and witches had access to magic.[12] In these cases, access to magical power was inherent. In all situations, magic could be used it for good or ill; however most publicly discussed or notorious instances appear to be when magic is used for ill.[13] We are also told that, in the pre-colonial customary order, the murder of a presumed sorcerer or witch was culturally approved if he or she had harmed, or was threatening to harm, members of the killer's family.[14]

Reading the cases about people accused of murdering harmful sorcerers or witches from the early colonial period to the present,[15] we discover that all of the defendants are men and many of the supposed sorcerers or witches they are accused of killing are women. Hence a theme of this chapter is that the witchcraft beliefs are a consequence of gender politics. Gender relations in many of PNG's traditional cultures were (and are) characterized by sexism and inequality.[16] Colonialism, the colonial courts and the laws introduced

---

[12] Although it is conventional in many societies to refer to men as sorcerers and to women as witches, the categories are not necessarily gender related. In Papua New Guinea, the gender-related convention is often followed, but the term 'sorcery' is also used to refer to any display of magic. Thus, the Papua New Guinea statute that outlawed both sorcery and witchcraft is titled the Sorcery Act. In this chapter, I tend to follow Michele Stephen in using the term 'sorcerer' to refer to someone who has voluntarily taken up magic as a way of life and who can choose to perform either helpful or harmful forms of magic, and in using the term 'witch' to refer to someone who is possessed by an evil spirit and who cannot help but do evil. Michele Stephen, ed., *Sorcerer and Witch in Melanesia* (New Brunswick: Rutgers University Press, 1987) 83–122.

[13] That might be because we who are not part of indigenous Papua New Guinea culture hear about sorcerers or witches only when their killers are arrested and tried.

[14] Or so we are told. And it might well have been true. But we are usually told this by the counsel for defendants in criminal trials, not by anthropologists, so we must wonder how recent the phenomenon may be. It has existed since early in the colonial era. See, e. eg., the 1898 report of Sir Francis Winter, at that time Chief Judicial Officer of British New Guinea, quoted in R. S. O'Regan, "Sorcery and Homicide in Papua New Guinea," *Australian Law Journal* 48 (1974): 76–82. O'Regan also quotes a former colonial administrator, David M. Selby, "Sorcery in New Guinea" *Australian Law Journal* 18 (1945): 306.

[15] Those cases are summarized in O'Regan, "Sorcery and Homicide" and in Bruce L. Ottley and Jean G. Zorn, "Criminal Law in Papua New Guinea: Code, Custom and the Courts in Conflict," 31 *American Journal of Comparative Law* 31 (1983): 273–278.

[16] The books and articles on this topic are far too numerous to mention. For an overview, see Strathern, *Dealing with Inequality*; Laura Zimmer Tamakoshi, " 'Wild Pigs and Dog Men': Rape and Domestic Violence as 'Women's Issues' in Papua New Guinea," in *Gender in Cross-Cultural Perspective*, ed. Caroline B. Brettell, Carolyn F. Sargent, 3rd ed. (Upper Saddle River: Prentice Hall, 2001), 565–580; Dorothy Ayers Counts, Judith K. Brown and Jacquelyn C. Campbell, eds., *To Have and To Hit: Cultural Perspectives on Wife Beating* (Urbana: University of Illinois Press, 1999).

during the colonial period did nothing to correct gender inequalities; in fact, the norms and institutions imposed on PNG by the colonial administration exacerbated existing inequalities and added new ones. Despite some gains, the status of women has not improved significantly in the post-colonial period. As a result, women, especially older women, continue to be called witches, and witches continue to be blamed for the ills that befall PNG's villages.

Defining 'Religion' and 'Law'

It is necessary to determine what the terms 'religion' and 'law' mean, at least for purposes of this chapter, before beginning to discuss in more detail the effects of these terms upon gender relations in PNG. That determination is made more difficult because the chapter concerns law and religion in two very different cultural contexts: in traditional village societies, still characterized to a large extent by customs inherited from the pre-colonial period, and in urban centers where institutions imported by the colonizing powers prevail. The religions and laws of customary societies are very different from the religions and laws of the societies from which the colonizers came, so different as to be unrecognizable. The extremity of the difference enabled missionaries to argue that Papua New Guineans were without religion, and colonial administrators and judges to convince themselves that PNG was without law.

Defining 'Religion'

Missionaries were able to believe that Papua New Guineans had no religion because the missionaries believed that 'religion' exists only in connection with the worship of the spiritual, thereby putting magic (and much else in the realm of the supernatural) outside the bounds of religion.[17] This dichotomy is useful to the members of those religions that do profess a belief in some kind of Supreme Being (or Beings), since it allows them to distinguish the supernatural (or counter-natural) results obtained by, or with the assistance of, their god(s) from those obtained through magic spells or other forms of arcane knowledge. It thus enables them to argue not just that Christianity and native beliefs are different, but also that Christianity is superior. That the natives

[17] In limiting their definition of 'religion' so that it included the beliefs and spiritual practices of religions like the major western religions, and very little else, the missionaries were not alone in their ethnocentrism. In agreement were those anthropologists, and there were many, who defined institutions according to their attributes. For them, as for the missionaries, 'religions' were institutions with a belief in a supreme being and an organized means of worshipping the supreme being. See, for example, E. E. Evans-Pritchard, *Theories of Primitive Religion* (Oxford: Clarendon Press, 1965).

themselves saw the supposed distinctions rather differently is a theme to which I shall return.

In this chapter, I use the term 'religion' in its broadest sense to include all of the supra-natural customs, beliefs and behaviors of the people of PNG's traditional village cultures, as well as the organized, spirit-worshiping religions brought to PNG by the missionaries.[18] In doing so, I include a very wide range of different customs, beliefs and moral systems under one umbrella. The various Papua New Guinean religions are as different from one another as they are from the diverse forms of Christianity imported during and after the colonial period; yet they are similar in that all fall outside the purview of what a Christian missionary in the colonial period would have considered acceptable.

The Role of Religion in Society

To say that the members of one organization believe in the existence of a spiritual father or mother figure and that the members of another do not is not to separate out religion from non-religion, but merely to demonstrate a difference in beliefs among different religions. What is important about religion—both to this chapter and to inter-cultural religious studies in general—does not reside in the belief systems of a religion's adherents, but in the functions that religion, as an institution, performs. What all religions in all societies do seem to have in common is a belief system that provides reasons for the occurrence of otherwise inexplicable events, especially reasons for unhappy events. A beloved person dies because 'God willed it,' because she made the mistake of angering a malevolent spirit, because a sorcerer or witch cast a spell, because germs have invaded her body, or because she was cruel or thoughtless in an earlier existence. An enemy gains power because he is in league with the devil, because he has powerful magic at his command, or because God sends these things to try us. These beliefs take away the accidentalist nature of human life and replace it with a meaning that believers find satisfying.

Religions do often involve a belief in a supernatural (or, at least, non-human) spirit or force of some sort, but that spirit is not necessarily to be worshipped. Highlanders in PNG believe that the ghosts of their dead kin lurk just outside the village, waiting to harm the unwary; however they do not worship them, any more than Americans worship the AIDS virus. The ghosts are invoked to explain unfortunate occurrences and to convince people to do what society wants them to do. Religion, then, provides some of the key

[18] In this, I am not alone. I take my cue from those anthropologists who define institutions as 'religious' according to their function in society. See Malinowski, *Magic, Science and Religion.*

motives for the behaviour that societies consider necessary or proper. Sometimes the motivating force is fear of punishment by sorcerers, spirits or the hands of an angry god. The existence of malevolent spirits, for example, means that few Highlands villagers stray far from home when alone or at night. Sometimes, the motivating force is the hope of a reward in the future, even if that future will not occur until after death—the promise of a brilliant after-life making up for the drabness of this one. Whatever the spiritual carrot or stick may be, religion, defined broadly, is an important element in social control. Since law is also pre-eminently an organ of social control, the perfectly calibrated society would consist of legal and religious institutions that support one another on all points.

Defining 'Law' and the Role of Law in Society

Just as foreign missionaries preferred to believe that they were replacing crude and destructive rituals with the comfort of a real religion, so too did the administrators of the territories of Papua and New Guinea wish to believe that they were bringing the benefits of law to a people who previously had obeyed nothing but the 'savage hand of custom'.[19] Just as the missionaries were supported in their beliefs about religion by the writings of prominent anthropologists, so too were the presuppositions of colonial administrators supported by anthropology. Cultural anthropology defines law as a system of beliefs and behaviors. In particular, it places law as an institution within an organized governmental structure, with legislatures to enact the norms, courts to apply them and an organized police power to enforce them.[20] Under this definition, of course, the traditional societies of PNG had no law. Functionalist anthropology, on the other hand, defines law (and religion) by the roles it plays in society.[21] Under that definition, every society has law of some kind, whether or not it has legislatures, courts or other formal structures. For functionalism, law's major roles are to maintain order and to resolve disputes.

---

[19] For a more detailed discussion of this topic, see Jean G. Zorn, "Making Law in Papua New Guinea," *Pacific Studies* 14 (4) (1991): 1–34.

[20] Robert Redfield, "Primitive Law" in *Law and Warfare: Studies in the Anthropology of Conflict*, ed. Paul Bohannan (New York: Garden City; American Museum of Natural History, Natural History Press, 1967), 4, is an example. This topic is further discussed in Jean G. Zorn, "Lawyers, Anthropologists, and the Study of Law: Encounters in the New Guinea Highlands," *Law and Social Inquiry* 15 (1990): 271, 276–278.

[21] Examples include Bronislaw Malinowski, *Crime and Custom in Savage Society* (New York: Harcourt Brace, 1926; London: Routledge, 2001); Karl N. Llewellyn and I. Adamson Hoebel, *The Cheyenne Way: Conflict and Case Law in Primitive Jurisprudence* (1941; reprint, Norman: University of Oklahoma, 1983).

The Mutual Effects of Law and Religion

Law and religion, then, are both means of maintaining the social order, and, in most societies, much of the time, are presumed to be mutually supportive. It can probably be said of most small, homogeneous societies that religion provides the primary motivation for lawful behaviour (both positive and negative), especially in societies without a strong governing authority. In these situations, sorcery and supernatural intervention are more real threats than are prisons or the police. It can equally be said about many societies that law provides the sanctions that maintain religious adherence.

Law and religion, however, do not always act in concert. In multicultural societies, or at any time that a society is undergoing change, the precepts of religion and the norms that we associate with the law may be at odds. In a multicultural society, such as the United States, many sub-cultures have religious beliefs that are different from, even antithetical to, those of the dominant culture.[22] In pre-colonial PNG, the different religious beliefs of different cultures seldom came into conflict, because there was little meaningful intermingling amongst Papua New Guinea's myriad culture groups. During the colonial period, a number of organizations, both Catholic and Protestant, mounted missionary movements into Papua New Guinea, and there was some conflict, primarily over territory, amongst the different Christian organizations.[23] The major conflict, however, was (and continues to be) between Papua New Guinea's traditional religions, on the one hand, and the introduced religions on the other. Colonial administrators and missionaries alike wished to do away with those beliefs and customs of native religions that they considered antithetical to Western morality, Christian ethics, or the political order that they were trying to impose.[24] As the cases discussed in this chapter illustrate, colonial administrators used the introduced legal system as a vehicle to do this.

---

[22] American law is in the difficult position of simultaneously enforcing the values of the dominant culture's religion and representing and enforcing contrary principles of the dominant culture—one of which is that differing religious beliefs should be respected and that the legal system, therefore, should not privilege any one of them above others.

[23] Excellent studies of Papua New Guinea's missionary history include Diane Langmore, *Missionary Lives: Papua 1874–1914* (Honolulu: University of Hawaii Press, 1989); Klaus Bade, "Colonial Movement and Politics: Business and Christian Missionaries under Colonial Rule," in *Papua New Guinea: A Century of Colonial Impact 1884–1984*, ed. Sione Latukefu (Port Moresby: National Research Institute and University of Papua New Guinea, 1989), 203–221. On this point, see especially John Dademo Waiko, *A Short History of Papua New Guinea* (Melbourne, Oxford University Press, 1993), 33–34.

[24] Nelson, *Taim bilong Masta*, 149–165; Waiko, *Short History of Papua New Guinea*, 37–39.

Women in a Changing Papua New Guinea

The changes that occurred in Papua New Guinea during the colonial and post-colonial periods were beneficial for women in some ways, but extremely deleterious in others. In the early colonial period, 'pacification' (the colonial term of the ban upon tribal warfare) was good for women, on the whole, since women had often been the victims of inter-tribal violence.[25] Even when war had not itself uprooted women and their children, many women had lived lonely existences as unwilling wives in villages populated almost entirely by the enemies of their clans. On the other hand, pacification destroyed many village societies. It left women with husbands who, with no village to guard or war to wage, no longer had a serious social role. Moreover, by introducing villagers to the lifestyles of the West, without permitting them to take part, pacification turned subsistence into poverty, and left men feeling even more angry and useless.[26] Given the built-in misogyny of Papua New Guinean traditional cultures, it is not surprising that men took out their frustrations on their wives. This situation was made even more perilous by the missions' destruction of the men's houses, so that, for the first time, husbands and wives were thrown together for most of their days.[27]

When a money economy was first introduced into rural areas, women benefited. Since they had always been the gardeners, they easily moved into growing coffee, cocoa and other cash crops. The colonialists' agricultural experts, however, rapidly put an end to that. In Western society at that time, men earned the incomes, and women lived private, domestic, decidedly second-class lives. The Australian administration saw no reason to change that rule, just because it was being enforced upon people of a different culture.[28] Colonial administrators thus trained men to grow the cash crops.[29]

In the later colonial and post-colonial periods, women have tended, on the whole, to receive less education than men, fewer opportunities for meaningful

---

[25] Gordon and Meggitt, *Law and Order in the New Guinea Highlands,* 162–169; Mervyn J. Meggitt, *Blood Is Their Argument: Warfare among the Mae Enga Tribesmen of the New Guinea Highlands* (Palo Alto: Mayfield, 1977), 98–99.

[26] Mike Donaldson and Kenneth Good, "The Eastern Highlands: Coffee and Class," in Denoon and Snowden, *Time to Plant,* 143–170.

[27] Lisette Josephides, "The Politics of Violence in Kewa Society (Southern Highlands)" in *Domestic Violence in Papua New Guinea,* ed., Susan Toft (Port Moresby: Law Reform Commission, 1985).

[28] Helene Barnes, "Women in Highlands Agricultural Production," in Denoon and Snowden, *Time to Plant,* 265–284.

[29] A number of anthropologists, beginning with Engels, have noted that gender differences are more marked, and violence against women often greater, in horticultural societies as compared to hunter-gatherer societies, and in societies characterized by capitalist agriculture as compared to subsistence horticultural societies: Frederick Engels, The *Origin of the Family, Private Property and the State* (1942; reprint, New York: International Publishers, 1972), 221.

employment, and lower incomes when they are employed. The percentage of women remaining in the village is much higher than the percentage of men. Yet moving to an urban area is not necessarily an improvement in the life of a woman either. Indeed, women have borne the brunt of social dislocation. While both men and women were doubtless frustrated by their second-class status under colonial regimes and the continuing problems of trying to make their way in the post-colonial era, it tends more often to be men who take out their frustrations by battering women than the other way round.

Women have also suffered more than have men from the confusion of cultures that is one of the results of enforced cultural change. The formal legal system recognizes two categories of marriage: a ceremony performed (either civilly or religiously) under the statute (called interchangeably, 'church' or 'statutory' marriages); and the diverse forms of ceremony that occur according to varying customary rules and processes ('customary' marriage).[30] Statutes provide that a marriage transacted according to either form entitles the woman to maintenance and the other perquisites of married status. However many couples have entered into unions that are neither statutory nor customary marriage. Sometimes this is because they come from different customary groups and do not share the same norms pertaining to marriage; sometimes it is because they are both living in urban areas, far from home, and slip into a relationship, presuming it will be formalized later. This situation works better for men, who are more mobile and more able to earn incomes, than for women, whom society still makes more dependent on fathers and husbands.[31]

Many men have one woman who is considered a 'wife' at home in the village and another in the town. While customary law recognizes polygyny, at least for wealthier men, this practice is unlawful under statutory law, unless the man's first marriage was customary.[32] Thus, it is likely that the formal courts would consider at least one of the two women not to be married, and thus not entitled to maintenance or other marriage benefits. Nor are most of these rural–urban forms of polygyny recognized under customary rules, at least under those of the husband's community, since it is probable that neither party in the urban relationship participated in any of the processes that the man's kin would recognize as constituting a valid marriage.[33] Even apart from those considerations, both

---

[30] Owen Jessup and John Luluaki, *Principles of Family Law in Papua New Guinea* (Port Moresby: University of Papua New Guinea Press, 1985), 16.

[31] There is no form of welfare or social security in Papua New Guinea. If women do not have a job or income from their husbands, then their only choice is to go back to the village and hope that their parents can provide for them.

[32] Jessup and Luluaki, *Principles of Family Law in Papua New Guinea*, 34–35.

[33] Jean G. Zorn, "Women's Rights and Traditional Law: A Conflict," *Third World Legal Studies* (1994–95): 169–205.

wives are likely to find themselves in an untenable position. Studies tell us that the husband is likely to leave his rural wife for years at a time, and her only source of sustenance during that period tends to be his family, who may or may not be concerned for her welfare. Any attempt on her part to rectify her situation by leaving him or by committing herself to another man may be seen as desertion or adultery.[34] In the meantime, her urban sister is no better off. Her husband is probably in a difficult work situation; he most likely has too little money, and too many demands on what he does have, and he probably drinks too much, and beats her when he does drink.[35]

In many traditional Papua New Guinean societies, the only major distinction made generally of people living in the same village was that between men and women.[36] Even a big-man or chief was more like his followers than women were like men. At least, the big-man and his followers lived in the same men's house, did the same work, and fought the same wars. Women and men tended to live in separate houses and to lead separate lives. Women's work was different from men's. Women's clan affiliations were different from those of their husbands. In Highlands societies, contact with a woman, especially sexual contact, was considered debilitating to men, and happened as infrequently as possible.[37] Wife-beating was frequent, and society generally supported the notion that cheeky women needed discipline.[38] It is easy to see how men might have characterized women as the 'other.'

During the colonial and post-colonial periods, some of the differences between men and women were erased.[39] For example, missionaries saw to the destruction of the men's houses, so men and women had to live together in what had once been the tiny houses allotted to women and small boys. Some girls went to school, where they received approximately the same education as their male counterparts were getting, and some of the schools were co-educational. But, as some gender distinctions disappeared, others arose to take their places.

---

[34] See the cases described in ibid., especially *Application of Wagi Non and In the Matter of the Constitution s. 42(5)*, unreported National Court judgment N 949 (1991); and *Application of Thesia Maip and In the Matter of the Constitution s. 42(5)*, (1991) PNGLR 80.

[35] James F. Weiner, "Diseases of the Soul: Sickness, Agency and the Men's Cult among the Foi of New Guinea," in Strathern, *Dealing with Inequality*, 255–277.

[36] See, generally, the articles collected in Strathern, *Dealing with Inequality*; Brown and. Buchbinder, *Man and Woman in the New Guinea Highlands*; and in Rick Marksbury, ed., *The Business of Marriage: Transformations in Oceanic Matrimony* (Pittsburgh: University of Pittsburgh Press, 1993).

[37] Weiner, "Diseases of the Soul', 255–277.

[38] Tamakoshi, 'Wild Pigs and Dog Men' 565–580; Counts, Brown and Campbell, *To Have and To Hit*.

[39] For an overview of changes in gender relations during the colonial and post-colonial periods, see, generally, D. Johnson, "Aspects of the Legal Status of Women in Papua New Guinea: A Working Paper," *Melanesian Law Journal* 7 (1979): 5 and sources cited therein.

As in Western societies, men received secondary and tertiary educations in far greater numbers than did women, and men obtained higher level employment, whereas women, for the most part, got no work at all. Attitudes about gender difference did not change; if anything, they hardened. All that happened was that men who considered themselves better than, and vastly different from, women were thrown into daily contact, sometimes into daily competition, with women. One result was that domestic violence, always a problem for women in Highlands societies, grew more widespread.[40]

There is a certain irony, I suppose, in the outcome. Women have, by and large, fared worse than men as a result of the vast social, economic and political changes that have swept over PNG, especially in the last half century. But they have also had to bear the brunt of men's anger and frustration at those changes, as the victims both of domestic violence and of witchcraft accusations.

Witchcraft and Gender

In those Melanesian societies where there were sorcerers and witches, it was generally, although not universally, the case that sorcery could be an honorable profession. In comparison, witches were considered possessed, usually against their will, by evil spirits.[41] It was also most often, although not always, the case that sorcerers were men and witches were women. It was furthermore generally believed that sorcerers could work their magic either for good or ill. Sorcerers could heal, and they could use the same, or similar, magic to kill. They could make a young man fall in love with one woman or out of love with another. They were certainly important during wars, as their spells and charms determined the outcome of the battle. Thus sorcerers were respected for the good they could do and feared both for the evil of which they were capable and for their power in general. The charms, spells and magic sayings of sorcery were, in some societies, handed down to the sorcerer's children or other kin. This knowledge was usually transmitted to the most talented, not necessarily to the eldest child. In other societies, sorcery spells and knowledge could be purchased. Most big men possessed the skills of sorcery; it was one of the many strategies at their disposal. In many societies, women also possessed various forms of magic, including spells and the knowledge of herbs

[40] See, generally, the articles in Toft, *Domestic Violence in Papua New Guinea* and also those in Susan Toft, ed., *Domestic Violence in Urban Papua New Guinea* (Port Moresby: Law Reform Commission, 1986).

[41] The following description of sorcerers and witches is taken, primarily, from various articles in Stephen, *Sorcerer and Witch in Melanesia*, especially Michele Stephen, "Contrasting Images of Power," 249–304; Marie Reay, "The Magico-Religious Foundations of New Guinea Highlands Warfare," 83–120, and Inge Riebe, "Kalam Witchcraft: a Historical Perspective," 211–245.

that promoted (or undid) love, caused pregnancy or abortions, and healed illness and injury; but, in most societies, women sorcerers were not considered to have the truly important knowledge possessed by men.[42] As can be seen from the list of the arts that women sorcerers practiced, it is evident that, in most societies, their practice was limited, for the most part, to the concerns and proper areas of interest, of other women.

Witches were reviled and feared. A witch could be a man, but was more often a woman. No one chose to be a witch; rather a woman was taken over by forces beyond her control. In some societies, it was said that the evil spirit could be felt as a hard lump in the woman's abdomen. A witch could be released of her demons, although most often the only way to release her was more than likely to kill her. A widespread way of dealing with a witch, for example, was to burn her with hot coals until the pain drove the demon out of her. In an odd collusion with European folktale, witches flew on branches through the night and kept small animals as familiars.[43] Witches tended to be solitary folks, widows, or people who behaved oddly. Witches were never perceived as doing anything good and all their spells were harmful. Again, however, this may be a matter of perspective. It was sometimes said that an errant husband would not abuse his wife for fear of the strong witchcraft that her family possessed.

A number of commentators have noted that the incidence of reported events of harmful witch-craft increased in Papua New Guinea throughout the colonial period and may well still be on the rise.[44] I see two causes for this increase. First, with pacification, roads, and the possibility of school and work far from home, many people in Papua New Guinea came into contact for the first time with people from different communities and cultures, and the knowledge about the existence of sorcery and witchcraft spread. People who once did not have witches in their own communities started to do so when they learned about witchcraft from neighboring cultures or brought it back from work in the mines or plantations.

A second cause, I believe, of the increase of evil (as opposed to good) witchcraft is the strain put on individuals and cultures by the enormous changes

---

[42] Let me qualify that. Men, in many societies, presume that women's magic arts are less important than men's. Women in those societies have a different opinion, but their voices are seldom heard outside their own circles: see, Annette Weiner, *Women of Value, Men of Renown* (Austin: University of Texas Press, 1976).

[43] I do not know whether the similarity to western images of witchcraft is a coincidence or an artefact of colonialism. I have found no author who comments on it.

[44] George D. Westermark, "Sorcery and Economic Change in Agarabi," *Social Analysis* 8 (1981): 89–100; Martin Zelenietz, "The Effects of Sorcery in Kilenge, West New Britain Province," Law Reform Commission of Papua New Guinea, Occasional Paper No. 11 (1979); Mervyn J. Meggitt, "Sorcery and Social Change among the Mae Enga of Papua New Guinea," *Social Analysis* 8 (1981): 28–41; and Inge Riebe, "Kalam Witchcraft: a Historical Perspective," in Stephen, *Sorcerer and Witch in Melanesia*, 211–245.

that occurred during and after the colonial period.[45] Many of these changes may ultimately be for the betterment of Papua New Guineans, and some, such as the enforced pacification of the early colonial period, may even have seemed positive to many Papua New Guineans at the time. However, many of the changes were disruptive of the traditional social order at best and utterly destructive of it at worst.[46] Moreover, whether or not the changes were for the better, change, especially when forced, is never comfortable. The insecurity, fear and lack of self-confidence which Papua New Guineans have experienced from first contact to the present cannot be over-emphasized.[47] Such an atmosphere is very likely to breed sorcery and witchcraft, as well as to increase the fear of such demons. Nor is it surprising that it would be witches, rather than sorcerers—women rather than men—who would take the brunt of punishment. In most

[45] There is a large and growing literature about the witch hunts in early modern Europe, focusing on the development of society-wide fears of witchcraft in periods of extreme social change and resulting stress, and more particularly on the way in which witch fears can be used to maintain male dominance in such periods of social upheaval. See, for example, Bengt Ankarloo and Stuart Clark, eds., *Witchcraft and Magic in Europe: The Period of the Witch Trials* (Philadelphia: University of Pennsylvania Press, 2003); Norman Cohn, *Europe's Inner Demons: An Inquiry Inspired by the Great Witch Hunt* (New York: Basic Books, 1975); Lyndal Roper, *Oedipus and the Devil: Witchcraft, Sexuality and Religion in Early Modern Europe* (London: Routlege, 1999). For a similar study out of American history, see Paul S. Boyer, *Salem Possessed: The Social Origins of Witchcraft* (Cambridge: Harvard University Press, 1976). These theories are of obvious relevance to Papua New Guinea. Interestingly, none of it seems to have had a great impact on scholarly or judicial writing in Papua New Guinea. There are also a number of legal scholars who wrote about the psycho-social underpinnings of the belief in witchcraft in the context of the African colonial experience. See, for example, Robert Seidman, "Witch Murder and Mens Rea: A Problem of Society under Radical Social Change," *Modern Law Review* 28 (1965): 46–61. This article, which, as its title suggests, discusses the increase in incidents of witch murder in times of extreme social duress, received less favourable attention amongst Papua New Guineans than did his other article, "Mens Rea and the Reasonable African: The Pre-scientific World View and Mistake of Fact," *International and Comparative Law Quarterly* 15 (1966): 1135–1164, which took the position that colonial courts are mistaken to dismiss customary beliefs on the grounds that, to the expatriate judges, they seem irrational.

[46] The political and economic disruption that colonialism caused is described in a number of sources. See, for Papua New Guinea, Azeem Amarshi, Kenneth Good and Rex Mortimer, *Development and Dependency: The Political Economy of Papua New Guinea* (Melbourne: Oxford University Press, 1979), which draws upon the work of dependency theorists, such as Samir Amin, *Accumulation on a World Scale: A Critique of the Theory of Underdevelopment* (London: Oxford University Press, 1974) and Andre Gunder Frank, *Capitalism and Underdevelopment in Latin America* (New York: Monthly Review Press, 1969).

[47] I don't know how to measure the reactions of the colonized to colonialism, and I don't know that anyone has tried. However, a number of writers, Frantz Fanon foremost among them, have tried to describe colonialism's psychic toll. Colonialism's psychic toll is most famously described by Frantz Fanon in *Black Skin, White Masks* (New York: Grove Press, 1967), originally published as *Peau Noire, Masques Blancs* (Paris: Editions de Seuil, 1952) and *The Wretched of the Earth* (New York: Grove Press, 1963). See also Jock McCulloch, *Black Soul, White Artifacts: Fanon's Clinical Psychology and Social Theory* (Cambridge: Cambridge University Press, 1983).

pre-colonial societies in PNG, women were considered inferior to men. Colonialism did not change this. If anything, it added to it.

Witchcraft and the Law

During the early days of the colonial period, the colonial administration was at pains to establish that its own laws, culture and religion were superior to any available in PNG. It did this in part by labeling Western beliefs as scientific and rational, in opposition to the superstition and ignorance that the colonizers understood to characterize Papua New Guinean beliefs. One of the results was that Papua New Guineans who were put on trial in the colonial courts for killing witches, thinking they were protecting their families or communities by doing so, were not permitted to plead any of the excuses—such as self-defense, provocation or even insanity—normally allowed to defendants whose victims had caused or threatened to cause harm to them or their families.[48]

In the late 1960s and early 1970s, as the colonial period came to an end, many prominent Papua New Guineans voiced the hope that an independent PNG would return to the norms, values and customs that had characterized Papua New Guinean societies prior to the colonial period.[49] If defendants were accurate about custom's approach to harmful witchcraft, this would have meant, amongst other things, an end to prison sentences for persons who killed witches. Moreover, essentially the same people who called for a return to customary norms also supported provisions for gender equality in the independent nation's new Constitution.[50] This should have required the courts to recognize the suspicious extent to which women, especially old women, were blamed for witchcraft, and to treat defendant witch-killers harshly, as a way of bringing home the importance of gender equality.[51] Neither has, in fact, happened. With two striking exceptions (both of which will be discussed later

[48] Ottley and Zorn, "Criminal Law in Papua New Guinea," 273–279; O'Regan, "Sorcery and Homicide in Papua New Guinea."

[49] Bernard Narokobi, "We the People, We the Constitution," in *Lo Bilong Ol Manmeri: Crime, Compensation and Village Courts*, ed. Jean G. Zorn and Peter Bayne (Port Moresby: University of Papua New Guinea, 1975), 19; (Prime Minister Sir) Michael Somare, "Law and the Needs of Papua New Guinea's People," in ibid., at 14.

[50] Ibid.

[51] A number of the commentators who wrote about the courts and witchcraft in the context of the African colonial experience noted the psycho-sexual origins of the fear of witches. See, for example, Alan Milner, "M'Naghten and the Witch-doctor: Psychiatry and Crime in Africa," *University of Pennsylvania Law Review* 114 (1966): 1134–1169; Kato, "Functional Psychosis and Witchcraft Fears: Excuses to Criminal Responsibility in East Africa," *Law and Society Review* 4(1969): 384–406. But this relationship between witch-craft accusations and gender issues was rarely commented upon in Papua New Guinea.

in this chapter), the courts have continued to treat witch killings precisely as they did throughout the colonial period: with a striking lack of concern either for custom or for the social and gender conflicts that might underlie accusations of witchcraft.

Colonial Cases

The rationalist judges, brought in from Australia to serve on the courts established by Papua New Guinea's colonial administration, had studied neither anthropology in general nor the culture of Papua New Guinea in particular. All they had studied was the common law. Confronted with accusations of witchcraft, they assumed that the benighted natives did not understand about science, germs, illness and its causes. The reality was very different, had the judges cared to ask. Papua New Guineans of course understood that illness and death had natural causes, but they asked the same question that Europeans ask: 'So, okay, I got ill. But why me?' Australians find the answer to that question in God's will or germs (the 'rationality' of science). Papua New Guineans find it in sorcery or spirits. Both Papua New Guineans and Australians are searching for an 'answer'; they just find the answer in slightly different places.

The colonial courts settled early upon their response to defendants who killed witches and sorcerers.[52] Although, under the Criminal Code, defendants found guilty of willful murder were liable for sentences of up to life imprisonment, those who had killed witches received sentences of only five to six years in prison. The judges' reason for meting out such short sentences did not suggest that they agreed with the defendants that the witches had posed a serious threat. Quite the opposite: the judges were staunch in their conviction that sorcery and witchcraft did not exist. Moreover, they saw it as their mission to teach the norms of this new and superior moral, scientific and legal system to Papua New Guineans, just as it was the missionaries' responsibility to teach the new and superior religion. Teaching the natives required that they go to prison for wrongdoing. But, right now, the judges believed the defendants were too uneducated, too primitive, and too irrational to understand the rules of the imported legal system or that they had broken those rules. After all, if they had been educated enough to understand modern law and science, they would not have believed in witchcraft in the first place. The judges certainly believed that they had to enforce the rules of the imported legal system—how else would Papua New Guineans ever learn to obey them? However, until defendants were sophisticated enough to understand what these new rules were, sentences should not be overbearing.

---

[52] O'Regan, "Sorcery and Homicide in Papua New Guinea;" Ottley and Zorn, "Criminal Law in Papua New Guinea."

In a number of cases involving killings of witches, defense counsel tried to convince the courts not just to set a lesser penalty, but to absolve the defendants entirely of guilt by holding either that defendants had been insane, or that they had acted out of self-defense. The courts, in a remarkable show of paradoxical reasoning, refused to accept either position. That is, the courts refused to find defendants insane, on the grounds that belief in sorcery was widespread in PNG and, therefore, it was not unreasonable for defendants to hold the belief.[53] At the same time, however, the PNG courts refused to find that defendants had acted in self-defense, on the grounds that self-defense requires a reasonable belief that one is about to be harmed, and a belief in witchcraft or sorcery is not reasonable.[54]

A third defense might possibly have been raised. Defendants could have argued the defense of provocation—that they killed the witch or sorcerer

> in the heat of passion caused by a sudden wrongful act or insult, done by the deceased to them or a close relative, of such a nature as to be likely, when done to an ordinary person to deprive him of the power of self-control and to induce him to assault the person by whom the act or insult is done, and before defendant's passion is cool.[55]

This might have been a more useful defense because the Papua New Guinea courts had held that, in other contexts, the victim need not have done a physical act in order for the defense of provocation to apply: words were enough.[56] Courts had also held (though, again, not in the context of acts or words connected with sorcery) that the act need not even have occurred in the killer's presence.[57]

However, as far as we know, no defendant ever raised the provocation defense in the context of the murder of a witch.[58] The most likely reason for not raising provocation as a defense was because, as illustrated in the cases discussed below, witches usually were not killed while a defendant was still in the heat of

---

[53] See for example *R. v. Womeni-Nanagawo* (1963) P&NGLR 72, discussed in O'Regan, "Sorcery and Homicide in Papua New Guinea," 77.

[54] See, e. g., *R. v. Manga-Kitai* (1967–68) P&NGLR 1, discussed in O'Regan, "Sorcery and Homicide in Papua New Guinea," 78. The seminal work on the unwillingness of colonial courts to admit that native beliefs about the supernatural can ever be reasonable is Seidman, "Mens Rea and the Reasonable African". This article was widely read and quoted by Papua New Guinean legal scholars—and did have an impact. It is footnoted by Narokobi in his decision in *State v. Gesie*, unreported National Court judgment, N254 (1980).

[55] Papua New Guinea Criminal Code, sections. 304 and 268

[56] See, for example, *R. v. Zariai-Gavene* (1963) P&NGLR 203, discussed in Ottley and Zorn, "Criminal Law in Papua New Guinea: Code," 267–268.

[57] *R. v. Rumints-Gorok* (1063) P&NGLR 81; discussed in Ottley and Zorn, "Criminal Law in Papua New Guinea," 268.

[58] O'Regan, "Sorcery and Homicide in Papua New Guinea," 79–81, mentions one case that discusses (and dismisses) the possibility of a provocation defense.

passion, but later, after the community or family had met, discussed matters, and had determined who the witch was and how they wanted to deal with her.[59]

The Sorcery Act—1970s

The Sorcery Act[60], passed in 1971, was promoted at the time as the answer to the problems raised by a court that refused to accept that a belief in sorcery might be reasonable. Papua New Guinea was nearing independence, and Papua New Guineans were talking about a return to a truer Papua New Guinean legal culture, a legal culture based upon the values, norms and processes of customary law.[61] There were sympathetic ears in the colonial administration, and the Sorcery Act was a result.[62]

Not that the drafters of the Act were willing to go so far as to state that they believed (or that anyone should believe) that sorcery is real. Indeed, the Preamble to the Act carefully refrains from saying that sorcery is real. The Preamble merely says that many people believe it is real:

> . . . there is a widespread belief throughout the country that there is such a thing as sorcery and that sorcerers have extra-ordinary powers which can be used sometimes for good purposes but more often for bad ones and because of this belief many evil things can be done and many people are frightened or do things that otherwise they might not do.

Still, the Act is an improvement on what went before, because it does permit provocation as a defense to willful murder on the basis of the customary belief in sorcery.

Section 20 of the Act specifically states that an act of sorcery is the kind of "wrongful act or insult" that the drafters of the Criminal Code were referring

---

[59] Bernard Narokobi, however, in *State v. Gesie*, unreported National Court judgment, N254 (1980), argues that the court should recognize the provocation defense in witch killings and should recognize that it can take days, even weeks, for the emotions caused by the death of a loved one to dissipate.

[60] In Papua New Guinea, sorcery refers to the actions both of males (sorcerers) and of females (witches), so the Sorcery Act was intended to cover both, and references in it to sorcery are meant to be taken as references both to male sorcery and female witchcraft.

[61] See Bernard Narokobi, "We the People, We the Constitution," in Zorn and Bayne, *Lo Bilong Ol Manmeri,* 19; (Prime Minister Sir) Michael Somare, "Law and the Needs of Papua New Guinea's People," in ibid. at 14; and other articles collected in that volume.

[62] Graham Freudenberg, *A Certain Grandeur: Gough Whitlam in Politics,* Rev. ed. (Ringwood, Vic.: Penguin Books, 1987), 189, points out that the Labour Government favoured making Papua New Guinea independent much sooner than its Liberal predecessors had expected to, and also supported making the criminal and other laws of Papua New Guinea better suited to the circumstances and culture of the indigenous people.

to when they were describing the kinds of acts that can provoke a person to murder. Section 20 of the Sorcery Act provides as follows:

(1) For the avoidance of doubt, it is hereby declared that an act of sorcery may amount to a wrongful act or insult within the meaning of section 268 of the Criminal Code.
(2) It is immaterial that the act of sorcery did not occur in the presence of the person allegedly provoked, or that it was directed at some person other than the person allegedly provoked.
(3) The likely effect of an act of sorcery relied on by virtue of this section shall be judged by reference, amongst other things, to the traditional beliefs of any social group of which the person provoked is a member.

As several commentators have noted, this formulation removes several of the impediments to use of the provocation defense in sorcery killings.[63]

Section 20(2) provides that, as with acts of adultery, acts of sorcery need not occur in the defendant's presence, and it adds that the act may be directed at someone other than the defendant himself. This is presumably intended to override the limitation to a defendant's near relatives, contained in section 268, and to permit provocation as a defense even when the witch is thought to have killed others in the defendants' village, and not their close kin. However, it seems possible that the two sections could be read together so as to retain that limit.

Finally, the Act explicitly takes away from the courts the opportunity to declare that a "wrongful act," sufficient to count as provocation, must be objectively wrongful (that is, either unlawful or physically harmful), reasoning that the courts might have otherwise been inclined to use such an argument should a defendant raise provocation as his or her defense. Section 20(1) undercuts the courts' intentions in this regard, in that it expressly declares that an act of sorcery may be provocation, and section 20(3) defines "wrongful" to mean not something that is wrongful under the introduced common and statutory law, but something that is considered wrongful according to "the traditional beliefs of any social group of which the person provoked is a member."[64]

The Sorcery Act is not, however, a complete or even certain defense for those who kill sorcerers. First, it retains the requirement from section 304 of the Criminal Code that the killing must occur sufficiently soon after the killer has learned about the act of sorcery so as to establish that the uncontrollable passion into which this information has plunged him has not had a chance to cool.

[63] O'Regan, "Sorcery and Homicide in Papua New Guinea," 80.
[64] But see ibid., 80.

Second, of all the defenses potentially available to those who kill sorcerers, the Sorcery Act recognizes only provocation. It does not by its terms recognize self-defense or insanity. I doubt that this was an oversight. If a court accepts the defenses of self-defense or insanity, the defendant is essentially judged not guilty and therefore escapes punishment. If a court accepts the defense of provocation, however, the charge is merely reduced from wilful murder to manslaughter, which means that the defendant will still be convicted of something and will still be liable for a prison term, although the term will be considerably less than it would have been if the defense had not been accepted.[65] The drafters probably intended exactly this result.

The judges[66] of the state courts of Papua New Guinea are positivists.[67] They believe in the sanctity of the rule. They do not believe that legal rules are to be interpreted according to the intent of the drafters, according to the rule's purpose, or even according to the most sensible reading of the rule. It is a tenet of their secular religion that rules are to be read exactly as written, unless so ambiguous as to have essentially no meaning on their face at all. Thus, if the Criminal Code requires for the defense of provocation to apply that it lead to a killing in the heat of the moment, then the courts will follow that rule, even when doing so might undermine the intentions, purposes and policies of the Sorcery Act.

However, the results that the drafters of the Sorcery Act hoped to attain, in relation to the treatment that should be meted out to defendants who have killed witches, actually match, to a large extent, what judges were doing all along. The Sorcery Act was intended to insure that defendants would get sentences less than life imprisonment—sentences, perhaps, of about five to six years—and that is pretty much what the courts had been doing throughout the colonial period.

---

[65] Ottley and Zorn, "Criminal Law in Papua New Guinea," 266–273.

[66] Only now are a significant number of judges being chosen from amongst the many Papua New Guineans educated in Papua New Guinea. Even though the University of Papua New Guinea Law Faculty has been in operation since 1972, the courts have continued to be staffed primarily by white Australians. Many of them are good and honest men, who wish to do good. However, they bring with them to Papua New Guinea a thoroughgoing belief in the superiority and universality of the common law—a belief based primarily on the fact that they have been educated in nothing else. There are, I believe, no judges remaining who were on the Papua New Guinea bench during the colonial period, but a number of the judges currently on the bench served with colonial era judges.

[67] Positivists are also called Austineans, after John Austin, the 19th century English legal philosopher credited with first developing the notion that the role of a judge is merely to apply the law as written. John Austin, *The Province of Jurisprudence Determined* (London: J. Murray, 1832; Cambridge: Cambridge University Press, 1995). Meant by Austin to be a safety measure, keeping aristocratic judges from picking "laws" out of thin air and applying them so as to send unlucky members of the thieving classes to Australia or worse, positivism became more conservative. H. L. A. Hart, "Positivism and the Separation of Law and Morals," *Harvard Law Review* 71 (1958): 593–629.

Post-Colonial Papua New Guinea

Papua New Guinea became independent in 1975 and adopted a Constitution that was intended to give a prominent role to customary law in the state legal system.[68] At the same time, the Preamble to the Constitution included two provisions—one relating to religion and the other to equality for women—which would, if followed, distinctly alter custom. The Constitution begins with a statement that the people of Papua New Guinea:

> Acknowledge the worthy customs and traditional wisdoms of our people—which have come down to us from generation to generation [and]
>
> Pledge ourselves to guard and pass on to those who come after us our noble traditions and the Christian principles that are ours now.[69]

Thus the Constitution proclaims that PNG is a Christian nation. It also provides for "equal participation by woman citizens in all political, economic, social and religious activities."[70]

The commandment that customary law become the underlying law of Papua New Guinea seems a moribund, if not entirely dead, letter. The courts have seldom, if ever, applied custom in preference to the imported common law.[71] Legislation to make those provisions operable was drafted by the Law Reform Commission as early as 1976, but was not adopted by Parliament until 2000, and, in the five years since that legislation came into effect, courts and lawyers have continued to act as if it does not exist.[72]

It is more difficult to assess the impact of the non-customary provisions. Papua New Guinea is nominally a Christian nation. Missionaries still abound in PNG, and new Christian sects enter the country all the time. The 2000 census suggests that 80 percent of Papua New Guineans identify themselves as Christian. However, even educated Papua New Guineans continue to believe in at least some aspects of their traditional religion. Moreover, PNG is still primarily a nation of small rural villages, where customary beliefs and norms continue to rule. The fact that witch-killing cases continue to be heard in the courts is itself an indication of the continuing belief in customary norms.

The status of women in the law is slightly better. There are now a number of cases in which the Constitutional provisions providing equality for women

---

[68] Constitutional Planning Committee of Papua New Guinea, *Report* (Port Moresby: Government Printing Office, 1975). Bernard Narokobi was a member of the Constitutional Planning Commission.

[69] Papua New Guinea Constitution, Preamble: Adoption of Constitution.

[70] Papua New Guinea Constitution, Preamble: National Goals and Directive Principles, 2(5)

[71] Jean G. Zorn and Jennifer Corrin Care, "Everything Old is New Again: The Underlying Law Act of Papua New Guinea" *Lawasia Journal*, 2002, 63.

[72] Ibid., 83–95.

have been used, usually to release a woman from some stricture placed upon her by custom.[73] For many supporters of PNG, including myself, the sexual abusiveness of Papua New Guinean customary law has always presented a problem. As PNG partisans and anti-colonialists, we have always argued that the formal legal system needs to be infused with custom in order to become a truly Papua New Guinean institution, receptive to the needs and culture that it serves.[74] At the same time, however, as feminists, we are critical of both custom and the courts for their continuing chauvinism. We have never found a way to merge successfully our belief in custom with our belief in equality.

Three Judicial Perspectives on Witchcraft

Since independence, the Supreme Court has continued to respond to witch killers much as it did during the colonial era: the criminal law is applied with strict exactitude to defendants. This means that, for the most part, defenses such as provocation or self-defense are not available; however, sentences are reduced to take account of defendants' lack of legal sophistication. For obvious reasons, I call this the post-colonial approach.

There are two other approaches, which I shall refer to as prelapsarian and post-modern. While these may be widespread among scholars, neither has had more than a single vocal adherent on the court. The decisions of Bernard Narokobi demonstrate the prelapsarian perspective, and those of Brian Brunton the post-modern view. Narokobi and Brunton were both anti-colonialist and pro-independence. Both were reformers. Both would probably agree on many of the issues that have faced PNG's villagers. However, their approach to sorcery murder could not be farther apart. To Narokobi, the murder of a witch is a part of the pre-colonial social and cultural fabric. To deny the power of witches is to denigrate the Melanesian spirit, mind and worldview. To Brunton, conversely, the murder of a witch is the same as any other attempt by the powerful to retain their power through acts of terror. The denigration of one person or group by another is always abhorrent to him, whether it is an act of the colonizers of Papua New Guineans generally, or the way in which men, both in customary and in Western societies, do violence to women.

---

[73] See the cases described in Zorn, "Women's Rights and Traditional Law", especially the discussion of *Application of Wagi Non and In the Matter of the Constitution s. 42(5)*, unreported National Court judgment N 949 (1991); and, *Application of Thesia Maip and In the Matter of the Constitution s. 42(5)*, (1991) PNGLR 80.

[74] Jean G. Zorn, "*Graun Bilong Mipela*: Local Land Courts and the Changing Customary Law of Papua New Guinea," *Pacific Studies* 15 no. 2 (1992): 1–38; Jean G. Zorn, "Making Law in Papua New Guinea," *Pacific Studies*, 14 no. 4 (1991): 1–34.

One finds strains of feminism in his writing, as well as a distinctly post-modern perspective.

I shall now analyze the written decisions of Narokobi, Brunton and the majority on the Supreme Court in three different cases involving the murder of witches, as a vehicle for examining these three perspectives more closely and for putting the debates over the legal treatment of witchcraft and witch murder into the context of the larger debates—particularly those over custom versus the common law, magic and pre-colonial religious beliefs versus science and rationalism, and tradition versus modernism—which have preoccupied the courts from the advent of colonialism to the present.

Bernard Narokobi and the Prelapsarian Perspective

In Narokobi's judicial opinions, pre-colonial custom is idealized as a lost but re-creatable system of laws, values and behaviours. According to this perspective, customary animism and traditional beliefs in sorcery were supplanted in PNG by positivism and rationalism, not because custom was inferior or in any way deserved to be replaced, but only because the colonists, who trumpeted the virtues of positivism and rationalism, had bigger guns. Narokobi sees the judge's proper role as actively working to refashion the legal system to take a fuller and proper account of custom.

It should not have surprised anyone that Justice Narokobi's decisions would reflect this viewpoint. In his long and deservedly distinguished career in public service, Mr. Narokobi has been a singular leader in a movement to return custom to a place of prominence in Melanesian jurisprudence. Raised in an Arapesh village and educated in Australia, Mr. Narokobi was an early member of Pangu, the Papua New Guinean independence movement that became one of its first political parties. He served on the Constitutional Planning Commission, and was probably the most important influence in ensuring that PNG's 'worthy customs' were enshrined in that document. After independence, he was the first leader of the Law Reform Commission. Under his tutelage, the Commission developed numerous initiatives for remaking the introduced legal system in custom's image. After his brief flirtation with a judgeship, he became a Member of Parliament. Although I have not spoken to him on this matter, I expect the latter position feels much more comfortable to a man of his talents and persuasion. As a judge, he was constantly overruled by the positivist judges to whom his decisions were invariably appealed. His attempts to educate the judiciary fell on deaf ears. As a Member of Parliament, however, he can function much more effectively as the educator that he has always truly been.

Legal scholars in the last years of colonialism in PNG focused on the inability of the colonizers' legal system to meet the needs or interests of the Papua

New Guinean nation. Influential voices from both the University and the Government espoused a return to customary norms on the grounds that they better mirrored Papua New Guinean cultural values. We were correct to denigrate the common law and statutes that had been received from England and Australia. The 'man of the Clapham omnibus' bore little resemblance to a Papua New Guinean, and was probably neither as sensible nor as kind. Nevertheless, as Kenneth Keesing has noted, in order to draw definitively the line between the common law and custom, we glorified the half-remembered pre-colonial past, describing custom as, perhaps, better than it had ever been.

Bernard Narokobi was amongst the scholars and political leaders arguing for a legal system based upon customary norms and legal processes. As a member of the Constitutional Planning Committee, he only partially succeeded. The Constitution, adopted in 1975, permitted the introduced legal system to continue, but contained provisions encouraging the courts and Parliament to integrate custom into statutory and common law. By 1980, however, when Narokobi was offered an Acting Judgeship, the courts had shown little inclination to use custom. The vast majority of decisions continued to be based almost entirely on the English common law, with little if any attention paid to whether the policies and purposes of that law fitted the Papua New Guinean experience.

Narokobi must have seen his appointment as a golden opportunity to educate his judicial colleagues about custom and, in that way, to turn the courts towards the recognition and use of custom. His decisions all seem to be written with that end in mind. The decisions do two things that the rest of the court needed in order to use custom in their decision-making. First, he explains the Papua New Guinean mind to the mostly expatriate judges; he attempts to familiarize them with custom from the inside out. Second, he shows the judges how they can interpret the Constitution and other laws in a way that permits them to base their decisions in custom, rather than in imported legal norms.

Narokobi's decision in *State v. Gesie* is just one example of this educational mission at work. In this case, two defendants, from a remote village in the Southern Highlands, are accused of the willful murder of an elderly woman from their community. Most judicial decisions include a brief narrative describing the circumstances that gave rise to the charge. Narokobi's judicial decisions are no exception—although even as he presents the State's evidence, he cannot forbear adding his own emotive touches. Here is an example:

> The primary facts can easily be stated in terms the State presented in evidence. The two accused got together with two other men the police have not been able to arrest, and planned to kill a woman. In the early hours of the next day, amidst the sound of the dawn birds, the four men entered a customary house. The customary house consisted of a single room, partitioned into two parts. One part

> was occupied exclusively by men. The four men entered the women's section and went for the deceased. The two accused held the woman's hands down while the other two men put a rope around the deceased's neck and "sikirapim nek bilong em na em i dai" which I take to mean . . . strangled her to death. The accused then pulled her out by the rope into the burial bush.[75]

A rationalist judge might consider that this paragraph constitutes a sufficient factual description. Narokobi does not. He starts from the premise that customary beliefs about sorcery are accurate—or at least as accurate as the explanations advanced by those who believe in science or other rationalist explanations for events. As a result, he includes in his decisions additional facts that expatriate judges might ignore or, at any rate, would describe with a very different emphasis:

> It all started when Yale Gesie was sleeping in his garden house one midday. In his sleep he had a dream. In that dream he saw the deceased come and carve out his son's eye with a knife. Shortly afterwards, the son developed swelling of his eye and died as a result of that swelling. Relatives and neighbours gathered to mourn according to good custom. It was during the mourning that the deceased came. Her purpose was also to mourn the dead child. Now something remarkable happened which was yet another link in the chain of events which led to the killing. As the woman [. . .] entered the house where the dead child lay, the eyes of the child were seen to pop up and down. That was followed by emission of urine and finally excreta.[76]

What is most remarkable about this description of the facts of the case is that, unlike the expatriate judges who decided sorcery murder cases during the colonial period, Narokobi writes as if these portentous events actually occurred—and, even more, as if the conclusions that the participants drew from the events are perfectly proper conclusions to draw:

> These strange events were given an interpretation by the accused. It was the deceased was responsible for the death of the child through her evil sorcery. This interpretation was held by the village folk. To them, it was a divine revelation that the child was killed by the deceased with her evil sorcery.[77]

Appellate judges write decisions because they understand that it is necessary to explain and justify their findings and conclusions—to the defendants, to the lawyers involved in the case, to judges of the trial courts, and, most importantly, to others who might be tempted to commit the same crime. Narokobi, it seems, is adding here another audience to that list. A trial judge, he is writing decisions which, he hopes, will educate the judges to whom this

---

[75] *State v. Gesie*, unreported National Court judgment N254 (1980), 1

[76] Ibid.

[77] Ibid., 2.

case will be appealed. He wants the judges to grasp significant truths about the people they are judging. He tries to get his judicial colleagues to rethink their relationship to Melanesian culture not by lecturing them but by becoming a model for them of the way in which they should approach their task:

> ... I am called upon to decide this case which arose exclusively within Melanesian legal order. And yet I am expected to judge these two men within the imposed legal system with its roots in the Austinean theory of jurisprudence. I say with all humility that I sit to judge with great anxiety and trepidation. Again I run the risk of judging these two men from Austinean jurisprudential cognitive lenses. To do justice to all manner of men without fear, without favour, affection or ill-will, according to law, is an oath easy to make, but quite difficult to live up to in cases of this nature. If men obey the law which springs from the hearts of man and act in violation of other laws, we face the challenge of having to harmonise the fresh water of a river with the salt water of the sea.[78]

It is evident, he writes, that the defendants did the acts with which they were charged. But ought those acts to be judged as criminal? Melanesian custom would say that these are not criminal acts; the imported legal system says that they are. An Austinean judge would see it as his duty to explain the rules of the imported law to the benighted Melanesians. Narokobi, however, takes upon himself the task of explaining custom to positivist judges:

> Custom is part of the nation's law. Law itself is an aspect of the Melanesian total cosmic view of life. In that Melanesian universe of existence, metaphysics which include dreams and secret knowledge are vital constituents of the society's fabric. They are vital aspects of human totality here as elsewhere.[79]

Narokobi goes further. He tries to explain to the judiciary that the events they label as dreams or magic are as real to Papua New Guineans, including to Narokobi himself, as their scientific, rationalist explanations are to Australians:

> Dreams in Melanesia are instruments through which the living spirits of ancestors reveal secret knowledge. Through dreams secrets of magic and ritual are revealed. Some of the best dances in Melanesia are revealed to the dreamers through dreams. In crime detection, Melanesians rely quite extensively on divination techniques.... Belief in dreams and fear of sorcery are aspects of the life of the nation state at this time. ... It is common knowledge among Melanesian that the secrets of knowledge concerning power, hunting, gardening, singsings etcetera are initially revealed to mortals through dreams. Among Melanesians, knowledge is secret, and it is revealed only to friends and relatives. Dreams are an important source of access to secret knowledge.[80]

[78] Ibid., 3.
[79] Ibid., 4.
[80] Ibid., 6, 7.

Moreover, Narokobi writes, magic and dreams are not merely, as some judges would have it, quaint aspects of Melanesian culture, to which the court should give deference as if out of some form of judicial politeness. Westerners themselves have in their own histories examples of reliance upon these ways of knowing:

> Sacred Scripture frequently testify that God does speak to his people through dreams. In the Middle Ages, it was a common feature for Christians to search for norms in the discernment of dreams.[81]

This quote about historical uses of dreams could suggest that reliance upon magic and dreams is something that Western knowledge has grown out of, or progressed beyond. Narokobi quickly asserts the opposite: Westerners were closer to the truth in the past than they are today. As Westerners have grown estranged from nature, they have lost this direct and important way of truth-seeking:

> I need say no more than refer to the work of Carl Jung in the modern sciences. The hyper-civilized man may be so estranged that he may have no need for dreams. . . . The world of cosmology exists at a level where we mortals have but a limited view. The psychic realm of Melanesians in close touch with nature may easily escape our minds, especially if we are used to clear cut scientific or jurisprudential divisions between spirit and matter, or of facts and law.[82]

The truths revealed by magic and dreams are as accurate as, maybe even more accurate than, those reachable by science and rationalism:

> Truths come from trial and error, from scientific investigation or from divine inspiration. In the context of Melanesia, the first and the last-mentioned are most important. Thus it is not difficult for me to see that upon dreaming, the accused Yale took the contents of his dreams to be the truth. . . . The realms of psychology and sorcery amongst Papua New Guineans transcend scientific and technological knowledge. Whilst these are difficult to quantify, their reality and continued existence leads men and women to do or refrain from doing certain things the written law might permit or prohibit.[83]

In the end, Narokobi decides that the accused are guilty of the killing, but that the circumstances are such that their sentences should be very short. He settles on sentences of imprisonment for less than a year, most of which time has already served as the defendants were, of course, held in custody prior to and during the trial. He takes note, in handing down sentence, that defendants have already paid customary compensation to the family of the deceased. As

---

[81] Ibid., 4.
[82] Ibid., 5.
[83] Ibid., 4, 5.

these sentences are considerably less than the sentences of imprisonment for five to six years that the Papua New Guinea courts normally hand down in cases of the murder of sorcerers, Narokobi therefore fully expects that his decision will be appealed to the Supreme Court.

Narokobi would prefer that custom be generally the law followed by the PNG courts. He recognizes, however, that, the majority of justices on the Supreme Court are unlikely to agree. Therefore, in his decision in the *Gesie* case, he endeavours to convince the appellate court that there are grounds for his verdict—not just in custom, but in the introduced law as well. He puts forward two legal theories to support the light sentences he has imposed: one is provocation, and the other is diminished responsibility. However, for either to be applied to the *Gesie* case, the court has to rethink and re-interpret statutes and the common law. Narokobi exhorts the court to do so:

> If the court in this jurisdiction was to treat the common law with inflexibility, we would not only be acting against legal history's experience, but we would run the risk of undermining the spirit of our home-grown Constitution. . . . We must look to custom to interpret the Code. . . . The fragile plant of the Criminal Law cannot be treated as an English Oak that must be pruned, but a coconut that must take root in Melanesian soil, if it is to blossom and flower . . .[84]

The defense of provocation is found in the PNG Sorcery Act and defined in the Criminal Code. A defendant who can prove that he was suddenly provoked—that is, that he killed whilst in the grip of a passion so strong that it deprived him of self-control, a passion brought on by having seen the victim do a terrible act—is guilty only of manslaughter, not of willful murder. The courts in PNG have usually held that, for provocation to be found, the killing must follow so immediately upon the defendant's sight of the victim doing a terrible act as to leave no time for the defendant's passion to cool and for reason to re-assert itself. Narokobi argues that, given the horror that acts of sorcery induce, particularly in a defendant whose own children were its victims, that it was not impossible to believe that the defendant's passion might have stayed white hot for several days, rather than for the few hours normally permitted by the law to those hoping to use this defense.

In the alternative, Narokobi suggests that the PNG courts should recognize the defense of "diminished responsibility killing," a defense totally new to Papua New Guinea jurisprudence. In a sense, Narokobi is saying, quite bravely, that if the common law as we know it cannot recognize custom, then

[84] Ibid., 19.

the common law will have to change. Narokobi fashions the defense out of a mixture of customary and common law principles:

> In this case, I find that the accused did participate in a material way in the killing . . . I also find that they did have the general intention to kill, but that the intention was greatly induced by a pre-existent state of mind brought about by fear of sorcery, sorrow and a general loss of responsibility. . . . By operation of s. 7(a) of the Native Customs Recognition Act, I am entitled to ascertain the existence or otherwise of the state of mind of the accused. . . . From the customary point of view, it is not unreasonable to believe in the power of witchcraft. Nor is it unreasonable to believe in what dreams tell. It is by custom equally reasonable to kill reputed sorcerers. But this is not to be encouraged as it is clearly repugnant to the general principles of humanity. Whilst on the one hand, the courts must resort to custom to ascertain the state of mind of the accused, we must not permit another Inquisition. . . . Proceeding under the Criminal Code, I find . . . the accused not guilty of willful murder, but guilty of manslaughter which I would describe as a diminished responsibility killing brought about by a state of mind induced by customary perceptions and beliefs.[85]

This is a remarkable paragraph. In it, Narokobi uses the statutes and common law of PNG to argue for a better appreciation of custom by the courts. He argues for a new legal standard that would apply to people who do criminal acts because customary beliefs and values impel them to do so. He points out that, from within the customary world view, killing sorcerers is not, as the colonizers would have it, the apex of irrationality. Rather, it is reasonable. However, he is willing, at the same time, to grant the Supreme Court judges the possible validity of their own most likely arguments against his position—that witch killing is a custom that violates the Constitutional prohibition against the recognition of customs that are "repugnant to the general principles of humanity".[86] He permits that, however, merely as support for his own argument. He is, in effect, telling the appellate court that they have the choice of accepting witch killings as entirely reasonable, and therefore letting defendants off completely, or accepting his new theory, which merely mitigates the sentence whilst still supporting the proposition that killing witches is unlawful.

Narokobi's brief tenure as a judge has not been sufficiently appreciated. He brought to the bench not only an appreciation of the role that custom should play in a Melanesian legal system, and excellent arguments about why custom

---

[85] Ibid., 18–19.

[86] This limitation on the recognition of custom has long been a source of frustration to Papua New Guineans, who point out that what is repugnant to one culture may not be to another, and the notion that nothing in English law is repugnant to the "general principles of humanity" (whatever those might be) whereas things in custom might be, is itself a notion repugnant to morality and clear thought. Narokobi himself has stated that position. Bernard Narokobi, *Lo Bilong Yumi Yet* (Suva: University of the South Pacific, 1989).

should play that role, but also a writing style that mirrored and modeled that customary image. His empathy for all parties to each case, his use of natural imagery and metaphor, his humility in the face of complex legal issues, his willingness to put himself as a first-person narrator into his decisions—these are themselves exemplars of the Melanesian way. He does not just describe customary approaches. He becomes what he argues for.

The Positivist Response

One reason for the lack of scholarly or other appreciation of Narokobi's judicial decisions is that they were instantly and tellingly attacked by the justices of Papua New Guinea's Supreme Court. The decisions of that august body did not merely express disagreement with the trial judge's verdicts. The appellate decisions amounted almost to derision of a trial judge who could have come up with verdicts so outlandish. After the Supreme Court had done its work, it would have been difficult for anyone to see Narokobi's decisions as anything more than charming but essentially wrongheaded aberrations from the true channels of judicial thought.

In each of the cases in which he found defendants guilty of killing a witch, Narokobi ordered prison terms of only a few months, coupled with the requirement that defendants pay customary compensation, just as he did in *State v. Gesie*. In PNG, the Public Prosecutor cannot appeal a trial judge's not-guilty verdict, should there be one; but that official can appeal a sentence deemed to be too lenient. The Public Prosecutor did just that in relation to most of Narokobi's sentencing decisions. One such appeal, *Acting Public Prosecutor v. Aumane*,[87] was heard by a five-judge panel of the Supreme Court. Three-judge panels are more common. Moreover, although each judge on the panel is free to write a separate decision, most judges do not avail themselves of the opportunity. In the *Aumane* case, every one of the five judges—three Australians and two Papua New Guineans—wrote an opinion, and every one of them criticized Narokobi's sentencing decision. In the end, all five justices agreed that the sentences of the four defendants in the case be increased from several months each to from five to six years each (the typical sentence usually handed down by the Papua New Guinea courts to defendants convicted of killing witches) and that the orders to pay customary compensation be reversed.

We learn the facts by piecing together bits of information scattered amongst the five opinions. The deceased was an elderly woman, accused of witchcraft. She and the defendants came from an isolated Highlands village. Until their arrest, the accused had had very little contact with the outside

[87] Unreported Supreme Court judgment, SC 190 (19 December 1980).

world. Suddenly and inexplicably, upwards of 20 villagers died in a short period. Villagers suspected that witchcraft had a part in the deaths, the old woman was accused, and a group of men set off to take her to the *kiap* (patrol officer) in Porgera, the nearest sizeable town. Somewhere along the way, she tried to escape, was recaptured, and once bound, was shot dead with three arrows.

Sir Bori Kidu, at that time the Chief Justice, wrote the first of the appellate court's opinions. His response to sorcerer murder typifies the court's views throughout the colonial period and beyond. Murder is a grievous crime, he says, and will not be deterred unless punished. It cannot be condoned merely because defendants say they killed in order to punish someone who was herself a killer; no government can permit its legitimacy to be undermined, as happens when people presume they can usurp the government's role in punishing wrongdoers. Nevertheless, the Chief Justice continues, a sentence significantly less than the maximum sentence of life imprisonment is in order, because of the cultural position of the defendants:

> His Honour the learned trial judge properly took into account the background of the respondents. I have no quarrel on that score. For instance he found that the respondents came from a remote part of the country with minimal contact with the outside world, that they encountered modern life style after they were taken into custody, that their area was sparsely populated and that what they did was out of fear of sorcery.[88]

In thus permitting a lesser sentence, the Chief Justice may seem to be agreeing with Narokobi, at least on the principle that the murder of witches is not a particularly heinous crime, even if he does not agree on the exact length of the sentence. However, the Chief Justice and the fledgling judge could not be farther apart. Narokobi directs that defendants serve only a short sentence because he believes in the value and validity of Papua New Guinean culture and customs. The Chief Justice permits the sentence to be mitigated precisely because he does *not* believe that this custom is of value. To him, a belief in sorcery and witchcraft is misguided, a sign that the believer is still a prisoner of a backward and inferior culture. He fully expects that, as Papua New Guineans gain more contact with Western values, as they become educated and urbanized, they will discard these beliefs. He sees the law's role as helping them in this educational process, by sentencing them when they act on the basis of these mistaken values: "It is the duty of the courts to bring home to those who take human lives that their taking such lives under whatever circumstances cannot be said to be honourable."[89] He also sees, however, that to be an effective educator, the law must be patient. It cannot sentence too harshly those

[88] Unreported Supreme Court judgment, SC 190 (19 December 1980), 2.
[89] Ibid., 3.

who come from villages so isolated that they have not yet been able to have the benefits of education into civic values.

William Kearney, who had been Secretary for Law for the last several years of the colonial period before becoming Deputy Chief Justice of the Supreme Court of an independent PNG, generally takes a somewhat more liberal position than many of his fellows on the bench. Nevertheless, he agrees with the rest of the justices in viewing the imported legal system not as an interloper, imposing foreign norms and anachronistic values on Papua New Guineans, but as an educational force, inducting Papua New Guineans into proper morality:

> The glue which holds together diverse peoples in one society has, as an essential element, respect for the sanctity of human life. The law must strengthen that element, inculcate that respect, as best it can. In practical terms, this is reflected in a sentencing policy for crimes of willful murder which will best enhance that respect.[90]

That is an utterly worthy and adequate sentiment to guide the decisions of a judge in Australia. In the Papua New Guinea context, it tells only half the story.

Justice Andrew, also an Australian, agrees with his brethren that the court's proper role is not to excuse Papua New Guineans who believe in witches, but to educate them out of that belief. He is much more assertive than Kapi or Kearney in insisting that villagers are wrong not only to kill witches, but to believe in witchcraft at all:

> I find that I am in agreement with the learned trial judge when he says that it is the genuine belief by the accused that the victim was a sorceress and responsible for numerous deaths, which makes the task of sentencing in these circumstances so difficult. . . . But the learned trial judge has found that the victim did in fact kill twenty people. . . . There is simply no evidence of this . . . .[91]

Andrew then turns to the legal aspects of Narokobi's decision. Andrew is, like almost every judge on PNG's courts, a positivist. That is, he is a judge who believes that it is the court's only proper job to apply the law as it has been written. He does not believe that courts should be swayed from following the written word just because that might interfere with the purpose that the law was intended to serve. He does not believe, in fact, that such a dichotomy would ever happen. He might believe that the written law can be uncertain or ambiguous—but only on the rarest of occasions. Most importantly, he does not believe that judges ever should, or do, make law: he does not believe that it happens by accident, and he certainly does not believe it should ever happen on purpose. He knows that the common law is evolutionary, that it changes

[90] Ibid., 8.
[91] Ibid., 19.

all the time. But, in order to believe, as he does, that judges do not ever make new law, he must never have asked himself how that evolution of the common law comes about.

Therefore, Andrew's major disagreement with Narokobi is over the new defense of diminished responsibility killing. Andrew is such a positivist that he refuses even to recognize that Narokobi seriously and intentionally was suggesting that the courts create a new common law defense:

> The second error in my opinion was that his Honour appears to have adopted the recommendations of the Law Reform Commission [that courts create the defense of diminished responsibility killing] as being the relevant law. . . . The [trial court's] judgment . . . proceeds to apply the facts of this case to those recommendations and I think that it is, at the least, implied that the trial judge treated this as a diminished responsibility killing. Such course is not open and amounts to an error of law. It may be a view of the law as one would wish it to be or an idealistic approach but it is not the law.[92]

Justice Greville-Smith, the third Australian on the bench, is even more of a positivist than Justice Andrew. He notes his agreement with the rest of the court about the appropriate sentence for defendants in less than a paragraph. His real interest is in another issue in the case, an utterly technical question about whether Supreme Court rules can modify a provision of the Supreme Court Act. Only an Austinean would care.

The last decision is written by Sir Mari Kapi, the Court's best judicial mind. He is a positivist, but a supremely thoughtful one. He decides against Narokobi, but in terms that show his respect for the learned trial judge. Whilst the other justices lecture at or about Narokobi, telling the reader how wrong he was, Kapi accepts Narokobi as a judge with ideas about the law that are worth consideration. Kapi begins his discussion of the sorcery murderers with an overview of the major theories behind sentencing—separation, rehabilitation, deterrence and retribution—and a discussion of which relates best to the circumstances of PNG. He decides that the trial judge did not have the power to order defendants to pay customary compensation, a finding with which the other justices agree. However the other judges had simply presumed this, whereas; Justice Kapi performed a careful study of the language of the Customs Recognition Act and other relevant statutes in order to reach the same conclusion.

Finally, Justice Kapi finds that the trial judge was in error in meting out such light sentence, but, again, in arriving at that conclusion, Kapi discusses each of Narokobi's arguments in the terms it which was written and with the gravity it deserves. Kapi's ability to respect a judge with whom he disagrees

[92] Ibid., 20.

[93] Ibid., 39.

may be due to his own ease with both custom and the introduced law. He does not believe that it is the task of the courts to educate Papua New Guineans towards the civilized heights of the common law, because he does not view the common law as any more civilized than custom: "Taking of life is against any system of law or custom," he writes.[93] Central to his judicial philosophy is the notion that custom is the equal of the common law; the difference between them is not, to his mind, that one is better than the other, or more sophisticated than the other, but that there is a separate sphere for each. The internal affairs of the family may be governed by custom, but criminal law is the purview of the common law.

In the end, Kapi returns to the themes with which he began his decision—the theories that lie behind sentencing. Notably, he does not include education on his list:

> . . . in imposing the sentence I have regard to the theories of retribution and deterrence. Whilst deterrence has its limitations on the ordinary villager because there might be difficulties of communicating the sentence, I have no doubt any deterrent sentence will have the impact upon their own community. . . . I also have regard to retribution. Taking of life is against any system of law or custom. . . . It is the duty of the court in imposing sentence to prove to others that it is wrong to take someone else's life under any circumstances. The law exists not only to protect the innocent but also those who are accused of doing wrong in the community. This is what our Constitution is all about. It is the duty of this court to impose an appropriate sentence to show that the law does not approve of killing of sorcerers.[94]

For Kapi, however, the law's disapproval of sorcerer murders does not come from any lack of belief in the power of sorcery. Whatever Kapi may himself believe, he does not overtly dispute, as Andrews did, the reality of witchcraft. For him, the question of the reality of witchcraft is not the law's business. It is not, he finds, relevant to the case. Instead, he reviews the facts with care—of all five justices, his fact description is the most thorough—and decides that the defendants were not trying to obey customary norms when they killed the victim. Therefore, they cannot use custom as a basis for mitigating their sentences:

> There is no dispute that the deceased was a reputed sorcerer. The respondents believed that she was responsible for the deaths of a number of people. They feared the deaths of more people. It was this fear which caused them to bring her to the Porgera Government station. . . . It is significant that at the outset, the respondents did not kill the sorcerer, as required by custom, but chose to take her to a Government station some five days' walk away. This, to my mind, is an indication of their knowledge of the law and Government influence on their lives.[95]

---

[94] Ibid.

[95] Ibid., 38

On balance, however, Kapi is a positivist. Even if he might approve of adding compensation and other customary remedies to the sentencing powers of the formal courts, he would not order it himself. A change of that magnitude, he concludes, is for the legislature to enact.

I have discussed two responses to those who kill witches. Bernard Narokobi, an activist judge who believed that the formal courts would not be appropriate forums for PNG until they had thoroughly accepted custom as their major source of law, sentenced defendants to only a few months in prison and added to their sentences the requirement that they offer compensation, in customary form, to the relatives of their victims. The Supreme Court retorted by overruling any of Narokobi's decisions that were appealed to them. The positivist judges did not credit the existence of any unwritten law—whether custom or a judge-made modification of the common law. Moreover, most of them strongly believed in the innate superiority of the English common law over any version of custom, especially over the irrationality of believing in sorcery.

There is yet a third response exhibited by a judge of the PNG National Court towards persons accused of killing witches. That is the feminist, post-modern approach of Brian Brunton which will now be examined.

Brian Brunton and the Post-Modern Perspective

Brian Brunton and Bernard Narokobi have much in common, although their views on the way in which the courts should respond to witch murder are poles apart. Like Narokobi, Brunton was a judge for a brief and, I suspect, dissatisfying (for him) portion of an otherwise long and useful career. Brunton was also, like Narokobi, a progressive thinker and scholar, and, therefore, an early anti-colonialist. Also like Narokobi, Brunton's legal education occurred in a culture different from that of his birth. But whereas the Papua New Guinean Narokobi traveled to Australia for his education, the Australian Brunton found himself, at a very young age, a *kiap* in PNG. His experience in that position bred in him a love for PNG coupled with distaste for anyone who would violate the rights of another, either in the service of colonialism or at the behest of custom. He chose to get his law degree at the then newly-formed University of Papua New Guinea in preference to returning to Australia, took Papua New Guinea citizenship immediately after independence, and, for the most part, has remained in Papua New Guinea ever since, teaching and leading a life of service to the country.

As a judge, Brunton's major case involving sorcery murder occurred when he learned that, after charging three defendants with the murder of a woman reputed to be a witch, the PNG Public Prosecutor had decided not to go ahead with the prosecution. As they do in other countries, Papua New Guinea's prosecutors have considerable discretion as to which cases they prosecute, so

Justice Brunton ultimately decided that he was unable to overturn the *nolle prosequi*.[96] However, he took the opportunity to discuss the approach he believed prosecutors and courts ought to take to the murders of women accused of witchcraft.

Judges reveal their attitudes towards a case not just in the reasons they give for their rulings, but even in the way that they describe the facts underlying the case. The differences between the facts on which Narokobi focused in his decision, and the facts upon which Brunton focuses, are significant. Narokobi tells his readers all about the events leading up to the murder—Gesie's dreams, the deaths of his son and daughter, just as his dreams suggested they would happen, the actions of the corpse when the old woman enters the room—but is spare in his description of the murder itself. Brunton's narrative is the opposite. He allots barely a sentence to the death that the villagers attribute to the 'witch', but describes her death in horrifying detail:

> Eight women were tied up at Kepai Village and left out in the sun for two weeks without food and water. . . . There was some indication that they were allowed indoors at night. . . . At one time during this period the women were brought to the house of the deceased Kauna Bosboi and were told to fetch water which had to be poured into the mouth of Kauna Bosboi. Seven of the women performed this act. One, the deceased Yanupa Kaupa refused and consequently was believed to be the person who was responsible for the death of Kauna Bosboi.[97]

After that, the women "were whipped with sticks all over our bodies."[98] The deceased was kicked repeatedly until she died.[99] Although only one of the accused admitted to killing the old woman, they all admitted to disposing of her body in the river. Brunton is not sure whether they did that to hide the evidence of their crime or, as one of the defendants testified, because a witch's body cannot be buried in a cemetery on account of the "bad spirit in her."[100]

Brunton recognizes the power of the prelapsarian argument, but he does not sympathize with this approach:

> There is now a body of sociological and historical scholarship which tends to the view that witch hunts were—or are . . . a society attempting to rid itself of what it considered to be a cause of death of illness. This view of witches, witchcraft, and witch-hunts still receives some sympathy within Papua New Guinea.[101]

---

[96] A statement filed by the Public Prosecutor with the court announcing the intention not to proceed with the prosecution of a defendant who has been indicted.

[97] *State v. Aigal*, unreported National Court judgment, N891 (1990), 6–7.

[98] Ibid., 7.

[99] Ibid.

[100] Ibid., 10.

[101] Ibid., 12.

For Brunton, witch-killings are nothing more than an attempt by men to retain their power over women:

> A more recent understanding of the social role of witch-hunts emphasizes their context in sexual politics. The political role of the witch-hunt is a form of terror that holds women in their place. . . . The power of older women, as against men, is limited by the threat of an allegation of witch-craft, and its consequences in coercion. As the surviving victims in this case showed—there is no defense to an allegation of witchcraft. The assertion proves itself, and the victims can only hope that they will not be killed.[102]

The "more recent understanding" to which Brunton refers is that provided by feminist jurisprudence, and Brunton's decision in this case is an example of the major service that feminism has done for legal thought and practice.[103]

By focusing on the voices and stories of women—voices and stories that had not previously been an acknowledged part of legal discourse—feminist legal studies have been the catalyst for significant change in legal policy. Until more recently than we care to acknowledge, the common law was a male institution. Women played a role in the legal system, if at all, only as plaintiffs and defendants. Since lawyers and judges did all the talking—at least all of it that was read, preserved, analyzed, and praised—women were, to all intents and purposes, silent. The culture, beliefs, and values of the legal system were male. Women's needs, interests, beliefs and values were, essentially, ignored. In PNG, the colonial legal system was intensely male-driven, and the post-colonial legal system has remained male-dominated long after women's voices have begun to be heard in the legal systems of other common law countries. It is telling, for example, that, in this article about the killing of witches, all the voices (except mine) belong to men. Even the sole judicial decision discussed

---

[102] Ibid., 12.

[103] A number of writers have discussed the political role that witch hunts play in maintaining male superiority over women. See, for example, those listed at notes 45 and 51, above. However, none of the writing has been expressly about Papua New Guinea, and very little of this scholarship seems to have reached any of the judges of the Papua New Guinea courts, except Justice Brunton. Given that a belief in witchcraft is probably more widespread at the moment in Papua New Guinea than anywhere else in the world, and given that cases about witch-killings continually reach the country's highest courts, one would have expected judges to show a great deal more interest in searching out the underlying causes for the continuing belief in witchcraft. If they have done any of this reading, it does not show in their decisions. One reason, perhaps, is that, as demonstrated by the decisions in *State v. Aumane*, unreported Supreme Court judgment, SC 190 (19 December 1980) even today when most of the judges are themselves Papua New Guinean, the court continues to view witchcraft as just another example of the general backwardness of rural Papua New Guineans. Another reason is that a jurisprudence which focuses judges on applying the law, as written, does not encourage in judges habits of thinking about the law and its purposes. This is one of the great limitations of positivism. By focusing judges on the text of the law, by not permitting them to go beyond it, positivism stunts judges' education and cramps judicial thought.

here that is from a feminist perspective was written by a man.[104] Moreover, the PNG legal system doubly disadvantages women, because customary law—at least in the form in which it enters the formal legal system—is also male-dominated.[105] For all we know, women in PNG's villages have been aware for centuries that the women most likely to be labeled as witches are those older, smarter, braver women most likely to stand up to men. But, so long as the law is interested only in male narratives, there was no way for this insight to become part of judicial decision-making.

By introducing the women's side of the legal story into the discourse, Brunton's decision should have done the PNG legal system a great boon. Women's voices are important to the legal system not only to help women—nor only because they make the legal worldview complete. As Brunton's decision demonstrates, the woman's perspective adds to the legal system experiences, truth, history and values that are crucial for everyone, male and female both. Without that perspective, the law is operating ignorant of the culture whose policies it is supposed to be furthering.

However, Brunton's decision failed to accomplish these objectives. It did not cause other judges or lawyers to listen to women or to include women's stories in their decisions or arguments. It was not discussed in law reviews or in the local press. It was neither praised nor derided. It was not overturned, or set aside, or argued against.[106] As far as I know, it fell on deaf ears. It was—like women in Papua New Guinea's legal system generally—simply ignored.

Conclusions and Afterthoughts

The differences amongst the judges are broader than just a legal spat. They demonstrate a divided nation. There are Papua New Guineans who believe in the power of witchcraft to do irreparable evil. There are judges who believe that witch killing is ignorant and savage, and that those Papua New Guineans

[104] In the time of which I write, only one of the judges of the Supreme Court was a woman. I have discussed one of her decisions in Jean G. Zorn, "Issues in Contemporary Customary Law: Women and the Law," in *Passage of Change: Law, Society and Governance in the Pacific*, ed. Anita Jowitt and Tess Newton Cain (Canberra: Pandanus Books, 2003). As discussed therein, she does not write from an overtly feminist perspective.

[105] On the changes that customary law undergoes when it enters the formal legal system, see Martin Chanock, "Neither Customary Nor Legal: African Customary Law in an Era of Family Law Reform," *International Journal of Law and the Family* 3 (1989): 72–88.

[106] Admittedly, the lack of serious mention in other judicial decisions is partly because, as noted above, it was not, and could not be, appealed from. But other National Court decisions have been cited, quoted or at least mentioned, if not by an appellate panel, then by commentators or scholars. The total lack of attention to this groundbreaking decision is itself a matter of note.

who do it are uneducated and in need of the modernization that only prison can provide. There are scholars and legislators—and, unfortunately, just one judge—who believe that, wrong as it may be to kill anyone, nevertheless, those Papua New Guineans are expressing something about the culture that the law is supposed to be listening to. And there are other scholars—and another judge—who believe that witch killing is a symptom of a society in serious disarray and of gender relations that are angry and unequal.

The judges' debate over the validity that should be accorded to witchcraft and sorcery is in part a debate between science and magic, between rationalism and religion, and between the Christian religion and other religious beliefs. The debate also goes beyond an argument over the issues specific to sorcery and witchcraft. When the debate turns to the role of women, it becomes part of the larger contest between tradition and modernity, and between hierarchy and equality. It also begins to reflect the dislocation and frustration that are still simmering consequences of colonial and post-colonial social, political, and economic policies. Finally, when the debate focuses on the proper way to interpret the Constitution, it becomes part of the more general tug-of-war between custom and the common law.

The law is always changing and judges are its shapers. Positivists would like to think that all they do is to enforce the law as it already is, but every case that a judge decides changes the law that little bit. Even positivists shape the law; they just have less conscious control over how it will be shaped. The worst that can be said about Narokobi and Brunton is that they tried to exert some control over the process.

Narokobi and Brunton drew very different lessons from their shared opposition to colonialism. The colonial intrusion bred in both of them a deep respect for Papua New Guinean culture and a preference for that culture over most things imposed on PNG by the colonial powers. The colonial hierarchy, based on the accidental difference between white and black, colonizer and colonized, also led both of them to embrace a thoroughgoing belief in equality for all. But these shared positions did not lead them to take the same position on witch-murders. Narokobi put his emphasis on supporting Papua New Guinean culture, and Brunton put his on supporting equality.

However, when they are read in tandem, as we have done in this chapter, their influence truly becomes apparent. Putting them together, I realize for the first time that support for traditional Papua New Guinean culture and a belief in equality, even in gender equality, need not be antithetical. Narokobi shows us how to bring traditional culture into the formal legal system. What Brunton's writing does is to show us that women's perspective is an integral part of that traditional culture. PNG's culture cannot be completely understood and encompassed until women's stories are included in it. Only when women's perspectives are included does the culture become whole.

CHAPTER FOUR

BETWEEN A ROCK AND A HARD PLACE: WOMEN, RELIGION AND LAW IN SOLOMON ISLANDS

Jennifer Corrin Care

Introduction

Traditional Solomon Islands society has been characterized as based upon values that are essentially conservative and patriarchal.[1] These values are echoed in customary law,[2] which is also based on male power[3] and emphasizes status[4] and duties towards the community.[5] However these bald generalizations obscure a complex relationship between the genders, which may often be governed more by local circumstances, such as the need to maintain inter-tribal

---

I should like to thank Dr Paula Heinonen of the International Gender Studies Centre (CCCRW), Queen Elizabeth House, University of Oxford, for her helpful comments on a draft of this chapter.

[1] Ben Burt, *Tradition and Christianity: The Colonial Transformation of a Solomon Islands Society* (Langhoren, Pa: Harwood Academic, 1994), 65; Ian Hogbin, *A Guadalcanal Society: The Kaoka Speakers* (New York: Holt, Rhinehart and Winston, 1964), 67, 84. See also, in relation to the Baruya in the Papua New Guinea highlands, Maurice Godelier, *The Making of Great Men: Male Domination and Power among the New Guinea Baruya* (Cambridge: Cambridge University Press, 1986), 59–60.

[2] For a definition of customary law, see text at note 23, below.

[3] Even in those parts of the region where title to land descends through matrilineal lines, power is still arguably in the hands of men: see further notes 106–8, below.

[4] Chief Justice John Muria, "Conflicts in Women's Human Rights in the South Pacific: The Solomon Islands Experience," *Commonwealth Judicial Journal* 11 no. 4 (1996): 7–12 where he observes that modern regimes in the domestic sphere are categorized as 'foreign' by ordinary islanders.

[5] It is not being suggested that the relationship between the sexes was uniform throughout the country. For example, Keesing points to a free and easy relationship between the genders in the Kwaio region of Solomon Islands and contrasts this with other areas of Melanesia. However, he concedes that even in the Kwaio area women are at a considerable disadvantage: Roger M. Keesing, *Kwaio Religion: The Living and the Dead in a Solomon Island Society* (New York: Columbia University Press, 1982), 224. Further, it is acknowledged that reference to Solomon Island 'women' is a generalization and that local and political specificity is necessary for a more detailed analysis.

harmony, than by a desire to exercise power over women.[6] More detailed analysis constantly reveals contradictions, including a certain prestige held by women within traditional society and a degree of cultural value placed on their skills.[7]

During the Protectorate era (1843–1978) the *araikwao* (foreigners) brought with them a very different set of values and norms. They introduced a different system of law that, at least by the time of independence, incorporated hard won reforms based on notions of formal equality.[8] At the same time, the *araikwao* introduced their own religions, which were also wrapped in Western culture, or at least the version of that culture carried by proselytizing missionaries.

The Protectorate era theoretically paved the way for a change of emphasis in law, religion and society generally. The Independence Constitution of 1978 suggests the culmination of such a change. Expressed to be established, "under the guiding hand of God,"[9] it displays a commitment to individual freedom and equality, in the form of provisions guaranteeing fundamental rights, including freedom of religion (section 11) and anti-discrimination (section 15). Yet the Constitution also expresses pride in custom and pledges to "cherish and promote the different cultural traditions," thus establishing a conundrum for the future. The reality beneath the rhetoric is that much of the patriarchal fabric of traditional society remains in place. Customary beliefs and practices are still strong.[10] There are strong indications that the promise of equality between men and women, held out by the introduced system of law and emancipatory understandings of the introduced religions, has not

[6] For an example of complex inter-clan exchanges, designed to balance the relationship between tribes in Papua New Guinea, see *In Re Miriam Willingal*, unreported, National Court, Papua New Guinea, Civ. Cas. N1506, 10 February 1997, www.vanuatu.usp.ac.fj/paclawmat/PNG_cases/Re_Willingal.html (accessed April 20, 2004).

[7] Colin H Allan, *Customary Land Tenure in the British Solomon Islands Protectorate*, Report of the Special Lands Commission (Suva: Western Pacific High Commission, 1957) 101, para 64. For a criticism of the stereotyping of Melanesians see Bronwen Douglas, "Conflict, Gender, Peacemaking an Alternative Nationalisms in the Western Pacific" *Development Bulletin* 53 (2000): 10–13.

[8] Historically, of course, the law of England was equally patriarchal. See, for example, the early divorce laws, where women had to prove adultery and a matrimonial offence in order to be entitled to a divorce: Matrimonial Causes Act 1857 (UK), section 27. Women were not placed on a similar footing to men as to the grounds of divorce until the Matrimonial Causes Act 1923 (UK).

[9] Constitution of Solomon Islands 1978, Preamble.

[10] It is a commonplace of much anthropological scholarship that the impact of colonization has adulterated customary law; see e.g., Roger M Keesing and Robert Tonkinson, eds, *Reinventing Traditional Culture: The Politics of Kastom in Island Melanesia* (Sydney: Anthropological Society of New South Wales, 1982). Scholars like Peter Fitzpatrick contend that customary law has actually ceased to exist: "Traditionalism and Traditional Law", *Journal of African Law* 28 (1984): 20–27.

been translated into practice in every day life. Rather, new values and ideas have been dispersed amongst the existing fabric of society, with scant regard for the frictions that inevitably result.

Commencing with a brief historical summary, this chapter examines the position of women in religion and law in Solomon Islands. After highlighting some aspects of pre-independence society, the events that transformed the country during the colonial period and in the transition to independence are outlined. The post-independence position of women, religion and law, according to the Constitution, is then analysed. The chapter proceeds to consider whether the notional positions of women, law and religion in Solomon Islands are echoed in practice. In particular, the impact of conflicting values relating to 'bride price' and custody are discussed. The dichotomy linking tradition with subjugation and Westernization with freedom and equality is questioned, as is the assumption that introduced law and religion promote freedom and gender equality in Solomon Islands society.

Background

Solomon Islands is made up of several hundred islands, situated in the Southwest Pacific, about 1,796 kilometres north-east of Australia. It is spread out over a sea area of approximately 1,340,000 square kilometres. The country was probably settled by explorers from Southeast Asia and New Guinea some time before 200BC.[11] Traditionally, the population on many islands was divided into 'bush people,' who lived in the hinterland, and 'saltwater people,' who lived on the coast.[12] There were marked differences between their ways of life. Bush settlements were not easily accessible and the people had limited interaction with outsiders. The inhabitants were hunter gatherers and gardeners and used traditional techniques to grow and track food.[13] Coastal dwellers had more interaction with outsiders. They fished the local waters and exchanged any surplus with the bush people for other types of food.[14]

The islands were 'rediscovered' by the Spanish in 1568 and exploration continued until the 1800s. In 1843, the Southern islands of the Solomon chain became a British protectorate. In 1885, Germany declared the Northern Islands to be under their protection. About five years later, the German Protectorate,

---

[11] Remains from Fotoruma Cave, the earliest settlement to be excavated, have been carbon dated to 1300–1000 BCE.

[12] Lawrence Foanaota, "Social Change" in *Ples Bilong Iumi* (Suva, Institute of Pacific Studies: University of the South Pacific Press, 1989), 68–69. See also, Allan, *Customary Land Tenure*, 10.

[13] Allan, *Customary Land Tenure*, 23–24.

[14] Ibid.

except for Buka and Bougainville, was transferred to Britain in exchange for recognition of German interests in Western Samoa. In 1893 the HMS Curacao sailed around the islands raising the British flag and declaring the Protectorate.[15] In 1896 the first resident commissioner, Charles Woodford, was sent to Solomons. The country was an area of intense fighting, both on land and at sea, during the Second World War, and was for a time occupied by the Japanese.

After the war, Solomon Islands continued as a British protectorate.[16] In 1960, a Constitution was brought into force by British Order, which established a Legislative Council. This Council was presided over, not by a Solomon Islander, but by the High Commissioner for the Western Pacific. Elected members were introduced in 1965. In 1967 a Legislative Council and an Executive Council were introduced. A new Constitution, which came into force in 1970, replaced these Councils with a single Governing Council. For the first time, the majority of members were elected locally. The British Solomon Islands Order 1974 introduced the new Constitution, which repealed the Governing Council with a Council of Ministers and a Legislative Assembly. The Governor and Deputy Governor were both appointed by the Queen of England. At Independence, the 1974 Constitution was repealed and replaced by the Constitution of Solomon Islands 1978.[17] Rather than permitting the Constitution to be prepared and enacted locally,[18] the Constitution was appended to the Solomon Islands Independence Order 1978 and brought into force by the British Privy Council.

In 1998, Solomon Islands began a steady decline into anarchy, fuelled by animosity between islanders from Guadalcanal and those from Malaita. The peace process stalled when arms decommissioning exercises failed. In late July 2003, an international peace keeping force of 2,200 police and military personnel (the Regional Assistance Mission to Solomon Islands, RAMSI) was sent to Guadalcanal and, at the time of writing, the rule of law is gradually returning.[19]

---

[15] The Pacific Order in Council 1893 (UK) provided the basis of government. Surprisingly, this Order still governs religious marriage by expatriates in Solomon Islands.

[16] The term 'colonial' is used loosely throughout this article to describe the relationship between Solomon Islands and Great Britain during the Protectorate era.

[17] Appended to the Solomon Islands Independence Order 1978 (UK).

[18] As was done the following year in Vanuatu: Exchange of Notes between Governments of United Kingdom and France (October 23, 1979). In Nauru and Samoa the constitution was dealt with by a special, locally constituted body: Constitution of Nauru 1968, brought into force by a Constitutional Convention in Nauru; Constitution of Samoa 1962, brought into force by a Constitutional Convention in Samoa (then called Western Samoa).

[19] For a more detailed background to the conflict, see Tarcisius Tara Kabutaulaka, "'Failed State' and the War on Terror: Intervention in Solomon Islands" *AsiaPacific Issues* 72 (March 2004) (Honolulu: East West Center, 2004). Regarding the role of women in peace building, see United Nations Development Fund For Women's Internet site on gender and conflict,: http://womenwarpeace.org/solomon_islands/solomon_islands.htm.

The present population of Solomon Islands is about 409,000.[20] Of these about 94.2 percent are Melanesian, 4 percent Polynesian, 1.4 percent Micronesian, 0.4 percent European and 0.1 percent Chinese. About 85 percent of the population still lives in rural villages.[21] The social structure of the country is extremely complex. Leadership hierarchies and customs vary from island to island, and even from village to village. The official languages are English and Pidgin, but there are also about sixty-five vernacular languages and dialects in existence.[22]

The Place of Women, Religion and Law In Pre-Colonial Solomon Islands

In traditional Solomon Islands' society, custom, law, and religion were bound up together. They were all part of a way of life and part of the relationship between the people and the land on which they lived. It is this inseparability, perhaps, that makes it so difficult to compare traditional and introduced concepts. The small village societies scattered throughout Solomon Islands prior to contact with the *araikwao* had their own rules governing conduct. These rules were bound up with survival and communal living. Local societies also had an array of mechanisms for resolving disputes and enforcing the rules of conduct. Collectively, these rules and mechanisms, governing the activity of communal life in traditional Solomon Islands society, are often referred to as customary law.[23]

The customary system was patriarchal[24] and, as under English custom, all women were regarded as "wives, potential wives, or former wives".[25] Generally, women were excluded from leadership roles[26] and major decision-making.

---

[20] This estimate is based on the 1999 Government Census. *Solomon Islands 1999 Population and Housing Census*, 2000, Solomon Islands Census Office, Honiara.

[21] Ibid.

[22] This information was supplied by Professor John Lynch and Dr Robert Early of the Pacific Language Unit, University of the South Pacific.

[23] This artificial distinction is made in order to contrast customary and formal law. The Constitution of Solomon Islands defines customary law as meaning "the rules of customary law prevailing in an area of Solomon Islands": section 144(1), which is not helpful, except to the extent that it dispels the colonial notion that customary law is rooted in ancient times.

[24] See Allan, *Customary Land Tenure*, 15, para. 11; see also note 1, above.

[25] Dorothy Stetson, *A Woman's Issue: The Politics of Family Law Reform in England* (London: Greenwood Press, 1982), 1. In relation to Vanuatu, Jeremy MacClancy points out that women were required to marry into nearby clans with a similar language and, "spent most of their lives among people who knew them only as the wife of one of their relatives": *To Kill a Bird with Two Stones* (Vanuatu: Vanuatu Cultural Centre, 1981), 35.

[26] Garry Trompf, "Pacific Islands," in *The Religions of Oceania*, ed. Tony Swain and Garry Trompf (London: Routledge, 1995), 145. In parts of Vanuatu, women had their own grades of authority, but the system was less elaborate: MacClancy, *To Kill a Bird*, 29, 31.

In some customary groups, they were regarded as a source of contamination that had to be cleansed during initiation ceremonies.[27] Some groups believed menstrual blood to have a defiling effect, to the extent that menstruating women were segregated during this period.[28] Women remained in their parents' village until a marriage was arranged for them, at which point they often had to move to their husband's village.[29] However, whilst women had little freedom in traditional Solomon Islands societies, they were often valued members by virtue of their role as childbearers,[30] producers of food and managers of domestic affairs. In the Kwaio area of Solomon Islands, Keesing writes of a counter-interpretation by women of the practice of isolation during menstruation and childbearing, which they considered as endorsing them as pure and sacred.[31] Furthermore, Pollard has observed that the chanting which occurs on the birth of a child in Are Are society reflects the esteem in which a female is held:[32]

> The chanting also demonstrates the girl child's value socially, politically and economically. She is not looked upon as a mere girl child but as one whose family can depend on for survival, power, fame and wealth.

This status carried with it the benefits of prestige and protection.[33] The social security of the close-knit, customary societies also gave all children affiliation to a family group. Where the mother was unmarried, affiliation was to the mother's group. Where she was married and bride price had been paid, affiliation was to the father's unit. Thus, the common law concept of *fillius nullius* was unknown. In some groups, women also had a special role in conflict resolution.

---

[27] See e.g., Burt *Tradition and Christianity*, 61; for PNG, see Godelier, *Making of Great Men*, 59–60.

[28] This belief endures in some parts of Malaita: see *Talosui v. Tone'ewane* (1985/86) SILR 140, where men from the *Toabaita* clan in Malaita were prevented from voting by their belief that they would be defiled if they entered the polling station which might have been occupied by a menstruating woman earlier in the day. See also Keesing, *Kwaio Religion* 222–224. Trompf, "Pacific Islands" 145, states that this segregation was due to the fact that women's bodies could 'dispossess' power from males.

[29] Foanaota, "Social Change," 70. In relation to Vanuatu, see MacClancy *To Kill a Bird*, 35.

[30] Trompf, "Pacific Islands," 145.

[31] Keesing, *Kwaio Religion*, 224, contrasted the Kwaio approach to segregation with that in other parts of Melanesia and in particular Lau, where he considered that it was used as an instance of "exclusion, subordination and denigration".

[32] Alice A. Pollard, "'Bride Price' and Christianity," (paper presented at the "Women, Christians, Citizens: Being Female in Melanesia Today Workshop" organized by the Australian National University's Society and Governance in Melanesia Project, Sorrento, Victoria, 11–13 November 1998), 1, http://rspas.anu.edu.au/melanesia/pollard.html.

[33] Julia Nesbitt, ed., *Development in the Pacific: What Women Say* (Canberra: Australian Council for Overseas Aid, 1986), iv.

For example, Pollard records that Are Are women could stand between warring parties and order them by saying that continued fighting would be equivalent to walking over their bodies. As male contact with a woman's body was 'tambu' (forbidden) the fighting would cease.[34]

Whilst beliefs and practices of traditional religion are still strong in Solomon Islands, little is known about the exact nature of religious beliefs before the arrival of Christian missionaries.[35] Part of the difficulty in identification is that traditional religion cannot be separated from other aspects of custom. Early suggestions that indigenous practices in Melanesia should be categorized as magic,[36] rather than religion, have been overtaken by less ethnocentric approaches to religion.[37] Traditional religion was a pervasive part of customary life. More than one god was worshipped, although some Solomon Islands myths acknowledge a high god as the creator of the universe.[38] According to one oral tradition, the first people who landed on Malaita knew the name of the creator, but it was too holy to be spoken. Accordingly, their children were told to address their prayers to their ancestors, who would pass the message on.[39] Ancestor worship was common. Fugui states that

> Spirits were generally believed to be in close attendance on human beings. Hence there was strong belief in magic, sorcery, witchcraft, shamanism and other expressions of spiritual power. The means by which the spirits might communicate with the living were dreams, visions, mediums and "signs" which might be discerned in many different actions and rituals.[40]

Spirits were of two kinds: the most venerated were spirits of remembered ancestors. The other type of spirits had never inhabited a human body.[41]

---

[34] Alice Pollard, "Resolving Conflict in Solomon Islands: The Women for Peace Approach," *Development Bulletin* 53 (2000): 44–46. See also B. Narokobi, "There's No Need for Women's Lib Here, because 'Melanesian Women are already Equal,'" in *The Melanesian Way* (Port Moresby: Institute of Papua New Guinea Studies, 1980), 71, where he describes the role of women in tribal war or inter-village battle in the Bukip area.

[35] For a study of religion in the Kwaio area, where traditional religion is still flourishing, see Keesing, *Kwaio Religion*.

[36] Bronislaw Malinowski, *Argonauts of the Western Pacific: An Account of Native Enterprise and Adventure in the Archipelagoes on Melanesian New Guinea* (London: Routledge & Keegan Paul, 1922), 392–407, writing about the Trobriand Islands in Papua New Guinea.

[37] See further, Roger Mortensen, "A Voyage in God's Canoe," in *Law and Religion* ed. Richard O'Dair and Andrew Lewis (Oxford: Oxford University Press, 2001), 511.

[38] Fugui, "Religion" 76. Some Polynesian beliefs involved great or supreme gods: Dorota Czarkowska Starzecka and Bryan A. L. Cranstone, *The Solomon Islanders* (London: British Museum 1974), 14.

[39] Fugui, "Religion" 76.

[40] Ibid.

[41] Starcezca and Cranstone, *Solomon Islanders*, 14.

Spirits might manifest themselves in the form of certain types of animal, most importantly the shark. Special respect was also paid to frigate birds, which were thought to be incarnations of ancestors, and some snakes and crocodiles.[42] It was generally believed that everyone had a soul. On death the soul departed the body or sometimes stayed in the skull of the deceased. Alternatively, it might inhabit the body of another person, usually a relative.

Some communities recognized the office of priest.[43] In others, there was no specific 'order' of priests, but some men were acknowledged to have particular skill in dealing with spirits.[44] People turned to religion to obtain assistance with their daily tasks, such as food production. The word usually used to describe the spiritual power that assisted individuals and communities to succeed in their endeavours is *mana*.[45] The importance of *mana* is one explanation for the indivisibility of custom, law and religion. If an individual possesses *mana*, this demonstrates approval by the spirits and provides the status, qualities and wealth to be a leader in the community. It has been said that all Melanesian religious practices, such as prayers and sacrifices, were aimed at acquiring *mana* for oneself.[46] Because of their *mana*, chiefs often played an important part in ceremonies. Sacrifices of food and animals were often made, accompanied by prayers and incantations. Human sacrifices were reserved for very special occasions.[47] Another link between law, religion and traditional society was sorcery. This was used to channel spiritual forces for good or evil purposes. Sorcery could be used to control the weather or restore good health; to impose misfortune on enemies; or defensively, as a means of protection from malevolent forces and bad luck.[48] As sorcery was greatly feared and could be used to 'pay back' or punish, it was a very effective means of social control.

The relationship of men and women in the community was reflected in religious beliefs and practices.[49] Keesing states that, in Kwaio society, religion

---

[42] Ibid.

[43] Harold M. Ross, "Leadership Styles and Strategies in a Traditional Melanesian Society," in *Rank and Status in Polynesia and Melanesia: Essays in Honour of Professor Douglas Oliver* (Paris: Société des Océanistes, 1978), 12. describes the '*wanen ifoa*' of the Baegu people as priests of ancestral spirits.

[44] Starcezca, and Cranstone, *Solomon Islanders*, 14.

[45] Fugui, "Religion" 78. In *Arosi* society it was referred to as 'mena': Charles Elliot Fox, *The Threshold of the Pacific: an Account of the Social Organization, Magic and Religion of the People of San Cristoval in the Solomon Islands* (London: Kegan Trench Trubner, 1924), 251–253.

[46] Robert Henry Codrington, *The Melanesians: Studies in their Anthropology and Folk-Lore* (Oxford: Clarendon Press, 1891), cited in Fugui, "Religion," 87.

[47] Starcezca and Cranstone, *Solomon Islanders*, 14.

[48] Fugui, "Religion," 77.

[49] Hogbin, *Guadalcanal Society*, 84.

was sometimes used as a means of reinforcing male authority, which was tacitly approved by the spirits and ancestors.[50] Impressive female gods were a rarity.[51] In the ceremonies, which were an integral part of religion and took place to commemorate all important events, only men offered sacrifices or participated in feasting.[52] There were no formal or group organized ceremonies for girls, such as there were for boys.[53] In most areas, women's contribution was restricted to food preparation, making traditional garments, weaving baskets, ropes and mats and preparing ornaments and dancing, and in some communities, being tattooed.[54] Women were excluded from certain ceremonies altogether.[55] In the Kwara'ae area, for example, only men were allowed to invoke the power of ghosts and this allowed them to assert and reinforce their own status in society.[56]

A Time of Change

Since the arrival of Europeans in Solomon Islands in the middle of the sixteenth century,[57] traditional society has changed. Much of the early contact was through Christian missionaries. The earliest of these were Catholics, accompanying Spanish explorers in the sixteenth century. However, the quest for converts did not gain momentum until the late nineteenth and early twentieth centuries. The early Marists provoked a hostile response in Isabel and Makira in the 1840s, but returned in 1898 expanding from Guadalcanal to Makira in 1909 and Malaita in 1912.[58] Meanwhile, the Anglicans had been proselytising from a safer haven, on board ship. Bishop Selwyn, in what

---

[50] Keesing, *Kwaio Religion*, 219. Keesing compares this to the process of 'celestialization', propounded by Marx.

[51] Trompf, "Pacific Islands," 125.

[52] Foanaota, "Social Change," 71.

[53] Ibid.

[54] Moffat Wasuka, "Education," in *Ples Bilong Iumi* (Suva, Institute of Pacific Studies: University of the South Pacific Press, 1989), 99. In the Kwaio area, Keesing, *Kwaio Religion*, 171, found that, "(p)articipation of women in the community rituals primarily staged by men is both significant and vital to successful performance".

[55] For an account of the restrictions on women participating in the Nagol (land diving) ceremony in neighbouring Vanuatu, see Margaret Jolly, "Kastom as Commodity," in *Culture, Kastom, Tradition: Developing Cultural Policy in Melanesia*, ed. Lamont Lindstrom and Geoffrey M. White (Suva, Institute of Pacific Studies: University of the South Pacific Press, 1994), 133. Women were also prohibited from kava ceremonies in parts of Vanuatu and the punishment for transgression of this rule was death by being buried alive: MacClancy, *To Kill a Bird*, 25.

[56] Burt, *Tradition and Christianity*, 61.

[57] Alvara de Mendana arrived in Solomon Islands in 1568, in search of King Solomon's gold.

[58] Fugui, "Religion," 85, 87.

became known as the Melanesian Mission, sailed around the country collecting young people to take back to Auckland to be trained before returning to pass on what they had learnt to their own people. In 1867 the Mission school was transferred to Norfolk Island and this remained the headquarters of the mission until 1919, when it was transferred to Siota, near Nggela.

During this time, nearly all of Isabel and Nggela had adopted the Anglican religion.[59] The Methodists, who arrived in 1902,[60] reached agreement with the Anglicans that they would work in the West, leaving the Eastern Islands to the Anglicans.[61] The Methodists monopoly was broken in 1914, when the Seventh Day Adventists arrived.[62] The first party of missionaries from the South Seas Evangelical Mission arrived in Solomon Islands in 1904, but the foundations of its teaching had already been laid by converts returning from labouring work in Queensland, Australia.[63]

The exposure to a different way of life, which occurred through these missionaries and other Europeans settlers in the nineteenth century, had a profound impact on the traditional ways of life and on religious practices. During the colonial era, customary practices were often condemned by the church as perpetuating heathen values. Some missions rigidly outlawed rituals and behaviour that they regarded as unchristian or even demonic. Christian missionaries endeavoured to "improve" the status of women by attempting to breakdown behaviour and values that they viewed, sometimes misguidedly, as demeaning.[64] A pertinent example of this was the attempt by the Methodists, South Seas Evangelical Mission and the Seventh Day Adventists to outlaw arranged marriages and the exchange of bride price, which they oversimplified as a process of buying and selling women like chattels.[65]

It is hard to say whether religious conversion was the cause or effect of this change. As Fugui puts it:

> Since traditional religion was intimately bound up with most elements of people's lives it followed that when their conditions of life changed people's attachment to their religion was likely to change. Conversely, it was likely that when people adopted a new religion that their behaviour would also change in various ways.[66]

---

[59] Ibid., 86, 87.

[60] The Methodists later became part of the United Church.

[61] Fugui, "Religion," 88, 91.

[62] Ibid., 88.

[63] Ibid., 88–89.

[64] See, e.g., below under the heading "Post Colonial Reality" and sub-heading, "Women," where the misunderstanding regarding bride price is discussed.

[65] For example, in 1932, a South Seas Evangelical Church Missionary claimed to have receives a message from God, saying that Christians should not practice bride price or smoke or chew betel nut: Pollard, "Bride Price and Christianity," 1.

[66] Fugui, "Religion," 81.

In any event, adoption of Christianity was often a "functional substitute",[67] as part of the process of adapting to a changing world, rather than conversion based on belief. For some, the Christian god was seen as a more powerful spirit, having proved this through healing where customary remedies had failed. As Fugui observes:

> [T]he new religion was adopted on much the same terms as the old one had been held. Thus belief in the power of magic and sorcery could survive the change of allegiance from the spirits to the Christian God. Indeed God could be seen as a more powerful sort of spirit, and be expected to act as one, and if he did not the people could easily revive old practices. It was as if a clean mat had been put over a dirty floor.[68]

These pragmatic 'converts' did not abandon their old beliefs, but merged one set of rituals with another.

From a legal perspective, the British administration brought with it the law of England.[69] English legislation, common law and equity were applied provided, in theory, they were appropriate to 'local circumstances.'[70] Between 1960 and the date of independence (1978), Ordinances were made locally by the Legislative Council.[71] This body of written law operated alongside customary law, which continued to be applied within 'traditional' society. To a large extent, these laws operated independently in their own spheres. Disputes at village level were determined according to customary law. The British administration encouraged this, as a means of social control that did not involve any expense.[72] In 1942, 'native' courts were, "constituted in accordance with the native law or customs of the area" in which they were to have jurisdiction.[73] They were to resolve disputes between indigenous parties, resident within the area in which they were established, on the basis of customary

---

[67] Ibid., 82.

[68] Ibid.

[69] Pacific Order in Council 1893 (UK), section 20; Western Pacific (Courts) Order 1961 (UK). Between 1893 and 1960, law was also provided by King's/Queen's Regulations, made by the High Commissioner of the Western Pacific in Fiji.

[70] Pacific Order in Council 1893 (UK), section 20. In practice common law was often applied without consideration of whether it was suitable to local circumstances. See further Jennifer Corrin Care, "Cultures in Conflict: The Role of the Common Law in the South Pacific," *Journal of South Pacific Law* 6 no. 2 (2002): 2.

[71] Between 1970 and 1974 this body was known as the Governing Council.

[72] Allan, *Customary Land Tenure*. 50, para. 64. See, e.g., Native Administration Regulation 1922, which provided for village and district headmen and the duties they would perform. However, the process of 'indirect rule' was limited in Solomon Islands, due to the fact that chiefly title was not easily determined: Allan, 62, para. 2.

[73] Native Courts Ordinance, Cap. 46, section 3.

law applying there.[74] As Solomon Islands was merely a protectorate, rather than a colony, the British administration laid no claim to land, which continued to be governed by the customary law.[75]

Some of the changes that occurred in Solomon Islands between colonization and independence were rapid and deliberate; others were gradual and unplanned. After World War II, social changes gathered force and this momentum continued up to the climax of independence. Women gained more freedom, as they were allowed to leave home before marriage to go to school. After leaving school, they might be allowed to remain in an urban centre for the purpose of pursuing paid employment. Movement by many people away from village life, into an urban environment for the purposes of work, education, or family commitments, has led to the weakening of traditional authority, particularly in urban areas. However, as is discussed later in this chapter, these changes did not necessarily benefit women.[76]

The Nominal Post-Independence Position

This section examines the nominal status of women, religion and law in post-colonial Solomon Islands, by reference to the Constitution, which has something to say about all three. The next section looks at how these three elements of society interrelate in practice. The Independence Constitution, which is declared in section 2 to be the "supreme law," contains conflicting principles in the preamble, requiring a delicate balancing of "worthy customs of our ancestors," the imperatives of "the guiding hand of God" and "principles of equality." Little guidance is given as to how this balancing act is to be performed, a matter that will be discussed further in the next section.

Protection from Discrimination

The Preamble to the Constitution pledges to "uphold the principles of equality." This is given substantive force in the Bill of Rights in Chapter II of the

---

[74] Native Courts Ordinance, Cap. 46, sections 6 and 10. These courts have been renamed as 'Local Courts' and an appeal to Customary Land Appeal Courts has been introduced: Local Courts Act, Cap. 19.

[75] The exception is Queen's Regulations No 4 of 1896, introduced to restrict he acquisition of land by foreigners. In 1959, a system of registration was introduced, but only 13 percent has been registered: Land and Titles Ordinance 1959 (SI). Earlier systems of registration existed, but conferred no guarantee of title: Proclamation of 8th November 1886; King's Regulation No 11 of 1915; King's Regulation No 6 of 1918 (Cap. 50).

[76] See text at notes 106–108, below.

Constitution, which is modeled on the Universal Declaration of Human Rights (1948), and of the European Convention for the Protection of Human Rights and Fundamental Freedoms (1953). Accordingly, the Bill expresses both the rights and freedoms, and also the exceptions to those rights and freedoms, in detailed terms. The Bill of Rights is to be given a generous and flexible interpretation unless the words are too precise to allow this.[77]

Section 15 is headed, "Protection from discrimination on grounds of race, etc." and prohibits different treatment on grounds including gender. It provides:

(1) Subject to the provisions of subsections (5), (6), and (9) of this section, no law shall make any provision that is discriminatory either of itself or in its effect.
(2) Subject to the provisions of subsections (7), (8), and (9) of this section, no person shall be treated in a discriminatory manner by any person acting by virtue of any written law or in the performance of the functions of any public office or any public authority.

. . . .

(4) In this section, the expression "discriminatory" means affording different treatment to different persons attributable wholly or mainly to their respective descriptions by race, place of origin, political opinions, colour, creed or sex whereby persons of one such description are subjected to disabilities or restrictions to which persons of another such description are not made subject or are accorded privileges or advantages which are not accorded to persons of another description.

The width of protection in section 15 is restricted by section 15(5), which contains seven paragraphs exempting certain categories of laws from the discrimination provisions. Section 15(5)(f) permits positive discrimination by stating that s 15(1) shall not apply to laws for the advancement of the more disadvantaged members of society. Paragraph (g) follows on from this by allowing special laws to be made for disadvantaged groups, whether advantageous or not, provided they are justifiable in a democratic society. Paragraph (a) exempts tax and revenue laws; paragraph (b) exempts laws relating to non-citizens; and paragraph (e) exempts land laws.

Paragraph 15(5)(d) provides that nothing in any law shall be held to be discriminatory to the extent that it makes provision for the, "application of customary law." It is not entirely clear whether this paragraph is intended to exempt all customary laws from the anti-discrimination provision or whether

[77] *Kenilorea v. Attorney-General* (1984) SILR 179, *Loumia v. DPP* (1985/86) SILR 158, following *Hinds v. The Queen* (1977) AC 195 and *Minister of Home Affairs v. Fisher* (1980) AC 319.

its protection is limited to laws designed to govern the *application* of customary law. The High Court has expressed a preference for the former interpretation.[78] However, the latter interpretation is supported by the two preceding paragraphs. Section 15(5)(b) exempts any law that makes provision, "with respect to persons who are not citizens of Solomon Islands," whilst s 15(5)(c) exempts laws providing for the "application, in the case of [non-citizens] of . . . the personal law applicable to [them]." If exemption of laws governing "application" was no different from exemption of all personal laws, s 15(5)(c) would be otiose. Rather, s 15(5)(c) is intended to legitimize legislation such as the Pacific Order in Council 1893,[79] which governs the application of certain British laws to British subjects.

A restrictive interpretation also coincides with s 75(1) of the Constitution, which directs Parliament to, "make provision for the application of laws, including customary laws."[80] However, until the High Court or Court of Appeal rules otherwise, customary law is shielded from attack on the basis of anti-discrimination, leaving women with an empty promise of protection.

Freedom of Religion

The preamble to the Constitution states that "the people of Solomon Islands ... do now, under the guiding hand of God, establish the sovereign democratic State of Solomon Islands." During the local discussion on proposals for the new Constitution there was concern about new evangelical religions attempting to establish a foothold in the country. Attempts to gain converts often involved a challenge to traditional authorities that endorsed one of the established churches. It was argued that freedom of religion should be restricted to churches established prior to independence. In the end, the view that this was a matter for legislation prevailed.[81] Accordingly, section 11

---

[78] *Tanavalu v. Tanavalu*, unreported, High Court, Solomon Islands, Civ.Cas 185/1995, 12 January 1998. The decision was upheld by the Court of Appeal: *Tanavalu v.Tanavalu*, unreported, Court of Appeal, Solomon Islands, Civ.App 3/1998. See also, *Minister for Provincial Government v.Guadalcanal Provincial Assembly*, unreported, High Court, Solomon Islands, CAC 3/97, April 23, 1997.

[79] SI 78 of 1893 (UK).

[80] Parliament's only attempt to fulfill its mandate under section 75(1) is the Custom Recognition Act 2000. This Act makes provision for proving customary law before a court. Its commencement has been postponed and, given the flaws in the Act, it is unlikely that it will come in to force. See further: Jean Zorn and Jennifer Corrin Care, "Proving Customary Law in the Common Law Courts of the South Pacific," Occasional Paper Number Two (London: British Institute of International and Comparative Law, 2002).

[81] Yash Ghai, ed., *Law, Politics and Government in Pacific States* (Suva, Institute of Pacific Studies: University of the South Pacific Press 1988), 45.

of the Constitution contains a guarantee of freedom of religion, under the banner of "Protection of Freedom of Conscience":

(1) Except with his own consent no person shall be hindered in the enjoyment of his freedom of conscience, and for the purposes of this section the said freedom includes freedom of thought and of religion, freedom to change his religion or belief, and freedom, either alone or in community with others, and both in public and in private, to manifest and propagate his religion or belief in worship, teaching, practice and observance.

The section goes on to entitle religious groups to set up schools (s 11(2)) and to include religious instruction in the subjects taught (s 11(4)). However, by section 11(4) religious instruction and participation in religious ceremonies or observances may not be made compulsory. Neither, according to section 11(6)(b), may any person be compelled to take any oath that is contrary to his or her religious beliefs. Furthermore, in that sub-section it is expressly stated that action may lawfully be taken to protect the right to practise and observe any religion without the unsolicited intervention of members of any other religion. Thus, domination by stronger Churches may be avoided. The width of protection in section 11 is restricted by section 11(6), which exempts laws made in the interests of defence, public safety, public order, public morality or public health, provided they are reasonably justifiable in a democratic society. Freedom of expression, which includes the right to express religious views, is also constitutionally protected in section 12.

There has only been one reported adjudication on the right to freedom of religion although there have been various appeals for restrictions on establishment of a foothold by additional religions.[82] Further there has been no reported case on the right to freedom of expression, in so far as it relates to religious views, although there has been the occasional objection to national radio broadcasts by the Baha'i Faith. Such disputes have always been settled and the Baha'i continue to broadcast. The Ministry of Home and Ecclesiastical Affairs has a nominal policy-making role concerning religion. The Ministry's policy objective in this regard is stated as, "to coordinate and promote more effectively ecclesiastical affairs of the people as provided for in the National Constitution for the freedom of association and worship."[83] All religious institutions are required to register with the Government. However, there have been no reports of refusal to register any group.

---

[82] *Lobo v. Limanilove and Others*, unreported, High Court, Solomon Islands, civ. cas. 101/2001, March 28, 2002. For examples of appeals, see, e.g., Constitutional Review Committee, *Report* (Honiara, 1987) vol. I, 348, 363, 368, 389, 392, 410, 415, 422, 424, 428, 472, 527, 535, 538, 583, 587.

[83] Solomon Islands Government Plan of Action, Para. 4.1.2, Policy Objective 3 (c).

Customary Law and Introduced Law

The components of the formal law are spelt out in the Constitution. Below the supreme law of the Constitution in the hierarchy is locally enacted statute law. This is followed by English statutes of general application.[84] Customary law is elevated to source of law in the formal hierarchy above the common law and arguably on a par with English statutes.[85] Common law and equity complete the sources of law that may be relied upon in the formal courts. This includes English common law and equity up to the date of independence, provided that it is appropriate to the circumstances of the country.[86]

English statutes and common law were retained as sources of law as a transitional measure. It was envisaged that they would gradually be replaced by more appropriate local enactments and judicial decisions. Unfortunately, this has been very slow to happen and English legislation and case law still play a dominant role in the law of Solomon Islands, applied in the formal courts, and particularly in the Supreme Court and Court of Appeal. Whilst, historically, the law of England was as patriarchal as customary law, reforms introduced in the wake of the suffrage movement and based on notions of independent rights and equality have been introduced.[87] Reforms in force in England prior to 1 January 1961 (in the case of statutes) and 7 July 1978 (in the case of common law) became part of the laws that were "saved" in Solomon Islands.[88]

Together with the introduced guarantees of freedoms and equality, discussed above, these reforms created a situation of conflict with the patriarchal norms of customary law. The potential for friction was, of course, increased by the elevation of customary law to a formal source of law. Surprisingly little thought appears to have been given to how the inevitable conflict would be resolved. The position is confused because the Constitution states that customary law is not to be applied if it is inconsistent with the Constitution or a locally enacted statute.[89] It might therefore be assumed that if a customary law is inconsistent with a constitutionally protected human right it will be void. However, as pointed out

[84] In force on January 1, 1961.

[85] Constitution of Solomon Islands, section 76 and schl. 3, para. 2(1)(c).

[86] Ibid., section 76 and schl. 3, para. 2(1)(b).

[87] Reforms between 1923 and 1937 established equal status for men and women in marriage and the anomalies of the separate property system were removed. See further Stetson, *Woman's Issue*, 9–10.

[88] These are the respective 'cut-off dates' imposed on introduced law: Constitution of Solomon Islands 1978, schl. 3, para. 1; *Cheung v. Tanda* (1984) SILR 108. Solomon Islands did not receive the benefits of the far reaching reforms of family law contained in the Divorce Reform Act 1969 and the Matrimonial Proceedings and Property Act 1970, which recognize that marriage is a relationship of shared responsibilities.

[89] Constitution of Solomon Islands, section 76 and schl. 3, para. 3(2). In the case of the Constitution this is supported by its status as supreme law: section 2.

above, according to the current interpretation by the High Court, discriminatory customary laws are shielded by section 15(5)(d).[90] On the other hand, religious freedom is protected from any attack founded in customary law, of the type that has been seen in Polynesia, where the traditional penalty of banishment has been used to prevent deviation from the religion endorsed by village chiefs.[91]

Post-Colonial Reality

Women and Law

In theory, independence heralded an era of liberation for women as constitutional guarantees were accompanied by a spirit of reformation. However, constitutional promise failed to evolve into tangible cultural change. As discussed above, the constitutional pledge in the Preamble to "uphold the principles of equality" has been restricted by an interpretation of the section dealing with discrimination that shields discriminatory customary laws from its protection.[92] Further, the Court of Appeal has shown a reluctance to strike down discriminatory laws even where they are not directly within that exemption. For example, it has refused to set aside legislation that restricted women's representation in local government.[93]

In any event, anti-discrimination provisions only apply in the public jural domain.[94] Most personal experience is in the private sphere. In this arena, it

---

[90] *Tanavalu v. Tanavalu*, unreported, High Court, Solomon Islands, Civ. Cas. 185/1995, January 12, 1998.

[91] The courts in Samoa have upheld the right to freedom of religion in a series of cases: *Mau Sefo, Osasa Aukuso v. The Attorney General & The Alii and Faipule of Saipipi*, unreported, Supreme Court, Samoa, July 12, 2000; *Tuivaiti v. Faamalaga and Others* (1980–93) WSLR 19; See, for example, *Tuivaiti v. Sila and Others* (1980–93) WSLR 19; *Lafaialii v. Attorney General*, unreported, Supreme Court, Samoa, April 24, 2003.

[92] See further Kenneth Brown, and Jennifer Corrin Care, "Conflict in Melanesia—Customary Law and the Rights of Melanesian Women," *Commonwealth Law Bulletin* 24 nos 3 & 4 (1998): 1334–1355. For similar observations in relation to Papua New Guinea, see *State v. Kopilyo Kipungi*, unreported, National Court, Papua New Guinea, N437/1983, where Los J. stated, "Although the equality of the sexes is now a constitutional principle in Papua New Guinea, at this stage it is more a matter for the books, rather than practice. For a contrary view, see Narokobi, "There's No Need for Women's Lib Here," 70.

[93] *The Minister for Provincial Government v. Guadalcanal Provincial Assembly*, unreported, High Court, Solomon Islands, CAC 3/97, April 23, 1997, 26. The Court's rationale for this decision was that, as Parliament was charged by the Constitution with providing for the position of traditional chiefs in local government, the fact that the formula it had devised for doing so was discriminatory was sanctioned by the constitution itself. This reasoning fails to take into account the fact that section 15(1) of the Constitution specifically outlaws discriminatory laws.

[94] The Court of Appeal has held that the fundamental rights provisions do not apply between private individuals but only to disputes involving the State: *Ulufa'alu (Prime Minister) v. Governor-General* (2001) 1 LRC 425.

would appear that the status of women in the post-independence State is not much improved. As Solomon Islands women's activist Dalcy Paina observes:

> The gender equality preached by women's organisations in Solomon Islands is sneered upon by Guadalcanal men. To them, it is a threat to their dominance and power over women. When men were interviewed, they admitted that they believe that a woman's role is in the kitchen and that she should not take over the role of head of the family, as supported by the Bible. Gender equality is thus never promoted in Guadalcanal. Our men are very resistant to changing their outlook on the role of women.[95]

Customary law and society are still male-dominated and, as Dalcy Paina's remarks indicate, Solomon Islands men are quick to use Christian scripture to reinforce and justify female subordination.[96] Traditional leadership roles are confined to men and decision making, except perhaps in relation to some household matters, is normally within their domain. To quote Paina again:

> [I]n any big decision making process, such as the sale of family land or other matters, women can attend and contribute but it is the men who have the final say.[97]

Even in those parts of the region where title to land descends through matrilineal lines, such as Guadalcanal, land disputes are generally litigated by men.[98] Many examples of women's continuing lack of power are apparent in the domestic sphere. As Polini Boseto remarks:

> Women are trusted as supervisors and implementaters of most household duties in relation to the preparation and distribution of food from the gardens, caring for every members' and visitors' comfort, and teaching the young girls on a day to day basis (boys are usually under the direct supervision of their fathers).... The burden of gardening, cooking, child-bearing, etc are women's primary task and must confine them to the home.[99]

---

[95] Dalcy Tovosia Paina, "Peacemaking in Solomon Islands: The experience of the Guadalcanal Women for Peace Movement," *Development Bulletin* 53 (2000): 47–48.

[96] See further Brown and Corrin Care, 'Conflict in Melanesia', 1334. In relation to Fiji, see e.g., submissions by the Fiji Women's Rights Movement and the Women's Crisis Centre, *Report of the Commission of Inquiry on the Courts* (Suva, Fiji, 1984), 172.

[97] Paina, "Peacemaking in Solomon Islands," 47.

[98] See e.g., *Maerua v. Kahanatarau* (1983) SILR 95. See also, A. Chowning, "Women are our Business," in *Dealing with Inequality: Analysing Gender Relations in Melanesia and Beyond*, ed. Marilyn Strathern (Cambridge: Cambridge University Press, 1987), 130–149. Land disputes must be dealt with by traditional leaders in the first instance: Local Court Act, Cap. 19, section 12. If no settlement is reached, application may be made to the local court, from which there is an appeal to the Customary Land Appeal Court: Local Court Act, Cap. 19 and Land and Titles Act, Cap. 133. These courts are presided over by local elders who are male. There is one female justice of the local court, but the court to which she was appointed is not currently operating.

[99] Polini Boseto, "Melanesian Women, Mothers of Democracy," (paper presented at the "Women, Christians, Citizens: Being Female in Melanesia Today Workshop" organized by the Australian National University's Society and Governance in Melanesia Project, Sorrento, Victoria, November 11–13, 1998), http://rspas.anu.edu.au/melanesia/polini.html.

The payment of bride price has often been misunderstood as being akin to buying and selling a woman like a chattel. Whilst it is now generally acknowledged as being a far more complex transaction, which may operate as an acknowledgement of the worth of a woman in traditional society, bride price may nevertheless have adverse implications for a woman. As Alice Aruheeta Pollard observes:[100]

> [T]he girl has little choice over the man she marries and is often dictated [to] by her parents and relatives. Shell money is used as a powerful tool in the whole system. Once the family's wealth through shell money is displayed, it is likely that the girl must give a positive answer towards the proposal. A negative response might result in harsh words and ill feelings.

It may also mean that a woman loses the right to custody of her children in the event of divorce or the death of her husband. In Solomon Islands' custom, custody is generally determined by reference to the payment of the bride price. If payment is made by the husband's family to that of the wife, the children prima facie remain with the father on dissolution or with his family on his death.[101] As Pollard points out:[102]

> [A]ny children born to the couple are already covered under the exchange of the gifts and it is considered that they belong to both tribes but more so to the male's side although they have equal access to their mother's side and land.

The case of *Sasango v. Beliga*[103] demonstrates this. When the husband died, his brothers took custody of his seven children and certain custom valuables, including pigs, shell money and porpoise teeth. The mother was compelled to apply to the formal courts for their return. The brothers argued that, according to Malaita custom, the children and the property passed to them after the death of the husband as the brothers had contributed to the bride price for the mother. The court awarded custody to the mother on the basis that this was in the best interests of the child, which according to the introduced statute law, is the paramount consideration in determining custody.[104] It was also ordered that the property be returned to the mother, on the basis that there was no impartial evidence of a customary law that a widow must give up all her personal property to the husband's relatives. Similarly, in *K v. T and KU*[105]

---

[100] Pollard, "Bride Price and Christianity," 2.

[101] See *In re. B* (1983) SILR 33, which sets out the basic position in Melanesian custom.

[102] Ibid.

[103] (1987) SILR 91.

[104] Guardianship of Infants Act 1925 (UK), section 1. This is in force as an act of general application, and part of the 'saved' introduced law. But see *Krishnan v. Kumari* (1955) 28 Law Reports of Kenya 32, where the court held that the Guardianship of Infants Act 1925 (UK) was not an act of general application in Kenya.

[105] (1985/86) SILR 49.

the mother was pursuing custody against paternal relatives, the father of the children having died. The magistrate regarded the mother's willingness to challenge customary law as demonstrating her, "courage and deep love for her children."[106] The welfare principle was applied and custody awarded to the mother.

Traditional practices have certainly changed since colonisation and indeed continue to change, however custom is being defined by men and it may be that in the process customs which benefit women are being lost.[107] It is arguable that women's position has worsened since independence. The importance of tasks such as tending a *sup sup* garden[108] has been diminished by Western influences, which regard such tasks as demeaning. As Sheyvens notes:

> Women are experiencing a decline in status and power as dependency on the cash economy and imported political and social systems become more entrenched [. . .] Pacific women often held a prestigious place in traditional society; they were economically active as producers, manufacturers, market managers and healers. Now women are increasingly marginalized. They are the least educated or consulted in the community.[109]

Further, freedom may be illusory when the benefits of communal living are no longer available. For example, a single mother living in an urban area can no longer rely on her relatives to assist her with bringing up her children. This may prevent her from working and ultimately force her to return to the village.

Outside the customary sphere, women have faired little better. The patriarchal underpinning of the social structure has been carried forward, through the colonial administration, into the present era. Colonial authorities sanctioned the entrenchment of male power in all three arms of the imported Westminster system of government. As demonstrated in the custody cases set out above, pre-1961 English legislation may sometimes be to the advantage of women. However, few women are likely to access the courts. Only 15 percent of the population are classified as 'urban dwellers'[110] and in rural areas

---

[106] Ibid., 53.

[107] A possible example of this from Vanuatu is mentioned by David Roe, Ralph Regenvanu, Francois Wadra and Nick Araho, "Working with Cultural Landscapes in Melanesia: Some Problems and Approaches in the Formulation of Cultural Policies," in Lindstrom and White, *Culture, Kastom, Tradition*, 127. Any sites of cultural significance to women were not recorded by field officers when a survey was done prior to the construction of a road linking villages on Malakula Island.

[108] Market garden, where vegetables are grown for food and trading.

[109] See Julia Nesbitt, ed., *Development in the Pacific: What Women Say* (Canberra: Australian Council for Overseas Aid, 1986), iv, cited in Regina Shyvens, "*Church Women's Groups and the Empowerment of Women in the Solomon Islands*," (paper presented at the "Women, Christians, Citizens: Being Female in Melanesia Today Workshop" organized by the Australian National University's Society and Governance in Melanesia Project, Sorrento, Victoria, November 11–13, 1998) http://rspas.anu.edu.au/melanesia/Scheyvens.html.

[110] *Solomon Islands 1999 Population and Housing Census*, 2000, Solomon Islands Census Office, Honiara.

customary law is far more relevant.[111] Moreover, the introduced law is not always of assistance to women because the welfare principle has not always been applied to the advantage of the mother. In *Molu v. Molu*,[112] for example, the court interpreted the welfare principle in a manner that endorsed the customary abduction of a two-year-old boy. The child had been taken by the husband's brother against the mother's wishes on the breakdown of the marriage. The husband's family's argument was that they "had paid [for] her already," meaning that bride price had been paid and consequently they were entitled to, at least, one of the children. Rather than condemning this *de facto* assumption of custody, the Court granted custody to the father and care and control to his relatives, justifying the decision on the ground that it was not in the best interests of the child to move from an environment in which he was allegedly happy and settled. In *Sukutaona v. Houanihou*,[113] the Chief Justice made it clear that the application of the introduced 'welfare of the child' principle did not render customary law irrelevant. Rather it was, "an important factor in deciding where that interest lies".[114]

Laws are often a compromise between the interests of different stakeholders, having been thrashed out over time and moulded by contemporary opinion over years, decades or even centuries. In the case of introduced law, this process does not occur. Rather, a whole body of law is transported to a different environment, in which the forces that originally shaped the law may not exist or may take a very different shape. Since independence, successive governments, suffering from a lack of cohesive policies and scarcity of resources, have been slow to enact 'home grown' legislation to replace the introduced law, as was intended. For example, the pre-Independence Islanders Divorce Act,[115] which is still in place, affords the wife no right to claim matrimonial property, but only to claim maintenance.[116] The husband, on the other hand, is entitled by section 18(1) to claim damages from the co-respondent where he is petitioning on the grounds of adultery. One piece of amending legislation that does stand out is the Affiliation Separation and Maintenance (Amendment) Act 1992. Based on an English model, the Act affords a straightforward avenue

---

[111] Law Reform Commission of Solomon Islands, *Annual Report* (Honiara, 1996), 10–11, para. 10.11.

[112] Unreported, Supreme Court, Vanuatu, Civ. Cas. 30/1996.

[113] (1982) SILR 12.

[114] Ibid.

[115] Cap. 48, section 21.

[116] The position has to some extent been remedied by judicial activism, which has made awards on the basis that equality is equity, although there appears to be no authority for doing so: *Kuper v. Kuper*, unreported, High Court, Solomon Islands, Civ. Cas. 12/987 and *Cheffers v. Cheffers*, unreported, High Court, Solomon Islands, Civ. Cas. 142/1990.

for obtaining *ex parte* injunctive relief, in the case of domestic violence. It incorporates supporting powers of arrest and remand. However, this Act is an exception to the general failure to introduce any legislation that might indicate a serious approach to gender equality.

The benchmark of equality set out in the Constitution requires specific legislation to make it a reality, but there is little sign of a structured program of reform. Lack of desire to change the status quo is also evidenced by Solomon Islands reluctance to become a party to the United Nations Convention on the Elimination of All Forms of Discrimination against Women (1979) (CEDAW). It finally became a State Party to the Convention on May 6, 2002, nearly twenty-four years after the pledge of equality was made in the Constitution.[117] It has yet to submit a National Action Plan[118] or a report to the CEDAW Committee.[119] In the most recent elections the one female Member of Parliament lost her seat.[120] The Ministry of Women, Youth and Sports has been dismantled. Few women hold high judicial or legal office.[121] There have been no women appointed as judges, only two as magistrates and one as a Local Court justice.[122] However, the number of women lawyers has dramatically increased within the last two years and women have been employed in the Attorney General's Department and Public Solicitor's Office.[123]

Women and Religion

In theory, Solomon Islands is founded on the Christian principles highlighted in the preamble to the constitution; it is a democratic State, "under the guiding hand of God". Ninety six percent of Solomon Islands are Christian. This includes members of the five major churches in the Solomon Islands, being the Church of Melanesia or Anglican Church (35 percent); the Roman Catholic

---

[117] Solomon Islands also ratified the Optional Protocol on May 6, 2002.

[118] The Beijing Platform of Action requires Plans of Action to be submitted to the UN Division for the Advancement of Women. Fiji Islands is the only South Pacific island country to have submitted a Plan.

[119] The CEDAW Committee was established under Article 18 to receive and comment on reports and make recommendations to assist countries to meet their obligations under CEDAW. To date Fiji and Samoa are only South Pacific island countries to submit reports.

[120] See statistics compiled by International Parliamentary Union, at October 20, 2003, http://www.ipu.org/wmn-e/classif.htm.

[121] There was an exception in the early 1990s, when the same woman lawyer was appointed as Registrar General and then as Chair of the Trade Disputes Panel. She has since returned to private practice.

[122] The Local Court in which she was appointed a justice is presently inoperative.

[123] In fact the Public Solicitor's office had a female legal officer from the early 1990's until she left to go into private practice. A recently qualified woman was taken on in 2003.

Church (20 percent); the South Seas Evangelical Church (18 percent); the United Church (11 percent); and the Seventh Day Adventist Church (10 percent).[124] The Baha'i faith and Jehovah's Witnesses also have a visible presence in Solomon Islands. There are a small number of Hindus and Muslims in the country, but neither group has an established place of worship. However, a numerical analysis of Church membership fails to reveal the unique features of Melanesian Christianity. Solomon Islands is usually proclaimed to be a predominantly Christian country. Certainly, 96 percent of the population declared themselves as Christian in the last census.[125] People announce their denominational allegiances proudly and publicly by their attendance at Church and contribution to fundraising.

However, Christianity and allegiance to a particular religious group may often be based on pragmatism rather than an intellectual or spiritual commitment.[126] A significant level of syncretism endures amongst many Solomon Islanders and customary rituals often take place alongside or combined with Christian worship.[127] Whilst noting that changes in conditions of life led to changes in attachment to traditional religion, Fugui acknowledges that:

> [E]lements of the traditional religion were often retained by people who had adopted a new faith. Even today, some Christians are still prepared to invoke the influence of spirit when they think it might be helpful to them.[128]

In this context, it is hardly surprising that emanicpatory readings of Christianity's central texts, which could be used to endorse equal relationships between men and women, have not been entrenched in every day life. In the event of conflict with customary norms, only those with an intellectual commitment to the Gospel are likely to prefer Christian values. In any event, the practical application of Christian ideals has not always been as attractive as the theory.[129] Equality bears the proviso that women must fulfil their domestic obligations by being a good wife and mother; the yoke in the gardens may have been replaced by apron strings in the home.

Further, during the move to independence, the search for national identity resulted in renewed emphasis on tradition. The Churches, particularly the

---

[124] Solomon Islands 1999 Population and Housing Census.

[125] Ibid.

[126] See further, Fugui, "Religion," 81.

[127] For example, in 1988, the consecration of the new Church was in Buala, Isabel Province, was accompanied by custom dancing and feasting. See also Boseto, "Melanesian Women, Mothers of Democracy."

[128] Fugui, "Religion," 81.

[129] As is well documented, religion, as well as 'culture', is often considered to be the source of women's oppression in many countries: Rebecca Cook, "Women's Human Rights Law: the Way Forward," *Human Rights Quarterly* 15 (1993): 230–61.

Catholics and Anglicans,[130] relaxed their approach to custom, allowing religion to operate in a cultural context. For example, bride price ceremonies were, generally, allowed, although conditions might be attached, such as the limit of 5 red money and $200, imposed by the South Seas Evangelical Church.[131] In return, Christianity was exempted from the taint of colonialism and imperialism, and allowed to increase its areas of influence. The extent of this influence cannot be explained by strength of membership alone. Due to the inattention of central and, to a lesser extent, provincial governments to the needs of rural societies, the Churches appear to have become a surrogate authority. They have filled the gap between the remote and unfamiliar Western style of government and the traditional authority of chiefs in remote villages. They have provided services and education, and they expect denominational allegiance to be given in return.

As shown in the statistics of affiliations, there is no one dominant Church. However, there are regional strongholds in Isabel and Temotu provinces, where the Anglicans are dominant and in areas of Western Province, where the United Church is strong. Whilst these regional affiliations could be regarded as entrenching local loyalties, perhaps even creating a new tribalism, Christianity seems to have acted as a uniting force. In areas other than those mentioned above, denominations cut across island, if not tribal, boundaries. For example, on Malaita there are congregations of Catholics, Anglicans, South Seas Evangelical Church and Seventh Day Adventists, albeit that the distribution will usually coincide with tribal groupings. Malaita is also the home of the *Kwaio*, who are followers of traditional religion.[132] Further, the uniting force of worshipping the same God and the Christian dictate to 'love thy neighbour,' may be gradually relaxing the demands of the *wantok* system.[133] Further, a platform for a united fellowship has been provided by Solomon Islands Christian Association, the umbrella organisation of the five longest established Christian churches of the country. Joint religious activities, such as religious representation at national events, are organized through this Association. Non-denominational worship is frequently encountered, for example in the form of prayers and hymns sung at major events.

Whilst Christianity purports to operate on the basis of equality, positions of authority within the church are usually dominated by men,[134] although there

---

[130] The Catholic and Anglican Churches only insisted on monogamy, respect for life, and the denial of the power of the spirits: Fugui, "Religion," 90.

[131] Pollard, "Bride Price."

[132] See further, Keesing, *Kwaio Religion*, 224.

[133] *Wantok*, literally 'one talk', refers to members of the same customary group who have an obligation to support each other.

[134] This is also the case in neighbouring Vanuatu: see Lissant Bolton, "Praying for the Revival of *Kastom*: Women and Christianity in the Vanuatu Cultural Centre," (paper presented

are signs of a very gradual change, particularly in some Churches.[135] However, whilst high office in the central hierarchy is denied them, women are allowed to form Church groups, such as the Mother's Union, a society of Anglican women; the Women's League, which is the Catholic equivalent;[136] and the United Church Women's Fellowship (UCWF), the women's arm of the Methodist Church. By way of example, the aims of the UCWF have been summarized as including the following:

> to express their love for Jesus Christ through Education, Devotion, Recreation and Service;
>
> to promote the educational standard of women and to uphold the dignity of women
>
> to help women to strive for freedom from all forms of oppression against women and humankind in general.[137]

In providing this opportunity, the Church brought about change for women incidentally. Women had an outlet for their organisational skills and a forum for networking and confidence building. The UCWF has also been instrumental in gaining better representation for women in the church hierarchy.[138]

However, there are limitations on the effectiveness of Church affiliated women's groups. The groups often operate within a context where the role of women is seen predominantly as one of wife and mother rather than as an individual or even community member, with identity outside the family.[139] There is evidence that this emphasis on family values prevents Church groups from joining women's political organizations, which are accused of undermining those values. Opponents to these organizations frequently cite the scriptures in support of their criticisms.[140] The recent conflict in Solomon Islands may

---

at the "Women, Christians, Citizens: Being Female in Melanesia Today Workshop" organized by the Australian National University's Society and Governance in Melanesia Project, Sorrento, Victoria, November 11–13, 1998) http://rspas.anu.edu.au/melanesia/lissant2.html. At footnote 5, Bolton records that there are exceptions to this, for example, there are two women pastors in the Presbyterian Church.

[135] In 1989 the synod of the United Church accepted a recommendation by the UCWF that at least one quarter of synod membership should be women.

[136] Foanaota, "Social Change," 71.

[137] Boseto, "Melanesian Women, Mothers of Democracy."

[138] See further, Sheyvens, "Church Women's Groups and the Empowerment of Women."

[139] W. Lee, "Women's Groups in Papua New Guinea: Shedding the legacy of drop scones and embroidered pillowcases." *Community Development Journal* 20 no. 3 (1985), 233. The same was true of women's church groups in England. The Mother's Union was one of the most vocal opponents to divorce reform in the early 1900's: Royal Commission on Marriage and Divorce 1912–13, *Report* (Cmnd 6478), 371.

[140] For a similar observations on women's church groups in Papua New Guinea, see Lee "Women's Groups in Papua New Guinea," 233.

have helped to break down some of these barriers and has seen some women's groups join together, under the banner of the National Council of Women, to call for peace and democracy. It has also seen women come together in Women for Peace (WFP), an interdenominational group of women, resident in Honiara. But the emphasis on the traditional role is still evident in the aim of WFP, which has been expressed to be taking a 'motherly approach' in working for peace.[141] The National Council of Women has also allied itself with the Church, holding a high profile service to pray for peace, reconciliation, good governance and democracy in the Anglican cathedral. Notwithstanding the continuing need to channel their voices though the medium of the Church and family, the conflict has been an important avenue for the development of the profile of women.

Further, whilst Christianity may not have overcome the traditional attitudes of men towards women, any more than it has in other countries of the world, it cannot be denied that it has at least passed on the ideal of equality. As Polini Boseto observes:

> The Christian Gospels message of equal participation of men and women in Church and society has opened the eyes of our women to discover their place and role in the Melanesian context today.[142]

Conclusion

In post-colonial Solomon Islands change has been inevitable. However, introduction of a veneer of Western ideology and institutions, which do not fit smoothly against the existing fabric of society, does not necessarily equate with progress. As far as women are concerned, constitutional pledges of freedom and equality have not produced tangible benefits and the extent to which they are capable of doing so is limited. Whilst written laws may signal an intention and serve as a symbolic affirmation of human rights, it takes more than statute law to change deeply imbedded structures and attitudes. Outside the main towns, life is still lived according to the rules of traditional society.[143] Both strength of will and means of support are required to disobey these rules, as the women in the cases discussed above were compelled by maternal bonds to do. In one of those cases, *K v. T and KU*,[144] the presiding Magistrate

---

141 Pollard, "Resolving Conflict in Solomon Islands," 44.

142 Boseto, "Melanesian Women, Mothers of Democracy."

143 The fact that those rules may have been adulterated by colonization does not alter the fact that they are still treated as binding within the community: see note 10, above.

144 (1985/86) SILR 49, 53.

commented on the, "remarkable tenacity shown by the mother" in fighting, "to keep her children and provide for them, in spite of financial hardship and strong male customary dominance." Meanwhile, the stability and protection offered to women by the customary system have arguably become more bitter than sweet, after the promises of equality and independence have failed to transpire.[145] As Parks cautions, there is a danger that, "Solomon Island women will become trapped within a new set of societal values that recognizes their need for greater autonomy, yet does little to alleviate or appreciate their workload."[146]

Solomon Islands is now faced with the challenge of rebuilding its society in the aftermath of the recent armed conflict (1999–2003). In order to move forward, answers must be found to some fundamental questions. How can trust and a sense of nationhood be engendered in a custom-based society, which has been divided along ethnic lines? Are traditional practices flexible enough to allow the benefits of the customary system to be retained, whilst the elements that lead to inequality and injustice are discarded?[147] Is it possible to encourage the development of a sense of national pride, balanced with a critical attitude to aspects of culture that do not promote the common good? Part of the overarching problem of finding an appropriate system of governance[148] is the question of how to find a legal system that accommodates both introduced and indigenous law and legal systems. Solutions based on moulding customary concepts to an approximate common law equivalent have proved to be completely inadequate. Areas of conflict require careful analysis[149] and

---

[145] There is still scant published research on customary law and traditional practices relating to women.

[146] Will Parks, "Blessed Maternity and Maternal Blame: The Paradox of Motherhood in Marovo, Solomon Islands," (paper presented at the "Women, Christians, Citizens: Being Female in Melanesia Today Workshop" organized by the Australian National University's Society and Governance in Melanesia Project, Sorrento, Victoria, November 11–13, 1998) http://rspas.anu.edu.au/melanesia/blessed.html.

[147] In *In Re. Miriam Willingal*, unreported, National Court, Papua New Guinea, Civ. Cas. N1506, February 10, 1997, www.vanuatu.usp.ac.fj/paclawmat/PNG_cases/Re_Willingal.html > (accessed 20 April 20, 2004), Injia J. considered that the framers of similar conflicting provisions in the Constitution of Papua New Guinea "were thinking about a modern PNG based on ethnic societies whose welfare and advancement was based on the maintenance and promotion of good traditional customs and the discouragement and elimination of bad customs as seen from the eyes of an ordinary modern Papua New Guinean."

[148] See further, Jennifer Corrin Care, "Off the Peg or Made to Measure: Is the Westminster System of Government Appropriate in Solomon Islands?" *Alternative Law Journal* 27 no. 5 (2002): 207–211.

[149] For examples of conflict arising in the field of human rights see Jennifer Corrin Care, "Reconciling Customary Law and Human Rights in Melanesia," *Hibernian Law Journal* 4 (2003): 53–76.

consideration of women's perspectives are a necessary part of this process. An original, even daring, approach is required to accommodate legal and cultural pluralism; a unique solution is required for a unique country.

Within this general debate, women are seeking to renegotiate their position in society, without losing important links with the past and the benefits of those aspects of custom that continue to have relevance for them. Religion may indirectly form a vital lifeline in this search, allowing women entry to debates on rebuilding government and seeking national identity. Just as Solomon Islands Christian Association spans religious and ethnic divisions, so have the women's church groups combined in the NCW and WFP as a powerful voice for women. Gradually, these platforms may bridge the divide between the traditional situation of women and a position where they may influence society at a national level without the need to channel their voices though the medium of the church and family. Additionally, religion serves as an outstanding example of how philosophy and argument may be indigenized to make it more meaningful to a local audience. The sharp division between religion and culture, which originally caused tension and resistance, has been blurred. Christianity has arguably become inseparable from other aspects of customary life in the same way that traditional religion once was and, to some extent, still is. In the same way, women may develop a human rights agenda with local resonance.[150] In a country where children are still dying of measles and malaria, political correctness is low on the list of concerns. Gender issues are likely to become less threatening to men and more accessible to women when placed in a context to which they can relate. Most men appear to support equal opportunity for women in education, although they may still struggle with the idea of women as leaders of traditional groups or organs of government. Women have already demonstrated their talent for repositioning debate by advancing their struggle for a voice in society within the boundaries of church and family. Now, perhaps, is an opportune time to extend this to a wider cultural context.

---

150 Ibid.

CHAPTER FIVE

WOMEN, RELIGION, AND THE LAW IN AOTEAROA/ NEW ZEALAND: THE COMPLEXITY OF ACCOMMODATING DIFFERENT VALUE SYSTEMS IN LAW

Margaret Bedggood and Leah Whiu

Introduction

From amongst the many stories that could be told about the relations between gender, religion, and law in Aotearoa/New Zealand, we chronicle two: an account of the dominant Pākehā (white settler) people's experiences (written by a Pākehā woman) and an account written from the perspective of the indigenous Māori women of Aotearoa (written by a Māori woman). These accounts, of course, are not reflective of the experiences of women who are neither Māori nor Pākehā, and they are not intended to be. Rather, our self-consciously binary approach has been adopted because it permits us to disrupt the falsely universal assumptions embedded in the old feminist slogan 'we are all women,' and to focus more sharply upon the differing experiences of, and sometimes fraught encounters between, settler Pākehā and the indigenous Māori.

This chapter, then, is in two distinct parts. It will be apparent that a major theme in both parts is the complex and sometimes paradoxical impact of Western law and values, particularly the formal anti-discrimination regime, upon the way that both Māori and Pākehā women experience their own cultures and faiths.

The first part begins by tracing the position of Pākehā women in law and society from 1840–1970, considering in particular the subtle influence of organized Christian religion upon that development. It then examines the more recent legal developments concerning the position of women from 1970 to the present, focusing in particular upon the extent to which New Zealand has adopted, recognized and implemented international human rights norms domestically. It then explores the relationship between women, law and religion in mainstream New Zealand society today through an examination of some recent anti-discrimination cases which illustrate the clash between law and religion and the way that this delineates current gender relations.

The second Māori part of this chapter commences by charting the historical role of Pākehā religion and law in the colonisation of Aotearoa/New Zealand, focussing on the period surrounding the signing of the Declaration of

Independence and the Treaty of Waitangi. These particular events starkly demonstrate the partnership of Pākehā religion and law in the colonisation project. Part Two then chronicles the role of Pākehā religion and law in the subsequent domestication of Māori women and the destruction of Māori social structures, and illustrates these conflicts through a close examination of a recent dispute at a building site in Wellington. Although seemingly trivial and ephemeral, this brief clash over the appropriate law governing women's presence on the building site—Western anti-discrimination law or *tikanga Māori* (Māori custom, law, values)—actually permits us to explore the complex relations between the regimes of gender, law, religion, and culture in Aotearoa/New Zealand and to ponder the missed opportunities for more fruitful engagement between them.

PART I by Margaret Bedggood

For a Pākehā Christian women like myself, the history of the development of religion and law in New Zealand is the story of the mainstream (or 'settler') culture to which I belong. In many ways this history and the place of women within it resembles that of other British-derived settler societies, but it has also been influenced by the parallel indigenous culture with which it has not yet fully come to terms. The history of that interaction and the challenges now facing both our *tikanga* in forging new partnership models in law and religion are perhaps the most interesting aspects of our study. However, understanding these current challenges requires some acquaintance with the history of mainstream Pākehā legal and religious development in Aotearoa/New Zealand.

That history has not been as dramatic as that of other countries in this region. Nor have there been major legal cases where religion and women's roles and rights have provided a central theme, such as the *McBain* litigation in Australia.[1] Rather, women's position in law has changed slowly as social attitudes have changed; the effect and influence which religion has had in that development has, for Pākehā women, been subtle rather than dramatic. For these reasons, I have chosen in this Part first to trace the history of that development as a prelude to a 'snapshot' of modern New Zealand, and then to consider one aspect of law, the anti-discrimination regime, which has the potential to come into conflict with religious values. The broader question of the relevance of such law in a different cultural context is left for the conclusion of this chapter.

[1] *Re McBain: Ex parte Australian Catholic Bishop's Conference* (2002) HCA 16 (18 April 2002); 209 CLR 372. In that litigation, the Roman Catholic Church supported a strict interpretation of the State of Victoria's Infertility Treatment Act 1995 which contravened the federal Sex Discrimination Act by limiting the provision of infertility treatment to heterosexual couples.

The Settler Society: 1840–1970

Following the Treaty of Waitangi (1840), British law[2] and religious traditions derived from Britain formed the basis of the new settler colony in Aotearoa/New Zealand.[3] This was despite the fact that from an early period other communities, with their own legal and religious values and practices, had been present and contributed to the mix of New Zealand society.[4] However, British religious traditions were not imported without modification. For example, although missionaries of the Church of England played a significant and often controversial role in the early years of settlement,[5] that denominational Church was not given any special status in New Zealand over other Christian denominations which were also represented in the early mission field, such as the Methodist, Presbyterian and Roman Catholic Churches, or over later arrivals such as the Mormons and the Salvation Army.[6] Thus, there was, and is, no 'established Church' in the New Zealand system, and this separation of Church and State is maintained in education, which (at primary level) has been officially 'free, secular and compulsory' since 1877,[7] and in a commitment (at least in theory) to 'freedom of religion.'[8]

---

[2] The English Laws Act 1858 (now 1908) proclaimed that the laws of England should be deemed to have been in force in the colony since January 14, 1840.

[3] See for example Brian Colless and Peter Donovan, eds., *Religion in New Zealand Society*, 2nd ed. (Palmerston North: Dunmore Press, 1985); Peter Donovan, ed., *Religions of New Zealanders*, 2nd ed. (Palmerston North: Dunmore Press, 1996).

[4] These include Dalmatian and Chinese settlers, a significant Dutch immigration after the Second World War, a constant influx from other Pacific Island nations and, more recently, increased immigration from neighbouring Asian states, as well as other smaller groups of displaced persons and refugees. See, for example, Christine Cheyne, Mike O'Brien and Michael Belgrave, *Social Policy in Aotearoa/New Zealand: A Critical Introduction*, 2nd ed. (Auckland: Oxford University Press, 2000).

[5] For the role of the Church Mission Society (CMS) in the early period including in connection with the signing of the Treaty of Waitangi, see Allan Davidson, *Christianity in Aotearoa. A History of Church and Society in New Zealand*, 2nd ed. (Wellington: New Zealand Education for Ministry Board, 1997), chap. 3; Allan Davidson and Peter Lineham, ed., *Transplanted Christianity: Documents Illustrating Aspects of New Zealand Church History* (Auckland: College Communications, 1987), chap. 1; below Part II.

[6] See, for example, Davidson, *Christianity in Aotearoa*, chaps 4 and 6; Davidson and Lineham, *Transplanted Christianity*, chap. 1; Donovan, *Religions of New Zealanders*, chaps. 1–5.

[7] Education Act 1877 section 84(2): the so-called 'secular clause.' See, however, Davidson, *Christianity in Aotearoa*, 65–7; Lloyd Geering, "Pluralism and the Future of Religion in New Zealand," in Colless and Domovan, *Religion in New Zealand Society*, 171–184; Ian Breward, *Godless Schools? A Study in Protestant Reactions to the Education Act of 1877* (Christchurch: Presbyterian Bookroom, 1967).

[8] Even the 'secular clause' (Education Act 1877, section 84(2)) was evidence of neutrality among religions rather than being 'anti-religious': see references in the previous note. The disputed Fourth Article of the Treaty of Waitangi was similarly intended to guarantee equality and neutrality: see the discussion below.

This does not mean, however, that New Zealand was a 'secular' society in the nineteenth century.[9] In many 'social' and 'moral' aspects it was considered to be a 'Christian society' as that term was understood in the Anglo-American home lands and colonies. Such customs as strict Sunday observance and control of gambling and drinking habits (by prohibition) were buttressed by reference to Christian precepts, as, less often, were such issues of social justice as opposition to 'sweating shops'.[10] The fact that many of those 'Christian' observances were culturally conditioned shaped the various ways that Christianity impacted on the indigenous populations. It is important, therefore, to draw a distinction between the influence of the institutional church (or churches) and the internalising of Christian faith (a distinction that is developed further in our conclusion). The institutional churches served to maintain women generally in a subordinate position and to secure their acquiescence in such a role. Although New Zealand, like other Western democracies, has now developed into a society which is more diverse and multicultural and therefore paradoxically both multi-religious and increasingly secular, traces of those earlier religious foundations remain and surface in sometimes surprising ways.[11]

Thus, from the beginning of colonization, the position of women was largely shaped and restricted by the religious and cultural traditions from which the settlers came. This did not mean that women were necessarily inactive in the Church and in society. It is worth noting that in the campaign for prohibition, the nineteenth century New Zealand Temperance movement (the Women's Christian Temperance Movement) was an early powerful example of a women's non-government organisation (NGO). It had international connections, was firmly based on evangelical Christian principles across denominational divides, and allowed women a social and political forum to express their faith.[12] It thus combined the Victorian era ideal of women as the guardians of 'purity,' moral standards and sanctity of the home, with calls for them to exercise that influence through the franchise.

---

[9] See Geering, "Pluralism and the Future of Religion," on the differences in the new colony from Britain; and especially, M. Hill's chapter in *New Zealand Society: A Sociological Introduction*, ed. Paul Spoonley, David Pearson and Ian Shirley, 2nd ed. (Palmerston North: Dunmore Press, 1994), 294 ff.

[10] See Davidson and Lineham, *Transplanted Christianity*, 229–333.

[11] See generally Davidson, *Christianity in Aotearoa*, chaps 15–16.

[12] See especially Phillida Bunkle, "The Origins of the Women's Movement in New Zealand: The Women's Christian Temperance Union 1885–1895," in *Women in New Zealand Society*, eds Phillida Bunkle and Beryl Hughes (Auckland: Allen & Unwin, 1980), chap. 3; Raewyn Dalziel, "The Colonial Helpmeet: Women's Role and the Vote in Nineteenth Century New Zealand," *New Zealand Journal of History* 11 (1977): 112–23; Patricia Grimshaw, *Women's Suffrage in New Zealand* (Auckland: Auckland University Press, 1972); Davidson, *Christianity in Aotearoa*, chap. 8.4 and p. 187.

This confusing mix meant that this powerful 'first wave of feminism,' including the granting of suffrage to women in 1893, did not lead to greater freedom or participation. Rather, until late in the twentieth century, the women of New Zealand were firmly cast as second class citizens in relation to education, marriage, ownership of property, inheritance, employment, and access to health care or reproductive rights.[13] Often, it was in the common law (and in subtle ways not susceptible to challenge) that prejudices, or conservative tendencies, were likely to prevail. If the law was to make any plausible claims to be in step with the society it reflected, major advances had to be introduced directly by the legislature.

The official position of women in the established churches generally reflected this pattern, despite the fact that in New Zealand, as elsewhere, the practical work of the churches from the time of the first arrival of Christian missionaries was carried forward by women at least as much as by men.[14] Until the middle of the twentieth century, for example, women were denied leadership position in the major Christian churches.[15] As a child growing up in the 1940s–1950s, I recall that girls were not allowed to serve at an Anglican altar, though no explanation of any kind, let alone a theological one, was ever provided for this exclusion. Girls were thus left to draw the conclusion, and internalize the belief, that females were in some way less acceptable in the sight or service of a male God. Writing in 1950, Mollie Whitelaw, a Presbyterian, summed up the situation thus:

> The Church at present offers to the world mainly 'a masculine façade' in structure and fabric of doctrine and worship. The interpretation of the Gospel, as far as theology and preaching go, is largely a man's. So far women have been forced to tread man-made paths and act according to the norms of a man-conditioned Church.[16]

This situation is neatly encapsulated in the title of a National Council of Churches (NCC) Women's Committee Studies booklet of 1965 "The Kiwi looks at Himself"!

---

[13] See, for example, M. Wilson, "Towards a feminist jurisprudence in Aotearoa," in *Feminist Voices: Women's Studies Texts for Aotearoa New Zealand*, ed Rosemary du Plessis (Auckland: Oxford University Press, 1992), chap 19. Married women, in particular, though they enjoyed a higher social standing, had few rights in law and even less in practice.

[14] See Donovan, *Religions of New Zealanders*, chap. 5; Davidson, *Christianity in Aotearoa*, chap. 8, and as late as the 1980s, at p.178.

[15] Davidson, *Christianity in Aotearoa*, chap. 8 and Chap. 14.2; with the notable exception of the Salvation Army.

[16] M. Whitelaw, *The Weaker Sex: The Work of Women in the Church* (Christchurch, Presbyterian Bookroom, 1950). See also Davidson and Lineham, *Transplanted Christianity*, 365 for a similar comment in 1975.

Advancing the Position of Women: 1970 to the present

From the mid twentieth century, the gradual liberation of women and the removal of the most blatant forms of discrimination were reflected in, and driven by, the law in New Zealand. Legal recognition of the right of women to equal pay with men started with the government service in 1960,[17] was widened to general coverage in the Equal Pay Act of 1972,[18] and briefly explored further in the Labour Government's legislation on employment equity in 1990.[19] Anti-discrimination legislation, applied to the ground of race in 1971,[20] was extended to include the grounds of sex, marital status, and religious or ethical belief in 1977.[21] A further advance for the protection of human rights, or at least of civil and political rights, was provided by the Bill of Rights Act 1990, the grounds on which discrimination is unlawful in New Zealand under the current human rights statute being also recognized in that context.[22] During the same period, New Zealand has striven to address domestic violence through both regulation and policy initiatives.[23] In these developments the law both reflects a gradual change in New Zealand society, and also parallels similar developments in other Western democracies and in international norms.

Perhaps the most significant of these developments was the passing of a broader human rights and anti-discrimination statute, the Human Rights Act of 1993. This Act, like its predecessors—the Human Rights Commission Act 1977 and the Bill of Rights Act 1990—explicitly linked New Zealand's human rights legislation to international human rights norms.[24] It extended the grounds on which it is unlawful to discriminate in New Zealand, in the areas set out in the Act,[25] to include disability (broadly defined),[26] age and sexual

---

[17] Government Service Act 1960.

[18] This was consequent upon a Commission of Inquiry into Equal Pay report entitled *Equal Pay in New Zealand* (New Zealand Government Printer, 1971).

[19] Employment Equity Act 1990. This was repealed by the later National Party Government. On the ineffectiveness of the equal pay statute in the current employment environment, see the discussion below.

[20] Race Relations Act 1971.

[21] Human Rights Commission Act 1977.

[22] Bill of Rights Act 1990, section 19.

[23] See Domestic Violence Act 1995.

[24] The long title to the Human Rights Act 1993 reads—"An Act . . . to provide better protection of human rights in New Zealand in general accordance with United Nations conventions or Covenants on Human Rights."

[25] Namely: employment, access to public places, and to educational establishments, land and housing, provision of goods and services.

[26] Section 21(i)(h).

orientation,[27] and it clarified the concept of indirect discrimination.[28] It also made clear that the Act addressed sexual harassment (section 62) and pregnancy discrimination (section 21(1)(a). The Act also sets out a comprehensive list of exceptions for each ground. Tellingly for our purposes, there is an exception under 'employment' which permits Churches to discriminate against women, and possibly, homosexuals, if they can base that decision on the "doctrines or rules or established customs" of their religion (section s 28(1) and 39(1)).

A notable development in this period has been an increasing awareness of, and willingness to recognize, international norms.[29] New Zealand has always regarded itself as a 'good international citizen' and has signed, ratified or acceded to many of the major human rights instruments,[30] including a large number of International Labor Organization (ILO) conventions,[31] among them the major conventions opposing discrimination against women. It ratified the Convention on the Elimination of All Forms of Discrimination against Women (CEDAW) in January 1985, although not without some opposition from conservative religious groups who argued that adherence to the Convention would undermine the family and its traditional values.[32] (Potential opposition on the same grounds to the ratification of the Children's Convention some years later was headed off by the government.[33]) The

[27] "Which means a heterosexual, homosexual, lesbian or bisexual orientation." This ground was introduced through a separate Supplementary Order Paper (SOP) which passed at the same time as the Human Rights Bill and was incorporated into the resulting Human Rights Act 1993: *Hansard Parliamentary Debates*, December 15, 1992: 13208.

[28] Human Rights Act 1993 section 65. Addressing such indirect discrimination often assists structural change.

[29] The long title to the Human Rights Act 1993 reads—"An Act ... to provide better protection of human rights in New Zealand in general accordance with United Nations conventions or Covenants on Human Rights."

[30] Convention on the Elimination of All Forms of Racial Discrimination, December 21, 1965, UNGA 2106 A (XX); *International Covenant on Civil and Political Rights*, G.A. Res. 2200A, 21 U.N. GAOR, U.N. Doc. A/6316 (1966) and Optional Protocols 1 and 2; *International Covenant on Economic, Social and Cultural Rights*, G.A. Res 2200A, U.N. Doc. A/6316 (1966); *Convention on the Elimination of All Forms of Discrimination Against Women*, G.A. Res. 34/180, 34 UN GOAR, Supp. (No. 46), UN Doc A/34/46 (1979); *Convention Against Torture and other Cruel, Inhuman or Degrading Treatment or Punishment*, December 10, 1984, U.N. Doc A/RES/39/46; *Convention on the Rights of the Child*, November 20, 1989, U.N. Doc. A/44/25.

[31] Although not, as yet, ILO Conventions 87 and 98.

[32] See Mai Chen, *Women and Discrimination: New Zealand and the UN Convention* (Wellington: Victoria University Press, 1989), 4; Ruth Low, "The United Nations Convention on the Elimination of All Forms of Discrimination Against Women (UNCEDAW) Debate: A Clash of Ideologies" (M.A. diss., Massey University, 1994); Rex Ahdar, *Worlds Colliding: Conservative Christians and the Law* (Aldershot: Ashgate, 2001), chap. 6.

[33] The announcement of the ratification of the CRC was made on a Saturday morning at a primary school function with no prior notice; for opposition see Ahdar, *Worlds Colliding* chap. 6.

requirement of periodic reporting to the CEDAW Committee has increasingly become a focus for women's advocates to raise issues of concern. As already mentioned, women's non-governmental groups in New Zealand have a long tradition of involvement and effectiveness. Historically, these were linked almost exclusively to religious activities or motivation, whether their concerns were 'moral' issues, employment issues, education, health, politics or women's concerns in general.[34] Today, although there are still Christian women's groups, most women's NGOs no longer have any religious affiliation.[35]

Women's NGOs have been paralleled more recently in the state sector by the establishment of a Ministry of Women's Affairs in 1984, (although the tenure of this Ministry has from time to time appeared precarious[36]), the brief appointment of an Employment Equity Commissioner,[37] the 'optional' alternative of an EEO (Equal Employment Opportunity) Trust, a Women's Commissioner in the Human Rights Commission[38] and recently an EEO Commissioner.[39] In recent times the Ministry of Women's Affairs has engaged in an extensive consultation process over its report to the CEDAW Committee both before presenting its report and in subsequent reports back, while NGOs have also taken advantage of the parallel reporting system, sending reports and delegations to the Committee hearings.[40] In the same period women have taken an increasing role in public life.[41] The barriers to formal equality are thus steadily being removed.

The churches have reflected the changes in secular society. Women were ordained in the Anglican Church in New Zealand in 1977, relatively early in

---

[34] Sandra Coney writes: "It was almost unthinkable in 1885 that any organization could exist independently of the patronage of the Church." Sandra Coney, *Every Girl: A Social History of Women and the YWCA in Auckland 1885–1985* (Auckland: YWCA, 1986) 7–8.

[35] The National Council of Women (founded 1896) or the New Zealand Federation of University Women are examples.

[36] It has been common for various political parties, in government or in opposition, to threaten the closure of the Ministry. For a recent example, see the comments of the then new leader of the opposition National Party, Dr. Don Brash, cited in Di Paton, "Specific needs of women still have to be catered for," *New Zealand Herald*, November 12, 2003 (Westlaw 2003 WL 67437393): "Don Brash has dragged out that old chestnut that there's no point in having a Ministry of Women's Affairs any more than there is a ministry of men's affairs."

[37] Under the Employment Equity Act 1990.

[38] Human Rights Amendment Act 2000.

[39] Human Rights Amendment Act 2001.

[40] See presentations following the combined third and fourth reports of New Zealand to the Committee (1998).

[41] Although women were eligible to be elected to the New Zealand Parliament in 1919, the first woman took her seat in 1933. Even today, despite women in some high profile roles, the percentage of women in Parliament remains low, as does their representation in the upper levels of law, business or education.

comparison with other parts of the Anglican Communion, and allowed to assume the role of Diocesan Bishop in 1990. However, their numbers in the higher counsels of that church remain few.[42] This is a pattern repeated for the most part in other Protestant churches.[43] So, again, the barriers to equality are no longer legal or doctrinal ones. The effect on all women in the Anglican church, for example, of the ordination of women to the priesthood has been to liberate all women, both lay and ordained, to take their full place in both the Church and the world. But whether substantive equality in fact has been achieved is another matter.[44]

Women, Law and Religion in Mainstream New Zealand Society Today

Mainstream New Zealand society at the beginning of the twenty-first century reflects a gradual emancipation and acceptance of the equality of women, first in law and more slowly in fact. But there remain signs of a more "conservative" tradition, which is hostile to women's equal participation, and which is now fuelled by the recent resurgence of a fundamentalist religious movement, both in particular fundamentalist churches and also as a constituency in the mainstream churches.[45] A third factor is also important when we consider New Zealand society as a whole: the changing demographic patterns. The Māori and Polynesian proportion of the population is growing, there is a significant Asian presence and there are also now groups of refugees of other faiths whose needs and customs must be taken into account by the law. In all

---

[42] The first woman was elected to the General Synod in 1972. See generally Davidson, *Christianity in Aotearoa*, chap. 14.

[43] Women were admitted to the position of Minister in the Presbyterian Church in 1965 and in the Methodist in 1959. In the Roman Catholic Church the subordinate status of women is even more marked, fuelled by the fact of their exclusion from the priesthood. See especially Christine Cheyne, *Made in God's Image: A Project Researching Sexism in the Catholic Church in Aotearoa (New Zealand)* (Wellington: Catholic Commission for Justice, Peace and Development, 1990); E. Isichi in Donovan, *Religions of New Zealanders*, chap. 6.

[44] Thus one woman writing in 1986: "Our experience, our culture, our voices have no authority": D. Danby, *Accent* (July 1986), 17.

[45] It should be noted that the views expressed here are from the so-called liberal wing of the Church. The other Pākehā voice not represented in our study is that of "conservative Christians": see Rex Ahdar, *Adrift in a Sea of Rights: A Report Prepared for the New Zealand Education Development Foundation* (Christchurch: New Zealand Educational Foundation, 2001); Rex Ahdar, *Worlds Colliding: Conservative Christians and the Law* (Aldershot: Ashgate, 2001); Bruce Patrick ed., *The Vision New Zealand Congress 1997* (Auckland: Vision New Zealand, 1997); C. Brown, "Church, Culture and Identity," in *Culture and Identity in New Zealand*, ed. D. Novitz and B. Willmott (Wellington: G.P. Books, 1989); J. Veitch in Donovan, *Religions of New Zealanders*, chap. 7; Colin Brown "How Significant is the Charismatic Movement?" in Colless and Donovan, *Religion in New Zealand Society*, 99–114.

of these groups the position of women may well be different from that in mainstream New Zealand as reflected in its legal system. This changing pattern will be considered in the concluding section of this chapter.

The effect of the conservative religious influence continues to be most noticeable around so-called moral issues, as it has in the past.[46] The argument is often centred on the concept of 'family values' or 'the breakdown of the family.' Recent examples include opposition to legislation to reform the law relating to prostitution[47] which also drew late criticism from some of the mainstream churches. Another example has been the defence of the smacking of children in the debate which has followed criticism of section 59 of the Crimes Act 1961[48] by the United Nations Committee on the Rights of the Child in their comments on New Zealand's 1997 report.[49] Politically these positions have been strengthened by the emergence of a minor party, United Future, as the Labour government's coalition partner after the 2002 elections.[50] One of the main planks of this party and of their success so far has been the establishment of a Commission on the Family, established in 2003, whose role is only slowly emerging. A current debate in New Zealand centres on the question of what constitutes a family.[51] A similar bias can still be detected in attitudes about and within the court system, for example in the controversy around the supposedly more 'liberal' Family Court and in discussions about domestic violence, where entrenched attitudes towards women and their role in the 'traditional family' are still to be found.[52] Even in the more mainstream churches the traditional 'family' continues to be privileged, often in quite subtle ways.

In law there have been some significant advances. For example, after the recent reform of property rights legislation,[53] the equal property division available to married couples is extended to de facto partnerships, including

[46] For example, homosexual law reform, contraception and abortion, the care and protection of children, opposition to the Domestic Purposes Benefit; see the authorities cited in the previous note.

[47] Prostitution Law Reform Act 2003.

[48] Which states that a parent is "justified in using force by way of correction" provided the force used is reasonable in the circumstances.

[49] See Ahdar, *Worlds Colliding*, chap. 8.

[50] As the successor to previous more overtly "Christian" political parties see Davidson, *Christianity in Aotearoa*, 186; J. Boston, "Christian Political Parties and MMP," in *God and Government: the New Zealand Experience*, ed. Rex Ahdar and John Stenhouse (Dunedin: University of Otago Press, 2000), chap. 6.

[51] See V. Adair and R. Dixon, eds., *The Family in Aotearoa/New Zealand* (Auckland: Addison Wesley Longman, 1998); Ahdar, *Worlds Colliding*, chap. 6.

[52] See for example of court attitudes *Quilter v. Attorney-General* (1998) 1 NZLR 523; also Spoonley, Pearson and Shirley, 302 ff.

[53] Property Relationships Act 2001.

same-sex ones. Another example is the recent move towards paid parental leave.[54] But these legal changes are not necessarily accompanied by changes in attitudes. Sometimes, they are simply not even legally effective, as in the case of equal pay.[55] Thanks to the Human Rights Act, discrimination is no longer overt, but it remains nevertheless. The broader question of women's access to justice, particularly access for the poor and for Māori women, has been examined in detail by the Law Commission, and it has been found wanting.[56] The role, and possible bias, of judges has also come under scrutiny.[57] Within the churches, even where equality appears to have been attained, attitudes may not have changed: within Tikanga Pākehā in the Anglican church[58] for example, women are still underrepresented in the bishopric or as full time parish clergy.

One area where potential clashes occur, either with fundamentalist religion, or with a different culture, is in anti-discrimination law, which enshrines this modern 'liberal,' 'Western' (Pākehā) cultural value. The clash with fundamentalist religion belongs properly in this section; the clash with different cultural values raises more difficult and disconcerting questions and will be discussed in the concluding section of our chapter.

Anti-discrimination Law: A Clash between Law and Religion?

By section 21, the New Zealand Human Rights Act 1993 prohibits discrimination on the grounds, inter alia, of sex, sexual orientation, religious belief or ethical belief. Discrimination is made illegal in relation to enumerated areas of public life such as employment (section 22), partnerships (section 36), professional associations and qualifying bodies (sections 37–41), access to public places (sections 42–43), the provision of goods and services (sections 44–52), the provision of land and accommodation (sections 53–3 56) and the access to educational establishments (sections 57–60). However, certain exemptions are permitted, including (in s 28) "exceptions for purposes of religion." Although there has not been much litigation on these exceptions, the cases have been controversial.

[54] New Zealand is still behind international standards: see art. 11.2(b) of CEDAW.

[55] The original Act (1972) having been premised on a system of industrial multi-employer awards.

[56] Law Commission Report 53, *Justice: The Experiences of Māori Women* (1999).

[57] For example the analysis of the underlying values of New Zealand society in *Quilter v. Attorney-General* (1998) 1 NZLR 523.

[58] The Anglican Church in New Zealand adopted a new Constitution in 1992; see Davidson, *Christianity in Aotearoa*, chaps 14 and 16.

The Human Rights Act 1993 and the 'Christian' Employer

In *Proceedings Commissioner v. Boakes*[59] the employer, a member of the evangelical Protestant Christian community of the Exclusive Brethren, dismissed a married female employee because of the employer's religious belief that married women should not work outside the home. In proceedings brought by the Proceedings Commissioner of the Human Rights Commission under section 83 of the Act, the Complaints Review Tribunal held that the employer had contravened the complainant's human right to be free from discrimination, there being no exception in the Act which would allow discrimination on the grounds of the *employer's* religious beliefs.[60]

The Human Rights Act 1993 and the Church as Employer

One of the exceptions to the section 22 prohibition on discrimination in employment is enumerated in section 28 (1), which provides:

> Nothing in section 22 of the Act shall prevent different treatment based on sex where the position is for the purposes of an organised religion and is limited to one sex so as to comply with the doctrines or rules or established customs of the religion whereby discrimination on the ground of sex is permitted in employment.

Thus the doctrine and practice of the Roman Catholic Church, which prohibits women's ordination, is deemed lawful because it is designed to "comply with the doctrines or rules or established customs of the religion." It had been suggested that a similar exception should be allowed for sexual orientation, but this, though part of the Supplementary Order Paper by which sexual orientation was introduced alongside the Human Rights Bill, did not survive into the final statute.[61] The other relevant exception is contained in section 28 (2)(b)(i) which permits:

> different treatment based on religious or ethical belief where ... the sole or principle duties of the position ... are ... those of a clergyman, priest, pastor ... or teacher ... or otherwise involve the propagation of that belief.

It can now be argued on good authority[62] that clergy are not 'employed' in terms of the Human Rights Act, since they are regarded in law as holding

---

[59] CRT 13 April 1994, 1/94 (unreported). See P Rishworth, "Coming Conflicts over Freedom of Religion," in *Rights and Freedoms: The New Zealand Bill of Rights Act 1990 and the Human Rights Act 1993*, ed. G. Huscroft and P. Rishworth (Wellington: Brookers, 1995) chap. 6.

[60] For the anxiety caused by such a decision see A. Turner, "The Human Rights Act 1993," chap. 22 in Patrick, *Vision New Zealand Congress*; for earlier examples, Ahdar, *Worlds Colliding*, chap. 5.

[61] See above n. 27.

[62] *Davies v. Presbyterian Church of Wales* (1986) 1 All ER 705; *Mabon v. Conference of the Methodist Church of New Zealand* (1997) ERNZ 690; *Ermogenous v. Greek Orthodox Community of SA Inc* (2002) HCA 8.

'offices' or 'callings' and therefore not intending to create a contractual relationship. If this is so, then of course section 22 does not apply. Alternatively, a female candidate for ordination might invoke section 38, which is concerned to prohibit discrimination by 'qualifying bodies' and therefore would apply to religious institutions approving candidates for ordination. However here, the exemption in section 39(1)[63] —which is similar to the section 28 exemption—could be used as a defence by a denomination which could point to a "doctrine, rule or established custom"[64] proscribing such an appointment.

Subsequent reaction to the interplay of these grounds (prohibiting discrimination) and exceptions (permitting it) by various groups and by the Human Rights Commission itself has proved enlightening. In particular, it has highlighted the possible clash between Western liberal values, as reflected in the search for formal equality, and the maintenance of a different set of values by conservative Christians. The effect of the passage of the Human Rights Act in 1993 appears to have taken a number of groups by surprise:[65] Conservative Christians who were not prepared for the narrowed scope of section 28(1),[66] and liberal Christians and gays who did not anticipate the ambiguities surrounding sections 28(2) and 39(1). The Human Rights Commission has endeavoured to resolve these ambiguities by commissioning three reports but has as yet issued no definitive statement which might lessen the fears of conservative Christians of intrusion into their affairs and attempts to override their values.[67] These issues have not been tried out on a particular set of facts, either in a complaint to the Commission or before the Courts. Probably wisely, the Churches have striven to keep their debates within their own structures, although divisions have arisen there also.[68]

---

[63] Section 39(1) reads:

Nothing in section 38 of this Act shall apply where the authorisation or qualification is needed for—a profession or calling for the purposes of an organised religion and is limited to one sex or to persons of that religious belief so as to comply with the doctrines or rules or established customs of that religion.

[64] Cf ICCPR art. 18 and General Comment No. 22 (Human Rights Committee).

[65] See above n. 27 for the confusing dual process on the passage of the Bill.

[66] Despite their attempt to broaden this in Parliament; it is clear the change of opinion since the defeat of attempts to outlaw homosexual discrimination in 1985 was unexpected. See R. Ahdar, *Worlds Colliding*, chap. 9.

[67] The three legal opinions are P. Rishworth, C. Pidgeon and M. Bedggood (May 1998); J. Dawson (November 1998); A. Duffy (September 2000). The Commission's Issues Paper "The Human Rights Act 1993 in Relation to Lesbian and Gay Clergy: An Issues Paper Prepared by the Human Rights Commission" can be viewed on the Commission's webpage by navigating from http://www.hrc.co.nz

[68] See Ahdar, *Worlds Colliding*, chap. 9; Patrick, *Vision New Zealand Congress*, chap. 22.

One of the thorny questions raised in this debate is that of determining who decides what are the "doctrines rules or established customs" of a religion? This difficulty can arise in two forms. In churches where there is division, the interpretation of the relevant doctrine may be an issue. In others there may be anxiety that the rules are not easily located, which raises the spectre of an outside body, a secular court, making the decision; although, to be fair, neither human rights bodies nor the courts have shown any inclination to take this course.[69]

This controversy highlights a number of questions about anti-discrimination law and allowable exceptions and the balancing of this right with another, namely freedom of religion. On what grounds and with what evidence should such exemptions be included? Who decides on the 'evidence'? Who has authority to speak for the group? What of the position of individuals within that group? In balancing rights, can there be some actions or attitudes which a society may find simply unacceptable?[70]

Although the focus of this controversy has largely been on questions of sexual orientation and the place, if any, of gay and lesbian people in the leadership of the churches, broader questions of the place of anti-discrimination law which underlie this particular controversy are relevant in considering the position of women. Put starkly, the central question is whether, and to what extent, religious institutions which recognize a perceived higher law or authority should be bound by the laws of their society and answerable to its institutions. The questions raised above are of course, enormous and crucial questions in today's world and lie at the heart of much of the debate about the universality of human rights. How these questions are dealt with will affect the lives and prospects of women in this region.

---

[69] This question of the 'reach' of anti-discrimination law in New Zealand has been considered in a recent case concerned with the recognition of same-sex marriages. In *Quilter v. Attorney-General* (1998) 1 NZLR 523 three lesbian couples challenged the refusal of the Registrar to issue to them a licence to marry under the Marriage Act 1955.

The Court of Appeal unanimously found that the Marriage Act reflected the traditional heterosexual concept of marriage between one man and one woman and that it could not be interpreted to include same-sex couples. The majority of the Court of Appeal also found that the Bill of Rights Act did not alter this position and that if this was discriminatory, then Parliament had expressly sanctioned it.

This case has been considered extensively elsewhere and its factual setting is somewhat peripheral to our discussion. But it is worth noting that the majority judgment in that case displayed a surprisingly narrow interpretation of the provisions and effect of the Bill of Rights Act and the Human Rights Act and the changes which they might have been supposed to have wrought in New Zealand law and society.

[70] Hate-speech, torture, slavery, for example. On the questions raised in this section in a broader context, see Peter Edge and Graham Harvey, eds., *Law and Religion in Contemporary Society: Communities, Individualism and the State* (Aldershot: Ashgate, 2000) chaps. 4, 8 and especially 9.

Part II: Māori Women's experiences of Religion and Law, By Leah Whiu

For Māori women in Aotearoa/New Zealand, the impact of Pākehā law and religion has been devastating.[71] Both Pākehā law and religion were, and continue to be, instrumental in the colonisation of Māori people. Pākehā law accompanied Pākehā religion to Aotearoa, and together these institutions set about civilising the natives by bringing God to them, while simultaneously and systematically destroying the social norms, structures, values, beliefs and knowledge that were meaningful for Māori. The role of the missionaries, and therefore of Pākehā religion, was necessary to provide the most receptive environment for the successful imposition of sovereignty by the British Crown over the Māori people through the Treaty of Waitangi in 1840. For Māori women and men, the preparation of the environment for the Treaty of Waitangi by the missionaries, together with its drafting, translation and ultimate execution on 6 February 1840, have been the site of the most destructive collusion of law and religion in Aotearoa. The role of missionaries and religion in this event were instrumental in the adoption and ultimate execution of this document which, according to the English language version, secured to the British sovereignty over New Zealand and its inhabitants, including the Māori people.

The colonisation project is also directly responsible for the deliberate destruction of Māori socio-political structures, such as the *whānau* (kin group). This was done to be rid of the power of the collective, while also facilitating a process for individualising land title, both of which were necessary to facilitate colonial land acquisition. The partnership of law, policy and religion in this project reconstructed the role, and thus the status, of Māori women so that it mirrored that of Pākehā women of the time. As Kuni Jenkins explains:

> Māori marriage was the despair of the missionaries. They made it a high priority for elimination and they preached hell-fire and brimstone to the sinful pagans who continued to practise it. They refused to accommodate or tolerate Māori marriage as being an alternative to their idea of the nuclear family and its demands on the colonial wife to be subservient, lacking in initiative and obedient to her husband. She had to prize highly her role of housewife and mother and believe it to be God's will . . . the Māori female had to be domiciled very quickly to the values of the new regime that had arrived to civilise her.[72]

---

[71] In this chapter I refer to Pākehā religion as encapsulating: the various forms of Christianity, the missionaries who brought their religion and the various institutions such as the missions. In so doing, I acknowledge that I have taken a very narrow view of what religion by focussing only on the role of organized, institutional religion.

[72] Kuni Jenkins, cited in Ani Mikaere, "Māori women: caught in the contradictions of a colonized reality," *Waikato Law Review* 2 (1994): 134, n. 40.

From a Māori perspective, the purpose of this relationship between law and religion has resulted in the subordination of Māori interests to the British colonial interests, and of the Māori people to the British colonials and settlers who subsequently arrived. Since the deliberate mistranslation of the Treaty,[73] this tactic and practice of oppression has continued to characterize, form and reproduce the dominant relationship of colonization between Māori and Pākehā, and Māori and the Crown, in Aotearoa. The dehumanising relationship of colonisation continues to limit both the coloniser and the colonized, since, as Paolo Friere writes, like any relationship of oppression:

> Dehumanization, which marks not only those whose humanity has been stolen, but also (though in a different way) those who have stolen it, is a *distortion* of the vocation of becoming more fully human. ... Because it is a distortion of being more fully human, sooner or later being less human leads the oppressed to struggle against those who made them so. In order for this struggle to have meaning, the oppressed must not, in seeking to regain their humanity (which is a way to create it), become in turn oppressors of the oppressors, but rather restorers of the humanity of both.[74]

It is in this context of considering our dehumanisation that, as a Māori woman, I found it difficult to think about the themes of this book without considering the violence of colonisation perpetuated in the name of both law and religion against Māori and other indigenous peoples throughout the world. In the journey of writing this chapter, I have perhaps somewhat inevitably been drawn to the apparent contradictions and tensions of what it means to be Māori, a woman, and a Christian. Speaking personally, I was raised as an Anglican by a family which considered itself to be Christian. However later in life, as I learned more about colonisation and the role of Pākehā law and of organized Christian religion in that process, I came to reject Christianity. I now acknowledge that, despite my attempts to disavow Christianity, I do have a relationship with the faith whereby it is firmly embedded in my family and myself. However it is a conflicted relationship: on one hand, I participate in some Christian rituals, and on the other hand, I feel sad and angry about the role of Christianity in the colonisation of my peoples and myself. A significant population of Māori people, along with their *tikanga Māori* (Māori law, custom) have embraced Christianity and other forms of Pākehā religion. One Māori man explained to me that, for him, Christianity is associated with peace and the end of war between tribes, and that this is a good thing for all Māori.

[73] Nan Seuffert, "Colonising Concepts of the Good Citizen, Law's Deceptions, and the Treaty of Waitangi," *Law Text Culture* 4 no. 2 (1998): 69–104. See below for further discussion of the mistranslation of the Treaty of Waitangi and its consequences.

[74] Paulo Freire, *Pedagogy of the Oppressed* (London: Penguin Books, 1972), 20–21.

Further, he explained, Christianity provided an easier way to access God in contrast to the very esoteric and difficult pathways to *ngā atua Māori* that were usually only accessible by *tohunga* (priests, skilled persons) and *rangatira* (chiefs). This complex and at times discordant relationship with Christianity resides uncomfortably within me and within other Māori. It is from that place that I offer this contribution. For to ignore this story of the complicity of Christianity with colonization is to ignore the realities and experience of a large proportion of both Māori women and men and other indigenous peoples, who have endured and survived such violence at the hands of our colonizers' religion and law.

Role of Pākehā Religion and Law in the Colonisation Project of Aotearoa

In 1839 when William Hobson, a representative of the British Crown, arrived in New Zealand to negotiate with Māori for the cession of sovereignty, the British and Māori had already experienced 70 years of contact, primarily through the frontiers of trade and Christianity.[75] Not surprisingly, during this period of contact Māori society "underwent substantial change," including the adoption of Christianity by some and the blending of Christian practices with traditional Māori *tikanga* and spirituality for many more.[76] As Claudia Orange observes, the promotion of "the belief that the Crown had a paternal interest in Māori welfare" by Samuel Marsden, a New South Wales chaplain who visited New Zealand many times was "[c]rucial in shaping Māori attitudes to the Crown".[77]

In 1833, in response to Māori and European appeals to the British Crown, James Busby was appointed as British Resident. While "[h]umanitarian reasons influenced the timing [of his appointment] ... protection of British trade was the decisive factor for the Colonial Office."[78] However, the success of Busby's engagement with Māori relied upon the missionaries' "network of contacts among northern Māori and, most importantly, their *mana* [authority]."[79] Further, Busby was also able to build upon Māori perceptions that the Crown was closely associated with the English church and thus "took a special interest in Māori."[80]

[75] Claudia Orange, *The Treaty of Waitangi* (Allen & Unwin: Wellington, 1987), 6.
[76] Ibid., 7.
[77] Ibid.
[78] Ibid., 10.
[79] Ibid., 16.
[80] Ibid., 12.

In his dealings with Māori, Busby had become convinced that only the development of a collective Māori sovereignty would achieve law and order and stop inter-tribal violence.[81] In addition to promoting the need for a national flag, Busby conceived and developed the Declaration of Independence (*He whakaputanga o te Rangatiratanga o Niu Tirene*) which was signed by 34 northern chiefs on 28 October 1835.[82] The key articles of the Declaration provided that the signatories declared: "their *rangatiratanga* (translated as independence) under the designation of The United Tribes of New Zealand"[83]; their "*kingitanga* and *mana* (translated as all sovereign power and authority)"[84]; and that they "would not permit any legislative authority (translated as *whakarite ture*) to exist apart from themselves; nor would they permit any function of government (translated as *kawanatanga*) to be exercised by anyone other than persons to whom they delegated such a task."[85]

The Declaration was translated by missionaries who had resided in New Zealand for at least 10 years. One of these was Henry Williams, who had assisted Busby with the text of the Declaration.[86] Two years later, in 1837, in response to a serious outbreak of tribal fighting "involving local European riffraff ",[87] a petition (promoted by the Church Missionary Society (CMS) with the support of the Wesleyan Missionary Society (WMS) and signed by over 200 British nationals) again sought intervention from the British Crown.[88] Claudia Orange observes that "[t]he missionaries had a vested interest in sponsoring this appeal. To hold the advances they had made, they were convinced that further government action was essential."[89] This approach was supported by Lord Glenelg, the Secretary of State for Colonies who "would have preferred to see the missions continue their task of civilising the Māori, possibly with increasing government support."[90]

---

[81] Ibid., 19.

[82] Ibid.

[83] Ani Mikaere "The Treaty of Waitangi and the Recognition of Tikanga Māori," (Unpublished paper, 2003), 5–6.

[84] Ibid.

[85] Ibid.

[86] Ranginui Walker, *Ka Whawhai Tonu Matou: Struggle Without End* (Penguin Books: Auckland, 1990), 88.

[87] Orange, *Treaty of Waitangi*, 23.

[88] Ibid., 24.

[89] Ibid.

[90] Orange describes Lord Glenelg as "an evangelical humanitarian who had been vice-president of the CMS, (who) considered that an injustice would certainly be done if any rights in New Zealand were granted by the British government before Māori consent was obtained." Ibid., 25–26.

The humanitarian and missionary concerns about the likely calamatious effects of colonization upon Māori had been influential in the policy of "no-colonization" of New Zealand. However, in the period from 1835-1839, significant development in the British Crown's policy concerning the colonization of New Zealand had occurred. These changes shifted official policy from a position of 'no-colonization' to one favouring colonization.[91]

In response to these concerns, in 1839, William Hobson arrived in New Zealand bringing instructions from the Colonial Office to "acquire sovereignty over either 'the whole or any parts' of New Zealand that the Māori wished to cede."[92] The desired vehicle for achieving this goal was the Treaty of Waitangi, a somewhat hastily-drafted and cobbled together document, comprising "Hobson's preamble, the articles developed by Busby from Freeman's [Hobson's secretary] skeletal versions, with the most important addition of the guarantee of land and other possessions, and finally, Busby's amended postscript."[93]

The role of the missionaries in the development and promotion of the Treaty of Waitangi was critical in helping influence Māori to surrender sovereignty.[94] Henry Williams, who had five years earlier translated the Declaration of Independence, was asked to translate the English version of the Treaty into *te reo Māori* which he did with the assistance of his son Edward, despite neither men being acknowledged experts in translation.[95]

There are two versions of the Treaty: an English language version, signed by 39 Māori chiefs, and a Māori language version, signed by between 530–540 Māori chiefs throughout the country.[96] The Treaty is comprised of a preamble and three written articles and a 4th verbal article that was included at least at Waitangi.[97] While the Māori text is supposed to be a translation of the English text, there are crucial differences between the two. Article 1 of the English text provides that Māori ceded sovereignty to the British and were guaranteed, in article 2, the "full, exclusive and undisturbed possession of

[91] Ibid., 29.

[92] Ibid., 29.

[93] Ibid., 37. There was also a further verbal commitment given with a fourth article stating "The Governor says the several faiths of England, of the Wesleyans, of Rome, and also the Māori custom, shall be alike protected by him." Ibid., 53.

[94] Ibid., 38–9.

[95] Ibid.

[96] Ibid., 259–60

[97] Article 2 of both texts also provided for the British Crown's exclusive right to purchase land from Māori and article 3 provided all the rights and privileges of British citizens to Māori. Article 4 was added during the discussions when the Catholic Bishop Pompallier urged that the various faiths of the Wesleyans, Rome and the customs of the Māori should be protected.

their Lands ... so long as it is their wish and desire to retain the same ...". However article 1 of the Māori text provides that Māori ceded *kawanatanga*, or government, to the British Crown and were guaranteed, in article 2, "*te tino rangatiratanga o o ratou wenua, o ratou kainga me o ratou taonga katoa*". *Te tino rangatiratanga* has been translated as "the highest chieftanship" or indeed "the sovereignty of their lands".[98] In the Declaration of Independence, Henry Williams had used the term *rangatiratanga* to translate the concept of independence. As Professor Ranginui Walker observes "[t]he chiefs are likely to have understood the second clause of the Treaty as a confirmation of their own sovereign rights in return for a limited concession of power in *kawanatanga*."[99]

The consequences of the mistranslation is that the establishment of the New Zealand state, law and society has been predicated upon an erroneous notion that in 1840 a population of 90-200,000[100] Māori gave away their sovereignty and independence to a handful of British colonists (numbering about 2000 at that time). This idea is clearly both logically and conceptually preposterous, since according to Māori worldview it was impossible to give away your own *rangatiratanga* and that of your people. Moreover, given the dominance of Māori at the time—why would they have done so?

The history of the acceptance and implementation of either version of the Treaty has been marked by a period of initially reluctant acceptance of the English version, until 1877. At that date, Chief Justice Prendergast, in an infamous decision, referred to the Treaty of Waitangi as a "simple nullity" since he considered that "[o]n the foundation of this colony, the aborigines were found without any kind of civil government, or any settled system of law [since the] Māori tribes were incapable of performing the duties, and therefore of assuming the rights, of a civilised community."[101] From 1877 until 1975, despite vociferous and constant protest by Māori and some Pākehā that the Crown was dishonouring the Treaty of Waitangi, the Treaty was largely ignored and erased from the New Zealand political, social, and legal context. However in 1975, in response to a national land march led by the prominent Māori woman activist Whina Cooper, as well as the work of a Māori member of parliament, Hon Matiu Rata, the then-Labour Government enacted the *Treaty of Waitangi Act 1975*, which established the Waitangi Tribunal to inquire into breaches of the principles of the Treaty of Waitangi. Since 1975, the discourse surrounding

---

[98] Waitangi Tribunal *The Motunui-Waitara Report* (Wellington: Brooker's, 1983), 59.

[99] Ranginui Walker, *Ka Whawhai Tonu Matou: Struggle Without End* (Penguin Books: Auckland, 1990), 93.

[100] Orange, *Treaty of Waitangi*, 7.

[101] *Wi Parata v. The Bishop of Wellington* (1877), 3 The New Zealand Jurist Reports SC 72, 77.

the Treaty of Waitangi has primarily developed around principles that have been unilaterally developed by the Government and the Courts.

Christian missionaries, then, played a prominent role in the establishment of colonial rule. On 5 February 1840, at Waitangi in the Bay of Islands, Hobson read out the English version of the Treaty of Waitangi to a gathering of chiefs. Henry Williams then read out the Māori translation.[102] There were no written versions of the Treaty circulated to Māori. Initially, there was significant vociferous opposition expressed by several speakers,[103] however "[a]t this critical juncture, Heke, Nene and Patuone, all long-time associates of the English missionaries, rose to speak [which] swung the mood of the meeting towards Hobson."[104] Heke pointed out that "good would derive from Hobson remaining to be 'all as one' with the missionaries; that it would be not unlike the benefit brought by the Word of God—Te Kawenata Hou, the New Covenant or Testament [and that] ... in the circumstances, [Māori] had to rely on the direction of their missionaries, their 'fathers'."[105]

The prominent function of Christian missionaries and the Christian churches in preparing Māori to accept their colonization is particularly evident in the participation of key missionaries such as Henry Williams in the translation of both the Declaration of Independence and the Treaty of Waitangi, and in the influence of the relationship of missionaries with Māori leading up to and during this period. As Claudia Orange argues "missionary influence was significant simply because many Māori trusted the missionaries' good intentions. This appears to have added a religious aspect to Māori understanding of the agreement."[106]

This alliance between Pākehā law and religion has been a common theme in the colonization project. In the next section I will discuss this relationship in the context of the domestication of Māori women and the deliberate destruction of the *whānau*.

Role of Pākehā Religion and Law in the Domestication of Māori Women

One of the dominant and frequently expressed perceptions of Māori culture is that it was and remains patriarchal, and that Māori women are not equal to Māori men. This perception has been assumed and imposed in the dominant

[102] Orange, *Treaty of Waitangi*, 45.
[103] Ibid., 49.
[104] Ibid.
[105] Ibid.
[106] Ibid., 90–91.

Pākehā culture's construction of Māori culture and, in particular, in its understanding of the relationships between Māori men and women. This Pākehā perception is used to legitimate and justify criticisms of Māori culture as archaic, and arcane—pejoratively 'traditional'—thus locking it in a time which is considered to be no longer relevant to modern secular New Zealand society. However these perceptions are now being challenged by Māori women,[107] who are actively engaged in developing ways of understanding, explaining and theorizing our experiences. In this section, I will give a brief outline of the role of Pākehā religion and law in the dominant construction of Māori women as domesticated assistants in the New Zealand capitalist economy and in the next section I will examine an ephemeral and seemingly fleeting incident which highlights the different ways that Māori women are constructed by the institutions of Pākehā law and culture.

The missionaries and early colonials who arrived in New Zealand in the late 1700s and early 1800s brought along with them their philosophy, ideology, law and norms, and these of course informed and underpinned their constructions of the role of women. The actual roles and status of women in Māori society must have been a complete anathema to the early colonizers who, in the name of Western civilization, set about rectifying the situation. For as Linda Smith observes:

> The first colonisers were men. They dealt with men and observed and studied men. The roles played by Māori women were marginalised because of the ethnocentric and phallocentric views of these early colonisers.[108]

One of the ways that this ethnocentrism and phallocentrism manifested was in the re-telling of our myths by Māori male informants to Pākehā male writers, who lacked understanding of the significance of Māori cultural beliefs. Ani Mikaere discusses the impact of this re-telling of our myths, pointing out that it has led to "a shift in emphasis, away from the powerful female influence in the stories and towards the male characters."[109] For instance, in the story

---

[107] Ani Mikaere, "The Balance Destroyed: The Consequences for Māori Women of the Colonisation of Tikanga Māori," (University of Waikato: Unpublished MJur Thesis, 1995); Linda Tuhiwai Smith, "Māori Women: Discourses, Projects and Mana Wahine," in *Women and Education in Aotearoa 2*, ed. Sue Middleton and Alison Jones (Auckland: Auckland University Press, 1997); Kathie Irwin, "Towards Theories of Māori Feminisms," in *Feminist Voices: Women's Studies Texts for Aetearoa/New Zealand*, ed. Rosemary du Plessis et. al. (Auckland: Oxford University Press, 1992); Patricia Johnson, and Leonie Pihama, "What Counts as Difference and What Differences Count: Gender, Race and the Politics of Difference" in *Toi Wahine*, ed. Kathie Irwin and Irihapeti Ramsden (Auckland: Penguin Books, 1995), 75.

[108] Linda Tuhiwai Smith "Māori Women: Discources, Projects and Mana Wahine" in Middleton and Jones, *Women and Education*, 48.

[109] Mikaere, "Māori Women," 131.

concerning the gift of fire, the central figure is the female guardian of fire, Mahuika, who is one of Maui's *kuia* (female elder). Because of her relationship to Maui and her love and promise to humanity, one by one Mahuika gives to Maui her children of fire, even though she is aware that Maui is killing her children. Finally, he asks for the last of her fingernails of fire, and in her anger she tells him "You ask too much" and throws the fire at his feet and subsequently asks the earthly trees to be guardians of fire forever.[110] However, in the retelling of this story, it is Maui's role in obtaining that fire through successful trickery that is valorised, while Mahuika is constructed as an "old woman" who continues to be tricked by him.[111]

The impact of this colonial hegemony was not surprisingly directed at Māori women by the colonial state which ". . . constructed Māori women as a group requiring domestication."[112] The colonial state policy required that:

> [t]hrough education, Māori girls were trained to fit the state categories of 'wives' and 'domestic workers'. . . . An openly espoused purpose of Māori education was to train Māori lads to be farmers and Māori girls to be farmers' wives.[113]

The successful domestication of women, including Māori women, "through their unpaid labour in homes and on farms, and through their roles as unpaid assistants to men",[114] was essential to the early beginnings of capitalism in New Zealand.[115]

The successful adoption and embodiment of these roles by Māori women was largely due to the combination of state education, policy, law,[116] and religion. Linda Smith observes that:

> [t]he role of the state in domesticating Māori women was also supported by the churches. Christian teachings stressed the importance of such notions as

---

[110] Patricia Grace and Robyn Kahukiwa, *Wahine Toa—Women of Māori Myth* (Auckland: Collins, 1984).

[111] Antony Alpers, *Myths and Tribal Legends* (Auckland: Longman Paul Limited, 1964), 57.

[112] Smith, "Māori Women," 44.

[113] Ibid.

[114] Ibid.

[115] Ibid.

[116] Mikaere, "Māori Women," 83, points out that "(t)he disruption of Māori social organisation was no mere by-product of colonisation, but an integral part of the process. Destroying the principle of collectivism which ran through Māori society was stated to be one of the twin aims of the Native Land Act which had set up the Native Land Court in 1865, the other aim being to access Māori land for settlement. Not only was the very concept of individual title to land destructive of collectivism, but the massive land loss brought about by the workings of the Native Land Court meant that, as the Māori population stabilised at a low point towards the end of the century and began to grow, Māori found that they had insufficient land left to support themselves. Whanau were eventually forced to break into nuclear families and move to towns and cities in search of work." Mikaere, "Treaty of Waitangi," 133.

> 'marriage', 'home', 'motherhood' and 'work'. Sexuality was, of course, confined to marriage. From what has been reconstructed of pre-Pākehā Māori society, we know that these notions were defined in quite different ways: individual mothers were not solely responsible for childcare; homes did not need twenty-four hour labour to keep clean; motherhood was probably important only as a developmental stage, and at the time of the birth itself; and work was communally focused.[117]

In summary, the relationship of religion with law and policy in the destruction of the collective social structures of Māori society, such as the *whanau* and its transformation or replacement with the Western nuclear family was seen by the missionaries and the state to be imperative to the success of the colonization project.[118] Central to this goal was the domestication of Māori women and their restriction to the home. As Linda Smith has so aptly observed:

> Māori women/girls were perceived either in family terms as wives and children, or in sexual terms as easy partners. ... Christianity reinforced these notions by spelling out rules of decorum and defining spaces (the home) for the carrying out of appropriate female activities.[119]

Māori scholar Ani Mikaere strongly argues that "these changes in perception of the role of women have come about as a direct result of colonisation" and that "evidence abounds which refutes the notion that traditional Māori society attached greater significance to male roles than to female roles".[120]

At the Intersection of Gender, Religion, Law, Colonisation and Culture

The dominant Pākehā perception of Māori society as patriarchal and founded on some outdated notions of inequality based on sex/gender was at the centre of an incident that occurred in the lower North Island of Aotearoa in 2003. This incident was subject to the intensive media, political and public debate that is the source of my analysis.

Briefly, on 28 March 2003 in New Zealand's capital city Wellington, the local newspaper reported that women had been banned from the construction site of the region's new Health Centre because the Health Centre's District Health Board had struck a deal with the local *iwi Te Ati Awa ki Whakarongotai*

[117] Smith, "Māori Women," 44.
[118] Mikaere, "Māori Women," 133–4.
[119] Smith, "Māori Women," 48.
[120] Mikaere, "Māori Women," 148, 125.

to ban women. It was reported in the *Dominion Post*, one of New Zealand's major metropolitan dailies, that:

> *Te Ati Awa ki Whakarongotai* spokesman Jack Rikihana said the ban was in keeping with *iwi* protocol for building sites, and any woman who set foot past the fence would "get a kick in the bum".
>
> The decision to ban women was made by *iwi kaumatua*, he said. The health centre was a "sacred site."
>
> "It's not my rules, it's rules that have been brought down through generations."
>
> Women could come on site once the structure was finished, he said.[121]

Jack Rikihana is also the current chairperson of *Te Runanga a Ati Awa ki Whakarongatai,* which claims to be the mandated representative entity for the *iwi* (descent group) of the area where this Health Centre is being built. He is an active *iwi* representative across a range of activities in this region, and was described by Judith Aitken, one of the Health Centre's District Health Board members, as someone who "works tirelessly on behalf of his people."[122] Jack Rikihana's position as a leader and spokesperson for his *iwi* is thus recognized and accepted by both his *iwi* and by the Health Centre's District Health Board.

A spokesperson for the District Health Board said: "The local *iwi* were insistent on that being the case and out of respect for their customs we complied."[123] The ban was apparently approved by a "health board official who thought it would have little practical effect as the project was small and there were no women in the construction crew."[124]

A New Zealand Human Rights Commission spokesperson said that while he was not familiar with the details "it sounds like a case that could be considered under the Human Rights Act if a complaint is received."[125] Subsequently, a complaint was lodged with the Commission about this ban by the Victoria University women's rights collective.[126] This Women's group is one of the representative groups of the Victoria University of Wellington Students' Association, and it is open to all female students. The group is served by an elected Women's Rights Officer and "welcomes all forms of feminism, encourages debate and

---

[121] Kathryn Powley, "Iwi bans women from worksite," *The Dominion Post*, March 28, 2003, p. 8.

[122] Judith Aitken, "Letter to the Editor- Much to learn from Māori," *The Dominion Post* March 5, 2003.

[123] Ibid.

[124] Martin Johnson, "Minister steps in as women banned" *The New Zealand Herald* March 29, 2003.

[125] Ibid.

[126] Kathryn Powley, "Site ban on women lifted" *The Dominion Post*, March 29, 2003, page 7.

discussion, liases with other women's groups on and off campus and is queer-friendly."[127] One of the collective members, Rae Robinson, said "she was "appalled" by the "misogynist" ban, which she said sent a poor message to young women considering careers in construction."[128]

This incident attracted considerable mass media, political, and public attention in New Zealand. On the next day, the District Health Board announced that it had retracted its ban on women setting foot on the new Health Centre site.[129] As the *Dominion Post* reported:

> The turnaround came after [the Minister of Health] Ms King criticised the ban, saying New Zealand was a "secular society", and she planned to visit the building site before it was finished. [She said] "I will expect to see women going about their business on the site when I make my own visit to it at some time in the future."[130]

While *iwi* spokesperson, Jack Rikihana could not be contacted, he was reported to have advised the District Health Board's chief executive "the custom should apply to privately owned dwellings, such as churches and marae, not public buildings."[131] However another District Health Board's chief adviser on *tikanga*, Naida Glavish, was reported to have "agreed with Mr Rikihana that building sites were *tapu*, and said she would enter 'only if it's life-and-death' and after appropriate *karakia* (prayers) had been recited by a *kaumatua* [elder]."[132]

In a later editorial, the *Dominion Post* wrote that:

> The ban was the latest in a series of conflicts between pseudo-religious rites practised by some Māori, who, like adherents of radical Islam, do not accept that the government has been founded on the separation of church and state, and secularism. Bans on women working construction sites are no more acceptable than, for example, mythical taniwha stopping road-building projects or new prisons.[133]

The editor continued:

> New Zealand is undergoing a healthy Māori renaissance—the wisest leaders of the *tangata whenua* are anxious to turn around appalling statistics in health, education and incarceration in jail. But Māori cannot do that by remaining wedded to ancient practices in a modern society where their own people have ample ability to succeed.[134]

---

[127] http://www.vuwsa.org.nz/representation/
[128] Johnson, "Minister Steps In."
[129] Ibid.
[130] Ibid.
[131] Ibid.
[132] Johnson, "Minister Steps In."
[133] Editor "Building site no place for prejudice," *The Dominion Post*, April 3, 2003, page 4.
[134] Ibid.

While this particular incident soon faded from public view, it is nevertheless worth further analysis as it raises several interesting issues concerning the intersection of women, religion, law, colonization, and culture in Aotearoa/New Zealand. On its surface, it appeared to the culturally dominant Pākehā media, public and politicians to be a simple case of discrimination on the grounds of sex/gender, and the inappropriate application of some "pseudo-religious rites"[135] by some intransigent Māori who are "remaining wedded to ancient practices".[136] Furthermore, consideration of this incident in the context of the relationship of colonization that characterizes interactions between Māori and the Crown, and between Māori and Pākehā in Aotearoa, reveals the presence of the dominant perceptions that Māori culture is both patriarchal and oppressive of women and that it is irrelevant and outdated in the modern age. This is evident in the editorial and reporting of the *Dominion Post* and also in the suggestion by the Human Rights Commission spokesperson that this incident, prima facie, warranted investigation by the Commission.

The comments reported to be made by the Minister of Health, Ms Annette King, and the musings of the editor of the *Dominion Post* reiterate the dominant view that New Zealand is a secular society and that "the government has been founded on the separation of church and state."[137] This separation of church or religion from the state and society is juxtaposed against the protocol or *tikanga* of this particular *iwi* of preventing women from entering construction sites, and is pejoratively described as "psuedo-religious" and "ancient". This process of holding *tikanga Māori* up against Pākehā ideology and practices in order to criticise and judge it is part of the armoury of the tactics and practices of colonization, the ultimate goal of which is the invalidation and subjection of *tikanga Māori* and *te ao Māori* to the superiority of Pākehā ideology and practices. This process is reminiscent of the colonial imposition of European constructions of civilization upon Māori, as Wayne Rumbles[138] argues:

> The universal value of sovereignty is based in the construction of European civilisation as the universal civilisation. This discourse is linked with words like progress, advanced, modern, rational, science, order and the rule of law. Indigenous peoples were seen in a state in opposition to that of the universal civilisation as primitive and in a state of nature.[139] Therefore to ignore Māori governance systems and Māori law was seen as an act of civilisation.[140]

---

[135] Ibid.

[136] Ibid.

[137] Johnson, "Minister Steps In."

[138] Wayne Rumbles, *Treaty of Waitangi Settlement Process: New Relationship or New Mask? Sovereignty; Tino Rangatiratanga; Identity and Postcolonialism: A Discourse Analysis Approach* (Waikato University: Unpublished LLM thesis, 1998), 38.

[139] Ibid., n. 159.

[140] Ibid., n. 160.

The word "modern" was used by the editor of the *Dominion Post* to describe the society "we" now live in, and it is contrasted with the description of Māori practices as "psuedo-religious" and "ancient". This polemic once again reinscribes the dichotomy of superior civilised European encountering inferior primitive Māori that has continued to form, reproduce and construct the relationship of colonisation between Māori and the Crown, and Māori and Pākehā, in New Zealand. What is also particular galling is the editor's selective approval of those parts of *te ao Māori* which delineate the successful adoption of this supposedly superior civilization by Māori. For instance, the editor notes that: "New Zealand is undergoing a healthy Māori renaissance—the wisest leaders of the *tangata whenua* are anxious to turn around appalling statistics in health, education and incarceration in jail." The editor seems to suggest here that at least one of the purposes of the Māori renaissance is to reverse the appalling social statistics (which of course Māori are concerned to do), but he totally ignores the context of colonization from which those appalling statistics have been borne and developed.[141] He also ignores the underlying goal of the Māori renaissance—cultural survival. For in ignoring the context of colonization and the goal of cultural survival, Pākehā in this country and colonizing peoples everywhere forget about the violence and any role and responsibility they and their ancestors may have in the perpetuation of cultural genocide. This practice of ignoring and forgetting is a fundamental source of alienation, division, and oppression in any relationship of colonization, and it is present in the hue and cry surrounding this particular incident.

Further, the same editorial suggests that Māori cannot undergo either a "... healthy Māori renaissance [or] ... turn around appalling statistics in health, education and incarceration in jail ... by remaining wedded to ancient practices in a modern society where their own people have ample ability to succeed." The clear message here for all Māori and also all Pākehā in New Zealand is that for Māori to be successful, to be better educated, healthier and remain out of prison, they must relinquish their cultural distinctiveness and *tikanga Māori.* In doing so, the editorial actually assumes that it is Māori and their culture, rather than the processes of colonization and domination, who bear the primary responsibility for the "appalling statistics". Moreover, the editorial reinforces the notion that *tikanga Māori* are inferior, primitive practices that have no place in the modern (read 'civilized' and 'superior' European) society. In other words the editorial is proposing: that these two worlds or ways of being are mutually exclusive; that Māori must give up being Māori to be

---

[141] That the social indicators are indeed 'appalling' is not disputed: see, for example, the findings of Ministry of Women's Affairs (New Zealand), *Māori Women: Mapping Inequalities and Pointing Ways Forward* (Wellington: Ministry of Women's Affairs, 2001).

successful; that Māori must forget our culture; and that to be a Māori who is "wedded to ancient practices" or who lives consistently with *tikanga Māori* is to be doomed. This is an example of the contemporary or modern form of colonization strategies that continue to construct, reproduce, and perpetuate relationships of oppression between Māori and the Crown and Māori and Pākehā in Aotearoa. As Linda Smith notes:

> We have lived through the processes of colonisation by church, by trade, by the gun, by the law and by the more subtle hegemonic processes of internalised self-abhorrence.[142]

What this incident also reflects is a lack of engagement between Māori and Pākehā, and Māori and the Crown in this country. In the context of colonization, this is not at all surprising; it is nonetheless profoundly disappointing. However, if instead of adopting intransigent positions, both parties had talked with each other, heart to heart; if they had been willing to explain why such a ban was necessary in terms of *tikanga* and why it applied to a Health Centre; if they had been willing to explain how such a ban might be inconsistent with anti-discrimination legislation to which the District Health Board is bound to adhere, and why this is concerning to the District Health Board; then perhaps, instead of polarization and reinforcement of the roles of colonization, the outcome might have been development of a relationship based on understanding, engagement, and respectful listening to each other. Crucially, the voices of Māori women were not heard. So, from the public, Pākehā account, we do not know whether Māori women understood their exclusion from the building site in hierarchical terms—as the feminist student collective at Victoria University and the Human Rights Commission spokesperson apparently did—or whether they might have understood it in a way that did not denigrate them as women. Pākehā colonization has rendered invisible Māori women's authority within their own culture. By listening to, yet only partially hearing, solely male Māori accounts of traditional law and custom, and interpreting these through the lens of patriarchal nineteenth century Christianity and the common law, the colonizers initially could not apprehend Māori gender relations and the positions of power and authority that Māori women had been accustomed to hold. By continuing these assumptions into the present, Pākehā institutions—as epitomized by the editorials in the *Dominion Post*—can apparently only accept Māori men in positions of leadership, and can still only interpret *tikanga Māori* in patriarchal terms.

---

[142] Smith, "Māori Women," 47.

Conclusion

We are conscious that the two accounts presented here do not tell the whole story of the complex interplay of culture, law, and religion for women in Aotearoa/New Zealand. One other strand which could be developed is the other effect of the encounter with Christianity, whereby Māori, bypassing or rejecting the increasingly settler orientation of the institutional churches, actively adapted and internalised Christian writing and teaching in ways more suited to Māori culture and orientation, and often arguably more consistent with Christian Gospel teaching. The life and work of Wiremu Tarapipipi Tamihana[143] provides one such example. Another is the story of the settlement at Parihaka, where a practical living-out of a theory of non-violence was brutally put down by the representatives of the "Christian" settlers. A consideration of the influences that shaped Parihaka and the thinking of its leaders, Te Whiti and Tohu, is a greater task than we can attempt here.[144] But it would give an indication of the complex religious and social context, and conflict, of nineteenth century New Zealand.

That complexity we would argue needs to be fully considered in the ways in which we now seek to address the challenges facing us at the beginning of the twenty-first century: how societies and faith communities may duly reflect the history of their founding cultures, while also accommodating groups of later arrivals. For, as mentioned above, the demographic patterns of New Zealand are changing and Māori will become a larger percentage of the population than they have been since the mid nineteenth century.[145] Furthermore, there are now other groups in New Zealand society, different often in both culture and religion from both Māori and Pākehā. There are now many settlers in New Zealand who have come from places in Asia. There is a visible Muslim presence [146] and relations between that community and the Christian Churches here have on the whole been positive and encouraged.[147]

---

[143] See Evelyn Stokes, *Wiremu Tamihana Rangatira* (Wellington: Huia Publishers, 2002).

[144] Davidson, *Christianity in Aotearoa,* Chaps 5, 7; Hazel Riseborough, *Days of Darkness: Taranaki 1878–1884* (Wellington: Allen & Unwin, 1989), Davidson and Lineham, *Transplanted Christianity*, 156–8; Donovan, *Religions of New Zealanders,* chap. 9.

[145] By 2016, 1 in 4 New Zealanders will have a Māori or Pacific Island background (NZ Herald 21/2/04).

[146] See Donovan ed., *Religions of New Zealanders*, chaps 14 and 18.

[147] For example, when Algerian refugee and former Member of the Algerian Parliament, Ahmed Zaoui was held in detention because of his alleged threat to New Zealand national security (despite the fact that the Refugee Status Appeals Authority had granted him refugee status), the campaign for his release was conducted on an inter-faith basis. When the Supreme Court ordered his release on bail in December 2004 he was given shelter by the Dominican Friars in Auckland. See the collection of press releases and information on the Human Rights Foundation of New Zealand webpage: http://www.humanrights.co.nz.

And there are now communities of immigrants of other faiths whose needs or customs the law must be able to take account of in one way or another, including accommodating, or deciding not to accommodate, differing views on the role and status of women.

One innovative example can be seen in the revised constitution (1992) of the Anglican Church in Aotearoa/New Zealand and Polynesia, with its three separate *Tikanga* Houses with independent resources and ministry units, but with a doctrinal 'common life'.[148] Similar models have been suggested for constitutional and legal reform.[149] In the legal context, the task may be harder than it is in a Church, which is united by a common belief system: how to accommodate different sets of values in one legal system and institutions? The examination of the Human Rights Act, above, indicates some of the difficulties to be faced here. Within the current legal system, we have seen examples of a possible clash between the human rights statutes and religious views. But the example in the second part of our chapter suggests a more fundamental difficulty: that the Human Rights Act is part of a legal system which is inherently non-reflective of the indigenous culture.

As it grapples with these questions of how to reflect different religious and social values, including those which address women's role and status, in law and its institutions, Aotearoa/New Zealand mirrors in microcosm the struggles of many other societies and jurisdictions in our region.

---

[148] Davidson, *Christianity in Aotearoa*, 137–9, 185.

CHAPTER SIX

THE ROMAN CATHOLIC CHURCH AND THE RIGHTS OF EAST TIMORESE WOMEN

Susan Harris Rimmer

Introduction

Timor Lorosa'e is the world's newest State, but it has inherited some complex problems from its history as a Portuguese colony (mid-sixteenth century until 1975) and an occupied Indonesian province (1975–1999).[1] In a State where educational opportunities are limited, poverty is widespread and contact with the outside world was curtailed during the period of Indonesian rule, the influence of the Catholic Church is pervasive. As one of the few institutions that remained intact during the occupation without collaborating with Indonesian forces, the Church has played, and will continue to play, an important role in helping Timor Lorosa'e become a fully independent, stable democracy.

For women, however, the crucial role played by the Catholic Church in East Timorese society has proved a mixed blessing. In many ways the struggle that the women of Timor Lorosa'e face in their dealings with the Church is a microcosm of the complex way in which the Catholic Church generally both supports women against certain types of oppression, but aids in perpetuating other forms of oppression. Since the Second Vatican Council in the 1962–1965[2] (if not earlier[3])

[1] The author wishes to acknowledge the valuable advice and assistance with this chapter received from Catherine Scott of the Catholic Institute for International Relations, the editors, and supervisors Professor Hilary Charlesworth, Professor Andrew Byrne and Dr Pene Mathew of Australian National University.

[2] See, in particular, *Gaudium et Spes: Pastoral Constitution on the Church in the Modern World* AAS 58 (1966), 1025–1120 which was formally approved by the Council on 7 December 1965, the second last day of the Council. Paragraph 26.1 reads: "(T)here is a growing awareness of the exalted dignity proper to the human person, since he stands above all things and his *rights and duties are universal and inviolable*. Therefore, there must be made available to all men everything necessary for leading a life truly human, such as food, clothing, and shelter; the right to choose a state of life freely and to found a family, the right to education, to employment, to a good reputation, to respect, to appropriate information, to activity in accord with the upright norms of one's own conscience, to protection of privacy and to rightful freedom, even in matters religious." (Emphasis added).

[3] For a collection of key Vatican documents dealing with human rights from as early as 1890 see Michael Walsh and Brian Davies, ed, *Proclaiming Justice and Peace: One Hundred Years of Catholic Social Teaching* (London: Flame HarperCollins, 1991).

the Church has increasingly been prepared to criticize governments for abuses of human rights. This is particularly the case when a predominantly Catholic population faces domination by a non-Catholic regime—a situation faced in Catholic Poland by Pope John Paul II during his younger days, and a situation in which the East Timorese found themselves during Indonesian occupation. But while the Church and its leadership has been prepared to call upon leaders acting in the public sphere to behave in compliance with human rights, it has been far more ambivalent with respect to abuse visited on women within the private spheres of Church and home, where women have generally been exhorted to be passive and patient in response to their suffering.

Both of these phenomena can be seen in Timor Lorosa'e. Where women's suffering under Indonesian occupation can be equated with that of men, the Church has been responsive and supportive of justice for victims. Indeed the Church has stood in solidarity with those who suffered so greatly under the occupation and has resisted attempts by the government to ignore past injustices. Yet, when women's oppression has been gender specific—involving rape by occupying forces or domestic violence in the home—the Church has often aligned itself with the violators rather than the victims. Moreover, this demarcation between the 'public' and 'private' realms to the detriment of women is reinforced by the response of international law to the transitional justice process in Timor Lorosa'e.

Women in Timor Lorosa'e

Timor Lorosa'e remains the poorest nation in Asia, with a total population of just under 990,000. The median age is 19 and 40 per cent of the population live below the poverty line.[4] The situation of women within this new nation is correspondingly bleak at the current time. One manifestation of the way in which this widespread poverty can have gender specific effects can be seen in World Health Organization figures, which show that twice as many women die in childbirth in Timor Lorosa'e as anywhere else in East Asia or the Western Pacific.[5] There are only 196 midwives available for a population of 800,000, which means that less than a quarter of Timor Lorosa'e's women have ready access to a health facility or a qualified midwife. The World Health Organization describes these figures as "an absolute tragedy."[6]

[4] United Nations Development Programme, East Timor National Human Development Report, *Ukan Rasik A'an: The Way Ahead* (Dili: United Nations Development Programme, 2002).

[5] World Health Organisation, *WHO's Contribution to Health Sector Development in East Timor* (Dili: World Health Organisation, 2001), 10.

[6] United Nations Development Programme, "More Women Die in Childbirth in East Timor than Anywhere in East Asia," Press Release, March 8, 2002, http://www.reliefweb.int/w/rwb.nsf/0/6c59b58c0921404949256b7d001e9c93?OpenDocument.

Some of the problems that continue to face the women of Timor Lorosa'e were graphically outlined by advocate Sister Maria de Lourdes. Sister Maria assisted many thousands of Timorese in the aftermath of the 1999 violence in Liquicia, Dili and West Timor, and founded the institute Maun Alin Iha Kristo ("Brothers and Sisters of Christ") to help the poorest people in Timor Lorosa'e improve their economic situation by reviving and preserving their culture. In a speech she made at a public event in 2002 to formally respect and honour the contribution of East Timorese women to independence, and the high price they paid during the Indonesian occupation, Sister Maria described how Timor Lorosa'e women are still "second class citizens" because girls do not receive "the same educational or employment opportunities as men", domestic violence is "rampant" and women are "slaves in their own homes" while the male leaders of independent Timor Lorosa'e are "still unwilling to accept [...] women as equals".[7]

A particular issue of concern for the women of Timor Lorosa'e is that domestic violence is pervasive and abuse within the home is so widespread that East Timorese authorities believe that it affects all families. Nearly half of the criminal cases in the country are crimes involving domestic violence and over half of all women interviewed in a recent study of domestic violence reported feeling unsafe in their relationships.[8]

Yet the position of the women of Timor Lorosa'e is not static and there are some causes for optimism. When Natércia Godinho-Adams addressed the UN Security Council, she pointed out that while the Indonesian occupation had been a tragedy for the women of Timor Lorosa'e, the crisis had also created a number of new opportunities for them:

> Men's and women's roles changed substantially during the years of conflict and social disruption since 1974. A significant number of women assumed active roles in the clandestine liberation front and the armed resistance. They were soldiers, they smuggled medication, food, armament, and information to the resistance movement hiding in the mountains. [...]. In the absence of the male household head, women assumed new responsibilities in traditional male income generation. East Timorese women want to build a society that will respect their newly acquired post-conflict roles, and will not force them to return to traditional powerless roles.[9]

[7] Curt Gabrielson, "East Timorese Women's Fight Against Violence," *Institute of Current World Affairs*, Letters, January 1, 2002: 3, http://www.peacewomen.org/resources/Timor-Leste/ETViolence2002.pdf.

[8] Sophie Boudre, "A Cruel History for East-Timorese Women," *Voices Unabridged: The E-Magazine on Women and Human Rights Worldwide* 1 (2004), http://www.voices-unabridged.org.

[9] United Nations, Press Briefing, "Headquarters Press Conference on Women in Peacekeeping", October 30, 2001, http://www.un.org/News/briefings/docs/2001/womenpkpc.doc.htm.

Thus the position of women is fluid. While in many ways Timor Lorosa'e remains a patriarchal and traditional society, there are social forces that suggest that women will start to play a greater role in the governing of the country as the strong showing of Fretilin [Frente Revolucionario de Leste Timor Independent] women in the recent elections demonstrates.[10]

The Catholic Church in Timor Lorosa'e

Timor Lorosa'e has a deep relationship with the Catholic Church. Ninety percent of the population identifies as Catholic, and there is almost universal attendance of weekly masses all over the island. Although the Church was prominent in the Portuguese colonial period, most East Timorese actually identified as animists until the 1975 occupation. However the Indonesian Government did not recognize animism as a religion on its census forms, and therefore many Timorese began formally to identify as Catholic only from the time of the occupation. During the Indonesian occupation, Church leaders such as Father Martinho da Costa Lopes and Bishop Carlos Filipe Ximenes Belo were seen to be not only independent, but also fiercely critical of Indonesian excesses. As Rowena Lennox points out in her biography of Father Lopes, "[t]he Catholic Church was the only organization in East Timor with infrastructure and independent links to the outside world."[11] However, the Church in Timor Lorosa'e was cut off from the outside world at the same time as the changes introduced by the second Vatican Council (1962–5) were beginning to percolate through the Church on a global level. Some trappings of the pre-Vatican II era therefore still remain, but as Timor continues to open up to the international community, the Timorese Church will inevitably be exposed to a variety of influences from within the Church internationally.

Since 1999, the Church has carefully defined its role in East Timorese politics. Bishop Belo stated in a circular on 11 February 2001 that "[t]he whole process of formation of this people as a nation, all the problems which it will meet, all the challenges it will face, are the problems and challenges of the Church. The Church is one with the people in the gigantic task of building a new East Timorese nation."[12]

---

[10] UNIFEM East and Southeast Asia Regional Office, "Support for Women in 2001 Elections in East Timor," http://www.unifem-eseasia.org/projects/easttimor/EastTElection.htm.

[11] Rowena Lennox, *Fighting Spirit of East Timor: The Life of Martinho da Costa Lopes* (Annandale: Pluto Press, 2000), 6.

[12] Quoted in Pat Walsh, *East Timor's Political Parties And Groupings: Briefing Notes* (Australian Council for Overseas Aid, 2001), appendix 3, http://www.asia-pacific-action.org/southeastasia/easttimor/resources/reports/etparpol.htm.

That the Church has played, and, given its influence, is likely to continue to play, an important role in shaping the culture of the newly independent country is undoubted. The question of the extent to which that influence will be of benefit to women is far more controversial. The ambivalence that many women's groups feel towards the role of the Church can be examined by looking at two case-studies—the proposed amnesty law and the Church's response to domestic violence.

Case Study One: Timor's Draft Amnesty Legislation

The role of the Church in relation to transitional justice demonstrates the extent to which it can provide powerful support regarding issues that are important to many East Timorese women. Yet the voices of the government, women and the Church are distinct and deserve separate consideration.

The Voice of the Government

Xanana Gusmão, the new President of Timor Lorosa'e, has consistently put the position that it may be better not to focus on righting past wrongs through trials of those guilty of offences during the occupation. He stated in 2002 that "[w]e must do our best to eradicate all sentiments of hatred, of revenge. If you still feel like this, then you are living with the ghosts of the past." This language is insensitive to the fact that in Timor Lorosa'e many women are living with the ghosts of past husbands, fathers, and sons who fell victim to the crimes committed during the occupation and, of course, many women were directly victims of the occupation themselves.

In early May 2002, a draft law on amnesty and pardons was prepared by President Gusmão. The draft law was introduced to the Constituent Assembly (the predecessor to the National Parliament) in the hope that it would be passed promptly on 20 May 2002 and thus form part of general independence celebrations. The Assembly, however, declined to discuss the draft in the limited timeframe allowed and instead referred it for redrafting. It has since been reintroduced to the National Parliament with some minor amendments. There has been significant NGO anxiety on the draft legislation.[13]

Of primary concern, the draft amnesty law seems to apply to serious crimes such as war crimes, genocide, crimes against humanity and torture set out in Regulation 2000/15. The draft law also provides for the reduction in sentences

[13] Judicial System Monitoring Programme, "What will be the Effect of the Draft Amnesty Law?" May 12, 2002, http://www.jsmp.minihub.org/Legislation/AmnEng.doc.

for people convicted of crimes against humanity. Therefore, even if (against enormous odds) a woman has secured a conviction as a victim of a crime against humanity, the convicted perpetrator could be released immediately. On 5 April 2004 the Parliament decided to give "general approval" to the draft Amnesty and Pardon law. The Parliament was supposed to consider each article of the draft law on 10 May 2004, but instead the debate was suspended until 2005.[14] The bill then lapsed, made redundant by the decision of the governments of Timor Lorosa'e and Indonesia in August 2005 to create a Joint Truth and Friendship Commission, granting immunity from prosecution for those invesitgated over the 1999 violence.

The issue is not only the substance of the draft legislation, but the fact that President Gusmão, and now the Government, seem eager to pass such an important bill without any consultation or involvement by the people who have the most to lose by it—the survivors and families of victims. While in Jakarta to invite the then-Indonesia President Megawati Soekarnoputri to attend the independence celebrations, Gusmão told a press conference:

> I believe if we talk about justice we see a few people to be judged, to be tried. But if we talk about social justice, we have all our people to gain [...]. I'm not saying I don't agree with justice. Justice, yes, justice. But what is my priority? Social justice. We suffered and died for what? To try other people or to receive benefits from independence? Our people are dying because of famine, because of disease. Women are dying, many children are dying, our elderly people are living in a very bad condition. It is a question of balancing the importance of issues.[15]

But even if this is an important perspective, President Gusmão and the Parliament of Timor Lorosa'e are under an obligation at least to consider the interests of the citizens who elected them, and that includes the voices of women who suffered under the occupation.

The Government of Timor Lorosa'e, however, seems to have now followed the President's lead and have all but given up on the issue of formal retributive justice for crimes committed in 1999, let alone during the occupation. Mari Alkatiri, the Prime Minister of Timor Lorosa'e, called in June 2003 for an amnesty for prisoners currently serving sentences in Timorese jails for crimes committed in 1999, but for reasons of avoiding hypocrisy rather than the imperative of reconstruction.[16] The charge of hypocrisy can be validly

---

[14] See further, Judicial System Monitoring Programme, "Parliament Gives Preliminary Approval to Amnesty Law," Press Release, May 7, 2004.

[15] AAP, "Gusmão to Focus on Freeing People from Poverty," *Sydney Morning Herald*, May 2002.

[16] "East Timor: PM Alkatiri Wants Amnesty for Crimes of 1999," ETAN (East Timor and Indonesia Action Network), June 12, 2003, http://www.etan.org/et2003/june/08-14/12etpm.htm.

made—in the absence of Indonesia making the most crucial defendants available to the Serious Crimes Court in Dili, and the Indonesian ad hoc Human Rights Tribunal failing to convict the commanding officers indicted for planning systemic violations, the few convictions by the Dili Court were lower level Timorese militia, while their Indonesian commanders have walked free.[17]

The United Nations also seems to have reviewed its position on formal justice. The Serious Crimes Unit of the United Nations Mission of Support in East Timor (UNMISET) issued eight important indictments, including former armed forces chief General Wiranto on 25 February 2003, in the knowledge that its mandate would expire in August 2004. On that same day, UN Spokesperson Fred Eckhard said that the UN had not issued the indictment and that the UN was only providing "advisory assistance" to the government of Timor Lorosa'e. The UN Commission on Human Rights also dropped its agenda item on justice for Timor Lorosa'e in its 59th session in 2003.[18]

The Voice of the Church

The government and UN position on amnesties has been challenged by a number of organisations in Timor Lorosa'e, including religious groups. For example, the Christian Consultation on East Timor (CCET), led by Catholic Church agencies, has accused the UN in explicitly biblical language of "washing its hands of responsibility for the indictments".[19]

The role of Bishop Belo has been particularly important. As co-recipient of the Nobel prize (with now-foreign minister Jose Ramos Horta) and a moral leader of the opposition to the abuses of the Indonesian government, he is one of the few figures with sufficient public respect and standing to credibly oppose President Xanana Gusmão's position on amnesties. Bishop Belo has been prepared publicly and emotively to put the case for the victims, even

---

17 Suzannah Linton, *Prosecuting Atrocities at the District Court of Dili* 2 *Melbourne Journal of International Law* 2(2001):456–8. A good summary of the current state of the case-law can be found at the Website of the Judicial System Monitoring Program, http://www.jsmp.minihub.org/courtmonitoring/ddc.htm

18 Commission on Human Rights, *Report on the Fifty-Ninth Session*, Economic and Social Council E/2003/23 E/CN.4/2003/135, Annexe 1 sets out the agenda where there is no mention of East Timor. In contrast, the discussion of the situation in East Timor was agenda item 42 in the 2003 session. See Commission on Human Rights, *Report on the Fifty-Eighth Session*, Economic and Social Council E/2002/23 E/CN.4/2002/200, 36.

19 Catholic Institute for International Relations, "Church Network Urges UN to Press Ahead with Timor Prosecutions," Press Release, March 18, 2003, http://www.jsmp.minihub.org/News/18_03_03etnews24feb03jr.htm.

when the government has wanted to move past the issue of criminal justice for atrocities. As Bishop Belo has said, "I hear the voices of widows, the complaints of raped women, of orphans. They don't like to live together and meet in the street their perpetrators."[20] In contesting the policy of government that comprises his former comrades, Bishop Belo puts the case for the victims and his words demonstrate an awareness of the gendered nature of the problem. The men in government make the decisions in regard to amnesties, but the Bishop argues the case for women victims—the 'widows, raped women and orphans.'

This advocacy is not new for the Bishop. He has consistently pushed first the Indonesians and now the indigenous government to take human rights seriously. In 2000 he wrote of "the path to freedom" and asked the international community to take heed of "the legacy of the past" when watching Timor Lorosa'e struggle towards a democratic society "founded on the values enshrined in the Universal Declaration of Human Rights". He wrote: "[u]p to 3,000 died in 1999, untold numbers of women were raped and 500,000 persons displaced—100,000 are yet to return."[21] The picture that he paints of the past suffering and future challenges for the country never excludes the "untold numbers" of women who have suffered under the occupation.

The Church, through both its formal leadership and through some of its associated bodies, has continued to be critical of the stance of the government and has stood firmly for the position that there can be no amnesties without the consent of victims. This criticism extends to the United Nations, as well as the new Timorese government. For example, Catherine Scott of the Catholic Institute for International Relations (CIIR) stated the network's opposition to the position of the United Nations to amnesties: "[n]ow that indictments have been issued against some of these persons, it is somewhat disingenuous of your spokesman to suggest that they are nothing to do with the UN. The crimes committed in East Timor were not only crimes against the East Timorese population, but were crimes against international law. They were crimes against the international community and against the UN itself."[22]

The Church in Timor and its international allies now appear to be a lone internal voice of power supporting the calls of Timorese non-government organizations for an international tribunal, and for material amendments to the amnesty laws. The Church has used the framework of international law

[20] Associated Press, "Revenge is Low on the List of Priorities," *The Weekend Australian*, May 18–19, 2002.

[21] Bishop Carlos Filipe Ximenes Belo, "To Forge a Future, Timor Needs Justice for the Past," *Sydney Morning Herald*, August 28, 2001, http://www.jsmp.minihub.org/Reports/Belo.htm.

[22] Ibid.

to explain its moral stance on justice in public statements. In a Pastoral Appeal in June 2002 entitled "On Amnesty and the Settlement of Crimes Against Humanity" that was timed to coincide with Parliament's reconsideration of the amnesty law, Belo said forcefully "[b]y international human rights standards, victims have a right to the truth and to indemnity, restitution, and reparation." The Bishop continued to take this stance, in clear contrast to the Government's view, until his retirement in November 2002.[23]

East Timor's new Catholic Bishop Alberto Ricardo da Silva has continued this rights-based opposition to the new Joint Truth and Friendship Commission. It was set up by Timor and Indonesian leaders to divert the UN from a damning Commission of Experts report, issued in July 2005, which called for the establishment of an international tribunal. He stated that "past crimes must be tried whatever Kofi Annan may say and whatever East Timorese leaders may want ... The position of the church is the same, it's clear and firm. We need justice, justice must be done."[24]

The Voice of Women

Women's groups in Timor Lorosa'e have a strong claim that it is women who have suffered the most from the time of the 1975 occupation until the present day.[25] It seems that Timorese women were targeted for gender persecution because of their centrality to the independence movement, including armed resistance. For example, Ana Lemos, chairperson of the resistance organization OMT in Ermera, was raped and murdered because, as one of her killers said, "she was the most courageous woman in Ermera".[26] Kirsty Sword Gusmão reports that many women put their lives on the line in the struggle for freedom:

> An untold number of women paid the price for their activism through torture, imprisonment, death and, more commonly, through the pain associated with the loss of husbands, children and other family members. The wives and children of Falintil soldiers and resistance leaders were particularly vulnerable to rape and sexual abuse by the Indonesian military, as they often lived alone or were left

---

[23] Bishop Carlos Filipe Ximenes Belo, *The Road to Freedom: A Collection of Speeches, Pastoral Letters and Articles From 1997–2001* (Sydney: Caritas Australia, 2001).

[24] *AsiaNews*, "Timor Bishop Opposes War Crimes Deal," February 7, 2005, http://www.asianews.it/view.php?l=en&art=2525.

[25] Kirsty Sword Gusmão, "Still Fighting To Be Free: East Timorese Women, Survivors Of Violence," Keynote Address at the Inaugural Domestic Violence And Sexual Assault Conference, Gold Coast, September 5, 2001, http://www.austdvclearinghouse.unsw.edu.au/Conference%20papers/Seek-soln/Gusmao,Kirsty.pdf.

[26] Galuh Wandita, "Left over from death," *Inside Indonesia* April–June (2001).

> without the protection of male members of the family for extended periods. In spite of this vulnerability, I have heard numerous tales of wives and mothers risking their lives by hiding members of the Falintil in their homes and by smuggling food and water to the guerrillas in their remote mountain hideouts.[27]

The phrase "untold numbers of women" is poignant, and literal—the story of women's experience before, during and after the 1999 violence remains largely untold despite the extraordinary efforts of Timorese women advocates. Evidence that gender-based international crimes in Timor Lorosa'e have been widespread since 1975 and were rife in the 1999 violence has been collected by the United Nations,[28] human rights NGOs such as Amnesty International,[29] an independent Indonesian Commission of Enquiry (KPP Ham),[30] Australian journalists,[31] and East Timorese NGOs themselves.[32] A joint United Nations fact-finding mission in November 1999 (consisting of the Special Rapporteur on Violence against Women, the Special Rapporteur on Extrajudicial, Summary or Arbitrary Executions, and the Special Rapporteur on the Question of Torture) found evidence of widespread violence against women in Timor Lorosa'e during the period from January 1999. It concluded that "the highest level of the military command in East Timor knew, or had reason to know, that there was widespread violence against women in East Timor."[33]

Many women have not merely relied on the advocacy of the Church in developing their responses to this violence, but have vigorously put forward a gendered perspective about the appropriate response to the crimes that were committed against them. Fokupers, a leading women's non-governmental

---

[27] Kirsty Sword Gusmão, "Still Fighting To Be Free."

[28] See especially *Report of the International Commission of Inquiry on East Timor to the Secretary-General*, United Nations Document A/54/726, January 31, 2000; *Report of the Security Council Mission to Jakarta and Dili*, United Nations Security Council Document S/1999/976, September 14, 1999; *Report of U.N. Special Rapporteurs: Situation of Human Rights in East Timor*, United Nations Document A/54/660, December 10, 1999.

[29] Amnesty International, *East Timor: Justice Past, Present and Future*, AI Index ASA 57/001/2001, July 27, 2001.

[30] Indonesian Commission of Enquiry (KPP-Ham) *Report on East Timor*, January 31, 2000, http://www.jsmp.minihub.org/Reports/KPP%20Ham.htm.

[31] Hamish McDonald et al, *Masters of Terror: Indonesia's Military and Violence in East Timor in 1999* (Canberra: Australian National University Strategic and Defence Studies Centre, 2002).

[32] See generally Natércia Godinho-Adams, *UN Security Council "Arria formula" Meeting on the Implementation of Security Council Resolution 1325*, October 30, 2001, http://www.pcug.org.au/~wildwood/01octwomen.htm; Fokupers, *Gender-based Human Rights Abuses during the Pre and Post-Ballot Violence in East Timor* (Dili, 2000). In September 1999, the office of Fokupers in Dili was attacked by militia, resulting in the looting and burning of the premises and to the staff of the organisation having to flee to save their lives.

[33] United Nations Economic and Social Council, Fifty-seventh Session, Commission on Human Rights, *Integration of the Human Rights of Women and the Gender Perspective: Violence Against Women*, prepared by Ms. Radhika Coomaraswamy, in pursuance of Commission on Human Rights Resolution 2000/45, E/CN.4/2001/73, January 23, 2001.

organization, made a series of demands of the United Nations in 2000. The demands made by the group included a thorough investigation of gender-based violence and support for those who will give formal testimony against perpetrators. They also want to see resources allocated for women and children affected by the violence and assurances that women's interests and equality will be taken into account in the future.[34]

If we accept that the greatest suffering during the violence was borne by women, and that their efforts in supporting the resistance to Indonesian occupation were important in achieving independence, then principles of equality and non-discrimination suggest that women should have substantial participation in determining what type of transitional justice is established. This justice (and, indeed, broader social policy) should be designed to fit, not exclude, the female experience. Therefore, women's experiences should directly impact on decisions about transitional justice. This position is forcefully put by activist Angelina Saramento:

> There are many contradictory ideas—for example, on the leaders' side, Xanana [Gusmão] a few months ago mentioned an amnesty—was he talking on the side of the victims or on the side of the political leaders, their perspective? For those who still really suffer, is not the leaders, but the main victims were the civilian people, so in order to make a decision as to how to bring the perpetrators to the court or whether to give an amnesty, the leaders have no right to decide it because they are not the ones who really suffered through the troubles.[35]

Gusmão is a revered figure in Timor Lorosa'e and there is no doubt that he has enormous empathy for the suffering of his people. But he was also a soldier, a man, the leader of the resistance movement that allegedly committed some of the crimes in question, and was physically absent in an Indonesian prison during many of the worst incidents of the occupation. His experience of suffering (significant though it was) is not easily equated to that of the women victims of the occupation. Many of the senior members of the current government were in exile during the occupation. The voices of women need to be heard in the debate over amnesties in Timor Lorosa'e or the resulting decision will only reflect the skewed perspective of the male leadership.

The Area of Tension—Sexual Crimes Against Women

In most aspects of the debate over amnesties, the Church and women's groups have spoken with one voice. Both have refused to let victims be sidelined in the transformation of Timor Lorosa'e into an independent country and both

---

[34] Fokupers. *Gender-based Human Rights Abuses.*

[35] Angelina Saramento of KSI, interview by author, Dili, January 23, 2002.

have spoken of the importance of formal judicial proceedings to right past wrongs. As the discussion above illustrates, the Church leadership has publicly acknowledged the suffering of women who were the victims of rape and other sexual crimes.

Yet sexual offences against women is an area in which the Church's influence has been ambivalent. On one hand, Church leaders have advocated the importance of reparations for women who have been raped. They have also stood against the notion that women are to be regarded as sinful or impure by virtue of being raped. One member of the Commission for Reception Truth and Reconciliation, Catholic priest Father Jovito, has consistently sided with women who were victims of the occupation. By his participation in the Commission, he and the Church offered pastoral care and also learnt about the gendered experience of occupation. One participant in the Women and Conflict hearings expressed concerns about the status of her marriage since her rape by a militia commander in 1999, and was reassured by Father Jovito that rape cannot nullify her marriage.[36] Such reassurance by a leading Catholic priest on the question of law and morality could prove invaluable for the particular woman, but the story should also bring home to the Church hierarchy the concern many women feel about these issues.

This understanding has spread to some of the population as well. A story reported from a "women to women" visit from 23 June to 1 July 1999 of the World Council of Churches and the Christian Conference of Asia details a horrific set of rapes, assaults, destruction of property and constant fear for the wife of a Falintil soldier, and then notes:

> Fortunately her husband understands that it was not her fault. He told her that they all face risks for the sake of freedom, and that she too, as a woman, needs to face risks.

What she said sounded like a theological statement:

> This experience has given me a new perception of my womanhood and my power. I know that almost every other woman in my village has had a similar experience of violence. I am determined to fight for the life of other women. Men may fight with guns, but as a woman I will fight with the power that I have gained out of my suffering, by raising my voice.[37]

But East Timorese women have not, in fact, been treated as heroes. East Timorese women clearly feel that because their resistance was based in their homes, it has been ignored by the UN administration and the government of

[36] Karen Campbell-Nelson, "E. Timor Women Must Tell of RI Atrocities," Commission for Reception, Truth, and Reconciliation (CAVR), Dili, posted to the Internet site on June 2003, http://www.jsmp.minihub.org/News/11_6nb_03.htm.

Timor Lorosa'e when public law and policy have been formulated. Media reports confirm that the "victims of militia rape and sex slavery continue to bear the scars of post-ballot violence in East Timor, facing ostracism on their return home."[38] Abuelda Alves of Fokupers bluntly states that women who are able to return home, often with babies who are the product of rape, "are viewed as rubbish. Their families are embarrassed. Women who were already married, their husbands reject them."[39]

While the official position of the Church is not to blame women for the sexual crimes committed against them, the Church has some degree of complicity in creating a culture in which victims of sexual crimes are mistreated. It is reported in one village, for example, that Church workers refused to allow baptisms for the babies born of rape, or confessions for their mothers.[40] More generally, the conservativism of Timorese Catholic society, particularly in relation to issues of sexuality, is partly generated from a religion in which sexual purity, particularly for women, is given great significance. In light of this, it is understandable that Ms Abrantes of Fokupers notes that the culture of Timor Lorosa'e is in large part to blame for the reluctance of rape victims to speak out, as the publicity means shame and humiliation: "Our culture does not allow women to speak out. For some it is very, very difficult. They feel great shame, they are shy and cry."[41]

More generally, Church has played a role in contributing to the culture of Timor Lorosa'e that leads to women being blamed for their victimhood and discouraged from being assertive of their rights to physical integrity. While the Church has officially encouraged women to stand up to those linked to the occupation who committed sexual violence, it has discouraged women from standing up to abuse and violence (including rape) within the home and family. The Church is itself a patriarchal institution wedded to ideas of hierarchy and obedience and has supported the patriarchal structure of East Timorese society. Despite the genuinely heroic struggle of the Church against the occupation and the fight by the Church for the rights of all victims of the occupation, it must accept some responsibility for creating a society in which women

---

[37] World Council of Churches (WCC) and Christian Conference of Asia (CCA), *Women to Women: A Solidarity Visit to Indonesia and East Timor*, June 23 – July 1, 1999, http://www.wcc-coe.org/wcc/what/international/indon.html.

[38] AFP, "Scars of Vote Violence Remain Real for Many East Timor Women," Dili, November 19, 2001, http://www.pcug.org.au/~wildwood/AFPScars.htm.

[39] Ibid.

[40] Seth Mydans, "Sexual Violence as Tool of War: Pattern Emerging in East Timor," *New York Times*, 1 March 2001.

[41] Asia Human Rights News, "East Timor: Sexual Violence including Rape was a Deliberate Military Strategy against East Timorese Women," April 7, 2001, http://www.ahrchk.net/news/mainfile.php/ahrnews_200104/1402/.

grow accustomed to violence and are blamed when they try to escape from abusive relationships. In such circumstances it is hard to expect women who have been encouraged to be subservient in their private lives suddenly to stand against the violence of the occupiers.

Case Study Two: "Bikan Ho Kanura Baku Malu" (The Plate And Fork Beat Each Other): Combating Domestic Violence In Timor Lorosa'e

The Problem of Domestic Violence

The issue of sexual violence in the home remains the key priority for Timorese women and non-government organizations, with frightening levels of domestic violence reported in every District.[42] A recent study by the International Rescue Committee (IRC) has provided troubling evidence of domestic violence in Timor Lorosa'e.[43] Disturbingly, the report found that family disputes and violence perpetrated by a husband to wife is considered as a "normal", yet very private, occurrence within the family. In an IRC study on the "Prevalence of Gender-Based Violence (GBV) in East Timor", 51 percent of women consulted stated that in the last 12 months they had felt unsafe in their relationship with their husband. In the "IRC Pilot Study on GBV in East Timor", it was found that 24.8 percent of women had experienced violence from an intimate partner in the past year.

Women's own attitudes to domestic violence were seen as significant, especially in relation to domestic violence campaigns which have taken place in Timor Lorosa'e and the drafting of the Domestic Violence Legislation in 2003. In the IRC study mentioned above, fifty-one percent of women surveyed strongly agreed that "a man has good reason to hit his wife if she disobeys him". Therefore, motivations for seeking assistance for violence are important to consider. Again, in this study, 84 percent of respondents strongly agreed with the statement that "family problems should only be discussed with people in the family", and 51 percent of women felt that the best way to cope was with support from their family. Most women who did seek help for domestic violence went to their family (32 percent), five per cent went to "traditional justice", three percent went to police, and nine percent tried to forget about it.[44]

---

[42] Manuela Leong Peirera, "Domestic Violence: A Part of Women's Daily Lives in East Timor," *La'o Hamutuk Bulletin* 2 no.5 (2001): 5–6.

[43] Aisling Swaine, International Rescue Committee, "Traditional Justice and Gender Based Violence Research Report," August 2003, http://www.jsmp.minihub.org/new/article.htm.

[44] Ibid., 34.

Timorese women experience this current violence in a particularly difficult and compounded context—they have not received the services they need to heal as survivors of torture. The International Rehabilitation Council for Torture Victims (IRCT), an independent international health professional organization, carried out a national psycho-social needs assessment in Timor Lorosa'e in June and July 2000. The aim was to assess the extent of 'torture and trauma and the health impact it had on the population.' The report found that torture was widespread. Thirty-nine percent of respondents said that they had been tortured, but a larger number, 57 percent, said they had experienced at least one of the six forms of torture included in the study, including rape or sexual abuse.[45]

The Legal and Governmental Position

In June 2003, the Timorese legal non-governmental organization Judicial System Monitoring Program (JSMP) summarized the way in which the legal system deals with domestic violence:

> Domestic violence accounts for approximately 40% of all cases before the Criminal Division of the District Court system—yet the justice system continues to undervalue the seriousness of such offences. Local communities, police investigators and prosecutors continue to treat many such offences inappropriately by referring them to mediation for resolution. Further concerns arise as to a substantial number of cases which are dealt with by the traditional justice system with reportedly highly varied, and, for the victim, unsatisfactory outcomes. Inadequate community education, together with a lack of support and counselling services for victims of domestic violence continue to mean that such offences often go unreported and/or inadequately managed.[46]

The relationship to the conflict and the tensions of transitional justice period make working on issues of domestic violence even more confronting than usual, especially if the Government treats it as a private circumstance rather than as a part of the transition. In the words of the Catholic Institute for International Relations, "[d]omestic violence against East Timorese women is an explosive issue which goes to the heart of gender equity."[47]

---

[45] J. Modvig et al., "Torture and Trauma in Post-Conflict East Timor," *Lancet* 356(9243) (2000): 1763.

[46] Judicial Systems Monitoring Programme, "Background Paper on the Justice Sector," June 4, 2003, http://www.jsmp.minihub.org/News/04_06_03.htm. See further JSMP, *Women in the Formal Justice Sector* (Dili: JSMP, April 2004); *Access to Justice for Women Victims* (Dili: JSMP, July 2004) and *Police Treatment of Women in East Timor* (Dili: J.S.M.P., January, 2005).

[47] Catholic Institute for International Relations, "Timor's Search for the Truth: Recovering from the Violence in East Timor," Press Release, March 1, 2000.

It is a situation made much more complex by the lack of clear legal principles and resources to prosecute violations. In 2003, draft domestic violence legislation was tabled in Parliament but it has not yet been passed. Prime Minister Alkatiri noted that "[w]e have to nip the problem in the bud" and stated that priests "will have a role to play", as will the whole community, in promoting awareness.[48] Alkatiri's Office for Promotion of Equality (OPE) also organized the "16 Days of Activism Against Gender Violence Campaign", supported by the United Nations Population Fund (UNFPA). The rallying call of the national campaign was that "Gender Based Violence is not part of East Timorese culture".[49]

The legislation is desperately needed. The UN introduced some important rights for victims of violence in its criminal procedure Regulation 30/2000. For example, an investigating judge has the power to prevent a perpetrator who has been arrested for domestic violence from living in the family home while the case is investigated and prosecuted; and when convicting a perpetrator of a crime of violence, the judge may order the payment of compensation to the victim.

However, pursuant to UNTAET Regulation 1, Indonesian law in operation prior to the referendum continues to apply in Timor Lorosa'e, except to the extent that it is inconsistent with specified international human rights standards, including the United Nations Convention on the Elimination of All Forms of Discrimination Against Women ("CEDAW").[50] Under the Indonesian Criminal Code, domestic violence is not a specific offence. Prosecutors must thus rely on the crimes of maltreatment and torture. There is no prohibition against threats of violence, attempted assault, or rape within marriage. Section 285 of the Indonesian Penal Code contains the legal definition of rape, which is limited to forced penetration of the vagina by the penis.

Added to this dilemma is the recent finding by JSMP that the justice system in Timor Lorosa'e is not yet functional, independent or affordable.[51] This can lead to reliance on the male-dominated traditional law system, which is responsible for judgments such as one case where the family of a 12-year-old girl who was raped by her uncle accepted as compensation a traditional dress for the child.[52] The uncle was later arrested and charged; however in other

[48] UNMISET, "Work Begins on Domestic Violence Legislation: Media Briefing Notes," November 20, 2002, http://www.etan.org/et2002c/november/17-23/20work.htm.

[49] Ibid.

[50] The omission of violence from the terms of CEDAW (despite Recommendation 19) raises the difficult international legal question of whether a legal system which does not criminalize domestic violence *per se* is strictly contrary to accepted international human rights standards.

[51] Judicial Systems Monitoring Programme "JSMP Background Paper on the Justice Sector." June 4, 2003, http://jsmp.minihub.org/News/04_06_03.htm.

[52] Amnesty International, *East Timor. Justice Past, Present and Future*, AI Index ASA 57/001/2001, July 27, 2001, para 7: 'Non-judicial mechanisms and the rights of women'.

cases victims have been pressured to marry the perpetrator to "save their own reputations".[53] Both the formal and the traditional legal system are clearly failing women who suffer domestic violence.

The Role of the Church

The Church does not condone violence against women and, as discussed above, will participate in initiatives to combat domestic violence in Timor Lorosa'e. Yet while the Church can be supportive of women as victims of crimes of violence, it places formidable hurdles in the way of women who seek to escape abuse and make independent lives for themselves. This can ultimately make the Church complicit in the violence, even if it does not expressly condone it.

Of particular importance in this regard is the strenuous opposition of the Church to divorce, except in a very limited number of cases. The official position of the Church is stated in the Catechism of the Catholic Church, which stipulates that divorce "is a grave offence against natural law. It claims to break the contract, to which the spouses freely consented, to live with each other until death." Remarriage and contracting other forms of union constitute a "situation of public and permanent adultery."[54] The section of the Catechism that deals with "Offenses Against the Dignity of Marriage" includes this condemnation of divorce and also includes strictures against adultery, incest, sexual abuse of children and polygamy; violence and sexual abuse of wives are not cited as offences against the dignity of marriage. Thus neither sexual nor physical violence constitutes grounds for annulment of a Catholic marriage.

At a local level, the Church has put great pressure on women's groups in Timor Lorosa'e that deal with domestic violence in an attempt to prevent them presenting divorce or separation as an option for abused wives. This is a position that the Church takes consistently in all countries; it presents abused women with very few options for escaping abusive relationships. In his address to the Roman Rota (the body that deals with requests for annulments of marriage) Pope John Paul II condemned the "divorce mentality" and urged a commitment to marriage for the good of couples, children, the Church and the whole of society. Those who might be thinking of divorce were urged by the Pontiff to "respond with the humble courage of faith" and to accept the indissolubility of the union. The way that the priests of Timor Lorosa'e deal with divorce as an option for marriages in trouble, therefore, only reflects central

[53] Ibid.

[54] Catechism of the Catholic Church, (2000) para 2384. A version of the Catechism can be found at: http://www.Vatican.va/archive/ENG0015/_P87.HTM.

Church teachings. The Pope has urged priests, when dealing with a couple that is "going through difficulties," to do so sympathetically but to emphasize that "conjugal love is the way to work out a positive solution to their crisis." This should allow the couple to "emerge from their moments of crisis renewed and strengthened."[55] The speech gives no guidance to—indeed evinces no understanding of—the situation of women caught in marriages that have not merely undergone a "moment of crisis", but that are sources of continuing, consistent and brutal physical and sexual assaults. For such women, who are all too common in Timor Lorosa'e, the Church can only offer the "humble courage of faith". This is in stark contrast with those women's groups that try to give women the option of living a life of greater independence and integrity.

This failure to understand the often grim realities of women's lives reflects the general difficulty the Church faces in coming to terms with roles for women outside the family—its inability to conceive of women as more than wives or mothers. This ambivalence is reflected in the letter sent by Pope John Paul II to women attending the Fourth World Conference on Women in Beijing. This letter shows remarkable development in the views of the Church: it condemns "exploitation and domination" and sexual violence against women, and recognizes that women have "dignity and rights" and play a role as workers in "every area of life". Yet throughout the letter, the Pope refers to the "mystery of woman" and implies that women bring emotional rather than rational qualities to the world and the workplace.[56] He spends far more time on women as wives, mothers, sisters, daughters and victims of male aggression than he does on their role as workers or rights bearers.[57] Even this rather arcane concept of womanhood is more progressive than that set out in his encyclical letter of 1981 on workers and workers rights. There are only two brief references to women in the lengthy letter, and they both refer to the importance of women as mothers. According to this letter, a mother should "devote herself to taking care of her children and educating them in accordance with their needs. . . . Having to abandon these tasks in order to take up paid work outside the home is wrong from the point of view of the good of society and the family when it contradicts or hinders these primary goals of

[55] All quotations from *Address of John Paul II to the Prelate Auditors, Officials and Advocates of the Tribunal of the Roman Rota*, January 28, 2002.

[56] Pope John Paul II, *Letter of Pope John Paul II to Women*, June 29, 1995, http://www.vatican.va/holy_father/john_paul_ii/letters/documents/hf_jp_ii_let_29061995_women_en.html, para 2: Women are acknowledged as working in many fields. "In this way you make an indispensable contribution to the growth of a culture which unites reason and *feeling*, to a model of life ever open to the sense of *mystery*" (emphasis added.)

[57] *Letter of Pope John Paul II to Women*, June 29, 1995.

the mission of a mother."[58] Moreover, and notoriously, the Church does not permit the ordination of women and women are excluded from its leadership and decision-making hierarchy.[59]

This concept of womanhood resonates deeply with segments of Timor Lorosa'e's patriarchal population, and it serves to legitimate male control and dominance of the household, including the use of violence to perpetuate that control. Even Father Jovito has admitted that Catholic doctrines can be mistaken in supporting the idea that men are dominant and that women should be "spiritual law educators".[60]

The Lobo Case

A case that illustrates the complications that arise in domestic violence cases and the obstacles facing women seeking justice in Timor Lorosa'e is that of Dr Sergio Lobo. Dr Lobo was detained in Dili on 10 July 2001 for physically assaulting his wife at a hotel. He is the former Minister for Health, a prominent surgeon at Dili hospital, former Chairman of the Department of Health for ETTA (East Timor Transitional Authority), the number three candidate for the UDT ticket in the recent elections and one of the few qualified East Timorese medical professionals. He stands accused of seriously assaulting his wife over a sustained period of time. The alleged abuse included beating his wife with a stick and injecting a sedative into her arm with a syringe he had brought for this purpose. She had gone into hiding in a convent, and several witnesses claimed that he hunted her down, attacked her in the convent with the syringe and also beat up a nun.[61] All this occurred while he was on release pending trial for the other crimes he was alleged to have committed against his wife. No action was taken against Lobo for breaking the terms of release and the victim remained in hiding. When she emerged to begin work in a Dili

---

[58] Papal Encyclical, *Laborem Exercens*, September 14, 1981, para 19.3 as reproduced in Walsh and Davies *Proclaiming Justice and Peace*.

[59] This position has been reiterated recently in a letter that also sets out the biological and biblical basis for differences between the sexes: Offices of the Congregation for the Doctrine of the Faith, *Letter to the Bishops of the Catholic Church on the Collaborations of Men and Women in the Church and in the World* May 31, 2004, para 16, http://www.vatican.va/roman_curia/congregations/cfaith/document/rc_con_cfaith_doc_20090731_collaboration_en.html. The letter deals with the different role of men and women in the Church and concludes: "In this perspective one understands how the reservation of priestly ordination solely to men does not hamper in any way women's access to the heart of Christian life. Women are called to be unique examples and witnesses for all Christians of how the Bride is to respond in love to the love of the Bridegroom".

[60] Jude Conway, "Fokupers: Women's Seminar Dili 25 Nov," Report on a seminar held on November 25, 1998, December 8, 1998, http://etan.org/et/1998/december/8-14/08fokupe.htm

[61] La'o Hamutuk, "Public Figure Detained Again for Domestic Violence," Press Release, July 12, 2001, http://www.etan.org/et2001c/july/08-14/12drl.htm.

hotel, the doctor found her out and allegedly beat her again. He was arrested again and this time detained.[62]

Dr Lobo appealed against the detention, arguing that according to East Timorese culture he had an entitlement to know where his wife was and to control her. The appeal was upheld on the grounds that the offender was needed by his community and that the victim was violating East Timorese cultural norms by working without permission from her husband. In addition, the defendant was granted custody of the couple's children. Dr Lobo was conditionally released, pending trial.[63] The concept of male control of his wife and the unseemliness of a woman working (and thus gaining for herself the financial independence essential if she is to leave her husband) was asserted by the judge and Dr Lobo, and these cultural values are also reinforced by many teachings of the Church.

At the time of writing, Dr Lobo's wife lives in a Fokupers domestic violence safe house, and Dr Lobo claims Fokupers is breaking up his home. He has refused his wife a divorce. Fokupers had previously supported a woman in her divorce proceedings, successfully arguing that her husband had not provided for the family, still the strongest grounds for divorce in Timor Lorosa'e. Commentators report that now Fokupers "suffers the wrath of the Church, a wrath made tangible through the great political power it holds."[64]

The Lobo case highlights the fundamental limitation on the Church's support for domestic violence survivors. The Church puts great pressure on women's organizations to avoid presenting divorce as an alternative, even in extreme cases of domestic violence like the Lobo case, and to focus all efforts on reconciling husband and wife. While women who suffered under the Indonesian occupation are encouraged by the Church to stand up to their violators, the same Church has effectively sided with the abusive husband in the Lobo case. By condemning the wife and the women's group that supports her, the Church has blamed the victim rather than the abuser for the problems of the marriage. The Church's teachings on divorce and the sacred nature of marriage lead to the Church being far more concerned to condemn the wife for leaving her husband than the husband for making the marriage intolerable for the wife. Notably absent from the Church's intervention in this case,

---

[62] For a defence of this detention see "Luis Carrilho: The Law Does Not Recognize 'Public Figures,'" extract from *Suara Timor Lorosae*, July 12, 2001, 1, http://www.pcug.org.au/~wildwood/01jullaw.htm.

[63] See further, Judicial Systems Monitoring Programme, "JSMP Comments to the Sergio Lobo Interlocutory Appeal," July 27, 200, http://www.jsmp.minihub.org/News/27-7.htm.

[64] Curt Gabrielson, "East Timorese Women's Fight Against Violence" *Institute of Current World Affairs*, Letters, January 1, 2002, 4–6, http://www.peacewomen.org/resources/Timor-Leste/ETViolence2002.pdf.

and its position on domestic violence more generally, is the same unequivocal condemnation of violence perpetrated against women and reliance on a rights framework that it has used so effectively in its stance on justice for female survivors during the Indonesian occupation.

Conclusion: Power, Presence And Platform—The Potential Of The Catholic Church In Timor Lorosa'e

As this chapter has shown, the Church as an ally has so far been a mixed blessing in transforming the lives of its female followers. Yet the potential for the Church to play a positive role in helping to transform East Timorese society remains significant. At times the Church and women's groups have spoken in unison, particularly on the issue of justice for victims of the occupation. Sadly it seems that, despite this coalition, the likelihood of formal justice for crimes under the occupation is beginning to look remote. Yet, despite the end of the occupation, violence against women continues in Timor Lorosa'e. And when the Church has been faced with husbands and fathers rather than occupying military or militia as the abusers, its response has been muted. It has been more concerned to shame women who leave their husbands than to assert the rights of those women to physical integrity and safety. However powerful a voice for women the Church might have been over amnesties, its interests are not always the interests of women. Groups such as Fokupers recognize the need for women to speak with their own voices and through their own groups rather than relying solely on the Church. Strategic alliances can and have been made between the Church and women's groups, but until the Church is prepared to see women as independent citizens and holders of rights in all contexts—including the home—then the positions of the two groups are likely to continue to diverge over time. This is a pity for the women of Timor Lorosa'e, for whom religion and the Church continue to play an important personal and spiritual role. It is also a pity for the Church that it does not seem able to seize this opportunity to transform itself to oppose abuse and violence in all their forms, and to reconceptualize the role of women in East Timorese society.

CHAPTER SEVEN

MUSLIM WOMEN'S POLITICAL STRUGGLE FOR MARRIAGE LAW REFORM IN CONTEMPORARY INDONESIA

Kathryn Robinson

Introduction: Religion, Law and Social Practice in Indonesia

Indonesia has the world's largest Muslim population: over eighty percent of its 217 million citizens profess Islam. That religion has been slowly penetrating the archipelago since the thirteenth century. The arrival of Islam followed the earlier introduction of Buddhism and Hinduism. All three of these cosmopolitan religions have been domesticated and accommodated by the pre-existing religious beliefs and practices in the region[1]. Daniel Lev's 1972 study of the operation of Islamic courts in Indonesia made this observation:

> Local rulers converted to Islam, but did not thereafter rule according to Islamic political principles or the *Sjariah* [Islamic law – *syari'ah*] . . . Islamic institutions—the kadi court for one—were adopted here and there, not everywhere, but always under the aegis of mixed myths of authority in which Islam represented only one ingredient.[2]

About half of Indonesia's Muslims are observant (*santri*), in the sense of expressing devotion to the 'five pillars'[3] that are the basis of Islamic practice. The number of observant Muslims has, however, been steadily growing in response to successive waves of Islamic reform. Two broad influences can be identified: international inspiration brought by pilgrims returning from Mecca from the early nineteenth century, and more recently the Islamic revolution in Iran in the 1980s. Domestic responses to this international Islamic enthusiasm has manifested in an explosion in Islamic education, much of it

---

[1] M. B. Hooker and Timothy Lindsey comment that vernacular texts show a "distinct regional Islamic response to Middle Eastern precedent" in "Public Faces of Syari'ah in Contemporary Indonesia: Towards a National *Mazhab*," *Australian Journal of Asian Law* 4 no. 3 (2002): 263.

[2] Daniel S. Lev, *Islamic Courts in Indonesia* (Berkley and Los Angeles: University of California Press, 1972), 5.

[3] The 'five pillars' are the five daily prayers, the confession of faith, the pilgrimage, the fast in Rhamadan, the payment of alms.

sponsored by the state, most importantly in the tertiary-level State Institutes of Islamic Studies, or IAIN.[4]

For Muslims, Islam provides an alternative source of authority to the state. In the early resistance to Dutch colonialism, Indonesian Islamic organizations were among the first groups to show an awakening of nationalism and anti-colonial consciousness, and in 1945 some of them sought to proclaim that the new republic was an Islamic state, with *syari'ah* legitimated as national law. However, the secular nationalist strand prevailed in debates over the constitutional form of the new republic. An attempt to reach a compromise over a constitutional preamble that obliged professed Muslims to abide by *syari'ah* (the so-called Piagam Jakarta, 'Jakarta Charter') also failed.[5] As a result, although Indonesia's constitution does stipulate in the preamble that all citizens profess a belief in God, Islam has no special status in national law. Monotheism, however, is guaranteed, as the foundational principles of state ideology (the five precepts of the Pancasila)[6] acknowledge belief in a monotheistic God as fundamental to national identity.

As the faith of the overwhelming majority of Indonesians, Islam has been awarded a central role in state administration through the establishment of the Ministry of Religion in 1946. The government department regulates and registers marriage and divorce for Muslims and organizes the Islamic courts. The establishment of the Ministry was the first in a series of strategies by the state to 'capture' Islam, rather than have Islam capture the state. More recently the Soeharto regime (1965–1998) sponsored the formation of the Indonesian Association of Muslim Intellectuals (Ikatan Cendiakawan Muslim se-Indonesia, ICMI) to harness the growing Islamic political consciousness to the regime.[7]

Islamic law has been unevenly adopted throughout the archipelago, but its principle influence has been in family law, especially the regulation of marriage and divorce. The slow process of Islamization has had diverse effects in different parts of the archipelago. Ethnographic studies show wide variation in the manner and extent to which Islam has become fundamental to the expression of gender differences, especially in terms of men's and women's

---

[4] See Hooker and Lindsey, "Public Faces of Syari'ah."

[5] M. C. Ricklefs, *A History of Modern Indonesia, c 1300 to the Present* (London: MacMillan, 1981); also Adam Schwartz, *A Nation in Waiting: Indonesia in the 1990s* (Sydney, Allen and Unwin: 1994), 168.

[6] The 'five principles' are: belief in God; nationalism; humanitarianism; democracy; and social justice.

[7] ICMI proposed a doctrine of Islamic intellectuals broadly participating in institutions and organizations across the board, rather than forming Islamic political groupings. In this approach they were influenced by Basam Tilbi (Personal Communication, 1999).

rights. Moreover localized practices are often justified in the name of Islam. These complexities can be seen in the following examples.

The Acehnese on the northern tip of Sumatra claim to be patrilineal 'like the Arabs'. They formally acknowledge the dual manifestation of Islam and custom (*adat*), in the distinction between *wali hukum*—relatives on one's father's side—and *wali adat*, or relatives on the mother's side.[8] While they "accept the 'patrilineal' bias of Islamic orthodoxy and reckon the kin of the father's side more extensively and value them more in formal terms", men live with their wife's matrilateral kin and depend for subsistence on rice provided by their wives.[9] The *wali hukum* inherit property, distributed with a bias in favor of men; but, in practice, property is more usually distributed by *hibah*, or gift (made by the parents to their children as they form their own families), so there is normally not much left for the *wali hukum*. Parents also provide houses for their daughters. In Bourdieu's terms, it would appear that while 'official kin' are *wali hukum*, reckoned on patrilineal lines, 'practical kin' are the *wali adat*, matrilateral relatives, and affines (for a man). [10]

In her study of the Javanese family, Hildred Geertz notes some "faint and structurally unimportant customs which stress paternal ties" which seem to indicate Islamic influence. These include division of property following divorce (in the ratio of two male shares for one female share), a similar ratio in inheritance, the notion of male guardianship for girl by agnatic kin, and the prohibition on marriage between paternal parallel cousins (i.e., between a man and his father's brother's daughter).[11] Javanese do not settle inheritance by recourse to "impersonal legal prescription", however.[12] Rather, each case is taken on its merits. The rules on property division "function mainly in authorizing alternative solutions to quarrels among kinsmen" and guardianship is rarely practiced.[13] The prohibition of marriage to parallel cousins is in fact not Islamic, but a folk belief which presumes it to be Islamic. Indeed, for some Arab societies it is a preferred form of marriage. Geertz concludes that except in cases of devout *santri*, "Islam as a legal system has hardly touched Java: its presence in the areas of marriage, divorce and heritance is due largely

---

[8] Chandra Jayawardena, "Women and Kinship in Acceh Besar, Northern Sumatra," *Ethnology* 16 no. 1 (1977), 24. The *wali hukum* correspond to the patrilineal clans, called Kawon, identified by Snouck Hurgronje: Jayawardena, 23.

[9] Jayawardena, "Women and Kinship," 33.

[10] Pierre Bourdieu, *Outline of a Theory of Practice* (Cambridge: Cambridge University Press, 1977).

[11] Hildred Geertz, *The Javanese Family* (New York: The Free Press, 1961), 76.

[12] Ibid., 46.

[13] Ibid., 77.

to the support given by the [colonial] Dutch [rulers] to Islamic religious officials in the courts".[14] (This is discussed below.)

For the Islamic Buginese of South Sulawesi (and many other Indonesians), marriage owes more to considerations of social connection and status than it does to Islam. Bugis marriage illustrates *par excellence* the gap between the idea of marriage as a contract (the Islamic *nikah*, between the groom and the *wali* with two male witnesses) at which in the past the bride was not present, and marriage as a socially legitimating performance of social connection (the *duduk bersanding*, with the bride and groom on display before the assembled guests). Islamic principles of inheritance (favoring male rights) have been encroaching on bilateral principles of inheritance, which recognise entitlements of both sexes.[15] In contested cases, a sharp difference of economic interest can pit male proponents of Muslim rules against women championing traditional norms.

What was common to Muslim societies across the archipelago at the beginning of the twentieth century was that principles in regard to marriage and divorce were uncodified, and regulated according to the peculiar mix of Islam and custom (*adat*) that pertained in particular localities. This was especially notable in practices relating to inheritance (as noted above) and polygamy. While polygamy and serial marriage following divorce by repudiation were common in Java, for example, in areas such as Sulawesi, polygamy has always been relatively uncommon.

The potential for women's rights in marriage and in property (recognized in many *adat* systems) to be undermined by literalist interpretations of Islamic law is demonstrated by the tendency for local Islamic practices to evolve to protect some of those rights. So, for example, in most parts of Indonesia, the *nikah* is followed by the utterance of the *talik* at *talak*, or provisional *talak*, in which the man's contractual obligations are made explicit. Failure to meet those conditions gives the woman a right to seek divorce through the court.[16] In Java, these terms include "if he does not feed his wife, sleep with her or provide her a place to live in, or if he abandons her for three months."[17] This practice, the *talik* at *talak*, has the effect of strengthening the woman's rights in marriage. Although Soewondo says the Acehnese did not practice this, Jayawardena noted that a man who went away trading (as he was expected to

---

[14] Ibid., 77.

[15] Mukhlis and Kathryn Robinson, *Agama dan Realitas Sosial* (Ujungpandang Indonesia: Hasanuddin University Press and the Indonesia Social Science Foundation, 1985).

[16] Cora Vreede-de Stuers, *The Indonesian Woman: Struggles and Achievement* (The Hague: Mouton, 1960), 34–5.

[17] Clifford Geertz, *Religion of Java* (New York: The Free Press, 1960), 56; see also Hildred Geertz, *Javanese Family*, 72–3.

do) but failed to send back money could legitimately be divorced by his wife.[18] These instances exemplify the general principle that the accommodation of Islam to *adat* has tended to soften the potential negative impact of literalist exegesis of Islamic doctrine on women's rights.

Reform of the law regulating marriage has been actively pursued by women's organizations. Public debates about religion and law have been inextricably bound with demands by women's groups that the state extend its grasp into the private domain of the family. In particular, women have demanded that the anti-egalitarian provisions of Islam in regard to family law be replaced by state regulations manifesting a more 'modern' sensibility.

This chapter traces the history of Islam and marriage law in the Indonesian archipelago, focusing on women's political struggle for reform, and the current threat to their gains (notably a secular marriage law and reform of the courts that have improved gender equity in marriage and divorce) in the current climate of political reform in the post-Soeharto period. Islam became a significant focus of opposition to Soeharto's regime—the self-titled 'New Order' (*Orde Baru*). In a climate where political expression was limited, but religious affiliation was mandated, and where Islam also provided a vision for a just society, Islam became a legitimate way to express political and social aspirations. For some, regime change has offered a promise for the realization of these Islamicist goals, of (re)turning Indonesia towards the path of becoming an Islamic state; while for others—including women's organizations—regime change has been embraced as an opening of democratic space to pursue equity goals.

The Colonial Period

Adat, Islam and Marriage in the Colonial East Indies

The constitution of the Dutch East Indies divided the population into Europeans, Natives and Foreign Orientals. The European group was subject to Dutch private law and the other two groups regulated according to their own unwritten customary laws which controlled the marital affairs of the majority of inhabitants of the East Indies.[19] In the codification of 'traditional' systems of law, the colonial government recognized the jurisdiction of Islamic courts in regard to family law whereas criminal and commercial law were

[18] Nani Soewondo, "The Indonesian Marriage Law and its implementing regulation," *Archipel* 13 (1977): 283–294.

[19] A Civil Code of 1847 covered Europeans and Chinese citizens and in 1861, a marriage law was passed for Christian inhabitants of the Moluccas.

handled by civil courts. The conditions of Islamic courts varied throughout the archipelago: in some places Islamic judges were appointed by local rulers, whereas in other places there were no distinct religious courts, with local religious leaders performing judicial services.[20] The courts faced a lack of formal independence and were subordinated to the colonial *Landraden* (colonial law courts for natives)—i.e., the civil courts.

Islam was contrasted with *adat* or custom as a way of ordering everyday affairs and Dutch scholars (who were influential in colonial policy) codified *adat* as an alternative regulatory system. In their formulation, *adat*, from an Arabic word meaning custom, is contrasted with *hukum* (law), which is that body of rules introduced by the colonial master and enforced by the colonial state. The Dutch *adat* law scholars Van Vollenhoven and Ter Haar argued that there were approximately nineteen different customary law spheres, or *adat* systems encompassing a variety of kinship systems for regulating marriage, residence, inheritance and related matters.[21] They claimed that the individualistic principles of justice that informed Islamic law were incompatible with the more communally-oriented principles of *adat* law: for example the differences in inheritance practices discussed above. Islamic principles would apply only if they had been accepted into *adat*.[22] The *adat* law scholars were interested in "securing and preserving the purity of what they understood as tradition" and they saw a need to avoid "alien accretions and influences", which included Islam.[23] The non-scriptural character of Indonesian Islam was taken as evidence that Indonesian Muslims were only nominal adherents to the faith.

The late nineteenth century witnessed a contestation between leading Dutch scholars on the *adat*/Islam relationship. L. W. C. van den Berg argued that in the East Indies, Islamic law should be applied 'in its integrity' to Muslims. He was opposed by the leading Islamicist Snouck Hurgronje, who argued that it should only be applied insofar as it was incorporated into *adat*. The question for colonial authorities was at heart political: the promotion of *adat* was fundamentally a challenge to Islamic authority, represented by the Islamic courts, and the inheritance laws which predominantly concerned the authorities represented the extent of the penetration of Islam. They were concerned to weaken the political potential of Islam as a unifying force, a view shared with domestic elites "who were forever hostile to Islam and fearful of

[20] Lev, *Islamic Courts in Indonesia*, 10.

[21] J. Katz and R. Katz, "The New Indonesian Marriage Law: A Mirror of Indonesia's Political, Cultural and Legal System," *American Journal of Comparative Law* 23 (1975), 655.

[22] Lev, *Islamic Courts in Indonesia*, 20; Nursyahbani Katjasungkana, "Perempuan dalam peta hukum negara Ibndonesia," in *Menakar "Harga" Perempuan*, ed. Syafiq Hasim (Bandung: Penerbit Mizan, 1999), n. 3.

[23] Lev, *Islamic Courts in Indonesia*, 17.

its expansion."[24] However, official debates over the relative priority to be given to *adat* or Islam did not represent a contest over issues of basic rights; yet these rights—particularly rights in family law—were, as we shall see, the dominant concern of women's organizations.

Women's Struggle for Reform

The politicized women's groups that developed as part of the nationalist movement in the early twentieth century saw improvement of women's position in regard to marriage and divorce as essential to improving women's welfare.[25] Polygamy aroused the disgust of many women, most famously, the nineteenth century figure Kartini, whose letters to Dutch friends were posthumously published and whose feminist vision influenced several generations of Indonesian women.[26]

The laws for Europeans and Foreign Orientals or Christians were viewed positively as reflecting modern sensibilities; but the women challenged the uncodified nature of the Muslim marriage law, which left women with few rights and little protection. The elision of Islam with custom meant there were no clearly articulated regulations for Indonesian Muslims on marriage, divorce and inheritance.[27] The principal issues of family and personal law taken up by the women's movement were child marriage, forced marriage, polygamous marriage that did not meet the requirements of Muslim law (in particular polygamy based on lust), arbitrary divorce by husbands (repudiation), and the lack of a requirement to pay alimony beyond the *iddah* period (the minimum waiting period before a woman can marry after divorce).[28] Women felt threatened by polygamy but also by 'successive polygamy' in which men discarded wives in order to remarry.

Age at marriage was also a contentious issue.[29] Under Islamic law, there is no stipulated minimum age, and girls could be married with consent of their male *wali-mujbir* (literally 'coercive guardian') regardless of their own consent.[30]

[24] Ibid., 27.

[25] Soewondo, "The Indonesian Marriage Law," 284.

[26] Raden Ajdeng Kartini, *Letters of a Javanese Princess*. Translated from the Dutch by Agnes Louise Symmers; edited and with an introduction by Hildred Geertz (New York, Norton, 1964).

[27] Soewondo, "The Indonesian Marriage Law".

[28] This is usually fulfilled at the onset of her next menstruation, indicating that she is not pregnant.

[29] Susan Blackburn and Sharon Bessell, "Marriageable Age: Political Debates on Early Marriage in Twentieth Century Indonesia," *Indonesia* 63 (April 1997): 107–41.

[30] Ibid., 109.

While in many situations, custom prevented the consummation of marriage until a girl reached puberty, there was concern at the possible damage to girls, as well as issues of rights and coercion. The practice was defended on grounds that it was better to marry off a girl while she was still young to avoid the damage that "the girl would make a choice from the heart and not the head", indicating an anxiety about the dangerous sexuality of young girls.[31]

The Enquiry into the Decline in the Welfare of Java and Madura in 1914 received submissions from nine women to the sub-report on the Improvement in the Position of Indonesian Women. Some submissions were from *santri* (observant Muslim) women who were critical of what they saw as abuses of women in practices justified in the name of Islam. Vreede-de Stuers quotes from an article published in the magazine of the Young Muslims, *El Fajar*, in 1927, which typifies the reforming tendencies of this period:[32]

> I am therefore persuaded that I am not acting against the spirit of Islam in expressing the opinion that we must, by all possible means, oppose polygamy such as it is practised in our time and in our country . . . the best method of combating polygamy is to be found in a careful study of Islam itself.

This early twentieth century article exhibits the same oppositional basis from within Islam and the arguments for diverse interpretations of Islamic law that we currently see in women's resistance to a resurgence of polygamy (discussed below).

In the early part of the twentieth century, several organizations supporting women's rights came into being. Nearly 30 groups met in the first national women's congress, held in 1928, which took up issues of polygamy, forced and underage marriage, and women's rights in *talak* (repudiation). Improvement in rights for women was linked to the broader goals of the nascent nationalist movement. Siti Sundari, a leading nationalist figure who edited the magazine *Wanito Sworo* (Women's Voice—founded in 1913), reported that she had received letters from women complaining about polygamy and arbitrary repudiation. She told the 1928 Congress:[33]

> Polygamy, child marriages, repudiation and divorces are unlimited in number . . . When a woman's independence disappears in marriage . . . it signifies the failure of the emancipation of our people.

---

[31] Raden Achmad Djajadiningrat Regent of Serang *Volkstelling 1030 Vol 1: West Java*, 44, cited in Blackburn and Bessel, 112.

[32] Cited in Cora Vreede-de Stuers, "On the Subject of the 'R.U.U.': The History of a Set of Marital Laws," in *Indonesian Women: Past and Present Perspectives*, ed. B. B. Hering (Courrier de l'Extreme-Orient No 62, 1976), 83.

[33] Cited in Vreede-de Stuers, "On the Subject," 83.

The necessity and right of the state to intervene in Muslim marriage was contentious. Ali Sastroamijoyo, a future Prime Minister of Indonesia, addressed the 1928 Congress on Islam and marriage explaining that Muslims had "the right to marry without the intermediary of a government official, provided that all the conditions of the Islamic law (*fiqh*) were fulfilled."[34] Three motions were carried at the congress, including a request that the government require the *penghulu* (celebrant) to explain the meaning of *talik* following the marriage contract (*nikah*).[35] The government responded with a requirement (in 1932) that the *talik* be explained to the *wali* at the conclusion of the marriage.

After 1928, women's organizations came together in a series of federations for holding national conferences on a regular basis, but it was many years before consensus on marriage reform was reached again. In particular, it was difficult to reach agreement between Islamic and secular nationalist organizations over the basic issue of the necessity and desirability of the government intervening in marriage. Nevertheless, the Second General Congress in 1935 achieved some compromise, when a decision was made to set up a Commission to Investigate Marriage Law which was to report back to the Congress.

Marriage Reform—Colonial Period

Colonial officials were, according to Lev, motivated by an interest in modernisation.[36] A Marriage Ordinance for Christian Natives (1933, amended 1936) established a minimum age of marriage—15 for women, 18 for men—and listed grounds for divorce.[37] In 1937, a draft set of rules for regulation of marriage in the Muslim population were presented to the women's congress for consideration. It was rejected by Islamic associations even though the regulation posed no threat to the controversial practice of polygamy. It was also rejected by the two largest nationalist groupings on the grounds that this was "intolerable interference on the part of the non-Indonesian government in such a delicate matter."[38]

---

[34] Vreede-de Stuers, "On the Subject," 80.

[35] The Indonesian practice of the man uttering the *talak* at *talik* at the time of the *nikah*, while not common in Muslim societies is legal according to the *fiqh* (the codification of legal principles from the Qur'an). The Indonesian practice strengthened the position of women as it provided some mitigation of the circumstance that "in Islam the woman is disadvantaged compared with her husband, as he alone holds the right of repudiation/divorce (*talak*) (Vreede-de Stuers, "On the Subject of the "R.U.U.," 81).

[36] Lev, *Islamic Courts in Indonesia*, 57.

[37] Vreede-de Stuers, "On the Subject," 80.

[38] Ibid., 84.

The Commission to Investigate Marriage Laws that was set up in 1935 reported back to the 1938 congress. The task fell to Maria Ulfah Santoso, who was one of the first Indonesian women to receive a law degree from a Dutch university (in 1933). She was a leading figure in the growing nationalist movement as well as the women's movement—the first in a line of distinguished women lawyers who have had a significant role in law reform for women's rights. Her two-hour long speech to the Congress "served as the basis in all the discussions that took place during the following years".[39] The recommendations were as follows: (i) before the husband delivers the *talak*, the couple should present themselves before the *penghulu* (official) who should attempt to reconcile them; (ii) the religious council (Raad Agama) must have the power to annul any *talak* (unilateral repudiations) uttered in a casual manner, before the reconciliation hearing before the *penghulu;* (iii) the *penghulu* must explain fully the implications of the conditions of the *talik* at *talak*; (iv) the form of the *talik* at *talak* should be comprehensive (as a basis for a divorce initiated by the woman). Maria Ulfah Santoso suggested the wording "where there is insurmountable disagreement between the parties" which Vreede-de Stuers describes as a "sign of a remarkable evolution in women's consciousness."[40]

The Post-Independence Period

Marriage and Family Law Reform in the 1950s

The nationalist leaders Soekarno and Mohammad Hatta proclaimed Indonesian independence in 1945, but it took another four years for the right to self-determination by the infant republic to be internationally recognized. During the period of resistance to the Dutch colonial forces, who were attempting by force of arms to return the newly independent Indonesian state to a colonial possession, the women's organizations continued to press for woman-friendly legal instruments in the new state. They succeeded in having the constitution of the new nation declare in Article 27 that all citizens have equal rights.

During the struggle for independence, the republican government established a centre of power in Jogjakarta, Central Java, and began a program of legislation for the nation. As mentioned above, a contentious issue was whether the new republic should be an Islamic state, but the compromise position (the *Piagam Jakarta*, (Jakarta Charter) which obliged Muslim citizens

[39] Ibid., 85.
[40] Ibid., 85.

to abide by *syari'ah*) was removed from the constitution one day after the proclamation of independence. Islamic groups have repeatedly tried to have it reinstated.[41] The political trade-off for organized Islam was the establishment of the Ministry of Religion in 1946. This made it possible to consolidate the administration of Islam into a single body which came to be controlled by the Islamic party Nahdlatul Ulama until the 1970s.[42]

The new Republican government issued Law No. 22 of 1964 Concerning Registration of Marriages, Reconciliation and Divorce. Marriage, Repudiation and Reconciliation (*nikah*, *talak* and *rujuk*, respectively) were henceforth brought under the formal supervision of registrars who were appointed by the Ministry of Religion and paid as civil servants. People who failed to register marriages or divorces were fined. Vreede-de Stuers comments that "it might have been expected that public affairs and religious affairs would be dealt with separately under the new Republic, which had declared itself to be secular."[43] By this law, the Ministry of Religion was staking a claim to control Islamic marriage affairs, "the one area of Islamic law that Muslims would not surrender without a fight."[44] The Ministry's claim was, however, contested in parliament as it was seen by some as an attempt to strengthen the position of Islam in the new state, because the Ministry was itself controlled by the Nahdlatul Ulama organization.[45]

It is noteworthy that new procedures addressed some of the concerns that had been expressed by women's groups. Ministerial Instruction No. 4 of 1947 directed registrars not to record child marriages, and to ensure compliance with conditions laid down by the *fiqh* in the case of forced marriages. In cases of polygamy, registrars should ensure the man knew of his obligations under *fiqh*; in cases of repudiation (*talak*), they should summon both parties, and try to persuade the husband not to pronounce the *talak*, or persuade him to retract it at the end of the *iddah* period.[46] The 1949 Women's Congress continued to press for new marriage regulations, but still could not agree on the need for a unified law.[47]

In response, the new parliament set up the Panitya Penjelidik Peraturan Hukum Perkawinan, Talak dan Rudjuk (The Investigative Committee on the Regulation of the Law on Marriage, Repudiation and Divorce—henceforth

---

[41] Lev, *Islamic Courts in Indonesia*, 43.
[42] Ibid., 44–5.
[43] Vreede-de Stuers, *The Indonesian Woman*, 125.
[44] Lev, *Islamic Courts in Indonesia*, 55.
[45] Ibid., 44–45.
[46] Vreede-de Stuers, *The Indonesian Woman*, 124–5; Vreede-de Stuers, "On the Subject," 85.
[47] Vreede- de Stuers, *The Indonesian Woman*, 117.

NTR Commission), which was charged with drawing up a bill "in keeping with the spirit of modern times".[48] A number of activist women were appointed to the NTR commission. Its Secretary, Nani Soewondo, was another prominent woman lawyer who sought the views of delegates to the 1950 Women's Congress on its deliberations, including on the familiar and still contentious issue of the desirability of a unified law.[49] Following this consultation, the NTR Commission decided to prepare a general act valid for all Indonesians, but incorporating special regulations applying to specific religious groups. The draft act included clauses addressing: the necessity of consent of both parties; minimum age to marry of 15 for a woman and 18 for a man; and equal rights for husband and wife in divorce. For those whose religion permitted polygamy, the second marriage could not be registered without the explicit consent of the first wife and the guarantee of support by the husband.[50] A prospective polygamist should demonstrate his capacity to support more than one family.

This draft act was sent to all women's organizations in 1952, but it was opposed: orthodox Muslim organizations found it "too indefinite", and Catholic organizations "could not support a law that allowed for polygamy and divorce".[51] Other groups supported the draft bill, however, proposing the insertion of Article 16 of the Universal Declaration of Human Rights relating to equal rights of men and women in marriage.[52] The federated women's organization, Perwari, organized a demonstration by several women's groups in 1953 to urge the Government to enact the proposed marriage law.[53]

The NTR Commission subsequently sent two draft bills to the Ministry of Religious Affairs in 1954, including one based on diversity of laws for different religious groups, but law reform stalled due to the apparent impossibility of reaching a consensus.[54] In 1954 the government endorsed the Law No. 22 of 1946 Concerning Registration of Marriages, Reconciliation and Divorce (discussed above) as a temporary statute for the whole nation. (It became Act No 7 of 1954.) Women parliamentarians opposed this move as a bloc, demanding the parliament consider the draft bills. The two bills were finally submitted to Parliament and debated in 1958–9, but no resolution was reached.[55]

While the quest for a new marriage law was stalled, other government decisions, particularly PP (Government Regulation) No. 19 of 1952 which extended pension rights to civil service widows in polygamous marriages raised women's

48 Vreede-de Stuers, "On the Subject," 85–6.
49 Vreede-de Stuers, *The Indonesian Woman*, 125.
50 Vreede-de Stuers, "On the Subject," 86.
51 Vreede-de Stuers, *The Indonesian Woman*, 126.
52 Vreede-de Stuers, "On the Subject," 86.
53 Soewondo, "Indonesian Marriage Law," 284.
54 Ibid.
55 Ibid.

ire. This move had support from Islamic women's groups (such as Masjumi Muslimaat and NU Muslimaat), but other women's groups opposed it. These latter organizations demonstrated in the streets in opposition to the regulation of polygamy, and demanding marriage law reform.[56] The women's cause against polygamy was dealt a further blow in June 1954 when President Soekarno (who had previously championed women's rights) took a second wife. Following the 1955 elections, "issues raised by the women's movement were largely disregarded".[57] However, women's groups continued to press for the law.[58] For example, the mass women's organization, Gerwani (affiliated to the Communist party) issued a statement demanding "the immediate enactment of a democratic marriage law, valid throughout Indonesia, which will protect the rights of women. The law should prohibit forced marriage, child marriage, rape, arbitrary divorce".[59] However, the issue was avoided by the government because of its potential to alienate the Islamic parties. Nani Soewondo has commented that between 1950 and 1960 the recurrent theme of the women's movement became "what has happened to the matrimonial legislation?"[60]

The 1974 Marriage law

No further change was achieved until the radical shift of government after the alleged communist coup in 1965, when the founding president Soekarno was replaced by General Soeharto as the nation's second president. The issue of family law reform was still alive for women's groups, however. The Gerwani journal *Api Kartini* continued to discuss the issue of marriage reform, publishing stories that emphasized women's vulnerability to arbitrary divorce or polygamy, and linking this to the necessity of women becoming independent through, for example, access to formal education.[61] They argued for a "democratic marriage law" that "guarantees the same position for the two sexes, as well as freedom in the right to choose the place of residence, and freedom to participate in work or community activities [. . .] (and) freedom to divorce. . . ."[62]

---

[56] Khofifa Indar Parawansa, "Institution Building: An Effort to Improve Indonesian Women's Role and Status," in *Women in Indonesia: Gender, Equity and Development*, ed. Kathryn Robinson and Sharon Bessell (Singapore: ISEAS, 2002), 70. N. Soewondo *Kedudukan Wanita Indonesia dalam Hukum dan Masyarakat* (Jakarta: Ghallia, 1981), 37.

[57] Indar Parawansa, "Institution Building," 70.

[58] Soewondo, "Indonesian Marriage Law," 284.

[59] *Harian Rakyat*, October 23, 1957, cited in Robyn Fallick, "Tradition, Innovation and Struggle: Gerwani 1950–1965" (paper presented the Second Women in Asia Workshop, Monash University, July 22–4, 1983).

[60] Soewondo, "Indonesian Marriage Law."

[61] Fallick, "Tradition, Innovation and Struggle," 11.

[62] *Api Kartini*, September–October 1962:23, cited in Fallick, "Tradition, Innovation and Struggle," 13.

The Parliament continued to debate the draft bills, but nothing was resolved, with Muslim groups still demanding diversity of laws. In 1972, however, President Soeharto announced his intention to proceed with a Matrimonial Bill and it was presented to Parliament on August 29, 1973. The draft bill proposed a unified law which recognized equal rights of women in marriage and divorce.[63] It was highly controversial, giving rise to heated debate in the parliament and the violent occupation of the parliament by young Muslim men who opposed the perceived secularizing of marriage and divorce which they feared would be achieved through the expanded jurisdiction of the civil courts.[64] While women generally supported the bill, some Islamic leaders argued that several articles were inconsistent with Muslim law. Compromise was reached on matters like age at marriage, and the role of the religious courts[65] and the legislation was passed on December 22, 1973 (the anniversary of the 1928 Women's Congress, which has since 1938 been celebrated as 'Mother's Day' (Hari Ibu)).

Enacted on January 2, 1974 as Law No. 1 of 1974 Concerning Marriage, its main points were as follows:

1. one law for all Indonesia;
2. marriage is valid if contracted according to the laws of the respective religions and beliefs of the parties, but every marriage will be registered. There is civil registration for religions other than Islam, and marriage according to the practices of their faith;
3. a minimum age for marriage of 19 for men, 16 for women;
4. explicit consent of both parties to the marriage is required protecting women from marriage against their will;
5. both parties can initiate judicial divorce. The grounds for divorce were set out in the implementing regulation. The judge must in the first instance try to reconcile the parties;

[63] Katz and Katz, "The New Indonesian Marriage Law," 653; Soewondo, "Indonesian Marriage Law."

[64] John Bowen, "Contextual Interpretation and Legal Pluralism in Indonesian Islamic Jurisprudence." (Unpublished paper, copy on file with author).

[65] Compromise related to: the minimum marriage age was reduced from 21 for men and 18 for women to 16 for women and 18 for men; the reasons for divorce were removed from the bill and only mentioned in the clarification. The article stipulating equal distribution of common property was changed to a stipulation that common property will be divided according to the law of the parties concerned. Muslim groups were anxious that the bill would weaken the religious courts. The compromise meant that the jurisdiction of Islamic courts was broadened rather than restricted, but not to the disadvantage of women (given the sympathetic interpretation they have taken in regard to divorce rights for women).

6. the principle of monogamy is paramount, but the law allows those permitted by religion (or the law of the country of their citizenship) to have more than one spouse;[66]
7. men are forbidden from taking second wives without the permission of the first wife;
8. the rights and responsibilities of spouses are stipulated in the law: the husband is the head of the family and the wife is in charge of the household;
9. the legislation increased the jurisdiction of the Islamic courts which "formerly were only competent to judge limited cases of marriage and divorce";[67] and
10. the final form of the bill gave women a more equal position vis-à-vis men in relation the equal division of common property.[68]

Where did the political will to finally enact the law come from? The modernizing regime of the New Order brought the 'private' aspects of women's lives into the state arena, with the state challenging the claims of other dominant ideologies—in particular Islam, but also local cultural traditions—to regulate personal and family relations. On the surface, the law was the act of a secular, modernizing regime, continuing the agenda of nationalist groups which aimed to weed out '*feodalisme*' (pre-modern unequal relations) from the personal realm as well as from society at large. Much of the political will to enact the law, however, came from the new government's commitment to overturn the pro-natalist policies of the Soekarno regime and establish a state-sponsored population control program. Limitations on early marriage were seen as an important measure to control fertility. The Family Planning program went ahead despite initial opposition from some Islamic groups (who held the line on abortion and on sterilization as officially sanctioned methods on the grounds that they were irreversible[69]) in large part because the major Islamic groups—NU and Muhammadiyah—supported fertility regulation for social welfare ends.

Effects of the 1974 Marriage Law

What has been the impact of the law on polygamy, the issue which women's organization identified as the strongest limitation on women's rights? While polygamy is permitted under Islamic law in specific circumstances, the weight

---

[66] Katz and Katz, "The New Indonesian Marriage Law," 653.

[67] Soewondo, "Indonesian Marriage Law," 289.

[68] Bowen "Contextual Interpretation," 6.

[69] Indonesian gynaecologists have trialed methods of reversible sterilisation in order that sterilisation could be officially programmed, with Muslim support. See M. B. Hooker, *Indonesian Islam: Social Change Through Contemporary Fatwa* (Sydney and Honolulu: Allen and Unwin and University of Hawaii Press, 2003), 166–78 for a discussion of the fatwa relating to contraception.

of sentiment in many Indonesian communities is against it as a common practice. Indeed, a common interpretation offered in Indonesia is that ordinary men would not be able to observe the requirement to treat all wives equally, therefore polygamy is in fact not normally permitted. While it would not be politically possible to outlaw polygamy, as it is discussed in the *Qur'an*, the Indonesian government has created significant impediments by making it legal only under specified conditions, and requiring judicial approval. The husband has to submit a written request to the religious court, which examines whether the wife/wives have consented; whether financial documents indicate that he will be able to support all his wives; and whether he will behave justly towards his wife/wives and children according to undertakings made on a form stipulated for the purpose.[70] The court summons the wife/wives and seeks their views and will then grant permission if it is satisfied there are sufficient reasons (in accord with the enabling regulations to the legislation). A polygamous marriage cannot be registered without court approval. Penalties for violation were set at three months gaol or a fine of Rp 7500. Women's organizations protested from the beginning that that there was not a sufficient deterrent; by 1998, the fine was only equivalent to A$1.25. Many men prefer to pay the fine, and others ignore the court system.[71] Although these procedures apparently establish formal barriers to polygamy, they do not effectively prevent it.

In a similar vein, while Islam recognizes the right of divorce through unilateral repudiation by the husband (*talak*), Indonesia, like many Muslim countries, recognizes that this can lead to women and children being left without financial support. The administrative procedures initiated with the 1974 law which required the registration of *talak* and the specification of valid reasons are all ways of creating delay, and allowing space for reconciliation. Hence, the implementing regulations that followed the passage of the law went some way towards acknowledging the concerns that had been expressed by women.

Soewondo, who has been a significant marriage reform activist since the 1940s, comments that the law has not necessarily curtailed polygamy, because polygamy has often been accepted by first wives as an alternative to divorce, since they would rather share a husband than not have a husband at all.[72] For women who prefer divorce to the suffering of polygamy, this has been difficult to obtain, since polygamy is not a ground for divorce. Butt cites a study which

---

[70] Katz and Katz, "The New Indonesian Marriage Law," 672.

[71] Simon Butt, "Polygamy and Mixed Marriage in Indonesia: The Application of the Marriage Law in the Courts," in *Indonesia: Law and Society*, ed. Timothy Lindsey (Sydney: The Federation Press, 1999), 132.

[72] Soewondo, "Indonesian Marriage Law," 287.

concluded that "judges of the Religious Courts often decided polygamy cases in accordance with Islamic law rather than the Marriage Law, and therefore usually allowed polygamous marriages".[73] Similarly, while the law mandates consent of both parties to a marriage, it is difficult for a young woman to act as agent of her own will and refuse her parents' wishes that she marry, even if she is underage; it is especially difficult if her parents' actions are seen as in accord with religion and custom.

The Soeharto government strengthened the restrictions on polygamy and divorce for civil servants through a 1983 regulation which required them to obtain the permission of their supervisors before seeking divorce or taking a second wife.[74] This regulation took precedence over customary law or the 1974 Marriage Law. It has had ambiguous benefits, as it has meant that many women have been kept as illicit second wives, with little security, in particular if the relationship breaks down.

On the basis of demographic data which indicates that the 1974 law has had little effect on age at marriage, Cammack, Young and Heaton question whether it has had any consequences for marriage practices.[75] They argue that the distinction in the act between marriages that are 'valid' and those that are 'legal' (part of the negotiated compromise to obtain passage of the 1974 legislation) allows an Islamic sphere of marriage outside state control. This issue has been raised by women's organizations, concerned at the lack of protection for a woman if a man fails to register the marriage.[76] But registration has become widely accepted as a practice throughout Indonesia: a major problem seems to be the lack of a centralized system, leading to the situation that women can be the unwitting partners to polygamous marriages with untruthful men.[77] Idrus describes the activities of '*imam liar*' or 'wild officiants,' whom she encountered in the South Sulawesi district of Sidrap.[78] These men, who are not registered by the state, preside at weddings, issue marriage certificates, and officiate in divorce proceedings. In their view, they operate according to Islamic law, valorising this above national law. They argue that

---

[73] Butt, "Polygamy and Mixed Marriage," 128.

[74] Government Regulation (PP) No 10 of 1983; Julia Suryakusuma, "The State and Sexuality in New Order Indonesia," in *Fantasizing the Feminine in Indonesia*, ed. Laurie J. Sears (Durham and London: Duke University Press, 1996).

[75] Mark Cammack, Lawrence A. Young and Tim Heaton, "Legislating Social Change in an Islamic Society: Indonesia's Marriage Law," *American Journal of Comparative Law* 44 (1996): 45–73.

[76] Sisters in Islam, *Report on Regional Workshop and Justice for Muslim Women, June 8–10, 2001*, http://www.muslimtents.com/sistersinislam/reports/810_062001.htm

[77] Kathryn Robinson, *Stepchildren of Progress: The Political Economy of Development in an Indonesian Mining Town* (Albany NY: SUNY Press, 1986).

[78] Nurul Ilmi Idrus, "To Take Each Other" (Ph.D. diss., Australian National University, 2003).

they provide a community service, marrying people polygynously (even polyandrously in the eyes of the state) in order to keep them free from sin. They issue certificates, and, interestingly, some women do not realise that their certificates are not legally valid. Marriage by way of the *imam liar* is not the same as the practice of living together out of wedlock where no registration is sought. While it is easier for men to take multiple wives through the services of the *imam liar*, it also enables women who have been abandoned by their husbands to obtain a divorce in his absence (by way of the *imam liar*) and even to remarry—hence it can have an enabling effect on women's agency.

Codification of Islamic Law and Reform of the Court System

The New Order regime further strengthened its grip on the Religious Courts, and hence the force of the secular marriage law, through the Law on Judicial Power (No. 14 of 1970) and the Law on Religious Justice (No. 7 of 1989) which brought the religious courts into a unified national system in which the Supreme Court is the ultimate court of appeal.[79] The Religious Court's function in regard to marriage is to regulate divorce, and thc 1989 law is "aimed at controlling the process of divorce by removing it from individual initiative and subjecting it to administrative procedures" thereby making it more difficult to obtain.[80]

The Compilation of Islamic Law (Kompilasi Hukum) was established as a guide for the judgments of the Islamic Courts, ratified by a Presidential Instruction in 1991. While this codification "purported to combine elements of classical Islamic texts, modern Islamic laws enacted by other Muslim countries, opinions and rulings of Islamic scholars and organizations, and decisions of Indonesia's Religious courts," the Kompilasi is a triumph of the executive, the secular power of the state, over religion.[81] There are three books, dealing with Marriage Law, Inheritance, and Charitable Foundations. The large chapter dealing with marriage incorporated the regulations under the 1974 Marriage Law, and reiterated that the Religious Courts had to make judgments based on the secular law, not just the *fiqh*. According to Butt, this has had the effect of making the Religious Courts rely more firmly on the 1974 Marriage Law, where they had previously been more inclined to base decisions on *fiqh*.[82] Cammack cites a Supreme Court judge opining that "the

[79] M. B. Hooker, "The State and *Syari'ah* in Indonesia 1945–1995," in *Indonesia: Law and Society*, ed. Timothy Lindsey (Sydney: The Federation Press, 1999), 104.

[80] Hooker and Lindsey, "Public Faces of Syari'ah," 277.

[81] Butt, "Polygamy and Mixed Marriage," 130.

[82] Ibid.

Compilation elevates family law matters to the status of enforceable civil law, and banishes forever the dogma that marriage and divorce is a private affair beyond the ambit of state control."[83] A judge of the Supreme Court (Mahkama Agung) "has asserted that the Islamic marriage law is now a state affair, as its principles are reflected in the Compilation, which has the force of positive law."[84]

The strategy used was not to go back to the *fiqh* but to provide a synthesis of the judgments of Indonesian courts, taking account of *adat*, national law and *syari'ah*. Islamic scholars in Indonesia have accepted the notion of legitimation, recognizing the possibility of reciprocal acculturation between Islam and local culture. For example, the liberal Muslim intellectual Nurcholis Madjid[85] wrote that "*adat* and a society's customary practices ... are a source of law in Islam".[86] Islamic codes do not usually incorporate notions of common property and the award of common proprietary rights is restricted to maintenance of a divorced woman for three months. However Indonesian civil courts declared maintenance to be a central part of *adat* (customary) law in many parts of the country, and so it was incorporated into the Kompilasi Hukum Islam. Within the Kompilasi, the Book on Marriage fundamentally supports the provisions of the 1974 Marriage Law in regard to marriage and divorce. Polygamy and divorce require judicial approval: *fiqh* is "subject to a secular process which actually determines its application."[87]

The Kompilasi can be seen as strengthening the rights of women in divorce, and negating the disadvantage they have under literalist interpretations of Islamic Law. There is evidence, however, that the courts were inclined to work in a way that was sympathetic to women's rights and interests, even prior to the 1975 law. Lev discusses the innovative manner in which the courts interpreted *shikak* (condition of irreconcilable disagreement) in divorce proceedings.[88] *Shikak* is a process of mediation by a third party for contested divorce and settlement.[89] Despite the fact that according to the *fiqh*, only the husband can initiate divorce, there has been an 'independent development'

---

[83] Cammack, Young and Heaton, "Legislating Social Change," 67–8.

[84] Butt, "Polygamy and Mixed Marriage," 130.

[85] Nurcholis Madjid is often described as one of Indonesia's leading Islamic intellectuals. He assisted in the establishment of ICMI in 1990 and has served a term on the Indonesian Human Rights Commission (Komnasham); he has been a lecturer at the Post-graduate Faculty of the IAIN Syarif Hidayatullah (Jakarta) and a distinguished member of the Indonesian Institute of Sciences; and has been Rector of the Paramadina Mulya University since 1998.

[86] Cited Bowen, "Contextual Interpretation," 13).

[87] Hooker and Lindsey, "Public Faces of Syari'ah," 280.

[88] Lev, *Islamic Courts in Indonesia*.

[89] Howard M. Federspiel, *A Dictionary of Indonesian Islam* (Athens, Ohio: Ohio University, Center for International Studies, 1995), 254.

in Indonesia dating from the 1930's in which the courts came to hold that that *shikak* gave women the option to initiate divorce, in circumstances where they had no grounds under *fiqh* and as "a way of ending marriages when women have exhausted other remedies against recalcitrant husbands."[90] It goes some way towards addressing the disadvantages of Islamic law for women, who have embraced the right to initiate divorce. Indeed, Hooker and Lindsey argue that there is evidence that women now more commonly initiate divorce proceedings than men.[91] The woman's refusal to grant permission for polygamy may be overridden by the court if the husband has grounds under the law, but he must be able to demonstrate his capacity to support all the wives and children.[92] There is also strengthening of women's common property rights, which is recognized in many Indonesian *adat* systems (*harta gono-gini*). One of the scholars involved in the Compilation is quoted by Bowen:

> maybe in Arabia the wife does not do anything, but in Indonesia it is not like that. If a man takes up a machete to go out to the fields, his wife comes with him, carrying a bundle on her back. So she had contributed to wealth, either by working on the fields or by taking care of the family, and she should receive some of the inheritance—and then we set specific amounts. Here, we differ from *fiqh*, we take account of culture.[93]

In Bowen's view, the effort by the government to unify a civil law code has resulted in a greater degree of equality between men and women.

The unification of the court system and the Kompilasi Hukum Islam brought some positive benefits for women, in bringing more legal certainty to some of the rights they hold under custom—especially in relation to property and inheritance—which may be in conflict with some literalist interpretations of Islamic law. It has also been significant in defining state authority in relation to Islam. In late 2004, the government announced its intention to upgrade the status of the Kompilas Hukum from Presidential instruction to law. This has given rise to a new wave of public debate, much of it initiated by the gender mainstreaming team in the Department of Religious Affairs, supported by the Commission on Women's Human Rights (KOMNAS Perempuan) who argue that the sections of the Kompilasi dealing with family law should be further revised to reflect principles of democracy and gender equity as well as contemporary Indonesian social practice. In particular, women's rights advocate criticize discriminatory clauses of the Marriage Law relating to age at marriage, the stipulation of male household heads, the

---

[90] Lev, *Islamic Courts in Indonesia*, 173.
[91] Hooker and Lindsey, "Public Faces of Syari'ah," 282.
[92] Ibid., 280–1.
[93] Bowen, "Contextual Interpretation," 14.

requirement for a *wali* to be male, differential divorce rights and the continued legal support for polygamy. They also want to revisit unequal inheritance.[94] That is, women are continuing to press the demands for state intervention to protect women's rights The concern for further advancing gender equity in the current (2005) process of legal revision has been given urgency by the current movement to legitimate *syari'ah* as the basis of state law in many parts of Indonesia, an issue which is discussed in the next section.

The Resurgence of Polygamy

The end of the Soeharto regime in 1998 was associated with demands for democratization, which included liberalizing political discourse and winding back the highly centralized executive concentration of state power. Soeharto's successor, his Vice-President Habibie, responded to these demands by returning some political and administrative power to the sub-provincial level districts (*kabupaten*). This devolution was intended to support democratization by re-empowering local political formations which had been subsumed under the New Order's uniform national model for local politics (implemented through the 1979 Law Concerning Village Government). It was also assumed that democratization would be served by bringing decision-making closer to the people. The emphasis on a return to *adat* as a basis of local governance has, in many places, opened the way for powerful groups to advance their interests in the name of a revival of distinctive traditions. Through this process, and under the rubric of *adat* and regional autonomy, gender relations are also being renegotiated.[95]

Some extremist Islamic groups have seized on the new climate of political freedom to push their cause for Islam as the basis of government, proposing *syari'ah* law be implemented in their districts.[96] The literalist interpretations of Islam that these moves have instantiated go against the strong emphasis on

[94] "Menyosialisasikan 'Counter Legal Draft' Kompilasi Hukum Islam," *Kompas*, Oktober 11, 2004, http://www.kompas.com/kompas-cetak/0410/11/swara/1316378.htm (accessed September 8, 2005); Anon, "Wawancara Dr Siti Musdah Mulia, M.A.: Kompilasi Hukum Sangat Konservatif!" *Jaringan Islam Liberal*, September 8, 2005, http://islamlib.com/id/index.php?page+article&id+408 (accessed September 8, 2005).

[95] Melani Budianta, "Plural Identities: Indonesian Women's Redefinition of Democracy in the Post-reformasi Era," *Review of Indonesian and Malaysian Affairs* 36(1) (2002): 35–50; see also Edriana Noerdin, "Women and Regional Autonomy," in Robinson and Bessell, *Women in Indonesia*.

[96] An attempt in 2002 to reinstate the Piagam Jakarta, obliging Muslims to abide by *syari'ah*, in the constitution was defeated: see Hooker and Lindsey, "Public Faces of Syari'ah," 265.

interpretation which has been the hallmark of the best known of Indonesia's leading Muslim intellectuals (figures such as Nurcholish Madjid and Abdurrachman Wahid[97]) and which characterizes the accommodative stance between custom and Islam in the Islamic courts.

The contentious issue of polygamy is now re-emerging in public debate. In the freer political climate of Reformasi, the men who have never accepted this limitation on their prerogatives have been publicly defending their right to have multiple spouses. While Indonesia may have achieved a milestone for women in the election of a female president, Megawati Soekarnoputi chose as her Vice–President Hamzah Has, the head of PPP (Partai Persatuan Pembangunan) the largest Muslim party in parliament. In a significant discursive shift from the public puritanism and hegemonic monogamy of the New Order, Hamzah Has has been announced on state television news broadcasts as attending functions "with his second/third wife". The legitimacy that change has given to polygamy was keenly felt by women activists, who have been critical of then-President Megawati's silent acceptance of his public polygamy. A number of activists pointed out to me that Megawati's own mother moved out of the presidential palace when her father took a second wife.

The most spectacular push by the pro-polygamy group is the institution of the 'polygamy awards' by a well known restaurateur, Haji Puspo Wardoyo, the self-styled president of Masyarakat Poligami Indonesia (the Indonesian People's Association for Polygamy). In July 2003 he hosted a night of celebrations at which he presented awards to high profile polygamists. Hamzah Has was an awardee but declined to attend.[98] A national newspaper reported that Puspo claimed "I know a lot of men who are embarrassed and keep secret the fact they have more than one wife. In fact, Islam allows polygamy, as long as you are just." His intention in establishing the polygamy awards was to give spirit (*semangat*) and a moral boost to practitioners of polygamy.[99] Of the hundreds of entry forms he distributed, only 50 had been returned. He argued that this was an indication that many men still felt embarrassed to join in. Their excuses included their status as civil servants and their fear of their wives.[100]

Puspo promotes legalised polygamy as positive for women, as otherwise they risk becoming secret "*simpinan*" (woman on the side) with no guarantee of their own or their children's rights. His goal is to make polygamy a common

---

[97] Abdurrachman Wahid, Indonesia's fourth President between October 1999 and July 2001, has also been leader of Nahdlatul Ulama, the largest Muslim organisation in Indonesia.

[98] Timothy Mapes, "Indonesian Restaurateur puts Polygamy on the Menu," *Wall Street Journal* November 24, 2003 (Westlaw: 2003 WL-WSJ 68129142).

[99] *Detik* July 25, 2003.

[100] Ibid.

and accepted practice. In his view: "A man who has the material wealth and is of moral character has the duty of taking more than one wife. ... If there are 20 million successful businessmen who are able to take a second wife, they can support 40 million women. So the problem of women overseas workers will be resolved. . . ."[101]

Puspo's public support for polygamy sparked outrage from women's groups, many of whom have been arguing since 2000 for a revision of the 1974 Marriage Law and a prohibition of polygamy. LBH-APIK (Legal Aid Institute of Justice for Indonesia Women) has been at the forefront of this campaign. Its founder, Nursyahbani Katjasungkana (a lawyer and member of the People's Consultative Assembly or MPR) has been a prominent advocate of revising the law to remove discriminatory clauses.[102] The umbrella organization, KOWANI, has also come out in support of marriage law reform.

The day of the awards ironically coincided with the 19th anniversary of Indonesia becoming a signatory to the International Convention on the Elimination of All Forms of Discrimination Against Women (CEDAW). The CEDAW Committee has raised the issue of the discriminative nature of a law allowing polygamy.[103] Women activists demonstrated against "the recent flowering of polygamy". Newspaper reports described demonstrators in Yogyakarta wearing the *jilbab* and carrying banners and posters with slogans like "Polygamy Transgresses Human Rights" and "Refuse Polygamy". The protest organizers problematized the legal status of polygamy, by linking it to Indonesia's obligations under CEDAW. They expressed a view held by many women's rights groups that no religions sanction polygamy. Yuni, from the Pro-Woman Alliance, was quoted as saying:

> In fact, the Qu'ran itself contains a universal appeal that the status of women is equal to that of men. Unfortunately religion has become a way of legalizing biological needs. Under the disguise of religion and using his wealth, an arrogant man (Puspo Wardoyo) has been able to wage a campaign in the mass media in support of polygamy, a form of violence against women.[104]

On the night of the awards, more women expressing the same concerns as the Yogya group demonstrated outside the venue, a luxury hotel in Jakarta.[105] Some of them gained entry to the hall. The women's legal rights advocacy

---

[101] *Kompas*, July 28, 2003.

[102] Their information materials on individual rights and on their political campaigns are posted at http://www.lbh-apik.or.id.

[103] United Nations, *Report of the Committee on the Elimination of Discrimination Against Women*, 18th and 19th Session, A/53/38/Rev.1, 26.

[104] *Suara Merdeka* July 25, 2003.

[105] Faiza Mardzoeki, 'We are against Polygamy', *Jakarta Post*, August 13, 2003; *Kompas* July 28, 2003.

group LBH-APIK—which has long been a supporter of marriage law reform and has acted for individual women who are victims of polygamy—articulated widely reported criticisms of Puspo Wardoyo.[106] For groups like LBH-APIK (and also organizations like Aisyiah, Kalyanamitra, Institut Ungu and the National Commission on Violence Against Women) polygamy constitutes a form of discrimination against women, based on male superiority and male sexual privilege which is clearly in contradiction with principles of equality and anti-discrimination enshrined in many national and international legal instruments.[107] LBH-APIK's campaign to amend the 1974 Marriage Law had to date principally focused on the clause differentiating the man as head of the household from the women as housekeeper. However, in response to Pospo's campaign to promote polygamy, the women's organization expressed a clear demand that it be abolished through amendment to the Marriage Law because polygamy is not in accord with CEDAW, since it unequally discriminates between the rights of men and women in marriage.

LBH-APIK's report on polygamy argued that polygamy often triggers domestic violence as well as other forms of physical, psychological, sexual, and economic abuse. They supported their argument by referring to the cases they had handled. Their experience in legal aid for women in polygamous relationships illustrated that polygamy in itself constitutes a form of domestic violence which is legitimated by law and by custom. Moreover, they argue that court data show that polygamy is the most common reason for women seeking divorce.[108]

They further argued that the clauses in the Marriage Law allowing polygamy assumed that the purpose of marriage is to satisfy the biological needs and the need for an heir of members of one sex only. There is an implicit assumption that one sex—the male sex—will never have a problem with its sexual capability. These clauses assume women are sex providers and reflect a phallocentric point of view. Polygamy, they argue, manifests a construction of male power as superior and a male desire to dominate women. It is a form of oppression of women that is not consistent with humanitarianism and justice. While some women do accept polygamy, it can be seen as a form

[106] See for example Linda Tangdialla, "Poligami adalah bentuk kerasan atas martabat perempuan," *Bisnis Indonesia*, July 25, 2003:, p 1.

[107] Such as: UUD 45 (The 1945 Constutition); UUHAM (The Law on Human Rights); UU no1/84 (the domestic law ratifying CEDAW); GBHN (Broad Outlines of State Policy) 1999; Deklarasi Penghapusan Kekerasana Terhadap Perempuan—Declaration on the Elimination of All Forms of Discrimination Against Women); also Mardzoeki, 'We are against Polygamy;' *Kompas* July 28, 2003.

[108] Muninggar Sri Saraswati, 'Men Forge Documents to Marry other Women', *Jakarta Post*, April 30, 2004.

of internalized oppression—as a consequence of their socialization into subordinated gender roles.[109]

Indeed, a number of women proclaiming themselves to be pro-polygamy entered into the debate. Some of them appeared on public platforms with Puspo Wardoyo. Sitoresmi Prabuningrat, the fourth wife of a rock star Deby Nasution, spoke out in favor of polygamy, saying that she was happy as a fourth wife, although she knew this was controversial, as most people saw it as a stigma. And rather than polygamy being the practice of the poorly educated, and not popular among women who had a modern outlook, she said it was precisely because she was an additional wife that she was able to be a "career woman": "If I were a sole wife, who would look after my husband?"[110]

The promotion of polygamy has sparked a noisy public debate in newspapers and on television, and has brought to public attention the division of opinion amongst Muslims, including Islamic scholars, on this issue. Progressive women's groups challenge literalist interpretations of the Qur'an and Hadith (traditions of the Prophet) with interpretive readings that contextualize apparently anti-woman verses historically, or in terms of other passages in the Qur'an. Moreover, it is not only women who argue for an interpretation of the Qur'an which is in fact a prohibition on polygamy, but also men. The debates often hinge on the possibility of polygamists treating all wives fairly, the impropriety of marrying for sexual satisfaction, and historical arguments about the circumstances of war pertaining in the Prophet's lifetime. For example, in a seminar on gender equity organized by the Islamic based women's rights group, Rahima (which is connected to the Malaysian group Sisters in Islam), Nasaruddin Umar addressed the interpretation of the Qur'anic passage, *Sura An-Nisa ayat 3* on polygamy. Although the passage states a man may marry up to four times, many *ulama* reject the interpretation that this provides a basis for polygamy. Their reasoning is that Islam basically affirms monogamous marriage, and accepts polygamy as an Arab tradition from the period prior to Islam that gave primary status and dominance to men. The (cultural/historical) bias in interpreting that *ayat* in many classic texts is the reason that polygamy is still practiced in many Arab countries. Even though the prophet Muhammad was polygamous, this cannot be used as an excuse by the *ummat* to support the practice because this was a special prerogative of the prophet. He used it in the course of *dakwah* (proselytising, disseminating his beliefs), to protect orphans of men who died in war, to strengthen his associations, to prevent ethnic conflict and to attract a particular

[109] Ibid.

[110] See further: Mapes "Indonesian Restaurateur puts Polygamy on the Menu."

ethnic group to convert to Islam. Out of his nine wives, only two were virgins. Most of them were widows and already menopausal.[111]

The Indonesian Islamic scholar Lily Munir cites Fatimah Mernissi and Riffat Hassan as 'opening our eyes' to misogyny in Muslim societies.[112] These scholars present what Kandiyoti refers to a 'progressive' reading of the Qu'ran, to challenge the exegetical approach of fundamentalists who argue that gender inequality is divinely ordained.[113] These progressive readings interpret apparently misogynist passages (regarding polygamy, women as witnesses, etc.) in historical cultural frames, and also point to passages in the Qu'ran that "support equality between men and women and that refer to women's rights . . .".[114]

So, for example, Lily Munir discusses the "classical exegesis" of *Sura An-Nisa* 4:34 which proclaims that men have authority over women.[115] Munir poses the question: "Have God's messages on gender and sexual equality been properly understood by the human? Is our understanding of the Qur'an in line with what God intends to express?"[116] While she is principally concerned in the paper to discuss sexuality, her argument is useful here as an example of the interpretive strategy which is used by women like herself, who are themselves well educated in the *pesantren* tradition, to challenge misogynist interpretations. She comments "[i]f these Qur'anic verses were so discriminatory against women, then how do they relate to the overarching message of the Qur'an that it is God's will for humanity to create a just society and institute a variety of social reforms, including raising the status of women?" She cites a number of verses which enjoin equality between men and women "in all essential rights and duties."[117]

Feminist activists have entered vigorously into the exegetical debates. For example, the Muslim feminist intellectual Lies Marcoes edits a weekly newspaper section on gender issues in the prestigious Jakarta metropolitan daily *Kompas* and she has commissioned a series of articles dealing with polygamy from prominent male Muslim intellectuals who have taken an exegetically based anti-polygamy stance.[118] The organization Rahima has published

---

[111] *Kompas* June 18, 2001.

[112] Lily Zakiyah Munir, "'He is your garment and you are his': religious precepts, interpretations, and power relations in marital sexuality among Javanese Muslim women," *Sojourn: Social Issues in Southeast Asia*, 17, no. 2 (2002): 191–220.

[113] Deniz Kandiyoti, "Introduction," in *Women, Islam and the State*, ed. Deniz Kandiyoti (Houndsmills, Basingstoke and London: Macmillan, 1991).

[114] Lily Zakiyah Munir, "The Koran's spirit of gender equality," *Quantar.de. Dialogue with the Islamic world* (2003) http://www.quantara.de/webcom/show_article.php/_c-307/_nr-19/i.html.

[115] Munir "He is your garment."

[116] Ibid., 213.

[117] Ibid., 210.

[118] Lies Marcoes, personal communication, July 2003.

similar articles by men and women on its Web-site, and a prominent figure in Rahima (Syafiq Hasyim) has published a book on *fiqui perempuan* (Islamic Law dealing with women). Rahima has also been monitoring the gender impacts of regional autonomy. These critiques of Islamic debates feed into political activism and demands for law reform, such as the debates about revising the Marriage Law referred to above.

Conclusion

In Indonesia, the demand for the protection of women's rights within marriage has brought women's groups into conflict with both Islamic groups and with the colonial and post-colonial states. The fundamental dispute has been concerning the right and/or obligation of the state to regulate the private domain of the family. To quote Iris Marion Young:[119]

> The feminist slogan 'the personal is political' does not deny a distinction between public and private, but it does deny a social division between public and private spheres, with different kinds of institutions, activities and human attributes. Two principles follow from this slogan: (a) no social institutions or practices should be excluded a priori as being the proper subject for public discussions and expression; and (b) no persons, actions or aspects of a person's life should be forced into privacy.

The private sphere has an ambiguous status in relation to the public/civil realm. Islam in particular, but also other religions, claims special status in regard to the regulation of personal life. The political task facing women is to challenge this covert anti-egalitarianism and to rupture the barrier which excludes matters of 'the private' from becoming the subject of public reflection and discussion.

Women have faced a political struggle to bring those arenas of life deemed private and hence excluded from public reflection and electoral politics into the public domain of political contestation, and achieved some success in the passage of the 1974 Marriage Law. Subsequent legal reforms by the government have strengthened the secular control of marriage and divorce in ways which have been positive for women. However, in accepting state regulation of marriage and divorce, the New Order also took upon itself the power to define women's primary social role as located in the domestic sphere. This was legislated in the same law that gave women protection in marriage and divorce.

---

[119] Young 1990, cited in Pauline Johnson, *Feminism as Radical Humanism* (St. Leonards New South Wales: Allen and Unwin, 1994), 86.

Women are utilizing the democratic space that has been opened up by *Reformasi* to demand that the state extend its authority on issues like domestic violence and rape in marriage. At the same time, Islamist organizations seeking to impose new forms of patriarchal authority in the name of Islam have captured state power in some of the newly empowered district governments. This poses a new challenge and threatens to unravel the gains for legal protection that women had already achieved, (paradoxically under the authoritarian and anti-woman New Order regime) while imposing new forms of restriction on personal autonomy hitherto unknown in the Indonesian archipelago.

CHAPTER EIGHT

ISLAMIZATION, MODERNITY, AND THE RE-POSITIONING OF WOMEN IN BRUNEI

Ann Black

Introduction

Since achieving independence in 1984, the Sultanate of Brunei Darussalam ('Brunei, the Abode of Peace') has been seeking to define its own particular national identity, while striving to be a leading nation amongst the states of Asia. The abundant political rhetoric announcing these dual aims is supported by strategies for practical implementation, and concrete initiatives in both directions are evident. To construct its national identity Brunei has implemented a national ideology, *Melayu Islam Beraja* (known as MIB) which translates as Malay, Islam, Monarchy (alternatively, 'Islamic Malay Monarchy'). This ideology permeates every aspect of life in the Sultanate. To become a leading state in Asia in political[1] as well as economic[2] terms, Brunei has used its petro-carbon derived wealth to improve the living standards of its people (currently second only to Japan in the region), has embraced high technology, and has been positioning itself as a leading banking and financial centre. However, there is a tension inherent in these choices: one path follows a route of modernization and development that is in line with the forces of globalization;[3] while

[1] In 1984, Brunei joined the following organizations: ASEAN (Association of Southeast Asian Nations); ARF (Asean Regional Forum.); APEC (Asia Pacific Economic Co-operation, as a founding member); ASEM (Asia European Meeting); PECC (Pacific Economic Co-operation Council). In 2000, Brunei hosted the annual APEC meeting. Brunei is a member of the Commonwealth of Nations, the United Nations, the International Monetary Fund and the World Bank. It is also a member of Islamic bodies such as OIC (Organisation of Islamic Conference) and ISESCO (Islamic Education, Scientific and Cultural Organisation).

[2] The Eighth National Development Plan in 2001 was designed to diversify the economy away from dominance of the oil and gas sectors, towards tourism and establishing Brunei as an offshore financial centre. The difficulty for Brunei in promoting itself as an International Financial Centre is that it has to compete with nearby Labuan (in Malaysia) as well as Singapore and Hong Kong.

[3] A prevailing view in Southeast Asia is that modernization inevitably means westernization or globalization. See Edwin Thumboo, "Introduction," in *Cultures in ASEAN and the 21st Century*, ed. Edwin Thumboo (Singapore: University of Singapore Press, 1996), xx.

the other charts a return to allegedly 'traditional' Malay customs and practices, a re-assertion of Islam as a religious and legal priority, and an endorsement of an undemocratic political regime.

The position of women in the Sultanate reflects the duality of national purpose. On the one hand, this is a time when women in Brunei have access to free education to tertiary level, are able to engage in a wide range of professional occupations and in business, have a free and internationally accepted high standard of health care, have comparatively high disposable incomes and are not subject to the social restrictions which occur in regions with *purdah* or women's seclusion zones. These benefits are the result of the nation's commitment to modernization, national unity, and economic development. However, these same Bruneian women are disenfranchised[4] and, if Muslim, are subject to the Sultanate's recently implemented policy designed for the 'Islamization' of laws and legal institutions.

Islamization is the process by which a society, generally with State support, and in line with Islamic revival and resurgence elsewhere in the Muslim world,[5] seeks to reassert its Islamic identity. It does so by according greater importance to designated Islamic laws, institutions, values, and practices than has previously been the case.[6] Given the centrality of law, described as the "the core and kernel of Islam itself,"[7] it is axiomatic that re-establishing Islamic law and legal institutions would be required by this direction. Given that women are seen as the symbolic role bearers of a society's cultural and religious values and traditions,[8] it was

[4] There have been no elections in Brunei Darussalam since 1962 when the state of emergency was declared. The Constitution of 1959 gave legislative authority to a Legislative Council, but Parts VI and VII of the Constitution, which set out the form and procedure for the Legislative Council, continued to be 'temporarily suspended' in the 1984 Revised Constitution at independence. Although the Sultan re-convened the Legislative Council in September, 2004, all of its 21 members were appointed. The Sultan has foreshadowed that there will be a minority of elected members (15 elected and 30 appointed) in the next Legislative Council though the time frame and details for an election have not been announced. However, as Ranjit Singh notes, "even if the Constitution was to operate *in toto,* the delegation of powers and functions to the various bodies is a façade." See D. S. Ranjit-Singh, "Executive Power and Constitutionalism in ASEAN States: The Brunei Experience," in *Constitutional and Legal Systems of ASEAN Countries,* ed. Carmelo V. Sison (Manila: Academy of ASEAN Law and Jurisprudence, 1990), 42.

[5] Obaid ul Haq, "Islamic Resurgence: the Challenge of Change," in *Islam and Society in Southeast Asia,* ed. Taufik Abdullah and Sharon Siddique (Singapore: Institute of Southeast Asian Studies, 1986), 332.

[6] Chandra Muzaffar, "Islamisation of State and Society: Some Further Critical Remarks," in *Shari'a Law and the Modern Nation State: A Malaysian Symposium,* ed. Norani Othman (Kuala Lumpur: SIS Forum, 1994), 113.

[7] Joseph Schacht, *Introduction to Islamic Law* (London: Oxford University Press, 1964), 1.

[8] This is a theme developed by Modhadam and is discussed later in this chapter. See Valentine M. Moghadam, ed., *Identity Politics and Women: Cultural Reassertions and Feminisms in International Perspective* (Boulder: Westview Press, 1994).

inevitable that women's roles and gender identity would be integral to the process. This is where law and religion directly intersect the lives of Muslim women in the Sultanate today.

The path of Islamization has even wider ramifications, as it also impacts upon the women in the Sultanate who are not Muslim, including the indigenous non-Malays. This is the focus of the last part of the chapter. While section 3 of the Constitution allows for other religions to be practiced in 'peace and harmony', law and policy informed by MIB act in practice to restrict the religious practices of the non-Malays. With strong government support for a robust *Melayu masuk* (becoming Malay) agenda, the result is that there are powerful disincentives for non-Malay women to freely adhere to their religious practices and to transmit these to their children. The steady numbers of indigenous non-Malays who are being absorbed, though Islamic conversion, into the Malay mainstream highlight the powerful mix that law and religion can exert over vulnerable and indigenous minorities.

Overview: Law, Women and Religion in Brunei

The area now known as Brunei Darussalam is just a remnant of the Sultanate of Brunei that has existed on the island of Borneo since 1360's. Although this date is disputed by some European historians,[9] its veracity is not to be questioned within Brunei. It is accepted that 1360 is the time of the conversion of Raja Awang Alak Betatar to Islam. As is the practice with conversions, he changed his name to reflect his new Islamic identity and to honour the Prophet, thereby becoming Sultan Muhammad Shah. The present Sultan, Haji Hassanal Bolkiah Mu'izzaddin Waddaulah, is his descendent.[10] In the centuries that followed, not all Borneans under the rule of the Sultanate converted to Islam. A minority of indigenous people retained their animistic Bornean beliefs and practices and today are still identified by their specific ethnic identity. Collectively they can be labelled indigenous non-Malays. The

---

[9] Robert Nicholl, "A Study in the Origins of Brunei," *Brunei Museum Journal* 7(1990): 20–31; Robert Nicholl, "An Age of Vicissitude Brunei 1225–1425," *Brunei Museum Journal* 6 (1989): 7–21; Mark Cleary and Peter Eaton, *Borneo: Change and Development* (Singapore: Oxford University Press, 1992), 25–45; Graham Saunders, *A History of Brunei* (Kuala Lumpur: Oxford University Press, 1994), xvii. Saunders claims that any opinion that disputes this date "impinges upon Brunei's status in the world today, upon the self image and identity of the Bruneian people, and upon the fundamental purpose of history as a discipline."

[10] It is claimed that the third Sultan, Berkat, was an Arab and a descendant of the Prophet. He married the daughter of the second Sultan of Brunei. This means the current Sultan can also claim lineage from the Prophet Muhammad—a factor which is significant for a ruler's Islamic credentials.

census indicates that there are 20,000 'other indigenous' non-Malays in Brunei and they comprise just 6 percent of the population. As is discussed later, while many have retained traditional animistic beliefs and practices, including longhouse living, there is a documented historical trend for indigenous (as well as Chinese) Bruneians to convert to Islam and thereby acquire the legal and cultural status of being Malay. Malays make up 70 percent of the population; 15–20 percent of the population is Chinese, and the 'other races' make up the remaining 10 percent, which mainly includes nationals from other Asian states, Europeans, and Australians. In terms of religious affiliation, the Chinese adhere to Buddhism, Taoism and Christianity and the 'other races' are a mix of Christians, Hindus, Buddhists and Muslims.

Religion

Islam is the State religion and to be a Brunei Malay is to be Muslim. Brunei is a Sunni state and, like most of Southeast Asia, adheres to the Shafi'i school.[11] Islamic teachings which deviate from "orthodox tenets of the Shafeite sect"[12] are condemned, as was demonstrated in the early 1990s when the Al-Arqam movement was banned[13] as a "heterodox Islamic sect."[14] The Sultan ensures that what the government labels "deviationist teachings" do not, in his words, "confuse the thinking and understanding of Muslims in Brunei"[15] nor

[11] Part II, section 3(1) of the Constitution states that the religion of Brunei Darussalam shall be the Muslim religion according to the Shafeite sect of that religion, and other legislation accordingly refers to rulings ordinarily following the 'orthodox tenets of the Shafeite sect.' Also contained in Religious Council and Kadis Courts Act (1984) section 43. This school adheres to the methodology and law of Imam As-Shafi'i and is one of the four remaining Sunni schools of jurisprudence that were founded in the eighth and ninth centuries.

[12] Religious Council and Kadis Courts Act (1984), section 43.

[13] The sect was declared unlawful under the Societies Act for promoting a belief contrary to those based upon the officially endorsed Ahli Sunnah Jama'ah creed. In the same *titah* it was announced that the authorities are to ban any foreigner who could be a threat to the country's religious harmony. See *Borneo Bulletin* 13 February, 1991 and more recently, warnings that there are people attempting to meddle with the meaning and words of the Qur'an, see Mohd Bahrin, "Muslims alert on attempts to meddle with Al-Quran," *Borneo Bulletin*, August 6, 2001. In 2003, six Bruneians were detained under the Internal Security Act for attempting to revive the Al-Arqam movement. See *Borneo Bulletin* September 23, 2003.

[14] Geoffry Gunn, *Language, Power and Ideology in Brunei Darussalam* (Athens, Ohio: Ohio University Press, 1997), 218. The movement was also banned in Malaysia three years later, and Case noted that the Sultan reminded the people that his vigilance against deviationist teachings outpaced others in the region. See William Case, "Brunei Darussalam in 1995" *Asian Survey* 36 (1996), 133.

[15] 'Be careful of Misleading Movements, warns Minister,' October 28, 2002, www.brudirect, com/DailyInfo/News/Archive/Oct02/281002/nite06.htm; "Beware of Deviationist Teachings, Warns Religious Minister," October 24, 2002, http://www.brudirect.com/DailyInfo/News/Archive/Oct02/241002/nite07.htm.

corrupt his subjects' devotion to "the true path."[16] It is likely, however, that political motives also underpin this approach. Al-Arqam promotes a return to a simpler, more spiritual life which, members argue, is closer to the way of life of early Muslims. It is possible that Government fears that if it allows free expression of divergent views within Islam, Bruneians might also query the justification for an authoritarian undemocratic State structure on the basis that it also diverges from the just and equal society expounded in the teachings of the Prophet Mohammad.[17] It is apparent, then, that the government believes that maintaining homogeneity of Islamic belief is crucial to preventing any challenge to its religious and political authority.

For these reasons, the government maintains control over all religious practice in the Sultanate. The Ministry of Religious Affairs is a powerful arm of government which regulates the practice and the protection of Islam. Apostasy has to be reported to the Secretary of the Majlis, the Religious Council,[18] and a period of detention for the apostate in a Religious Rehabilitation Centre follows in order to 'assist' the apostate's return to correct Islamic adherence.[19] Furthermore, there are prohibitions on Muslims accessing information about other religions,[20] and a series of offences that prohibit "misuse"[21] or "derision"[22] of the Qur'an and Islamic teachings.

In addition, there are restrictions on the religious practice of non-Muslims. The Internal Security Act (1960), modeled on the infamous law of neighboring Malaysia, is employed to prevent any religious activities that are regarded by the government as attempting to promote a religion other than Islam, or

---

16 Malai Hassan Othman and Mohd. Bahrin, "Shun deviationist teachings," *Borneo Bulletin* August 16, 2000. Also in his *titah* for *Aidil Adha*, March 7, 2001 the Sultan reminded Muslims to not let "deviants influence them" www.bruneisultan.com

17 Kesseler writes of the paradox in modern Southeast Asian States where Islam is being used to support oligarchical structures, when Islamic teachings could be interpreted as encouraging Muslims to resist a society based on such inequality. Clive Kessler, *Islam and Politics in a Malay State: Kelantan 1838–1969*, (Ithica: Cornell University Press, 1978).

18 Religious Council and Kadis Courts Act (1984), section 169.

19 This is contrary to The Universal Declaration of Human Right, in which article 18 lays down the principle that "everyone has the right to freedom of thought, conscience and religion," and clearly states that such a right "includes freedom to change his religion or belief and freedom, either alone or in community with others, and in public or private, to manifest his religion or belief in teaching, practise, worship and observance."

20 Under the Religious Council and Kadis Courts Act (1984) section 186, it is an offence to publish, issue, sell or bring religious books which are against Islamic teachings (six-month imprisonment or $4,000 fine with the books or documents could be confiscate); Section 188 it is an offence to conduct teachings, religious talks or a ceremonies that are against the Islamic teachings (three-month imprisonment or $2000 fine. See also the Undesirable Publications Act (1982).

21 Religious Council and Kadis Courts Act (1984), sections 189–90.

22 Religious Council and Kadis Courts Act (1984), section 191.

which might "deviate the belief of the Muslim population".[23] This means that proselytizing or outreach activities, such as public prayer meetings, are penalised. Like its Malaysian counterpart, the Act allows the government to detain suspects without trial for up to two years. It has been employed to detain Christians and members of the Baha'i faith, Qadianis and followers of a cult known as Silat Lintau.[24] There are restrictions on the importation of non-Islamic religious materials such as bibles and religious icons, including the Christian cross, and statutes of the Buddha and Hindu gods.[25] Non-Muslim religious bodies must be registered with the government, and to establish or extend a church, temple, shrine or other place of worship requires government approval, which is not always easy to obtain.[26] Despite these restrictions upon the practice of other faiths, there is a Chinese Buddhist temple, an Anglican church and a Roman Catholic church in the capital, Bandar Seri Begawan.

Women

The United Nations Human Developer Indicators, released in 2003 and based on data collected in 2001, indicate that women in Brunei have a high standard of health,[27] are as well educated as males in the Sultanate,[28] and are entering the workforce in increasing numbers. Today woman comprise 40 percent of the workforce; however, they receive only half the income of their male counterparts.[29] This is because there are not equal pay scales for men and women, and because women are under-represented in the higher

[23] "Brunei detains 3 for pushing Christianity," *The Australian*, March 26, 2001. It has been reported that twenty-five people associated with the Borneo Brunei Bible Council were investigated under the Act for 'disrupting religious harmony'. Kazi Mahmood, "Brunei Cracks Down On Christian Group," Islam Online, January 2003: http://www.islam-online.net/English/News/2001-03/23/article15.shtml.

[24] Azlan Othman, 'Six deviationist activities found in Brunei' *Borneo Bulletin* August 28, 2003.

[25] See US Department of State, *Country Reports on Human Rights Practices 2002*, www.state.gov/g/drl/rls/hrrpt/2002.

[26] Bureau of Democracy, Human Rights and Labour, US Department of State, "International Religious Freedom Report, Brunei, 2003," http://www.state.gov/g/drl/rls/irf/2003/23822pf.htm.

[27] The high standard of health care is reflected in the female life expectancy rate of 78.7 years with men slightly lower at 74.0 years.

[28] Female adult (15 years of age and over) literacy rate is 88.1 percent, with the male rate slightly higher at 94.6 percent, the discrepancy being a reflection of earlier education policies as current youth literacy rates (15–24 years) show 99.8 percent of women are literate. The combined primary, secondary and tertiary educational enrolment ratio shows females at 84 and males at 81.

[29] Men on average receive US$26,122 compared to US$11,716 for women (2000) and there are not equal pay scales.

echelons of the government and private companies. Speeches,[30] reports[31] and Internet sites on women's groups in Brunei[32] show that women are well represented in small and micro-home based enterprises, known locally as SMEs. Their lesser representation in middle to top level positions in the workplace is officially explained as arising from a 'cultural orientation that constrains women's ability to perform on an equal basis'.[33]

Women are encouraged to wear the *hejab*, the local version being the *tudong* (traditional Malay head-covering). While there is no legislation compelling women to veil in public places and many chose to wear Western clothes, nevertheless, in government schools a *tudong* is part of required uniform for all girls. Furthermore, in some workplaces, such as the Department of Religious Affairs and the University of Brunei Darussalam, strict dress codes apply.

Laws, Courts and Other Legal Institutions

Brunei was legally pluralistic[34] even prior to the arrival of Islam, as each of the indigenous ethnic groups had its own *adat* (custom) to regulate the lives of its members. The Islamic model of law and dispute resolution that was adopted by the Muslim Malays has been described as a derivative of Islam because Muslim legal orthodoxy was blended with indigenous *adat* elements, so that Islamic law was in a form that was compatible with the local Bruneian culture.[35] Thus, from the outset, Islamic law in Brunei was imbued with distinctive Malay, as opposed to Arabic or South Asian, characteristics. Furthermore, in keeping with the practices of Borneo, the Malay cultural tradition was less patriarchal than in the Muslim heartland of the Middle East and South Asia.[36] This meant that Muslim women in the Sultanate had greater rights than, and were not as confined as, women in the purdah zones of the Middle East and South Asia. This situation has continued to the present.

---

[30] APEC Second Ministerial Meeting on Women in Mexico, 2002.

[31] Brunei Darussalam's Delegation Report to 23rd Special Session of the United Nations General Assembly on "Women 2000: Gender Equality and Development and Peace for 21st Century," 2000.

[32] Women's Business Council, www.bruneiwbc.com, and Council of Women of Brunei Darussalam, http://www.womencouncil.org.bn.

[33] Brunei Darussalam's Delegation Report to 23rd Special Session of the United Nations General Assembly on "Women 2000: Gender Equality and Development and Peace for 21st Century," 2000.

[34] For an overview of dispute resolution in Brunei see Ann Black, "Finding the Equilibrium for Dispute Resolution: how Brunei Darussalam balances a British legacy with its Malay and Islamic Identity," *International Trade and Business Law Annual* 8 (2003): 185–214.

[35] M. B. Hooker, *A Concise Legal History of South-East Asia* (Oxford: Claredon Press, 1978), 49–51.

[36] Wazir-Jahan Begum Karim, *Women and Culture: Between Malay Adat and Islam* (Boulder: Westview Press, 1992).

The establishment of the British Residency[37] in Brunei in 1905 led to the transplantation of a new secular legal order into the Sultanate. English laws and common law courts were introduced at that time. Nevertheless, Islamic law pertaining to religious duties and to family, marriage and succession survived because, although the Resident's advice "must be taken and acted upon on all questions in Brunei', there was an exception for matters 'affecting the Mohammedan religion."[38] However, Islamic law was reduced to the status of a private religion and a private law, to be administered separately under the religious authority of the Sultan through a separate court system known as Kathis Courts[39] (later as Kadis Courts[40]).

Today, the Islamic legal system continues to operate in parallel with the secular, transplanted common law system. The co-existence of these two quite distinctive legal systems, one religious and one secular, is symbolic in many ways of the duality that permeates so many facets of life in Brunei and contributes to the creative tension that exists between the imperatives of modernization and Islamization.

Islamization in Brunei: Consequences for Muslim Women

Why Islamization?

For almost 100 years, Brunei straddled two cultures as well as two systems of law. This duality was the legacy of the competing and complementary forces that had interacted there over the preceding century. Once able to chart its own course in the post-Independence era, the Brunei government re-evaluated this legacy and decided to reclaim what it saw to be its own unique Bruneian identity. This gave rise to the ideology of MIB. This state ideology provided a map for conceptualizing and rationalizing what should be the desirable values and priorities in public and private life, as well as in economic and non-economic life. Being so small in size, population and infrastructure, this

[37] A Residency was a special form of colonial Protectorate, in which a British Resident is appointed to advise the Sultan on all matters pertaining to his Sultanate, apart from those concerning the Malay religion. The Sultan was obliged to accept and act upon the Resident's advice. Technically, Brunei was not a colony, but the difference was purely semantic—for all practical purposes Brunei lost her independence as all power resided with Britain.

[38] Supplementary Treaty to the Protectorate Agreement was signed by Sultan Hashim and his *wazirs* in December 1905.

[39] The Courts Enactment (1908); Religious Council, State Custom and Kathis Court Enactment (1955).

[40] Religious Council and Kadis Court Act (Rev. Ed.) (1984).

became imperative not only because of the colonial inheritance and the dominance of English laws and institutions, but also because of the continuing hegemony of Western values and practices. This impact of the West was intensified by the forces of globalization, especially the internationalization of commerce and communications, and the international pressure brought by agencies such as the United Nations for conformity with designated 'universal' norms and standards.[41] MIB was to be the filter through which such offerings from the West would be accepted or rejected. Whilst detractors contended that MIB was invented to sanctify the consolidation of absolute political, economic and spiritual power in the hands of the current Sultan and a self-consolidating elite,[42] there is no doubt that the state ideology drew on three components—Malay culture, Islam, and the Monarchy—that had been dominant in shaping pre-colonial Bruneian institutions, practices, and sense of identity. Just as official state ideology has been used in other post-colonial Asian nations,[43] MIB was employed to maintain cohesion within Brunei society against further inroads from monolithic western, democratic and secular culture.

At the heart of MIB is Islam. This is not Islam in the narrow sense of 'religion' that is employed in secular countries. Siddique explains that the inadequacy in seeking to understand Islam as *merely* a religion is that it leaves unanalysed Islam's political, economic, legal and social aspects.[44] He argues that Muslims do not conceptualize Islam in terms of Western, and thus Christian, derived sociological categorization of religion, which inevitably places the individual at the centre of all analysis. Rather than a focus on the personal relationship between God and the individual, Islam's mission extends beyond the individual dimension to direct all economic, political and legal processes towards an entire Islamic social order.[45] This is the imperative of

[41] An example of a response to international pressure relating to women is Brunei's 'Women 2000' report to the United Nations General Assembly (see above, n. 31). The Chairman of the delegation from Brunei, Ambassador Jemat Haji Ampal, reported on progress made in his country in fulfilling United Nations recommendations. These included increasing the number of women in tertiary education institutions and in the civil service; prioritising preventive health programs for women, infants and children; and implementing legislation to protect women, such as the Emergency (Married Women) Order, 1999 and the Emergency (Guardianship of Infants) Order, 1999, which cover non-Muslim women in the Sultanate. The Islamic Family Law Order provides for Muslims.

[42] G. Braighlinn, *Ideological Innovation under Monarchy: Aspects of Legitimation Activity in Contemporary Brunei* (Amsterdam: V. U. University Press, 1992).

[43] Indonesia has the *Pancasila*, Malaysia has *Rukun Negara* with its 'the Four Pillars', and Singapore promulgates Confucianism as defining its national values.

[44] Sharon Siddique, "Conceptualizing Contemporary Islam: Religion or Ideology?" in *Readings on Islam in Southeast Asia*, ed. Ahmad Ibrahim, Sharon Siddique and Yasmin Hussain (Singapore: Institute of Southeast Asian Studies, 1985), 338.

[45] Ibid., 338.

Islamization described by the Sultan as: "a concept which upholds Islamic principles and values based on the Qur'an and Hadith as the basis of *all* activities" [italics added] in the Sultanate. It resulted in the legal prohibition on the sale and importation of alcohol (1991) and pork production (1992), laws for Islamic banking and finance[46] (from 1993) and the restructuring and upgrading of the Kadis Courts into to Syari'ah Courts (1998). Whilst Islamization occurred across many aspects of life in the Sultanate, the Islamic blueprint for life meant that there were to be consequences for women in the Sultanate.

Brunei's Model of Islamisation

Islamization is not a uniform process whereby the same model is replicated in each nation that reaffirms its national commitment to implement Islamic law. Whether it is Iran, Pakistan, Nigeria or Indonesia, the re-affirmation of commitment to Islam occurs but the re-assertion of each Islamic identity is distinctive and culturally specific. Throughout the twentieth century there have been different interpretations of the sources of Islamic law, as some scholars challenge restrictive interpretations whilst others passionately confirm the veracity of orthodox *fiqh* in the respective schools. Integral to choice between orthodox[47] and modernist[48] interpretations of Islam is the issue of gender differentiation, or, more precisely, inequality, between men and women in Islamic law. If the country pursues that mode of Islamization which adopts literalist, patriarchal or Arabic interpretations of Islamic law, the consequence will be increased differentiation of women's rights, duties and entitlements from those of men. It also would countermand those aspects of modernization based on contemporary internationally-derived conceptions of gender equality and of women's inherent rights, as declared by the United Nation's Charter and the Universal Declaration of Human Rights as well the specific Convention on the Elimination of All Forms of Discrimination against Women (CEDAW).

---

[46] This provides services to clients free from the giving or taking of 'interest', as this may be classified as *riba*, which is prohibited under the Qur'an and *Sunnah* in Islamic law. The opening of the first Islamic Bank of Brunei was in 1993, followed by the Islamic Trust Fund (Tabung Amanah Islam Brunei), Islamic Insurance (*takaful*); the conversion of the Development Bank of Brunei from conventional banking to a '*riba*-free' full Islamic system. For a detailed analysis see Abdullah Saeed, *Islamic Banking and Interest* (Leiden: EJ Brill, 1999); M. K. Lewis & Latifa M. Algoud, *Islamic Banking* (Cheltenham: Edward Elgar, 2001); Mohammad Ariff, ed., *Islamic Banking in Southeast Asia* (Singapore: Institute of Southeast Asian Studies, 1988).

[47] Orthodoxy can be defined as doctrine embodied in the Syariah around the tenth century CE., It refers to Sunni doctrines of belief and practice. The orthodox view does not seek to compete or be compared with West but aims to preserve the status quo to safeguard Islam and Islamic law.

[48] Modernism proposes that Islam can be interpreted in a way that is dynamic, modern and able to compete with Western secularism with no sacrifice of its essentially Islamic character.

Brunei chose the orthodox path to Islamization. However it permitted some modifications, in acknowledgment of strong arguments from modernist Islam and in deference to its own modernization agenda more generally. Whilst Brunei did not become a signatory to CEDAW,[49] it did endorse the equality of women in the economic and educational and vocational spheres. At the same time, it rejected Western style equality in matters pertaining to the family, such as marriage, divorce, custody, succession and in the law of evidence. In keeping with MIB, the nation wanted to retain and 'tighten' the Islamic model of laws for family relations so that the law reflected the orthodox position of the Shafi'i school. This, it was argued, was in keeping with the significance of Islamic family law for most Muslims. Poulter reasons that family law embodies the "quintessential culture of a distinctive group ... which cannot be discarded lightly" and that as many other aspects of Islamic law, notably in the commercial and criminal spheres, have "given way to" Western models it has made family law more "precious and worthy of preservation worldwide."[50] That was true in Brunei because family law as contained in Parts VI and VII of the Religious Council and Kadis Court Act had been a complete compilation of all Islamic laws on marriage, divorce, maintenance, and custody of children for Muslims and were applied in the *Kadis* Courts (Islamic courts). As one of the few remaining components of Islamic law preserved through the colonial era, family law was the symbol of the syari'ah in the Sultanate. As well, Poulter notes that many Muslims sincerely believe that the best way to preserve their own families from what are seen as the corrupting forces and 'evils' in Western societies—prostitution, pornography, child abuse, abortion, marital breakdown, extra-marital affairs, single mothers, same-sex relationships, neglect of the elderly—is to operate on the scale of family values embodied in Islamic law.[51] This perspective is reflected in Brunei, where it is frequently argued at official and popular levels that such social ills will be reduced by "tightening religious laws"[52] and when Islam assumes a greater role in Brunei.[53]

---

[49] Other Muslim countries who refrained from signature/ratification of the Convention include Bahrain, Djibouti, Mauritania, Niger, Oman, Qatar, Iran, Kazakistan, Saudi Arabia, Somalia, Sudan, Syria and the U. E. A.

[50] Sebastian Poulter, "The Claim to a Separate Islamic System of Personal Law for British Muslims" in *Islamic Family Law*, ed. Chibli Mallat and Jane Connors (London: Graham and Trotman, 1990), 147.

[51] Ibid., 147.

[52] Mohamad Yusop bin Awang Damit "Negara Brunei Darussalam: Light at the End of the Tunnel," *Southeast Asian Affairs* (2002): 81–99.

[53] Malai Hassan Othman "Increasing Social Ills Jolt Religious Authorities into Action," *Brudirect News*, www.brudirect,com/DailyInfo/News/Archive/Oct02/051002/nite01.htm; C. T. Haji Mahmod, "Public awareness in a Caring Society," *Borneo Bulletin*, October 31, 2002.

In taking this course, there was acceptance of the validity of those orthodox interpretations of the primary sources of Islamic law—the Qur'an and Sunnah—regarding the differential rights and obligations of men and women in Islamic family law. At the same time, there was sensitivity to transnational discourse and to international movements that demanded an end to religious laws and customary practices that treated women and men unequally. Brunei's solution was to adhere to orthodoxy, but to modify particular components in order to avoid perceived, or actual, injustice to women. Such compromises are a recurring theme throughout the new legislation on family relationships.

The Brunei Compromise

The ways in which Brunei has retained but modified the orthodox Shafi'i school of Islamic law to reduce the unfairness to women illustrates both Brunei's form of Islamization and its selective modernization. The modifications to the laws dealing with marriage are quite minor, but they still provide some safeguards against what could be unreasonable outcomes for women. Polygyny is a case in point. Although the term polygamy is used in the English version of the Islamic Family Law Order (1999), it is technically only polygyny[54] that is lawful in Brunei. In the Order, the classic Sunni right of a husband to four simultaneous marriages[55] has been retained. Although the number 'four' is not actually specified, the phrase 'in accordance with the *hukum Syari'ah* (Islamic law) allows for this. But there is a modification. Now, additional marriages can only occur with the written permission of a syari'ah judge.[56] According to section 23(2) of the Order, this may be granted after the judge has reviewed the husband's application stating why the polygynous marriage is 'just and necessary,' and also stating the husband's 'present income', 'current ascertainable financial obligations and liabilities', the 'number of dependents

[54] Polygyny is one category of polygamous marriage. It allows for a husband to have more than one wife at the same time, and is contrasted with polyandry which allows for a woman to have more than one husband. Polyandry is prohibited in Islam.

[55] Surah 4:3 "... then marry such women as seem good to you, two and three and four; but if you fear that you will not do justice (between them), then (marry) only one... .". Polygyny is also supported by the Prophet's own *sunnah* of marrying more than one wife.

[56] Islamic Family Law Order (1999) section 23. If a marriage occurs without permission a $2000 fine or imprisonment for 6 months can be imposed. It has been noted in Malaysian states with similar provisions that some men contract polygynous marriages without court permission and simply pay the fine and retrospectively register the marriage, obviating the need to make a court application. See Nik Noriani Nik Badlishah, "Country Report Malaysia: Polygamy," at Sisters in Islam, "Report on Regional Workshop and Justice for Muslim Women," held Kuala Lumpur, June 8–10, 2001, http://www.sistersinislam.org.my/reports/810_062001.htm

as a result of the proposed marriage' and whether the 'consent or views of the existing wife' have been obtained.

Through this modification, Brunei has adopted a compromise position on a law that has engendered considerable debate in Muslim countries, and been the subject of considerable advocacy by Islamic women's organizations because of its differential treatment between men and women. Reformers criticise the practice on the basis that it makes 'gender relations uneven',[57] in that the mere existence of such a unilateral right shifts the power balance away from equality in the marriage. Whether employed or threatened, the potential to exercise this right puts the husband in a more powerful position in the marriage. Such concerns have meant some Muslim countries such as Tunisia have decreed polygyny unlawful[58] on the basis that it is inconsistent with the Qur'anic verse: "Ye are never able to be fair and just as between women, even if it is your ardent desire"[59] which is taken as an affirmation of monogamy in Islam. Brunei has rejected that modernist interpretation, but has recognized possible detriment for wives and hence has employed the syari'ah court to scrutinized applications for additional wives and to ensure that a husband can be fair and treat each wife equally (at least in terms of housing, material goods and time). Although not widespread, polygyny is accepted and condoned in Brunei. In the last two years, there had been 164 applications submitted to the court.[60] It is probable that if living standards continue to improve, so will the polygyny rate,[61] since multiple wives can be a status factor for men and symbol of wealth. As the male members of Royal family, including the Sultan, have married more than one wife, there is no overt or public criticism of the practice. However, the Malaysian based women's organization Sisters in Islam argues that Muslim women should be empowered to curtail the practice by being made aware at the time of marriage of the option to stipulate in their marriage contract a condition that legally binds a husband not to take a second wife during the duration of their marriage.[62] In some Islamic nations, such as Iran, such clauses are a standard feature of marriage agreements.

---

[57] "Southeast Asia's Islamic women seek reforms" *Asia Times* August 1, 2001.

[58] Tunisia has made polygamy a criminal offence. Turkey and Albania have eliminated polygyny through the adoption of a purely civil (not Islamic) code of personal laws.

[59] *Surah* 4:129.

[60] These statistics were provided in a speech "Polygamy According to the Brunei's Islamic Family Law Perspective," by Datin Dr Hjh Saadiah D. W. W. Hj Tamit, Brunei Academic Studies lecturer at U. B. D. on August 14, 2003, http://www.nccibd.com/NewsArchieve/2003/August/14/news9.html.

[61] Gavin W. Jones, *Marriage and Divorce in Islamic South-East Asia* (Kuala Lumpur: Oxford University Press, 1994), 271 and Jamila Hussein, *Islamic law and Society* (Leichhardt: Federation Press, 1999), 73.

[62] "Add no-polygamy clause in marriage contract, says SIS" in *Star News* January 18, 2003 at: http://www.polygamyinfo.com/intna1media%20plyg%20168star.htm.

Brunei has an integrated, well educated, relatively affluent, skilled or professionalized female population. In such a context, the retention of the legal requirement for a woman to have the consent of a male marriage guardian (*wali*) for the marriage to be valid demonstrates the continuing priority given to Shafi'i[63] orthodoxy in the Sultanate. This is especially so given that it is not a Qur'anic requirement, but one based on *hadith* of the Prophet[64] which coincided with existing patriarchal customary practices Islam encountered as it spread through the Middle-East, Africa, and Asia. Getting her *wali's*[65] consent means permission from her father, paternal grandfather, brother or other male relative (determined in the order of agnatic inheritance laws). A woman cannot perform the role of a *wali*.

As with polygyny, Brunei has adopted a compromise position in relation to the function of the *wali*. If her *wali* "refuses to give his consent without reasonable grounds"[66] a woman can go to the Syari'ah Court where a *wali Hakim* (a syari'ah judge who inquires into the issue of consent) will be appointed. Of course, the gender differentiation remains. A women's consent to marriage still requires validation by a man, either by her *wali* or *wali Hakim*, whereas there is no such limitation on men, who, regardless of age at the time[67] are legally able to give their own consent to a marriage contract. It arguable that this provision is difficult to justify in present day Brunei, where the educational standard, economic independence, and employment rates for women are comparable to those of men, and where, furthermore, child marriages are relatively rare. On this basis, Islamic reformers such as Norma Maruhom[68] question the need for continuing patriarchal assumptions about a woman's inability to make decisions about her life.

One aspect of Islamic family law where there has been major modification of the orthodox position is *talaq* divorce. This is also possibly the most criticized

[63] The Hanafi school does not have this requirement.

[64] "Take ye care that none contract women in marriage but their proper guardians, and that they be not so contracted but with their equals," cited in Shaheen Sardar Ali, *Gender and Human Rights in Islam and International law: Equal before Allah, Unequal before Man?* (The Hague: Kluwer Law International, 2000), 164.

[65] Section 12 (a) Emergency (Islamic Family Law) Order (1999).

[66] Section 12 (b) Emergency (Islamic Family Law) Order (1999).

[67] The new Order does not establish a legal age for marriage between Muslims. Thus the classic Syariah position applies that a person of either sex who has reached puberty can consent to marriage. The general marriage age under civil legislation in Brunei is 13 years, but data from the Ministry of Religious Affairs for 2000 shows that there were just eight girls under 15 who were married and that the most popular age was 20–29 years. Ignatus Stephen, "Brunei's 14-year Itch Causes Marriage Breaks," http://www.brudirect.com/DailyInfo/News/Archive/Jan03/200103.02.htm

[68] Sisters in Islam, "Report on Regional Workshop"

aspect of Islamic family law in the West, because *talaq* divorce gives a husband alone the unilateral right to extrajudicial divorce, without cause, simply through the pronouncement of one, two or three *talaqs* (statements of intention to divorce).[69] Although the Qur'an was progressive in its time by providing divorce options for wives, the fact that a *talaq* divorce was the preserve of a husband has been condemned in the present day as discriminatory. This is so because, in comparison with the ease by which a husband may initiate a *talaq* divorce, a wife must attend a court and convince a judge that she had genuine grounds for divorcing her husband; otherwise she faces the difficult task of buying her way out of the marriage.[70]

What the new Order has done is to abolish the unilateral and extrajudicial components of *talaq* divorce. Now, either husband or wife can present an application for *talaq* divorce to the Court, setting down the reasons for the application and particulars of the marriage.[71] This is a radical reform. Other aspects of the *talaq* law are retained, in that it remains a revocable divorce requiring a period of time *iddah* (three menstrual cycles)[72] in which it is possible, and in fact encouraged, that there be *ruju*, or reconciliation. Both husband and wife will be counselled by a Family Adviser to "achieve a reconciliation" and "resume conjugal relations"[73] and the traditional role laid down in the Qur'an[74] for family members to act as arbiters for both sides (*hakam*) is also retained.

Despite the significance of this reform of *talaq* divorce, which would seem to obviate the need for other Islamic divorce procedures, these other forms are all retained essentially unchanged from their classic form. They include

[69] After three *talaqs* there can be no reconciliation and remarriage to each other unless the wife has an intervening marriage. Qur'an, *surah* 2:229.

[70] In *khulu* or *cerai tebus talaq* (divorce by redemption) a wife with the court's permission could buy her way out of an unhappy marriage by returning the marriage gift to her husband. It could be a severe financial impost because she would lose not only her marriage gift, but possibly also her maintenance entitlement.

[71] Islamic Family Law Order (1999), section 42. After the application, the court serves a summons on the other party and a copy of the application and requires both to appear before the court. If the other party consents to the divorce and the court is "satisfied that the marriage has irretrievably broken down," the judge will advise the husband to pronounce *talaq* before the court.

[72] Per the Qur'anic requirement in 2:228: "Divorced women shall wait concerning themselves for three monthly periods. Nor is it lawful for them to hide what God Hath created in their wombs, if they have faith in God and the Last Day. And their husbands have the better right to take them back in that period, if they wish for reconciliation."

[73] Emergency (Islamic Family Law) Order (1999), section 41(10).

[74] Surah 4:35. On Islamic arbitration in Brunei see Ann Black, "Alternative Dispute Resolution in Brunei Darussalam: the Blending of Imported and Traditional Processes," *Bond Law Review* (2001): 305–339.

khulu divorce,[75] divorce by *li'an* or oaths[76], divorce by *ila*[77] divorce by *cerai ta'liq*[78] and dissolution or annulment *fasakh*,[79] on a range of eleven different grounds, the majority being applicable to the conduct or condition of the husband[80] and two of the wife.[81] One inexplicable provision, given the seemingly progressive nature of the reform, is the inclusion in the Order of *zihar*. This is a virtually extinct Arabian (and pre-Islamic) form of divorce not used elsewhere in South-East Asia.[82]

Women as the Transmitters of Culture and Religion

Where there is a context of "intensification of religious, cultural, ethnic and national identity" as is occurring in Brunei, researchers such as Moghadam argue that there will inevitably be a "politization of gender, the family and the position of women."[83] Thus women become important to achieving the new Bruneian national identity. With Brunei's articulated national identity centred

[75] Emergency (Islamic Family Law) Order (1999), section 48. See note 71.

[76] Emergency (Islamic Family Law) Order (1999), section 49. This is used when a husband accuses his wife of infidelity and she denies it. A series of oaths are sworn in court by both husband and wife.

[77] Islamic Family Law Order (1999) section 50 and is based on Qur'an 2: 226. This section enables a court to grant a divorce when a husband takes an oath swearing that he has not had sexual intercourse with his wife for four months or more and has been ordered by the court to have intercourse with his wife and refuses.

[78] Islamic Family Law Order (1999), section 45. This applies when there is a breach by the husband of one of the terms in the marriage contact. Terms may be deserting her, moving away from their village, or taking a second wife. As was noted earlier in later is rarely used in marriage contracts in Brunei or in Southeast Asia.

[79] Islamic Family Law Order (1999), section 46.

[80] That the husband is absent (s46 (a)) or in detention (section 46(b)) or in prison (section 46 (d)); he is impotent and the wife was unaware of this at the time of marriage (section 46 (f)) or he is suffering from insanity, leprosy, AIDS, HIV, or venereal disease (section 46(g)).

[81] That the wife is incapacitated and unable to have sexual intercourse (section 46(j)) or did not freely consent to the marriage (section 46(i)).

[82] It comes from the pre-Islamic practice among Arabs to degrade their wives by declaring them 'like their mothers,' in the sense of being prohibited to them sexually, and then abandon them, but on occasions return to them later. *Zihar* is mentioned in two verses of the Qur'an (33:4 and 58:2–3) which stipulate that if men declare their wives like their mothers and abandon them, they cannot return to them until they have freed a slave. Modern jurists have argued that as such practices do not exist in other Islamic societies, and since there is no longer an institution of slavery, *zihar* should be considered to have no contemporary application. More orthodox jurists hold that instead of freeing a slave, a husband can fast 'for two consecutive months' as a form of atonement or proceed with divorcing his wife by statements of *zihar*.

[83] Valentine M. Moghadam, ed., *Identity Politics and Women: Cultural Reassertions and Feminisms in International Perspective* (Boulder: Westview Press, 1994), 18.

on Islam and Malay culture, it is inevitable that the idealized woman is the embodiment of Muslim Malay identity. Within this Muslim Malay ideology, 'virtue' is considered integral to the relationship between husband and wife and supports the longstanding cultural and legal requirement that a wife be obedient to her husband. This ideal of loyal and obedient wife and good mother then mirrors the ideal relationship between caring ruler and loyal obedient subject.

The requirement for loyalty and obedience is reinforced by the Islamic legal concept of *nusyuz* (disobedience, not fulfilling one's marital duties). For a husband, *nusyuz* is failing to maintain and support his wife; for a wife, it is her refusal to obey her husband's lawful wishes or commands. It arises from one of the most debated verses in the Qur'an—Surah 4:34.[84] The orthodox interpretation has been that Allah has given men authority and control over women and so women are to be obedient to men—be they husbands, fathers or brothers. It also has been interpreted to allow for (mild) physical punishment to be given to a disobedient woman. Modernist writers and Islamic women's groups challenge these interpretations;[85] for example Sisters in Islam write that this Qur'anic verse actually "focuses on the responsibility of men to treat their wives fairly, especially when women follow their suggestions."[86]

The new Order in Brunei retains the legal categorization of *nusyuz*.[87] Not only is it an offence for a wife to 'wilfully disobey an order by her husband in accordance with *Hukum Syari'ah*'[88] but she faces the consequence that by refusing 'to obey the lawful wishes or commands of her husband', she may lose her basic entitlement to maintenance from her husband.[89] The notion of 'disobedience'

---

[84] The text reads:

> Men are the protectors and maintainers of women, because Allah has given the one more (strength) than the other, and because they support them from their means.
>
> Therefore righteous women are devoutly obedient, and guard in (the husband's absence) what Allah would have them guard.
>
> As to those women on whose part ye fear disloyalty and ill-conduct, admonish them (first), (next), refuse to share their beds, (and last) beat them (lightly); but if they return to obedience, seek not against them means (of annoyance): for Allah is Most High, Great (above you all).

An outline of arguments in this debate on interpreting 4:23 can be found in Shaheen Sardar Ali, *Gender and Human Rights*, 63–70.

[85] Shaheen Sardar Ali, *Gender and Human Rights*, 65.

[86] Sisters In Islam, *Are Muslim Men Allowed to Beat their Wives?* (Petalang Jaya: SIS publishing, 1991), 5.

[87] It should be noted that disobedience is a separate legal category from ill-treatment of a husband or of a wife. The new order makes 'ill-treatment' an offence where either spouse is found by a court to 'ill-treat her husband or wife'.

[88] The section provides an escalating scale of punishment: the *nusyuz* wife is liable to a fine not exceeding $500 for the first conviction, and $1000 for any subsequent offences.

[89] Islamic Family Law Order (1999), section 61.

can refer a range of behaviour and attitudes, such as a wife's refusal to respect her husband's directives regarding whether or not she work, or his sexual 'wishes and commands'. In keeping with the reforming pattern already established, the determination of *nusyuz* no longer remains at the husband's discretion alone, but is to be decided on the advice of the syari'ah judge.

In a similar way, the laws of custody and guardianship reflect the significance of women as transmitters of values and culture to their children and nation. Papanek postulates a nexus between national identity and women's identity, so that the "Ideal Women and the Ideal Society"[90] go hand in hand. The patriarchal perspective of the ideal society led by the caring ruler is mirrored in the requirement that legal guardianship of children[91] rests with the father as "the first and natural primary guardian of his minor child"[92] just as, in national terms it rests with the Sultan and the male *ulama*. The importance of transmitting Islamic values and practices is seen in laws dealing with custody of young (*mumaiyiz)*[93] children during marriage and after dissolution. Custody is given to the mother at least until the child attains puberty; however, a woman can lose custody if her role as transmitter of proper values becomes suspect. Hence the order provides that if she remarries,[94] is of bad conduct in a "gross and open manner," changes her place of residence so as to make it difficult for the father to exercise necessary supervision of his child, neglects or abuses the child or becomes an apostate,[95] then custody will be lost. The inclusion of apostasy as an automatic ground for losing custody of one's child shows the significance of the mother as the transmitter of Islam and its practices, ethos and values.

The role of women in Brunei's Islamization agenda

To what extent can Bruneian women participate in the debates and institutions shaping the national priorities and laws that govern their lives and relationships? In general, women in Brunei have not participated in this discourse, though there is a pervasive acceptance at official as well as individual level that Islamization was welcomed and is appreciated by all Brunei

---

[90] Hanna Papanek, "The Ideal Women and the Ideal Society: Control and Autonomy in the Construction of Identity" in Moghadam, *Identity, Politics and Women*, 42–75.

[91] *Islamic Family Law Order (1999)*, section 95(1).

[92] A minor is a child who has not turn 18 years according to the Islamic calendar.

[93] Defined as a 'child unable to differentiate a matter,' but in practice this means a child who has not attained puberty. Generally in Islamic law this is considered about 9 years of age.

[94] Section 90 (a) where the man she marries is not related to the child "thereby prohibiting him from marrying the child."

[95] These are contained in section 90 (b)–(e).

Muslims. Islamization was first enunciated in broad statements in *titahs* of the Sultan and in speeches by his Ministers, which were then transmitted to Bruneians through reposts in the mass media. The details of what would be entailed in the 're-enactment of the syari'ah judicial system' were never publicly clarified. Without parliamentary debate,[96] without effective political parties,[97] without 'green papers' enabling a community consultative processes, the women of Brunei had no input into the legislative agenda that would impact directly upon their lives. Unlike their Muslim counterparts in Malaysia and Indonesia, the women of Brunei are denied a vote and thus a voice—either in support or in rejection—of social and legal Islamization. Whilst this is true for men (who were disenfranchised since the declaration of the State of Emergency in 1962) the significance for women has been greater, as the authoritarian and paternalistic nature of the political process ensured the perpetuation of male discourse and dominance. This is because there are almost no women's voices in the corridors of powers. The appointment of 21 men as the 21 members of the 2004 reconstituted Legislative Council re-enforces this view. There are no female Ministers in Cabinet and few in the higher echelons of government. Except for a handful of Permanent Secretaries and a female ambassador (the Sultan's sister, HRH Princess Hajah Masna) the steering of the government is in male hands. In keeping with the dominance of the Royal family in public life,[98] the women selected to speak publicly on behalf of the women of Brunei are typically members of the Sultan's family.[99] Women too are absent from the consultative process set up in 1992, known as 'grass-roots democracy,' through which government decisions are explained

[96] Parliament has not met since 1962. Brunei has remained in a state of Emergency since that time.

[97] Brunei's two registered political parties, Brunei National Solidarity Party (PPKB) and the People's Awareness Party (PAKAR) have had dwindling memberships down to less than 100 members. Whilst the PPKB has been gently advocating democratic reform it was cautious to not want 'anything that is outside MIB'. See Rosli Abidin Yahya, "Brunei's Political Scene in Disarray following Mass Resignations," *News Express* February 24, 2001. However, the recent reconstitution of the Legislative Council and the official statements that in future there may be elections for additional members to join the appointed and nominated members on the Council, may serve to revive these parties. Political debate may also be stimulated. Government regulations forbid public servants from becoming members of political parties even if the parties recognize the supremacy of the institution of monarchy. See: B. A. Hussainmiya, Brunei Darussalam: A Nation at Peace, http://www.niu.edu/cseas/outreach/bruneipaper.htm.

[98] The Sultan is also the nation's Prime Minister, Minister of Defence, Minister of Finance, Chancellor of the national University, Superintendent General of the Royal Brunei Police Force, and leader of the Islamic faith.

[99] For example: HRH Princess Hajah Masna presented the report for Brunei at the APEC Second Ministerial Meeting on Women, Mexico, September 2002.

to the people and popular responses are received back by government.[100] The village elected headmen (*ketau kampong*), who are given the role of government 'mediating agents'[101] are also male.

One of the repercussions of Brunei's lack of democracy is that vigorous debate on matters of faith, law and social policy, and gender issues does not occur; or, if it does, this is never made public. Again, this situation stands in contrast with neighbouring Malaysia and Indonesia, where Muslim women can, and do, use the political process directly, and where they use women's organizations to project a voice that reaches both the public and the government. Women's participation in the process of reform (*reformasi*) in both Malaysia and Indonesia is a good example of women being heard and involved. In Malaysia, for example, Dr Wan Azizah Ismail is a leader and founder of the Malaysian Justice Party (Keadilan); and groups such as Sisters in Islam[102] openly advocate legal reform of discriminatory practices against women[103] and create public awareness about issues of equality and justice for women within the framework of Islam. Through their efforts, Qur'anic verses[104] are being re-interpreted to provide a construct which is more egalitarian and less discriminatory towards women.[105] Similarly in Indonesia, the Coalition of Indonesian Women for Justice and Democracy is a vocal advocate for reform, and other groups such as Women's Solidarity for Human Rights and Volunteers for Humanity articulate a women's perspective on issues and events that challenges the government stance.[106] Such women's

[100] A. Mani, "Negara Brunei Darussalam in 1992: Celebrating the Silver Jubilee" *Southeast Asian Affairs* (1993), 99. See also Mark Cleary and Shuang Yann Wong, *Oil, Economic Development and Diversification in Brunei Darussalam* (London: St Martins Press, 1994), 126.

[101] B. A. Hussainmiya, "Philosophy for a Rich, Small State," *Far Eastern Economic Review* 10 February 1994, 31. District officer, Dato Paduka Hj Dani outlined their role as ensuring "harmony and peace is attained in their respective communities," listening "carefully to grievances," and "implementing government guidelines and policies at the grass root level"—see Bahreen Hamzah, "New Village Heads Appointed," *Sunday Borneo Bulletin* January 28, 2001.

[102] http://www.muslimtents.com/sistersinislam/home_mission.htm.

[103] There have been a series of submission papers to the government including one on reform of Islamic family laws, and the Women's Agenda for Change which details changes in eleven areas of needed reforms.

[104] As well as the Qur'anic text it is accepted that the Prophet Mohammad consulted widely with women. They were amongst the first to know of the revelations and to follow the new religion and were influential in the early Islamic community. His wives gave *hadiths*, which become *sunnah* and one wife Aiyesha assumed military command leading massed troops into battle.

[105] Shaheen Sardar Ali, *Gender and Human Rights*, 42– 86. Also generally Fatima Mernissi, *Beyond the Veil: Male-female Dynamics in Modern Muslim Society* (Bloomington: Indiana University Press, 1987) and Abdullahi Ahmed An-Na'im, *Toward an Islamic Reformation: Civil Liberties, Human Rights, and International Law* (Syracuse, N.Y.: Syracuse University Press, 1990).

[106] Kathryn Robinson, "Indonesian Women: from *Orde Baru* to *Reformasi*," in *Women in Asia: Tradition, Modernity and Globalisation*, ed. Louisa Edwards and Mina Roces (St. Leonards, Allen and Unwin, 2000), 139–165.

voices are missing from Brunei. Apart from restrictions on political parties and activities[107] there is no prohibition on such discourse. But it seems there is a culture self-censorship, in which adherence to MIB has become the major test of citizen loyalty.[108] Loyalty to the Sultan as head of State and head of the Faith means supporting what is decreed and implicitly trusting what is done is in one's best interest. The Council of Women, the country's national women's body, states that its first aim is 'to uphold the aspirations of the Malay Islam monarchy concept in any activity' it undertakes.[109] Whilst other aims include 'unit[ing] and strengthen[ing] women force through women's organizations, welfare bodies and individuals' and 'encourag[ing] women to realize and undertake their responsibility towards society and country' the focus is to complement, not to critique, the government.

The absence of effective political parties and women's organizations to express opposition or alternative views on women's issues is compounded by the media's compliance with the government. The licensing requirements for locally printed newspapers, as well as the unfettered power of the Minister for Home Affairs to refuse or revoke printing permits and to prevent overseas publications from entering Brunei, means that only those views are aired that uncritically accord with MIB, and thus with the government's particular Islamization policy. Even the advent of the Internet and its on-line chatrooms, such as BruNet, has not allowed for totally open political debate and commentary. If postings are too critical of the government the lines are closed down.[110] Press[111] and media censorship silences women's (and men's) views that may dissent, question, or challenge any aspect of three tenets of MIB. The consequence for Bruneian women is explained by Moghissi who argues that the absence of a truly free press and independent media allows a male-serving value system to decide what comes to public attention.[112]

---

[107] See n. 98 and Rosli Abidin Yahya, "Brunei's Political Scene in Disarray following Mass Resignations," *News Express* February 24, 2001.

[108] An Observer, "Negara Brunei Darussalam in 1991: Relegitimising Tradition," *Asian Survey* 32 (1992), 128.

[109] http://www.womencouncil.org.bn; There is also the Women Business Council which gives assistance and support to women engaging in business and commerce.

[110] Mohammad Yusup Haji Damit 'Brunei Darussalam: Steady Ahead' *Southeast Asian Affairs* (2004), 63, 66.

[111] All newspapers must be owned and all directors of a newspaper company must be Brunei citizens or permanent residents. Publication can only occur with a government permit is required which requires payment of B$100,000. There is self-censorship anyway as the Sultan's brother Prince Mohamed's QAF Group owns the *Borneo Bulletin*. The Sultan's other brother Prince Sufri is a partner in the Company that owns the *News Express*. See Roger Mitton, "Waiting for Dawn," *Asiaweek*, August 13, 1999):17. More strident censorship is through the Undesirable Publications Act (1982), Censorship of Films and Public Entertainments Act (1962) and the Internal Security Act (1960).

[112] Haideh Moghissi, *Feminism and Islamic Fundamentalism* (London: ZED Books, 1999) 82.

This acquiescence of Brunei women to government policy and apparent acceptance of Islamization as being in their best interests has meant that the stage appears set for the introduction of syari'ah criminal law. The implications of this would be very serious for Brunei's women, if the experience of women in nations where it is currently in force (such as Pakistan, Sudan and the northern states of Nigeria) is any indication. Unlike Islamic family law, Islamic criminal law and its controversial and very harsh punishments have not been a part of Brunei's legal tradition. Paving the way for this possible new phase of Islamisation was the Syari'ah Courts Evidence Order (2001), which is already in force in Brunei. This Order stipulates the number and gender requirements of witnesses in particular *hudud* offences. For example, a conviction for *zina* requires evidence of four male *syahid*;[113] for theft, highway robbery, false accusations and consuming alcohol, evidence of two male *syahid* is needed[114] whilst corroboration of wealth requires three male *syahids*.[115] The Order makes the classic distinction between *bayyinah* and *syahadah* evidence with women (and non-Muslims) excluded from giving *syahadah* evidence, except in matters pertaining to designated women's issues: 'matters relating to menstruation, birth, breastfeeding and of embarrassment to a female'.[116] Additionally, the principle that the evidence of a woman is weighted at half that of a man prevails through the Order, since, with the exception of those offences specifically referred to,[117] *syahadah* evidence shall be given by two male *syahid* or one male and two female *syahid*.

The desire for Islamic criminal laws to apply in Brunei was first publicly articulated in the Sultan's Birthday *titah* in 1996, in which he proclaimed that the Syari'ah Courts were not just for the implementation of family laws, but were to apply the "*Qunun Jina'I Islam* (an Islamic Criminal Law Act) in its entirety as required by Allah, the Almighty".[118] He justified this on grounds of erosion of moral values and the proliferation of social ailments such as drug addiction and HIV/AIDS, and lamented that the current secular laws and penalties were not curbing these social diseases. "We are confident" he said "that this good intention (to enact Islamic criminal law) will become a source of blessing to the country and to the people."[119] There have been several subsequent public announcements in this vein with the deputy Minister of

[113] *Syahids* are persons the court finds are able to give *syahadah* evidence, Syariah Courts Evidence Order (2001), section 106(1).

[114] Syariah Courts Evidence Order (2001), section 106(3).

[115] Syariah Courts Evidence Order (2001), section 106(2).

[116] Syariah Courts Evidence Order (2001), section 106(5).

[117] Section 106 (1)–(5).

[118] *Titah* delivered from the Throne Room at *Istana Nurul Iman* on July 16, 1996. Reported in *Borneo Bulletin* July 16, 1996.

[119] Ibid.

Religious Affairs in June 2003 advising that "a new Islamic Criminal law Order is in the process of enactment. The law will provide for certain offences such as murder, causing hurt, adultery, rape, theft, robbery and drinking intoxicating liquor."[120]

The prospect of introducing Islamic criminal law concerns many non-Muslims in the Sultanate, including the indigenous non-Malays who already feel their traditional practices, religion and way of life is threatened by the committed policy of Islamization.

Impact of Islamization on Non-Malay Indigenous Women of Brunei

Although non-Muslims in Brunei are not subject to the jurisdiction of the Syari'ah Court and to the specific statutes discussed above,[121] the impact of Islamization reaches all residents in the Sultanate. This is because the aim of MIB is to promote one culture (Malay) and one religion (Islam). The ethnic and religious diversity that was apparent on the island of Borneo from earliest times is thus suppressed, as assimilation into Malay culture is encouraged in order to create a mono-cultural Brunei. A Brunei educationalist explained that although:

> multi-racial and multi-cultural in character, this does not mean that the government is pursuing social policies in favour of the development of multiracialism and multiculturalism in the country. The government has definite ideas about the country's socio-political status . . . Brunei Darussalam will forever be a Malay, Islamic Sultanate.[122]

The government acknowledges that Brunei is 'a poly-ethnic society,' but is firm in its resolve that the national culture is Malay and the national religion is Islam. For the indigenous non-Malays whose culture and religion pre-dates the arrival of Islam, the policy of Islamization threatens the survival of their way of life. For these women, it not the intersection of Islamization with goals of modernization that causes tension, but the impact of Islamization on their indigenous Bornean traditions and spirituality. Their religion extends in a continuum to Borneo's pre-Islamic, pre-European, animistic way of life. Animism is a system of beliefs used to explain the natural world, and how humans should interact with each other and with natural phenomena. In the dense and rugged tropical rainforests, the early peoples of Borneo constructed

---

[120] Pehin Dato Ustaz Awing Haji Yahya's speech reported in "Brunei to Maintain Tranquil and Moderate Islamic Laws," www.brudirect.com/DailyInfo/News/Archive/June03/100603.

[121] This is in general terms as non-Muslims can be called to give *bayyinah* evidence in the Syari'ah Court: *Syariah Courts Evidence Order* (2001), section 103(2).

[122] Abdul Ghani Bujang, "Education for Nationhood," *Southeast Asian Journal of Educational Studies* 24 (1987):43.

a belief system where the natural and supernatural merged, and where the souls or spirits of people, animals and the deities constantly interacted. The concepts and procedures for the settlement of disputes were intimately linked with the spiritual, so that ritual redress complemented the secular. Animism supported egalitarian notions including gender equality, and relied on established practices for maintaining harmony between people and their natural environment. Women were always important transmitters of these cultural and religious values and in some cases women were bearers of high religious office, mediums for communications with the spirit world, and custodians of religious ritual. The Dusun of Brunei is one indigenous group where religious leadership was almost exclusively female through the *belian*, or Dusun priestesses. *Belian* conduct ritual ceremonies and perform exorcisms and essentially are the agents of religious transmission.[123]

Despite constitutional guarantees that 'other religions may be practiced in peace and harmony,' there are significant restrictions on the practice of any religion other than Islam. However animism which is polytheistic and linked with the supernatural spirit world is of particular concern to the authorities in modern Brunei, just as it was earlier Muslim leaders, who considered that peoples without holy scriptures, the 'non-believers' or *kafirs*, were not entitled to the protections that were afforded *dhimmis* (people of the book).[124] Given rules for modesty in dress, Muslims can be offended by the clothing of indigenous non-Malay women and find their practices living in longhouses, hunting and eating *haram* foods of concern. In addition, governments in Southeast Asia generally consider the indigenous religious practices as primitive or backward, as commentators like Winzeler have observed.[125]

There are particular obstacles for the indigenous people of Brunei in retaining their own identity and religious practice. The first is the legal categorization of six of the distinctive indigenous ethnic groups as Malay for the purposes of Bruneian nationality.[126] The word Malay, as we have seen, signifies adherence

[123] For a detailed study of Dusun religion and in particular the role played by women see: Eva Kershaw, *A Study of Brunei Dusun Religion: Ethnic Priesthood on a Frontier of Islam* (Borneo: Borneo Research Monograph Council, 2000).

[124] Abdullahi Ahmed An-Na'im, "Towards an Islamic Reformation: Islamic Law in History and Society Today" in Othman, *Shari'a Law and the Modern Nation State,* 17. In orthodox Muslim communities the subjects are classified as Muslims, *dhimmis,* 'People of the Book' because they believed in revealed scriptures from God, and *kafirs* or 'unbelievers'. *Dhimmis* were granted some rights of citizenship, provided they paid a special tax (*jizyh*), and could practice their religion provided they did so in private and did not attempt to convert Muslims. They could not hold positions of authority over Muslims. Unbelievers had fewer rights and at times were killed unless granted safe conduct (*aman*) by Muslims.

[125] Robert L. Winzeler, ed. *Indigenous Peoples and the State: Politics, Land, and Ethnicity in the Malayan Peninsula and Borneo* (New Haven, Conn.: Yale University Southeast Asia Studies, 1997), 12–13.

[126] Brunei Nationality Enactment (1961) section 4(1). The Constitution of Brunei recognized seven indigenous ethnic groups as *puak jati* (original tribes) which includes these six groups plus the Brunei Malays.

to Islam. Despite that, under the nationality law, the indigenous Kedayan,[127] Tutong,[128] Belait,[129] Dusun,[130] Bisaya,[131] and Murut[132] peoples are also classified as Malay. Although most of the Kedayan, Tutong, and Belait had converted to Islam by the time of the independence, the Dusun, Bisayas and Murut remained predominately non-Muslim, having either retained their animistic beliefs or converted to Christianity. By using the legal categorization of 'Malay,' the Bruneian state condescendingly overrules indigenous peoples' adherence to other belief systems and ignores their cultural self-identification.[133]As these six indigenous groups are counted with the Brunei Malays as Malays for census purposes it is difficult to calculate their respective numbers in the total population. The 20,000 indigenous people, categorized in the census as 'other indigenous' are from contiguous parts of Borneo who came to reside in Brunei during the early part of the twentieth century.[134] They are mainly the Iban,[135] Kadazan, Punan[136] and Melanau.[137]

A second repercussion of Islamization is the barrier it provides to inter-ethnic marriage. It impacts upon the indigenous Bruneians because marriage between

---

[127] See Allen R. Maxwell, "The Origin of the Brunei Kadayan in Ethnohistorical Perspective," in Winzeler, *Indigenous Peoples and the State*, 153.

[128] The Tutongs were part of a linguistic and cultural group in the Lower Baram basin and in western Brunei. Most have converted to Islam and been assimilated with the Malays, forming a totally Islamic group of 12 000 people. See Victor T. King, *The Peoples of Borneo* (Oxford: Blackwell, 1993), 194.

[129] See: Peter Martin, "The Orang Belait of Brunei: Linguistic Affinities with Lemeting (Meting)," *Borneo Research Bulletin* 22 (1990), 131.

[130] See A. Bantong, "Brunei Dusuns," *Brunei Museum Journal* 8 (1993): 11–16. The Dusun refer to themselves as *Sang Jati*, which means indigenous people or 'our people' and consider themselves to be a distinct race. Jay H. Bernstein, "The De-culturation of the Brunei Dusun," in Winzeler, *Indigenous Peoples and the State*, 164.

[131] The Bisayas share a common language and cultural affinity with the Dusuns and are predominately non-Muslims.

[132] Victor T. King, "What is Brunei Society? Reflections on a Conceptual and Ethnographic Issue," *Southeast Asia Research* 2 (1994): 176–198.

[133] Braighlinn, *Ideological Innovation under Monarchy*, 19 ascribes to this view, detecting an imputation that non-Malay indigenous groups lack 'enough authentic culture or valuable culture to be considered anything better than 'sub-groups' of the dominant Malay population.'

[134] Brunei Nationality Enactment (1961) denies automatic citizenship on the grounds of their Sarawak origin.

[135] The Iban are the largest of the non-Malay indigenous group in Brunei.

[136] The Penan/Punan are traditionally nomadic or semi-nomadic people of Sarawak, who made temporary camps in groves of sago palms, supplementing their hunting for wild pig and deer with collecting fruit and plants. There is a small settled Penan community in the Belait District of Brunei, but as Martin and Sercombe report that intermarriage with the local Dusun and Iban is frequent, and their traditional pursuits of blowpipe production and hunting and gathering is becoming less common. See Peter W. Martin and P. Sercombe, "An Update on the Penan of Brunei," *Borneo Research Bulletin* 24 (1992): 86–91.

[137] The Melanau were coastal people to the south of Brunei, on whom the Sultanate exerted considerable influence, particularly on their social stratification and on the progressive conversion to Islam. See H. S. Morris, "The Coastal Melanau," in King, *The Ethnic Groups of Borneo*, 48–73.

a Muslim and non-Muslim is not lawful until the non-Muslim converts to Islam.[138] Any children of the marriage are automatically Muslim, thus sealing the end of affinity to indigenous religion and culture. This is because the conversion does not only mean observance of a new religion, but also: a new identity through the taking of an Islamic name;[139] changes in outward appearance by the wearing of Brunei Malay clothes;[140] new daily practices;[141] dietary change from regular consumption of pig to all *halal* foods; and no alcohol (rice wine is integral to many indigenous ceremonies and festivals).

The third factor that has adverse consequences for the indigenous non-Malays and their religion is the law on proselytizing. While law is used to prohibit and punish the proselytizing of any religion other than the Shafi'i sect within Islam, there is no prohibition in reverse. In accord with the state ideology of MIB, the government actively pursues and funds the propagation of Islam to non-Muslims. The Islamic *Dakwah* (Propagation) Centre of the powerful Ministry of Religion exists solely for this purpose. A conversion to Islam automatically accords the convert Malay status as well as provides tangible benefits, such as cash payments,[142] promotion at work, grants of land and houses and improvements in public works.[143] Representatives from the *Dakwah* Centre visit longhouses and villages, concentrating firstly on obtaining the conversion of the headman, and then the remaining members of the longhouse or village.

[138] Religious Council and Kadis Courts Act (1984), section 134 required both parties to profess Islam, however, The Emergency (Islamic Family Law) Order (1999), section 10 states that "A marriage shall be void unless all the necessary conditions, in accordance with *Hukum Syara'* have been satisfied."

[139] Report from *Brunei Bulletin* June 3, 2000 under "Two families embrace Islam" states that two Iban families from Ulu Belait converted and sets out the new names of each. "The family of Dyg Kalong Anuk Gindau, 43, is now known as Dyg Nur Rashidah bte Abdullah Gindau and her 11 year old daughter, Chin Yuk Moi, as Dyg Nurhafizah bte Abdullah."

[140] Dress of *tudongs* (veils) and angle-length loose gowns for women and girls, and *songkit* or MIB shirts for men.

[141] A Muslim is required to observe the five pillars of Islam, which include prayers five times a day, and fasting during the month of *Ramadan*, as well as the annual payment of *zakat*, a pilgrimage to Mecca during one's lifetime, and belief in God and Mohammad as his messenger.

[142] Bernstein, "The De-culturation of the Brunei Dusun," 174 indicates that the figure of B$200 per month is given to each convert.

[143] Azaraimy H. Hasib also reports that are financial incentives given to new Muslim converts and quotes Awang Hj Jaman bin Ali, a Religious Propagation Officer from the Ministry of Religious Affairs, as stating homes valued at around $42,000 are being built and given to converts in the hope of improving 'their well-being and living quality', together with 'water tank supply and power generators which may cost around $2500 to $5500 each'. See Azaramy H. Hasib, "Brunei Takes Giant Strides towards Islamic Conversions," http://www.brudirect.com/Daily Info/News/Mar01. Bernstein similarly reports that road and other public improvements do not occur until the conversion to Islam of a household, when the work is immediately executed. See Bernstein, "The De-culturation of the Brunei Dusun," 174.

The conversion of a family or individual is accompanied by public ceremony, at which the Sultan may, on occasions, personally officiate.[144] Certainly, the new convert receives newspaper and often television coverage, which, given that the numbers converting some years exceed 600,[145] gives a powerful statement to the non-Malays that they are going against the religious tide. Employers are encouraged to ask non-Muslims if they are planning to convert to Islam, and it is not discriminatory for an employer to request that only Malays apply. School students are frequently converted to Islam: indeed, once fourteen and a half, they can convert without parental consent. All students may attend Government schools; but once there, all of them, non-Malays included, must take subjects on Islam and MIB and wear Malay dress, including the *tudong*. There are no classes on non-Malay indigenous culture, languages or practices. The steady conversion rate[146] suggests that the survival of non-Muslim indigenous groups in Brunei is precarious. One researcher has predicted that by 2050 all the ethnic groups in Brunei will have been converted to Islam and thereby assimilated into the official Malay state sponsored culture.[147]

Conclusion

Brunei became independent just twenty years ago, and during that time the Sultanate has focused on reclaiming its Islamic Malay identity while striving to be a modern and influential nation in the region. Modernization comes in different forms, and in Brunei the aim is not to jettison the past and replicate the West but to modernize whilst retaining its Islamic and Malay character.

---

[144] Report in the *Borneo Bulletin* August 26, 2000 explains that at their ceremony for Islamic converts from Temburong District on August 25 "the new converts were most fortunate to proclaim their new religion in front of His Majesty," which was accompanied by the Sultan's presentation of keys for their new homes as part of the housing scheme of the Dakwah Islamic Centre.

[145] Report in the *News Express* April 14, 2000 titled "Steady Increase in Converts" gives the figures from the Ministry of Religious Affairs as 351 in 1995; 426 in 1996; 601 in 1997; and 618 in 1998. A subsequent report gives the figures for 1999 as 467—see J. Obina, "More Islamic Women Convert in Brunei than Men," *News Express* February 1, 2001. It also reported that more women than men converted.

[146] In 2000 it was reported that 222 atheists or non-believers (terms used for those adhering to indigenous animistic religions) converted to Islam. The figures for 2000 also show that 121 Iban, 104 Dusuns, and 10 Murut converted. However, it has been suggested by some Iban that a percentage of conversions take place in order to receive the monetary advantage, but in practice, earlier beliefs (animistic or of another religion) continue to operate. This is not unlike the notion of the 'rice Christian' conversions in Asia.

[147] This is the prediction of Maxwell, cited in Bernstein, "The De-culturation of the Brunei Dusun," 177.

Similarly, Islamization, as a re-assertion of Islamic identity, takes distinctive cultural and political forms. However, the intersection of the two—Islamic resurgence and modernization — creates inevitable tensions and creative solutions.

In the last decade, the choices the government of Brunei has made for women in the Sultanate reflect the inherent tension in reconciling modernization and Islamization. Three themes have been apparent in this chapter. One is that women themselves have been largely excluded from the debate — they have not informed it, nor have they had any decision making role in the choices being made about law and religion. The choice that Brunei's modernization route would eschew democratization and revive an autocratic, patriarchal, even anachronistic, political construct of a Sultanate has ensured an inherently male dominated system and a culture of acquiescence to authority, or civic apathy.[148] In rejecting democracy, Brunei chose not to adopt a key plank of the Western modernization agenda and signalled a leaning to conservative Islam. The consequent effect of paternalism for women in Brunei goes beyond denying them a right to vote and to participate in government. It has restricted what information can be accessed, what organizations are allowed, and whether they can change their religion or practice it openly.

The second theme relates to choices made in formulating legislation in accordance with Islamization and the extent to which modern concepts — whether derived from Western or international norms or from reformist Islam — should prevail over the orthodox Shafi'i interpretations. In matters of family law, Brunei has essentially retained the orthodox stance but, cognisant of particular inequities and wider criticisms, made modifications to reduce injustice. This pattern of compromise can be seen in laws on polygyny, *wali* consent and disobedience of a wife. Greatest revision occurred in the case of *talaq* divorce which has been made available to both husband and wife. In contrast, the introduction of the pre-Arabic *zihar* divorce shows the competing influences in the sensitive area of family law. Possibly the greater impact of law and religion on women in the Sultante could come if Islamic criminal laws were to be introduced. This has been foreshadowed in official pronouncements by the Sultan and by the enactment of Islamic laws of evidence which differentiate between the evidence of males and females. This is a necessary precursor to criminal law. Given the gender equality in educational attainment and economic standing in the Sultanate, the retention of such differentials clearly signals a conservative leaning in the Islamization process in Brunei.

[148] A study by Crane, Gillen and McDorman found several Asian cultures display civic apathy or a lack of civic consciousness, which relates to issues of constitutionalism. C. Crane, M. Gillen and T. L. McDorman, "Parliamentary Supremacy in Canada, Malaysia, and Singapore," in Douglas M Johnston and Gerry Ferguson, *Asia-Pacific Legal Development* (Vancouver: UBC Press, 1998), 155–217.

The third aspect of the tension between Islamization and modernization is the impact for indigenous non-Malay women. Those who adhere to their animistic beliefs which were essentially egalitarian, some with sacred roles reserved for women, find these belittled and under challenge. Modernization renders their religion and way of life 'backward and primitive', being out of keeping with modern development in the technological age. Islamization, which under MIB strives for a monoculture of the Muslim Malay, necessitates the absorption of the indigenous Borneans into the dominant Malay, a process which can only occur through conversion to Islam. Positive discrimination in favour of the Islam and of the Malay, coupled with inducements to convert and restrictions on other religious practices, means the choices for indigenous non-Malay women are limited. This outcome is not unique to Brunei Darussalam but has been identified as occurring in other post-colonial situations in which the dominant ethnic group subsumes indigenous or tribal people.[149] The phrases 'Fourth World colonialism'[150] and internal colonization[151] have been coined to label this recurring process.

It can be seen that as the Sultanate attempts to reconcile prioritizing of Islam with the demands of modernization, women can be caught in conflicting, and sometimes, shifting ideological paradigms. Yet it becomes clear that the main direction for law and religion in the twenty-first century is towards the Islamic world and its solutions. In keeping with the tradition attributed to the prophet that 'whosoever imitates a community, is actually part of it',[152] Brunei Darussalam is veering away from its inherited secular colonial model to join other Muslim states[153] on the route to greater Islamization.

---

[149] Government policies are facilitating this process in the indigenous non-Malays including the Semelai and Dayaks of Malaysia. Also threatened are the Dayaks in Kalimantan, Indonesia. The Thai government as well has a similar policy for its tribal mountain people (Hmong).

[150] Winzeler, *Indigenous Peoples and the State,* 1; also Bernard Nietschmann , "The Third World War," *Cultural Quarterly Survival* 11 (1987) 1–16.

[151] Robert Denton, "How the Malaysian Ruling Class constructs Orang Asli," in Winzeler, *Indigenous Peoples and the State*, 98–134.

[152] Ravindra S. Khare, *Perspectives on Islamic Law, Justice, and Society* (Lanham: Rowan and Littlefield Publishers, 1999), 166.

[153] Islamization has been taking place in Libya, Pakistan, Sudan, Nigeria, Iran and the Malay states of Kelantan.

CHAPTER NINE

'SHE'S A WOMAN BUT SHE ACTS VERY FAST'[1] : WOMEN, RELIGION AND LAW IN SINGAPORE

Li-ann Thio*

> One of the hallmarks of a modern, progressive society is the status of its women—how equally they are treated, how well they are respected, how educated they are, how much opportunity they have to be economically active, and how much say they have in family, community and national affairs . . . a society which neglects or mistreats its womenfolk is competing in the race of nations with one leg hobbled.
>
> Deputy Prime Minister Lee Hsien Loong[2]

> In the old days, girls did not go to school, women did not work and, in the Chinese community, the tradition of feet-binding prevailed. But today, girls go to school . . . and large numbers of women are in the workforce . . . Therefore, one comes to the conclusion that the only feet-binding that remains is in the mindset of the Government. . . .
>
> M.P. Halimah Yacob, challenging the discriminatory civil servant medical benefits regime[3]

Introduction

The multicultural and multi-religious city-state[4] of Singapore is a study in ambivalence when one examines law's treatment of women, and religious

[1] Mr. Yow Kuan Hong, general manager of Bukit Timah's Community Development Council, commenting on the appointment of new mayor Mrs. Yu-Foo Yee Shoon: Chua Lee Hoong, "Time to be Fair to the 'Fairer' Sex," *Straits Times* March 7, 2001 (hereafter, "Straits Times").

* B.A. Hons (Oxford); LL.M (Harvard); Ph.D. (Cambridge); Barrister (Gray's Inn, UK), Associate Professor, Faculty of Law, National University of Singapore. I thank Lee Ti-Ting, for her cheerful and invaluable research assistance.

[2] "Hallmark of a Modern Society is the Status of its Women," Speech, D. P. M. Lee Hsien Loong, Singapore Government Press Release, March 7, 2003, http://www.sprinter.gov.sg (visited 7 July 2003).

[3] 76 *Singapore Parliament Reports*, 13 March 2003, col. 558 at 556 (hereafter "SPR").

[4] A June 1997 census puts Singapore's ethnic composition thus: Chinese (77.15 percent), Malay (14.11 percent), Indians (7.4 percent) and Others (1.34 percent): Ministry of

influences in this respect, within a quasi-secular constitutional order. Rejecting an antagonistic stance and favoring a respectful one towards religion, the government seeks to safeguard religious harmony by adopting a neutral, even-handed posture in relating to different religious groups. Religion is considered a 'positive factor,' a source of spiritual strength and moral guidance.[5] A primary advocate of 'Asian values'—which is associated with patriarchal Confucian values as pragmatically qualified by modernity's demands—this espoused national ideology shapes laws and public policy.

In contemporary Singapore, a few women occupy top public or government-related offices, such as the US ambassadorship[6] and CEO of Temasek Holdings,[7] a major government investment company.[8] Gender issues are raised in public discourse by non-government organizations, such as AWARE,[9] formed in 1985. Government recognized women's organizations are served by the Singapore Council for Women's Organizations,[10] an umbrella body promoting women's interests in the fields of education, economic participation and social involvement. Its members include women's associations organized along religious affiliations, including Christian, Muslim and Baha'i groups.

Community Development and Sport (MCDS), *Singapore's Initial Report to CEDAW Committee*, January 2000, CEDAW/C/SGP/1 ("Initial Report"). A 1995 General Household Survey showed that 86 percent of Singaporeans profess a religious belief. Of residents aged 15 and above, the religious affiliations were as follows: Buddhists (31.9 percent); Taoists (21.9 percent); Muslims (15 percent); Christians (12.9 percent) and Hindus (3.3 percent): Initial Report, part I, para. 1.5. Of the Muslims, 86.3 percent were Malays, 90 percent of Christians were Chinese and 99.3 percent of Hindus were Indian: at para. 1.6. Indeed, Christianity has overtaken Taoism as the second most important religion for the Chinese, next to Buddhism: Jason Leow, "Christianity Popular among Chinese Here," *Straits Times*, November 18, 2000, H7. The Singapore Census of Population (2000) provided these percentages in terms of religious affiliation: Christianity (14.6 percent); Buddhism (42.5 percent); Taoism (8.5 percent); Islam (14.9 percent); Hinduism (4 percent); Other Religions (0.6 percent); No Religion (14.8 percent).

[5] White Paper, Maintenance of Religious Harmony Bill (Cmd. 21 of 1989), paras. 5–6.

[6] Professor Chan Heng Chee is Singapore's current US ambassador. MCDS, *Singapore's Second Report to CEDAW Committee*, 2001, CEDAW/C/SGP/2, para 5.5 ("Second Report").

[7] Ms. Ho Ching, wife of Deputy Prime Minister Lee Hsien Loong. Mr. Lee became Singapore's third Prime Minister in August 2004 when Goh Chok Tong stepped down from this post, becoming Senior Minister in Mr. Lee's new cabinet.

[8] The Prime Minister, in responding to parliamentary questions, noted that as of March 2003, some 10 percent of 630 statutory board directorships were held by women; of the 593 directorships of government-linked companies, 9.9 percent were held by women: 76 *SPR*, 14 March 2003, col. 901.

[9] Association of Women for Action and Research (AWARE), founded in 1985. Its website is at http://www.aware.org.sg. For a succinct overview of their agenda, see their paper *Remaking Singapore: Views of Half the Nation*, available at http://www.onlinewomeninpolitics.org/sing/aware.pdf (visited 4 June 2003) ("*Remaking Singapore*").

[10] The SCWO website is at www.scwo.org.sg. This has been active since the 1980s, having a network of some 45 affiliates, with some 100,000 women members.

Singapore signed the ASEAN[11] Declaration on the Advancement of Women on 5 July 1988. The Declaration lists promotional goals rather than being rights-oriented,[12] consistent with its antipathy towards cultivating an adversarial 'rights culture,' thought corrosive to the national priority of social harmony and political stability.[13] Nevertheless women's issues received some prominence when Singapore acceded to the Convention for the Elimination of All Forms of Discrimination against Women (CEDAW) in 1995, and Singapore has commenced engaging with the UN human rights regime through the state reporting process before the CEDAW Committee.[14]

However, the image of Singapore women abroad is perhaps refracted through the lens of the iconic 'Singapore Girl,' the flight attendant subserviently and gracefully ministering to the in-flight needs of Singapore Airlines passengers, an "enchanting, adorable, inviting nymph in an irresistible Balmain creation".[15] The political marginalization of women is evident from the absence of female Cabinet ministers,[16] with female politicians currently falling far below the 30–35 percent 'critical mass' needed for genuine gender-sensitive political change.[17] The CEDAW Committee was concerned about the "very low level of representation of women in politics and decision-making,"[18] urging corrective measures (such as quotas[19]); however these reforms are resisted by the government

---

[11] Association of South East Asian Nations (ASEAN).

[12] Text available at http://www.aseansec.org/8685.htm.

[13] This is reflected in the Shared Values White Paper (Cmd 1 of 1991), "Consensus over Contention" ("Shared Values White Paper").

[14] These reports are available at the website of the Ministry of Community Development, Youth and Sports (MCYS), formerly known as the MCDS, at http://app.mcys.gov.sg, under 'Individuals (About Women'): Initial report submitted on 12 January 1999 (CEDAW/C/SGP/1). For a non-government report, see http://iwraw.igc.org/publications/countries/singapore.htm.

[15] Cherian George, "Leading Advertisers Could Set the Trend for Less Sexist Ads," *Straits Times*, November 5, 1995, 14. Sexist advertising images were criticized for perpetuating "the West's romantic stereotypes about gentle Asian girls."

[16] Tan Tarn How and Neo Hui Min, "Where are you, Madam Minister?" *Straits Times*, March 8, 2003. Two female parliamentarians were appointed to cabinet positions by Singapore's third Prime Minister, Lee Hsieng Loong who assumed office in August 2004. These are Mrs. Lim Hwee Hwa, who is Minister of State for Finance & Transport and Mrs. Yu-Foo Yee Shoon, Minister of State for Community Development, Youth and Sports. 'Mr. Lee names his Cabinet,' *Straits Times*, August 11, 2004, 1. A third woman appointed to political office is Dr. Amy Khor as mayor of Southwest Community Development Council.

[17] CEDAW Committee, General Recommendation 23, (16th Sess., 1997), *Political and Public Life*, U.N. Doc. A/52/38, para.16.

[18] *Report of the Committee on the Elimination of Discrimination against Women*, 24th–25th Sess., GAOR 56th Sess. Supplement No. 38 (A/56/38), (2001) paras. 87–88. Female parliamentarians remain low at 6.5 percent: para. 62 ("2001 CEDAW Report").

[19] 2001 CEDAW Report, para. 88.

because they transgress state-sponsored meritocratic policies.[20] The gender-insensitivity of high-ranking male politicians is captured in a comment related to a gender-biased government policy, that this might be altered "as time changes . . . perhaps one day when you have women in the Cabinet, we will discuss this again."[21] The AWARE President criticized this signal that "men in positions of power may take and enforce decisions that are detrimental to women without justification, explanation or cause."[22] As noted, the "convention in Singapore has yet to catch up with reality" insofar as certain men considered women the less competent, weaker sex.[23]

Singapore has no national human rights institution, let alone a dedicated Women's Ministry.[24] However, the Ministry of Community Development and Sports (MCDS) declares itself "the lead agency for women matters in Singapore," dealing with health, education and employment issues or providing services to needy women.[25] However, its website does not have a section devoted to 'Women' but rather 'Celebrates Women' under the heading of 'Families.'[26] As an example of measures adopted to support women, married women receive special tax incentives.[27] The economic necessity of having working women has spurred the adoption of 'family friendly' policies,[28] such as promoting dual parental responsibility. Women are thus perceived as situated beings within marital and familial contexts, rather than individuals. This is consistent with the government's declared "pro-family"[29] policy, although such policies "seem to cast women in a secondary role" as passive beings whose "paramount mission is to fulfill the roles of a wife and mother."[30]

---

[20] Deputy Prime Minister Lee opposed female parliamentary quotas: "Govt to Work Harder to Get More Women into Parliament," *Straits Times*, March 8 2003, H9. It was suggested that the Nominated MP scheme would enable women to participate in politics without having to represent an electoral constituency: Irene Ng, 74 *SPR*, April 5 2002, col. 602.

[21] "Ask When There Are Women in Cabinet," *Straits Times,* March 14 2003, H4.

[22] Tisa Ng, President, AWARE, "Aware Slams Discrimination against Women," *Straits Times,* March 15, 2003, 35.

[23] Chua Lee Hoong, "Time to be Fair to the "Fairer" Sex," *Straits Times,* March 7, 2001, H11.

[24] There have been calls to institutionalise agencies, including a women's agency, to review and provide redress for discriminatory acts through formalised channels: 75 *SPR*, April 2, 2002, col. 181.

[25] Within this Ministry there is a dedicated section serving as the focal point for the formulation and review of national policy on women's issues, bearing in mind CEDAW obligations.

[26] See http://www.mcds.gov.sg.

[27] Initial Report, para. 1.3.

[28] These include flexible work hours, working from home and job sharing: Second Report, part II, para. 7.22. See also 75 *SPR*, July 22, 2002, cols. 430ff; 72 *SPR*, November 14, 2000, cols. 1173ff.

[29] Initial Report, para. 3.1 declares that many policies specifically designed for the family benefit women. Second Report, part II, paras. 8–9, lists "pro-family" measures including allowing married male civil servants 3 days paid leave on the birth of his first three children.

[30] Irene Ng, 75 *SPR*, October 1, 2002, col. 1131. AWARE has criticised the policy allowing only married women civil servants to take a certain amount of paid sick child leave as reinforcing a sexual stereotype of a wife and mother as the care provider: *Remaking Singapore*.

Nevertheless, there appears to be a minor sea-change in the mindset of the People's Action Party (PAP), which has governed Singapore since Independence on 9 August 1965, as it recently fielded three single women as parliamentary candidates in the 2001 General Elections.[31] These female MPs have argued that gender issues are treated and marginalized as 'women's issues' rather than structural issues affecting society. Further, they state clearly that "a national identity . . . based on patriarchy excludes women."[32]

Advances in the women's rights agenda within a depoliticized society are not achieved through constitutional litigation, but 'granted' where economically pragmatic to do so, perhaps in response to soft non-confrontational lobbying and low-key advocacy. For instance, the December 2002 removal of the one-third female medical student quota, justified by appeal to scarce human resources,[33] was motivated by statist economic imperatives such as promoting Singapore as a medical hub, rather than concerns for gender egalitarianism, personal welfare, and self-determination.[34] Perennial policy bugbears fuelling women's rights advocacy have included disparate citizenship rights for children born of Singapore men and women with foreign spouses[35] and differentiated medical benefits for male and female civil servants, despite the ratification of the ILO Convention on Equal Pay for Equal Work in 2002.[36]

---

[31] Han Fook Kwang, "What No SAF Scholars in New PAP Line-Up?" *Straits Times*, October 24, 2001, H4. B.G. Lee noted a shift in PAP policy preference for married women candidates as 25 percent of female graduates were single and "it's not their fault." AWARE criticised the stereotypical images of women parliamentarians with respect to marital status, calling for a review: Khoo Heng Keow, President of AWARE, "Remove Set Images of Potential Women MPs," *Straits Times*, August 4, 1999, 36.

[32] Irene Ng, 75 *SPR*, October 1, 2002, cols. 1130–1.

[33] Since more women doctors tended to stop work to raise children, the quota was justified and did not violate the right to equal access to education, guaranteed by art. 10, CEDAW. 75 *SPR*, November 25, 2002, cols. 1518–22.

[34] "Lifted: Quota on Women in Medicine," *Straits Times*, December 6, 2002, (available on LEXIS). The Health Minister stated that with greater resources and a narrowed gender gap between trained doctors exiting the profession, the quota could be lifted; also, that Singapore's aging population needed more doctors who would also support its push into the life sciences: 75 *SPR*, December 5, 2002, col. 1969.

[35] This contravenes art. 9, CEDAW. Parliamentarians have cited population decline as an instrumental reason for changing citizenship policy: Liang Hwee Ting, "Long Hours, Hard Work, Disturbed in the Middle of the Night But...This Woman Doctor has No Regrets," *Straits Times*, December 7, 2002, (available on LEXIS). For the CEDAW Committee criticism and Singapore response, see Initial Report, para. 10.2; 2001 CEDAW Report, para. 75; Press Release, WOM/1293, CEDAW Committee, 25th Session, 522nd Meeting: "Singapore Delegates, Describing Compliance with Women's Convention, Say Account must be Taken of Cultural Tradition, Need for Stability" (July 13, 2001), available at: http://www.un.org/News/Press/docs/2001/WOM1293.doc.htm; ("CEDAW Press Release").

[36] "Women May Fight For Same Pay as Men," *Straits Times*, March 9, 2002. Despite gender income disparities, the Manpower Minister considered Singapore was in "full compliance" with the ILO Convention: 75 *SPR*, 22 July 2002, cols. 440–1. The rationale was that in Asian

Government policies are wont to display a startling bias in buttressing female stereotypes, as where a non-gender-neutral sex education curriculum urges only girls not to have pre-marital sex, likening a girl's (not a boy's) loss of virginity to removing a magazine from its plastic cover.[37] The Singapore Armed Forces has also blithely commissioned sexist advertisements.[38]

While the world's major religions are represented in Singapore, where religious faith is recognized as forming "a major part of Singapore's cultural ballast,"[39] this chapter discusses the relationship between law, religion, and women in relation to two systems of religious belief, broadly defined.[40] The first discussion relates to neo-Confucianism of the Singapore variety, as this apparently founds the preferred PAP authored national ideology, particularly in its appeal to 'Asian values' to legitimate policies. The second discussion considers the position of Islam in Singapore, as the need to protect minority culture and religion rationalizes legal pluralism. To safeguard religious particularities, the general law does not apply to the minority Muslim community in limited fields, which is significant for women insofar as certain Islamic laws discriminate against women, contrary to CEDAW norms and the constitutional guarantees of equality.

---

societies like Singapore, "it is the husband's responsibility to look after the family's needs." Exceptionally, female employees who were sole breadwinners would be eligible for the same medical benefits for her dependents: 75 *SPR*, October 31, 2002, cols. 1461–3.

[37] This related to a sex education CD-Rom released in October 2000. "Messages are Sexist, Says Aware President," *Straits Times*, October 21, 2002, 60. The AWARE President was criticised by Minister of State Aline Wong for her views that these discriminatory messages eroded equality, arguing that virginity should be promoted as a value in both boys and girls, as double standards constituted "criminal" "psychological damage". A disenchanted *Straits Times* reader opined that female politicians were "not doing their own gender any good," being mere "mouth pieces" for the chauvinistic political party: Chen Siow Ying, "Need More Women in Power," *Straits Times*, January 2, 2001, 1.

[38] Member of Parliament Irene Ng complained that a website recruitment clip portrayed men as purposeful leaders and women in a fashion reminiscent of "a high-class karaoke hostess": "SAF Recruitment Clip for Women 'Demeaning'," *Straits Times*, March 15, 2003, H6. Initial Report, para. 6.2 asserts "there is equal portrayal of women in leadership roles in the media." Furthermore, the Singapore Broadcasting Authority's Free to Air TV Programme Code contains clauses addressing the stereotyping of females and the commercialization of sex: Second Report, para. 2.3. When an advertisement targets young single women as property owners, rather than preying on their insecurities, this is cause for note: Ong Soh Chin, "Not a Man's Property," *Straits Times*, May 17, 2003, (available on LEXIS).

[39] Shared Values White Paper, para. 45.

[40] The Supreme Court has not exhaustively defined 'religion' although the Court of Appeal narrowly defined it as faith in a personal God, excluding declarations of allegiance to a state, in *Nappali Peter Williams v.Institute of Technical Education* (1999) 2 SLR 569. Thus, secular ideologies fall without Religion's ambit. Notably, Confucian Ethics was practically treated as part of the short-lived Religious Knowledge programme in schools: Dr Tony Tan, 54 *SPR*, 6 October 1989, cols. 628–34.

This chapter first sets out the constitutional framework and socio-legal context, including Religion-State relations and general policies towards women. It then discusses the influence of neo-Confucianism and how its patriarchal notions shape policies that rest on the secondary status of women within family and community. Finally it examines how the State adopts a 'hands-off' approach towards gender inegalitarianism within the Muslim community insofar as this is regulated by Islamic law, mandated by the limited legal pluralism practiced in this common law jurisdiction under the Administration of Muslim Law Act (AMLA) (Cap. 3). It considers the regime of Muslim women's rights, disparate internal views over female circumcision practices and contentious issues including wearing *tudung* in public schools and banning public performances which apparently disparage Islam.

The Legal Framework and Political Culture of Singapore

The Constitutional and Legal Framework of Singapore with Particular Reference to the Role of Religion and Women's Rights

Singapore practices a modified form of Westminster parliamentary democracy. Through extensive constitutional engineering, the institutional creation of unelected parliamentarians,[41] an electoral system which has resulted in most wards being uncontested[42] and transforming the ceremonial presidency into an elective office with minimalist oversight powers over primarily fiscal matters,[43] political power has effectively been concentrated in the PAP, within a dominant one party state. The 2001 General Elections saw the PAP controlling 82 of 84 parliamentary seats.[44]

---

[41] The Non-Constituency MP and the Nominated MP scheme were created in 1984 and 1991 respectively. See Thio Li-ann, "The Right to Political Participation in Singapore: Tailor-Making a Westminster-Modelled Constitution to Fit the Imperatives of 'Asian' Democracy," *Singapore Journal of International and Comparative Law*, 6 (2002): 516–24. See also Thio Li-ann, "The Constitutional Framework of Powers," in *Singapore Legal System*, ed. Kevin Y.L. Tan, 2nd ed. (Singapore: Singapore University Press, 1998).

[42] The electoral system is organised along the lines of a mixture of team (Group Representation Constituencies or GRC) representation constituencies and 8 single member constituencies as statutorily mandated by section 8A (1A), Parliamentary Elections Act (Cap 218).

[43] See Thio Li-ann, "The Elected President and Legal Control: Quis Custodiet Ipsos Custodes," and Kevin Y.L. Tan, "The Presidency in Singapore: Constitutional Development," both in *Managing Political Change: The Elected Presidency of Singapore*, ed. Kevin Y. L. Tan and Lam Peng Er (London and New York: Routledge, 1997).

[44] Most GRC wards were and continue to be uncontested. See Kevin Y. L. Tan, "Constitutional Implications of the 1991 General Elections," *Singapore Law Review* 26 (1992): 26–59.

Singapore has a written, supreme constitution,[45] although this is easily amendable, given the PAP's control of over two-thirds of parliamentary seats.[46] Chapter IV contains a short fundamental liberties list, including personal liberty, criminal due process rights, equality, free speech, religious freedom, and minimal educational rights. Broad public order exceptions judicially construed in a 'pro-communitarian' fashion in deference to state goals qualify these liberties.[47]

State and Religion

Singapore's quasi-secular constitutional order[48] is distinct from Malaysia's confessional constitution which enshrines Islam as the Federation's religion, and privileges it by prohibiting the propagation of other religions to Muslims.[49] Article 15 guarantees the right to profess, practice and propagate religion and while there is no textual endorsement of the principle of secularity, its adoption is evident from various sources,[50] being a deliberate move in forging a distinct post-Independence national identity.

Article 152(1) enjoins the government to care for the interests of racial and religious minorities and while article 152(2) recognizes the 'special position' of Malays as 'indigenous people,' they are not entitled to special rights like those enjoyed by Malaysian Malays as *bumiputras* (sons of the soil). Instead, minority concerns are addressed through individual, not group rights.[51] The constitutionally established Presidential Council of Minority Rights[52] provides limited legislative

---

[45] Article 4, Republic of Singapore Constitution.

[46] Since 1965, the Constitution has been amended some 36 times.

[47] On the judicial approach towards constitutional interpretation, see Thio Li-ann "'An i for an I': Singapore's Communitarian Model of Constitutional Adjudication," *Hong Kong Law Journal* 27 (1997): 152–86; and "Trends in Constitutional Interpretation: Oppugning Ong, Awakening Arumugam," *Singapore Journal of Legal Studies* (1997): 240–90. See also Kevin Y. L. Tan, "Economic Development, Legal Reform and Rights in Singapore and Taiwan," in *The East Asian Challenge for Human Rights* ed. J. R. Bauer and D. A. Bell (Cambridge: Cambridge University Press, 1999) 264, 268–70.

[48] The introduction of religious knowledge as part of the school education caused concerns that it was inconsistent with the secular basis of government and state: Tan Cheng Bock, *SPR*, 6 October 1989, col. 585.

[49] Articles 3 and 11, Federal Constitution of Malaysia. The High Court in *Daud bin Mamat v. Majlis Agama Islam* (2001) 2 MLJ 390 held that as art. 11 only expressly referred to the right to profess and practice religion, Malaysian Muslims had no constitutional right to renounce religion.

[50] Report of the 1966 Constitutional Commission, ("Wee Commission Report"), affirms that Singapore is a "democratic, secular state": para. 38. The Report is reproduced in Kevin Y. L. Tan and Thio Li-ann, *Constitutional Law in Malaysia and Singapore* (Asia: Butterworths, 1997), 1025. See Shared Values White Paper, para. 45; White paper, Maintenance of Religious Harmony Bill (1989), para. 21.

[51] See Wee Commission Report, para. 12.

[52] Constitution, part VII. See Thio Su Mien, "The Presidential Council," *Singapore Law Review* 1 (1969): 2.

review over bills "disadvantageous to persons of any racial or religious community." There is no constitutional conflation of ethnicity with religion, in contrast with the Malaysian Constitution.[53] Article 153 authorizes legislative enactments to regulate Muslim religious affairs and constitutes a Council to advise the President on the Muslim religion. The Muslim Affairs Minister, a cabinet post, oversees the welfare of 14 percent of the total population.

Excessively politicized religious groups are considered pressing security concerns, precipitating laws empowering the Minister to impose non-justiciable restraining 'gag' orders on religionists deemed to be intruding into politics.[54] The government preserves discretion to define the non-self evident terms of 'religion' and 'politics' although the apparent chief motive is to confine religious groups to 'educational, social and charitable work,' avoiding "radical social action"[55] associated with the so-called 'Marxist Conspiracy' in the late 1980s.[56]

The primacy of maintaining religious harmony was heightened after members of Jemaah Islamiah, a group of fundamentalist terrorists, were preventively detained in 2001 after the discovery of a plot to bomb foreign embassies. The Singapore government sought to disassociate terrorism from Islam[57] to forestall any eruption of inter-ethnic tension, such as that associated with the 1960s race riots.[58] Terrorism waged in Religion's name would undermine communal solidarity. In 2003, Muslim Affairs Minister Yaacob Ibrahim

---

[53] Article 160 of the Federal Constitution of Malaysia defines "Malay" as "a person who professes the religion of Islam . . .". This conflation is absent from the art. 39A, Singapore Constitution, definition of "Malay" for electoral purposes.

[54] Maintenance of Religious Harmony Act (Cap 167A). See Valentine. S. Winslow, "The Separation of Religion and Politics: The Maintenance of Religious Harmony Act," *Malaya Law Review*, 32 (1990): 327–331.

[55] White paper, Maintenance of Religious Harmony Bill (1989), para. 2.

[56] A group of 20 socially minded Catholics allegedly sought to bring about a Marxist state, which they denied, and were preventively detained under the Internal Security Act (Cap 143). See generally "The Conspiracy Theory," *Far Eastern Economic Review*, 22 October 22, 1987. The leading cases are: *Chng Suan Tze v. Minister of Home Affairs* (1988) SLR 132 (Singapore, Court of Appeal), *Vincent Cheng v. Minister for Home Affairs* (1990) 1 MLJ 449, *Teo Soh Lung v. Minister for Home Affairs* (1989) SLR 499 (High Court); (1990) SLR 40 (Court of Appeal). See also White paper, Maintenance of Religious Harmony Bill (1989), Annex, paras. 30–31.

[57] See Foreign Minister Jayakumar, parliamentary remarks, "Strategic Review of the World, Including the Situation in Iraq and Asia-Pacific Region," 14 March 2003, para. 13, available at Ministry of Foreign Affairs Website, 'Press Releases,' http://www.mfa.gov.sg/internet/; 76 *SPR*, March 14, 2003, cols. 848 at 851–862.

[58] On the 1950s Maria Hertogh and 1960s Geylang riots, see C.M. Turnbull, *A History of Singapore 1819–1988*, 2nd ed (Singapore: Oxford University Press, 1992), 242 and 283 respectively. On non-Muslims' mistrust of Muslims, see Wong Kan Seng, 75 *SPR*, 20 January 2003, col. 2035 at 2043–44. On the Muslim community's efforts at strengthening inter-ethnic ties, see Yaacob Ibrahim, 75 *SPR*, 21 January 2003, col. 2229ff. See also Prime Minister's National Day Rally 2002 Speech in Malay, urging Malays to reject extremism and retain their moderate image (Singapore Government Press Release, 18 August 2002). See David Chan, *Attitudes on Race and Religion: Survey on Social Attitudes of Singaporeans 2001* (Singapore: MCDS, 2002).

cautioned the Muslim community against warped religious teachings, urging it to be a "progressive, integrative" community.[59] This bears geo-political implications, as Singapore is a "red dot" in a "sea of green",[60] a predominantly Chinese city-state surrounded by Muslim nations.[61] The 2003 Declaration on Religious Harmony[62] seeks to preempt religious conflict and radicalism by promoting pacific co-existence among religious groups.

The government considers that Religion should help its adherents accept change, not obstruct it.[63] Nevertheless, religious groups are regularly consulted on controversial issues like living wills and organ donation.[64] However, the government is pragmatic in policing morals, tolerating vices like prostitution[65] and the muted homosexual scene, which social and religious conservatives oppose.[66]

---

[59] Sue-Ann Chia and K. C. Vijayan, "Blind Followers...Like JI Detainees, They May Be Misled by Warped Religious Teachings: Yaacob Ibrahim," *Straits Times*, 30 June 2003, 3.

[60] Former Indonesian President B. J. Habibie made this derogatory reference: "President Unhappy with Singapore, Says AWSJ," *Straits Times*, August 5, 1998, 16.

[61] Thio Li-ann, "Recent Constitutional Developments: Of Shadows and Whips, Race, Rifts and Rights, Terror and Tudungs, Women and Wrongs," *Singapore Journal of Legal Studies*, (2002): 328 at 352–5. Malaysian newspapers have invoked anti-Muslim images in criticising Singapore policy: a December 2002 editorial entitled "Singapore Behaving like the Jews in Claiming Batu Putih Island," adding that "just like Israel that is surrounded by Arab countries, Singapore is like a Jewish state surrounded by Malay states." Cited by Irene Ng, 75 *SPR*, 21 January 2003, col. 2121.

[62] "Declaration on Religious Harmony," Press Statement, 9 June 2003, http://www.mcys.gov.sg; Neo Hui Min, "More Than Words, a S'pore Way of Life," *Straits Times*, June 10, 2003. See Thio Li-ann, "Constitutional 'Soft' Law and the Management of Religious Liberty and Order: The 2003 Declaration on Religious Harmony," *Singapore Journal of Legal Studies* (2004): 414–443.

[63] "Religion Should Help People Cope with Change: PM," *Straits Times*, June 23, 2003, H3.

[64] However, religious groups were not consulted over the sex education Growing Years Series educational programme: "We Are Aware of Differing Views, Says Ministry," and "Sex-education Package Gets Blessing from Religious Groups," *Straits Times*,1 October 21, 2000, 61. Government leaders have assured religious leaders that feedback on policies on gambling casinos, a law requiring Sunday work, easier divorces and compulsory cremation would not be construed as mixing religion and politics: Joseph Tamney, *The Struggle over Singapore's Soul: Western Modernisation and Asian Culture* (Berlin and New York: Walter de Gruyter, 1996), 36.

[65] Unlike religious policing in Malaysia, Singapore pragmatically adopts a policy of "containment" in relation to prostitution, solicitation of which is a criminal offence: 71 *SPR*, March 6, 2000, col. 1142. Prostitution was discussed in relation to various Women's Charter provisions: see 70 *SPR*, May 5, 1999, col. 1343–1447. The radical PAS government of the Malaysian state of Terengganu has actively attacked vice by closing entertainment and gambling outlets and enacting Islamic criminal laws: 'Terengganu an Islamic state, says PAS leaders' *Straits Times* April 25, 2003.

[66] Social conservatives and members of the faith community, including Christians and Muslims, expressed concern over the implications of a further liberalisation of the homosexual agenda with respect to public morality and health issues, after the June 2003 government announcement that it had relaxed its policy of hiring homosexuals in key civil service positions, subject to sexual orientation disclosure. The Prime Minister clarified he did not "encourage or endorse a gay lifestyle" and was pleased that mainstream social conservatives and religious groups had expressed their concerns about a militant homosexual agenda "clearly and responsibly". "From the Valley to the Highlands", National Day Rally Speech, (August 17, 2003), at Singapore Government Press Release, http://www.gov.sg/nd/ND03.htm.

Case law manifests consistent deference to government assessments of public order concerns, limiting religious liberty. Yong CJ in *Chan Hiang Leng Colin v. PP* considered that actions motivated by religious beliefs could not run counter to Singapore's "sovereignty, integrity and unity,"[67] the Constitution's "paramount mandate."

Any discussion on women and religion in Singapore must appreciate that government policies are formulated with the conscious need to maintain 'religious harmony' and not to agitate Muslim sensitivities,[68] especially given enhanced ethnic-religious awareness in a post 9–11 political landscape.

Women and the Singapore Legal Framework

Article 12(1) of the Constitution declares that "all persons are equal before the law and entitled to the equal protection of the law." Article 12(2) prohibits discrimination against Singapore citizens in any law, in public or professional employment and in relation to property laws on four specific grounds: religion, race, descent, place of birth.[69] Gender is notably absent from this list. However, the MCDS' website declares that "women enjoy equal status as men in Singapore"[70]as the generality of article 12 "necessarily encompasses the non-discrimination of women."[71]

Singapore has no specific sex discrimination or sexual harassment laws[72] and no specific laws were enacted to give effect to Singapore's CEDAW

---

[67] (1994) 3 SLR 662, 684F-G.

[68] For example, Muslims were extensively consulted in relation to "national" matters like SARs, and Muslim-specific matters like compulsory education. Muslims were granted an exception to SARs control measures, being allowed immediate burial in 2 sealed body bags rather then the mandated cremation of victims: "No Wakes for Suspected SARs Deaths," *Straits Times*, April 24, 2003, H4.

[69] In contrast, art. 8(2) of the Malaysian Constitution was amended in 2001 to prohibit gender discrimination.

[70] <http://www.mcds.gov.sg/web/faml_enablewomen.asp?szMod5faml&szSubMod5enablewomenmain> (Celebrating Women). It states: "In the 21 Century, a woman's place is no longer relegated to the home . . . She can contribute to the community, home, workplace and nation."

[71] Initial Report, para. 4.11.

[72] AWARE has urged the conducting of a study on the extent of workplace sexual harassment with a view to drawing up a code or law to deal with the problem, which appears evident from anecdotal evidence: *Remaking Singapore*. Dr. Kanwaljit Soin, a past AWARE president raised the issue in Parliament in 1996, noting that the new section 13 of the Miscellaneous Offences (Public Order and Nuisance) Act addressed the problem: 65 *SPR*, February 27, 1996, cols. 701–3. In contrast, the Malaysian Ministry of Human Resources launched a Code of Practice on the Prevention and Eradication of Sexual Harassment in the Workplace in 1995 which is voluntary and contains no grievance procedure: Honey Tan Lay Eean, (Women's Centre for Change, Penang) "Measuring Up to CEDAW: How Far Short are Malaysian Laws and Policies?" http://www.wccpenang.org/CEDAW-SUHAKAM-honey.htm.

obligations.[73] General laws confer some protection upon women, such as the censorship regime banning pornography, which degrades and objectifies women, perpetuating sexual stereotypes.[74] The Criminal Procedure Code has gender-sensitive provisions allowing witnesses under 16 years of age to give testimony through live TV links for certain sexual offences, lessening the trauma of confronting their assailants.[75] Other gender-protective legislation includes the Women's Charter, authorizing courts to issue a Personal Protection Order (PPO) to family violence victims on the basis of a "balance of probability," the breach of which constitutes a criminal offence.[76] Further, the public/private dichotomy is not maintained in domestic violence cases[77] where hurt is caused or threats uttered as these are punishable in the same manner as hurt and criminal assault committed in non-domestic settings.[78] The Penal Code was amended in 1998 to impose harsher penalties for assaults upon foreign domestic workers or maids, who are mostly women.[79] Indeed, the High Court in *PP v. Chong Siew Chin* recognized that vulnerable women like domestic maids needed legal protection for abuses committed "in the privacy of the home where offences are hard to detect". Yong C. J. treated mental abuse as an aggravating sentencing factor, considering deterrent sentences necessary to inhibit maid abuse and to address the erosion of Singapore's international reputation flowing from the "disgraceful conduct" of maid abuse.[80]

Prior to Independence, the PAP actively campaigned on a socialist platform which included promotion of women's rights.[81] Its 1959 manifesto criticized patriarchy, promising to enhance women's status within a socialist society

---

[73] Foreign Affairs Minister Jayakumar stated in 1996 that CEDAW's provisions accorded with existing law, there being no "imminent need to take any further measures": 65 *SPR*, 18 January 1996, col. 444. The Singapore representative in presenting the country reports admitted there was "room for improvement": 2001 CEDAW Report, para. 56.

[74] Initial Report, paras. 6.4–6.9. The Advertising Practice Code provides that "no advertisement should, by claim or implication, unfairly discriminate against, cast in poor light or denigrate any race, religion or sex."

[75] Section 364A of the Criminal Procedure Code, was first utilised in *PP v. Norli bin Jasmani* Criminal Case No. 17 of 1996 involving an uncle's alleged rape of a minor girl.

[76] Women's Charter (Cap. 353), sections 64, 65.

[77] See generally Kumaralingam Amirthalingam, *A Feminist Critique of Domestic Violence Laws in Singapore and Malaysia*, Asia Research Institute, Working Paper Series 6 (July 2003), http://www.ari.nus.edu.sg/wps/2003wps06ft.pdf.

[78] Women's Charter (Cap 353), para. 19.5.

[79] Pang Gek Choo, "Tougher penalties for maid abuse," *Straits Times*, 21 April 1998, 1.

[80] *Public Prosecutor v. Chong Siew Chin* (2002) 1 SLR 117 at 127A-H.

[81] Its election programme stated that the emancipation of women was part of the PAP's five year plan, including the passage of monogamous marriage laws although "(s)uch law however will not apply in those cases where there is a conflict with their religious beliefs." Dr. Toh Chin Chye, 12 *Singapore Legislative Assembly Debates, Official Report*, January–June 1960, col. 469.

and to ensure equal pay for equal work. PAP Member of Parliament Chan Choy Siong blamed "feudalistic" and "colonialistic" ideas and systems for oppressing women who were regarded as "suitable for work in the home and not outside in society", treating career women as "beautiful decorations"[82]and women generally as "pieces of meat put on the table for men to slice."[83] In 1961, the PAP government adopted the Women's Charter in satisfaction of electoral promises, although care was taken to ensure that solutions to women's problems did not contravene "their religious beliefs".[84]

The Charter essentially regulates marriage rights and responsibilities, ensures both spouses' legal equality and safeguards women's and children's rights. It departed sharply from existing practice by institutionalizing monogamous marriages as the societal norm, eradicating "the previous evil custom"[85] of polygamy, while carving an exception for Muslims.[86] Although polygamy was considered part of the Chinese religion of ancestral worship by a colonial Straits Settlement Court of Appeal, no similar exemption was made for the Chinese community in independent Singapore.[87] By outlawing polygamy

---

[82] Chan Choy Siong, 12 *Singapore Legislative Assembly Debates, Official Report*, November–July (1960–61), col. 1200.

[83] Chan Choy Siong, 12 *Singapore Legislative Assembly Debates, Official Report*, January–June 1960, col. 443 quoted in Zuraidah Ibrahim, "Women, Where Art Thou?" *Straits Times*, July 17, 1999, 53.

[84] Chan Choy Siong, 14 *Singapore Legislative Assembly Debates, Official Report*, November–July (1960–61), col. 1201. Polygamous marriages were permitted under Chinese customary law but while the Chinese were to abide by modern norms, the Muslim community could retain its Islamic traditions.

[85] Chan Choy Siong, 12 *Singapore Legislative Assembly Debates, Official Report*, January–June 1960, col 443. The Straits Settlement Courts had recognized Chinese polygamous unions for purposes of succession and legitimacy among native inhabitants whose religion permits polygamy: see *In the matter of the Estate of Choo Eng Choon, Deceased, Choo Ang Chee v. Neo Chan Neo, Tan Seok Yang, Cheang Cheng Kim, Lim Cheok Neo, Mah Imm Neo and Neo Soo Neo*, (1911) XII SSLR 120.

[86] Islam endorses polygamy under certain conditions. A Muslim M. P. stressed that while Islam permits polygamy, the law itself does not encourage this: Inche Yaacob bin Mohamed, 12 *Singapore Legislative Assembly Debates, Official Report*, January–June 1960, cols. 463–4.

[87] Braddell J, in interpreting a Civil Procedure Code (1907) allowing widows "who were of a religion 'allowing polygamy'" to prepare petitions for probate and administration, stated that this provisions was not confined to Muslims or the Mahomedan religion. He stated: "The basis of the Chinese religion is ancestral worship, and their marriage laws appear to me to be directed to creating a line of male issue to perform this worship, the justification in a moral sense for a man taking a secondary wife while his faith casts upon him of securing the performance after his death of the worship of his ancestors, and therefore polygamy may be said to be an element in the religion of the Chinese." *In the matter of the Estate of Choo Eng Choon, Deceased, Choo Ang Chee v. Neo Chan Neo, Tan Seok Yang, Cheang Cheng Kim, Lim Cheok Neo, Mah Imm Neo and Neo Soo Neo* (1911) XII SSLR 120 (Straits Settlement Court of Appeal). See Leong Wai Kum, "Chinese Customary Marriages," in *Family Law in Singapore* (Singapore: Malayan Law Journal, 1990), 62–95.

to reflect "modern views of society,"[88] preventing easy divorces and declaring the same rights in running the house, the Charter sought to re-align the gender power imbalances at home and court. It regulates divorce-related matters, enforces maintenance orders and addresses domestic violence.[89]

Official Policy Towards Women in General

Although promoting women's issues constituted an integral part of PAP election strategy in pre-Independence Singapore, between Independence and 1984 there were no female parliamentarians. In July 1989, the PAP established a Women's Wing to focus on women's issues.[90] The official current policy[91] is to consider women, comprising over 50 percent of the total population as of June 2000,[92] as part of the mainstream of society pursuant to the espoused policy of 'meritocracy,' consonant with Confucianist values (*ren ren wei xian*). This is distinguished from treating women like "a minority or disadvantaged group,"[93] a special interest group[94] accorded affirmative action.[95] This peculiar understanding of meritocracy extends to providing equal access and opportunity for all in relation to education, employment and health care, thus creating an 'enabling environment' wherein women can realize their potential in public life.[96]

Reference is made to 'traditional Asian values' in conjunction with 'the importance of the family' to justify government policy, although these values are not specifically identified.[97] In the educational context, the initial state

---

[88] Lee Siew Choh, 12 *Singapore Legislative Assembly Debates, Official Report*, January–June 1960, col. 454.

[89] 1996 amendments to the Women's Charter brought these provisions into force: Initial Report, para. 4.7. There has been some public debate about the possibility of renaming it the Family Charter, to eradicate its chauvinistic elements, particularly in relation to the provisions of the maintenance of wife and children. The government's rationale was that since Asian values placed husbands as household heads, male pride would not allow men to claim maintenance. On discussing the needs of the 1800 househusbands in Singapore, see 75 *SPR*, 1 October 2002, cols. 1091–4. A Family Charter would seem apt, given that many men work for female superiors or marry women with higher incomes: "Time to Rename It the Family Charter," *Straits Times*, January 27, 2002.

[90] This revived the PAP Women's League, formed in 1956.

[91] For an overview, see Jean Lee, Kathleen Campbell and Audrey Chia, *The 3 Paradoxes: Working Women in Singapore* (Singapore: Association of Women for Action and Research, 1999).

[92] As of June 2000, Second Report, para. 3.

[93] Initial Report, para. 3.2.

[94] 2001 CEDAW Report, para. 57.

[95] Article 4 CEDAW contemplates the adoption of temporal special measures which Singapore eschews, apart from employment regulations aimed at protecting maternity: Initial Report, paras. 1–5.2.

[96] Ibid., para. 22.2.

[97] Ibid., para. 6.1.

report before CEDAW affirms that family life education recognizes the mutual parental child-raising responsibilities.[98] In reversing past policy, to underscore that home-making is not solely a woman's responsibility, from 1993 both boys and girls could study home economics and technical studies in schools.[99]

Certain inegalitarian gender-biased policies[100] contrary to the espoused meritocracy policy have, in the past, been justified as consonant with Asian values,[101] three of which were regularly raised in public discourse: the one-third quota on female medical students; providing certain civil servant medical benefits (MSO) to males only (even though females constitute 54 percent of civil servants);[102] and providing automatic citizenship for spouses and children of male Singaporeans but not the foreign husbands or children of female Singaporeans.[103]

For example, the 'basic philosophy' of the MSO scheme was that this "should reflect the values and practices of our Asian society where the husband

---

[98] Ibid., para. 6.16.

[99] Ibid., para. 6.22. Previously in 1984, the government had barred secondary schoolgirls from taking technical studies, requiring them to take home economics to train them for their future roles as wives and mothers. Tamney, *Struggle over Singapore's Soul*, 136.

[100] It would be remiss not to note that certain policies discriminate against men such as that of compulsory military service for male Singaporeans, which nevertheless entitles men to certain salary and tax benefits and to form social networks, unavailable to women: 61 *SPR*, 3 December 1993, cols. 1193–5 and a shorter period of paternity leave for fathers (3 days), as compared to maternity leave (2 months): "Three Days' Paternity Leave for Civil Servants," *Straits Times*, August 28, 2000.

[101] Dr. Anne Kendrick Tan, President, Association of Women Doctors (Singapore), "Why the Discrimination?" *Straits Times*, June 20, 2003.

[102] In 1993, Minister Richard Hu justified this policy as preserving "the social structure by supporting the principle of husband as head of household," noting that men traditionally are the chief breadwinners: 61 *SPR*, 11 November 1993, col. 1009ff. This was reiterated in 2000 by Deputy PM Lee Hsien Loong who said that the government policies should "follow, rather than lead social changes" in matters as basic as "the family structure": 75 *SPR*, 31 October 2002, col. 1461. AWARE criticised this policy as constituting a blot of Singapore's "reputation and image": Tisa Ng, President, AWARE, "Unequal Benefits a Blot on Government Image," *Straits Times*, May 25, 2002. In September 2002, a parliamentary committee stated that the civil servants medical benefits policy breached the ILO Equal Remuneration Convention, which Singapore ratified in 2002. The official response was that differences involved were minimal and that if a female MSO officer is divorced or widowed or her family's sole supporter, she also receives this subsidy. Joyce Chia (for Permanent Secretary, Prime Minister's Office) and Ong-Chew Peck Wan (for Permanent Secretary, Ministry of Home Affairs), "All Officers Get Similar Perks," *Straits Times*, June 27, 2003.

[103] The Ministry of Home Affairs is apparently reviewing Singapore's citizenship laws, engaging in comparative study to "keep up with the times while still preserving our traditional values": "All Officers get Similar Perks," *Straits Times*, June 27, 2003. Initial Report, para. 2.3 justifies the necessity of reservations to art. 9(2) "to ensure our immigration policy remains in line with our Asian tradition where husbands are the heads of households". For the instrumental justification for refusing to review art. 122(1) of the Constitution which differentiates between overseas birth by granting citizenship by descent only to children of male Singaporeans, see Wong Kan Seng, 75 *SPR*, October 1, 2002.

is responsible for taking care of the family." While appreciating the importance of families as basic social units, the CEDAW Committee expressed concern that granting the husband legal status as household head might be interpreted "to perpetuate stereotyped gender roles in the family,"[104] reinforcing discrimination against women.

The government has indicated that not all policies are writ in stone and that "societal values change."[105] However, one might argue that the economic progress Singaporean women have achieved is not consonant with the social-political state of affairs as "the Government insists in upholding and preserving the patriarchal system, choosing tradition over civic values enshrined in the Constitution and embedded in our national pledge."[106] Nevertheless, recent policy reversals relating to the female medical quota, gender-biased citizenship laws and the MSO scheme indicate a progressive mindset which is willing to slaughter culturally entrenched 'sacred cows' which elevate the man as household head, as where medical benefits for all civil servants were recently equalized. In announcing this policy reversal, Prime Minister Lee Hsien Loong in August 2004 noted that "Norms are changing. Ten years ago, we could not imagine a young women's team wanting to climb Mount Everest."[107]

The Legal-Politico Culture and the Lack of a 'Rights Culture'

Appreciating the political context helps contextualize the enquiry. First, the PAP's political hegemony (and particularly that of Senior Minister Lee Kuan Yew) is such that their opinions must be accorded greater weight, as these are easily translated into law and policy.[108] The PAP has long discarded its original socialist leanings,[109] abandoning its pragmatic approach to government in the

---

[104] 2001 CEDAW Report, para. 79.

[105] Joyce Chia (for Permanent Secretary, Prime Minister's Office) and Ong-Chew Peck Wan (for Permanent Secretary, Ministry of Home Affairs), "All Officers Get Similar Perks," *Straits Times*, June 27, 2003.

[106] Irene Ng, 75 *SPR*, October 1, 2002, col. 1130.

[107] "Major Changes ahead with PM's bold vision," *Strait Times*, August 23, 2004, 1.

[108] For example, Senior Council and PAP MP K Shunmugam cited before a judicial proceeding Prime Minister's Lee Hsien Loong's 2004 National Day Rally speech as though it was determinative to argue that Singapore welcomed the setting up of a casino as part its tourism initiative, even though this matter is controversial and was in September 2004 subject to ongoing public debate: 'Court rules in favour of foreign casino', *Straits Times*, August 26, 2004. The relevant case is *Liao Eng Kiat v. Burswoods Nominees Ltd* (2004) Singapore Court of Appeal (SGCA) 45.

[109] As noted by Tamney, *Struggle over Singapore's Soul*, 29, the 1959 PAP's Manifesto spoke of the need to abolish "unjust inequalities of wealth and opportunity" while the 1982 Manifesto promised a society where rewards are "in accord with each Singaporean's performance and contribution to society."

1980s and articulating a new neo-Confucian or 'Asian values' communitarian-based ideological approach to governance.[110]

The possibility of seeking a remedy for an article 12 equal protection claim through judicial review has been alluded to officially.[111] However prospects of constitutional litigation remain minimal. In fact, no test cases on gender discrimination have been brought and AWARE considers that the lack of an explicit gender discrimination clause in article 12 has facilitated the construction of non-gender-neutral policies.[112] Several factors may explain the paucity of civil rights litigation. First, the general population lacks rights consciousness, perhaps due to unfamiliarity with legal processes or the lack of empirical success in suits challenging the constitutionality of government action. The government has won all notable constitutional cases, even in the exercise of broad executive powers which denude criminal process rights in order to safeguard public order.[113] Given the judicial deference to communitarian concerns like social order, judicial review is not an attractive option.[114] Consequently, activist groups have generally adopted a more low-key persuasive approach when seeking reform.[115]

The second factor is the political culture, associated with 'Asian values' or the 'Singapore school' that is constructed and espoused by the political elites. These values include deference to community interests, social harmony and respect for authority.[116] For example, the government urged dialogue over litigation to resolve the 2002 '*tudung* controversy', where four Muslim schoolgirls who wore headscarves were suspended from attending school for breaching educational policy.[117]

---

110 See generally Chua Beng Huat, *Communitarian Ideology and Democracy in Singapore* (London: Routledge, 1995).

111 Initial Report, part I, paras. 1.2, 4.2. Minister Lee Yock Suan, in defending the challenged constitutionality of the female medical quota, said that N.M.P. Kanwaljit Soin could "put this to a test in a court of law": 63 *SPR*, August 25, 1994, col. 486.

112 *Remaking Singapore*. The CEDAW Committee has expressed concern about wage differentials and the possibility that this was due to gender discriminatory attitudes in public and private sectors: 2001 CEDAW Report, paras. 85–6.

113 See Michael Hor, "Singapore's Innovations to Due Process," *Criminal Law Forum*, 12 (2001) 25–40.

114 Thio "'An i for an I'".

115 Li-ann Thio, "Rule of Law within a Non-Liberal Communitarian Democracy: The Singapore Experience," in *Asian Discourses of Rule of Law*, ed. Randall Peerenboom (London and New York: Routledge, 2004) 183, esp. 193–201.

116 See generally Anthony J. Langlois, *The Politics of Justice and Human Rights: Southeast Asia and Universalist Theory* (Cambridge: Cambridge University Press, 2001).

117 As yet, this matter has not been litigated. "Muslims Urged to Discuss Tudung Issue: Legal Action Is Not the Way to Resolve Matters Says MP Zainul Abidin Rasheed" *Straits Times*, January 28, 2002.

This cautiousness towards cultivating a rights-oriented culture translates into a reticence towards institutionalizing complaints mechanisms, as focal points for specific concerns,[118] because these might exacerbate ethnic tensions.[119] Aggrieved citizens are urged to utilize informal *ad hoc* general feedback channels or raise matters with Members of Parliament, and to eschew adversarial litigiousness.[120] Further, the government position is that possible rights claims and concerns could be addressed through soft regulatory codes and mediation rather than through binding legal regulations.[121] A proposal to create a complaints-handling watchdog body, similar to an Equal Opportunity Commission was rejected; instead, the current piecemeal 'promotional and educational approach' that seeks to 'nudge employers down the path' is preferred.[122] Further, no specific body was given the responsibility for examining gender discrimination complaints after Singapore became party to CEDAW and the ILO Equal Remuneration Convention on Equal Pay for Equal Work in 1995 and 2002 respectively, despite calls for a Women Affairs Ministry or dedicated national body to promote women's full participation in society.[123] The government, in refusing to accede to CEDAW's individual communications optional protocol,[124] prefers to limit its international obligations to submitting periodic reports before international bodies.

---

[118] M. P. Irene Ng noted that Singapore prefers to promote employment standards by persuasion rather than coercive institutionalised methods: 75 *SPR*, April 2, 2002, col. 179.

[119] Irene Ng, "Discrimination: Maybe Watchdog Body Can Help," *Straits Times*, February 18, 2001, 37.

[120] The Committee on the Family, which reports to MCDS, is a feedback avenue for women's issues: Initial Report, para. 3.4. When Opposition MPs raised the issue of establishing a Board of Equal Rights to allow all citizens to complain of unfair discrimination, the official response was that sufficient redress availed through judicial review or through contacting MPs or government ministries who take appeals concerning rights violations "very seriously": 69 *SPR*, June 30, 1998, cols. 380–1.

[121] For example, a set of tripartite guidelines on Non-Discriminatory Job Advertisements were adopted in response to complaints expressed in national newspapers, by the Manpower Ministry, National Trade Unions Congress and Singapore National Employers' Federation. Text available at http://www.mom.gov.sg. Prohibited grounds of discrimination (subject to exceptions) include age, gender, marital status, race or religion. Second Report, para. 7.6, avers the efficacy of these guidelines; as of October 2000, less than 1 percent of such advertisements stipulate criteria such as gender, age or race.

[122] This Manpower Minister rejected this, fearing it would make workplace culture more litigious: "'No' to Legal Body to Fight for Equal Opportunities," *Straits Times*, April 4, 2002.

[123] Irene Ng, 75 *SPR*, April 2, 2002, col. 181.

[124] Mrs. Yu-Fu Yee Shoon explained that Singapore had always maintained its right to sovereignty over domestic policy, contradicting the view that human rights are matters of international concern: Braema Mathi, "UN Convention on Women: Govt Has Reservations," *Straits Times* July 11, 2001, H10. The CEDAW Committee encouraged Singapore to improve its complaints procedure regarding constitutional equality rights, urging that it become party to the Optional Protocol: 2001 CEDAW Report, paras. 89, 94.

Neo-Confucianism, The Law and Women

Neo-Confucianism as the State Ideology

While Malay culture is closely related to Islam, Chinese ethnic identity is not affiliated with any specific religion, with the majority Chinese community, comprising more than 75 percent of the population, variously practicing Buddhism, Taoism, folk religion, Islam and Christianity.[125] Nevertheless, the government's current advocacy of Confucianism or neo-Confucianism, which shapes and informs public policy and law, seeks to draw strength from its close, if not exclusive identification with the Chinese community. This is so despite the universalist pretensions of neo-Confucian advocates.[126]

Background to the Shared Values White Paper

This espousal of 'Asian values' is most evident in the PAP government authored 1991 Shared Values White Paper, perceived as a backdoor attempt to re-introduce neo-Confucian values,[127] after the failed promotion of Confucian knowledge as part of the Religious Knowledge programme in secondary schools.[128] This White Paper declared itself a secular document, rejecting 'belief in God' as a shared value because the government was 'strictly neutral' on religious matters; it also correctly recognized that 'the faiths themselves are fundamentally different'[129] despite sharing certain virtues.

---

[125] Tamney, *Struggle over Singapore's Soul*, notes that Chinese parents are broadly accepting of their children's conversion to non-traditional Chinese religions, e.g., Christianity: at 34.

[126] Professor Wang Gung Gu, Director of the East Asia Institute, asserted that Confucianism was "a rational approach to cultivate a moral awareness" rather than a religion. In his opinion, one could be "a Confucian-Buddhist, Confucian-Christian or a Confucian-Muslim": Jason Leow, "Is Confucius Too Subtle for the Singapore Mind?" *Straits Times*, June 21, 1997. This view is clearly incorrect, as Confucianism as an ideology is incompatible with theistic faiths like Islam or Christianity. For example, see Leo Shirley Price, *Confucius and Christ: A Christian Estimate of Confucius* (New York: The Philosophical Library, 1951).

[127] Jon T. S. Quah, *In Search of Singapore's National Values* (Singapore: Times Academic Press, 1990).

[128] This was introduced in 1984 in an attempt to ground moral education, but abandoned by that decade's end: Tamney, *Struggle over Singapore's Soul*, chapter 2, "The Religious Studies Experiment," 25. The chief ministerial architects of this moral education programme, Lee Kuan Yew and Goh Keng Swee, appeared to ground it on their belief that world religions shared common core ethical values which would combat negative "hippy" values, "a libertine pre-occupation with self-gratification, the cult of living for today and for myself and to hell with others" (quoting the *Straits Times*, December 3, 1982): Tamney, *Struggle over Singapore's Soul*, 26. The Religious Knowledge programme included a module on Confucian ethics which proved to be unpopular: Tamney, *Struggle over Singapore's Soul*, 37. Only 17.8 percent of the Chinese community took Confucian ethics, as compared to 44.4 percent who took Buddhist Studies: Aline K. Wong, 54 *SPR*, October 6, 1989, col. 603. This programme was terminated and replaced with a civics/moral education programme in 1989: 54 *SPR*, February 22, 1990, col. 1040.

[129] Shared Values White Paper, para. 46.

Singapore imported Confucian scholars in the 1980s to draft a Confucian educational syllabus, in a non-organic top-down initiative to promote an ideology comporting with the ruling elite's dominant political values, "specifically in terms of paternalism, communitarianism, pragmatism and secularism."[130] Confucianism, which is oriented towards preserving tradition, was presented in curricular materials as capable of accommodating modernity[131]—the instructions were to modify the tradition to accommodate gender equality, in recognition of the women's movement and female contributions to economic development.[132]

The White Paper was a reactionary attempt to halt what were perceived to be the corrosive, degenerative values associated with Western liberalism, including excessive individualism, an adversarial distrust for government authority and litigiousness. The five essential but non-exhaustive 'core' values identified are 'communitarian' in orientation ("Nation before community and society above self" and "Family as the basic unit of society"); the emphasis on social order is evident ("consensus instead of contention" and "racial and religious harmony"). The individual is not the atomistic individual of the West (an island) but a situated being ("regard and community support for the individual"), existing in the centre of relationships (a flowing stream), defined by duties owed to family and nation.[133] Thus, the ideal family writ large is transposed as the operating societal framework, where the government head as *paterfamilias* discharges the trust of his citizen-charges by safeguarding their welfare. Indeed, while alluding to his predecessor's style of governance as "a stern father," the second Prime Minister sought to govern "like an elder brother."[134]

Confucian values supportive of the PAP's favoured political values were identified as 'relevant' while others, such as rebuking rulers stepping beyond

---

[130] Eddie C. Y. Kuo, "Confucianism as Political Discourse in Singapore: The Case of an Incomplete Revitalization Movement," in *Confucian Traditions in East Asian Modernity: Moral Education and Economic Culture in Japan and the Four Mini-Dragons*, ed. W. M. Tu (Cambridge, Mass, Harvard University Press, 1996), 304, 307.

[131] Tamney, *Struggle over Singapore's Soul*, notes that the Secondary Three text at page 5 states that "Confucian ethics cannot be lived out in Singapore in exactly the same way as in ancient China, even though the principles behind its teaching are valid for all time and place": 31–43.

[132] Tamney, *Struggle over Singapore's Soul*, 119. Thus, the Confucian programme was instrumental towards serving the economy and had to be consistent with a 'support for capitalism, tolerance of other creeds...and a modern view of women': Tamney, *Struggle over Singapore's Soul*, 26. For an apologetic defence, see Martin Lu, *Confucianism: Its Relevance to Modern Society* (Singapore: Federal Publications, 1983).

[133] Tu Wei Ming, "A Confucian Perspective on Human Rights," *Wu Teh Yao Memorial Lectures* (Singapore: UniPress, Centre for the Arts, 1995), 21.

[134] "Spore 'Strict, Not Authoritarian'," *Straits Times*, October 9, 1996. Goh made his "Big Brother" analogy in a *Le Monde* interview: "PM to Forge Europe–E. Asia Link Deeper Insight into What Makes Switzerland Tick," *Straits Times*, October 20, 1994.

heaven's mandate, were underplayed. This is evident in lauding "the concept of government by honourable men (*junzi*)" duty-bound to "do right for the people" and possessing the population's "trust and respect" in preference to Western notions of limited government.[135]

Confucianism and the Historically Subordinated Status of Women

The White Paper displays ambivalence towards wholly endorsing Confucian values, selectively de-emphasizing the less savory or democratarian aspects, revealing itself as a utilitarian exercise in appropriating legitimating values, driven by capitalist impulses,[136] serving the project of economic development and political control under strong PAP leadership.

Confucianism, an andro-centric brand of secular humanism[137] forged in a patriarchal agrarian society, has historically attributed an inferior status to women. The male superiority myth was perpetuated by 'cultural emphasis on continuity of the male lineage', 'filial piety' and 'the religious practice of ancestor worship'.[138] In times past, the Confucian filial piety ideal condoned polygamy and concubinage to facilitate the maximum production of family name-carrying male heirs.[139] Women were subjugated and devalued in this noxious environment, accorded lowly familial and societal status[140] and treated not as friends and partners but as unpaid labor and male baby producers.[141]

This cultural preference for male children, inspiring female infanticide or abortion of unborn female babies in countries like China,[142] continues.

---

[135] Shared Values White Paper, para. 42.

[136] For example, the "Confucian contempt for money-making" is regarded anachronistic. Downplaying the right to question authority may be seen as an attempt to legitimise an authoritarian state: Tamney, *Struggle over Singapore's Soul*, 38. Tamney notes that the Confucian and PAP political ideals differ as the former exalts moral development while the latter, economic gain: at 183.

[137] Confucius was notably reticent about life after death, focusing on how to live life: see Leo Shirley-Price, *Confucius and Christ*, 47–75.

[138] Aline Wong, *Women in Modern Singapore* (Singapore: University Education Press, 1975), 15.

[139] Notably, the failings of filial piety are evident in enacted laws requiring children to support their parents: Maintenance of Parents Act (Cap 167B). See "Parent's Tribunal an Important But Sad Milestone," *Straits Times*, May 30, 1996.

[140] The inferior traditional status of women also resulted in the sale of Chinese daughters to prostitution, as befitted familial interests: James Francis Warren, "Chinese Prostitution in Singapore: Recruitment and Brothel Organisation," in *Women and Chinese Patriarch: Submission, Servitude, and Escape*, ed. Maria Jaschok and Suzanne Miers (Hong Kong University Press, 1994), 77–107.

[141] Price, *Confucius and Christ*, 106–7.

[142] Toh Chin Chye, 12 *Singapore Legislative Assembly Debates, Official Report*, January–June 1960, col. 469 noted that the "female sex" had been taken for granted "out in the East (and) . . . in the past, girl babies were at a discount in China" such that it was "past practice that girl babies were disposed of by drowning."

Having female children in a Chinese family was commonly considered "very despicable."[143] Even in contemporary Singapore, the desire for male children has been invoked by men to justify bigamous liaisons[144] or caused women to lament the birth of second daughters.[145]

The traditional Chinese family as a corporate unit was accorded priority over individual happiness.[146] Pursuant to Confucian tenets, relations were hierarchically structured and inferior females were always dependent on a man, as a child, wife or widow, to her father, husband or son.[147]

The Smorgasbord or Selective Approach to Confucian Values in the Shared Values White Paper

The Confucian prejudice against women, apparently resting on the idea of the lofty and low position of men and women respectively (*nan zun nu bei*),[148] is repugnant in an age of human rights and egalitarianism. Indeed, the authors of the White Paper were conscious of treading upon two sensitivities. First, the suspicions that the paper chauvinistically constituted "a subterfuge for imposing Chinese Confucian values" on non-Chinese Singaporeans (and indeed, Chinese Singaporeans who reject Confucianism) had to be allayed.[149] Imposing 'Confucianism by another name'[150] would elicit disquiet. Second, that it would import harmful values traditionally associated with it, like gender subordination. To assuage these concerns, the paper declared Confucianism had "no monopoly of virtue" and required updating to suit national goals.[151]

Two Confucian-related values were expressly rejected. First, the 'Confucian concept of family ties' and differentiating between blood relatives

---

[143] Chan Choy Siong, 12 *Singapore Legislative Assembly Debates, Official Report*, January–June 1960, col. 443.

[144] "Serial Bridegroom," *Straits Times*, May 7, 2003.

[145] An irate Straits Times reader recounted the story of a woman who cried after having her second daughter; when asked why a son was so important she said "because everyone said so." Chen Siow Ying, "Need more women in power," *Straits Times*, January 2, 2001. Notably, the government's 1970s population control programme bore the slogan: "boy or girl, two is enough."

[146] Tamney, *Struggle over Singapore's Soul*, 117.

[147] Aline Wong, *Women in Modern Singapore*, 19.

[148] Kao Chen, "Is Confucianism Relevant in the New Economy?" *Straits Times*, February 7, 2001. Confucius had apparently complained in his analects that "women and petty men are hard to get along with, for they turn sullen if kept at a distance, but turn insolent when kept close."

[149] Shared Values White Paper, para. 39.

[150] Ibid., para. 42.

[151] Ibid. See also Neil Englehart, "Rights and Culture in the Asian Values Argument: The Rise and Fall of Confucian Ethics in Singapore," *Human Rights Quarterly*, 22 no. 2 (2000): 548–68; "Confucius' Teaching Needs to Be Updated: PM Goh," *Straits Times*, April 24, 1993. For example: "Women were not valued; only sons were valued. I think this is not applicable in today's context in Singapore or China."

and outsiders (*qin shu you bie*), manifesting in nepotism,[152] inimical to a clean, efficient bureaucracy.[153] Second, the "strictly hierarchical" structuring of traditional Confucian family relationships whereby "males take precedence over females, brothers over sisters and the first born over younger sons"[154] was inapt in Singapore where "sons and daughters are increasingly treated equally."[155] The fivefold basic familial relationships (*wulun*) were replaced with the White Paper's prescription that the ruler-ruled relationship should rest upon "trust,"[156] without explicitly addressing gender issues. Influential Senior Minister Lee Kuan Yew in 2001 noted that 'the Confucian practice of male over female, of a patriarchal society—this has to change.'[157]

Policy and Patriarchy

Despite the declared commitment to gender egalitarianism best embodied by Singapore's accession to CEDAW, a clear patriarchal mindset which Confucianism sustains is reflected in various structural and administrative policies and practices. For example, holding the man as household head 'is held up as a truth here.' This appeal to 'Asian values' at home and abroad as policy justifications is manifest in various practices sustaining a degree of 'enforced dependency', for example, preventing a woman from filing taxes because her husband was away, and where grants of subsidies, rather than welfare benefits, are structured "to reinforce the Confucian tradition that a man is responsible for his family."[158] This buttresses traditional gender roles within marriage and entrenches, rather than dismantles, cultural stereotypes which seek to control their subjects by assigning labels and roles, contrary to article 5(a) of CEDAW. Gender discriminatory laws and policies regarding citizenship and civil servant medical benefits co-existed uneasily with policies seeking to recognize women's economic contribution in the public sector and to support this

[152] Kao Chen, 'Is Confucianism Relevant in the New Economy?" *Straits Times*, February 7, 2001.

[153] Shared Values White Paper, para. 43.

[154] Ibid., para. 44.

[155] Ibid.

[156] Ibid., para. 41.

[157] Chua Lee Hoong, quoting Senior Minister Lee "Asian Attitude Towards Women 'Has to Change'," *Straits Times*, January 31, 2001. S. M. Lee apparently said, "We educated them. There is no turning back." In 1996, SM Lee apparently expressed the view that the rapid education of women had liberated them too quickly from "their traditional roles as wives, mothers and custodians of the next generation," upsetting traditions too rapidly: Tom Plate, "More Homeowners than Hard-liners: Singapore's Lee Kuan Yew Explains a Prosperity that Easily Abides Social Restrictions," *Los Angeles Times*, October 8, 1996.

[158] Lee Kuan Yew, *From Third World to First: The Singapore Story: 1965–2000* (Singapore: Singapore Press Holdings: Times Edition, 2000), 126.

through government-sponsored child care services[159] and the official characterization of parenting as a shared responsibility.[160] This reflects the ambivalence between traditional and modern views about women's role in society.

Islam, The Law and Women

The Muslim Community in Singapore: Conservative v. Progressive or Monolithic?

Given the global reach of the systemic subordination and oppression of Muslim women's human rights, which is of course not solely explained by religion, the compatibility of Islamic values with human rights standards remains heavily debated.[161] In rejecting the Universal Declaration of Human Rights as an imperialistic Western imposition, an Islamic Declaration of Human Rights has been adopted.[162]

Despite calls by scholars like Abdullahi An-Na'im[163] for cross-cultural discourse pursuant to filtering through the patriarchal cultural norms shaping the application of Islam values,[164] others maintain Islam was a "patriarchal

---

[159] Member of Parliament Lily Neo, in calling for better child care facilities, observed: 'Today women are not seen as housewives alone, but are expected to contribute to the two-income families of modern Singapore': 76 *SPR*, June 2, 1997, cols. 116–17.

[160] To help women to balance careers and family life, Prime Minister Goh asked that all Civil Servants be accorded unrecorded leave at full pay to look after sick children, warning that without a "mindset change" about male/female roles and shared child-rearing responsibilities, declining birth rates would continue: "Age Cap for Child-sick Leave Up from 6 to 12," *Straits Times*, July 7, 2002. The progressive extension of sick leave provisions to male civil servants was noted at 2001 CEDAW Report, para. 70.

[161] See generally Maznah Mohamad, "Feminism and Islamic Family Law Reforms in Malaysia: How Much and to what Extent?" *Asia Journal of Women's Studies*, 4 no. 1 (1998): 8–32; Jamal A. Badawi, *Gender Equity in Islam* (Plainfield, Indiana: American Trust Publications, 1995), http://www.jannah.org/genderequity/.

[162] The Islamic Conference of Foreign Ministers adopted the Cairo Declaration on Human Rights in Islam on August 5, 1990. All rights are subject to Islamic Syari'ah and certain rights privilege men, e.g. article 6 states that while woman is equal to man in human dignity, the husband is responsible for family welfare.

[163] He advocates intercultural discussions to revive the authentic Islamic values compatible with human rights norms, including women's rights: An-Na'im, ed., *Human Rights in Cross-Cultural Perspectives: A Quest for Consensus* (Philadelphia: University of Pennsylvania Press, 1995).

[164] This would include pre-Islamic Arabic culture. Writers and Islamic clerics have pointed out that Islam actually uplifted the status of women in these cultures: see, e.g. Mary Ali and Anjum Ali (Institute of Islamic Information and Education), "Women's Liberation through Islam," http://www.nusms.org.sg; MUIS Sermon, "Negative Perceptions Towards Muslim Women," November 3, 2000, http://www.muis.gov.sg/websites/khutbah/ser-031120.asp (visited September 5, 2003). The imperative of differentiating between practices oppressing women stemming from traditional customs, as opposed to those stemming from Islamic teachings, was stressed in MUIS Friday Sermon, "Women the Backbone of Society," February 28, 2003, http://www.muis.gov.sg/rservices/oom_files/K1024.doc (visited September 5, 2003).

religion from the beginning," given the unequal gender treatment in the divine text. Today, Muslim communities debate correct interpretations of Qur'anic law, as the examinations of Islamic law in Brueni and Indonesia in other chapters in this book demonstrate.[165] However, within Singapore, any such debates receive little media publicity. Independent voices purporting to represent an Islamic viewpoint not affiliated to Muslim government MPs or official religious bodies have been swiftly rebuked.[166] There is no active dissenting voice in relation to perspectives on Islam and human rights in modernity,[167] nor a dedicated female non-government organization comparable to Malaysia's Sisters of Islam, a group of professional Muslim women seeking to promote women's rights within the Islamic framework, or Indonesia's *Nahdlatul Ulama*, the biggest moderate Muslim group seeking to empower Muslim women.[168]

Notably in Singapore, a degree of self-critique is evident in the tone of certain apologist MUIS (Majlis Ugama Islam, or Islamic Religious Council of Singapore) sermons asserting that "Islam never terrorized the rights and status of women" and in fact "uplifted the status of women." Chauvinistic views of women as "a trial and enemy" stemmed from false, myopic misinterpretations of Islam by insecure men "trying very hard to defend their manhood by misinterpreting the *Al-Quran* and *Hadith*."[169] Indeed, sermons have urged men to share in household responsibilities while remembering their primary role to maintain their wives, and to "act kindly towards women"[170] who by nature are "in need of men's protection," even in an age of the working woman, many of whom may earn higher incomes then men.[171]

A female Singapore Member of Parliament asserted it "imperative" to hear the "progressive voices of Muslim women" in the "ongoing debate on the

[165] And see also: Jaclyn Neo Ling Chien, "Anti-God, Anti-Islam and Anti-Quran: Expanding the Range of Participants and Parameters in Discourse over Women's Rights and Islam in Malaysia," *UCLA Pacific Basin Law Journal*, 21 (2003): 29–74.

[166] For example, the views expressed on a website for Muslim news, Fateha.com (the voice of the Singapore Muslim Community), relating to such matters as the war against terrorism or the tudung controversy were criticised by government officials: "Leaders Warn against Fringe Groups," *Sunday Times*, January 20, 2002, 1. Other Muslim organisations have also been critical of Fateha: "Muslim Groups Slam Fateha," *Straits Times*, January 22, 2002, 1. See also "Muslims Here Reject Fateha Chief's Remarks," *Straits Times*, January 24, 2002, 1.

[167] There are various Muslim groups in Singapore, including the Federation of Indian Muslims, Pergas (Singapore Islamic Scholars and Religious Teachers Association), Mendaki and the Young Women's Muslim Association.

[168] Irene Ng, 75 *SPR*, April 2, 2002, col. 2125.

[169] MUIS Friday Sermon, "Cosmopolitan Women," 16 August 2002, http://www.muis.gov.sg/rservices/oom_files/K903.doc (visited September 5, 2003).

[170] MUIS Friday Sermon, "Cultivating the Seed of Love in Our Marriage," August 11, 2000, http://www.muis.gov.sg/websites/khutbah/ser-110820.html (visited September 5, 2003).

[171] MUIS Friday Sermon, "Women the Backbone of Society," February 28, 2003, http://www.muis.gov.sg/rservices/oom_files/K1024.doc (visited September 5, 2003).

interpretation of Islam."[172] The Muslim community's lack of spirited engagement in public debate is evident in the insular framing of official MUIS pronouncements on public policy matters like homosexuality in the public sphere[173] and reticence on matters like equal pay for equal work.[174] In pronouncing that SMS divorces were permissible, consonant with United Arab Emirates practice, Singapore's Syari'ah Court's Registrar nevertheless displayed ambivalence by stating "no right-thinking Muslim man" should consider "such an unethical act."[175]

Moderation is paramount in Singapore, particularly after the exposure of the *Jemaah Islamiah* bomb plot in December 2001,[176] prompting subsequent government declarations that Singapore Muslims were of the moderate persuasion[177] and assurances about the security of the Malay/Muslim community.[178] Certainly, no Singapore politician has publicly defended any Taliban-like

---

[172] Irene Ng, 75 *SPR*, April 2, 2002, Tenth Parliament (Threat of Terrorism) col. 2125.

[173] The MUIS statement on homosexuality stated that this was a sin in Islam and urged Muslims to reach out and coax people in their community out of their homosexual lifestyle: "Muis Spells Out Its Stand on Gay Issue," *Straits Times*, August 2, 2003. In contrast, the National Council of Churches spoke against the promotion of homosexual lifestyles in general: "Rejected Gay Practices not People: Church Council," *Straits Times*, July 30, 2003.

[174] Singapore signed the ILO Equal Pay for Equal Work Convention in 2002 although no dedicated national body was created to supervise its implementation. In contrast, the Malaysian political party PAS, which governs Terengganu and Kelantan states, considers that men with children should be paid more so that their wives could stay home and rear children, stating that the idea of working women was based on 'western concepts' and discouraged in Islam. The ruling UMNO party retorted that this degraded women and placed limits on their contesting elections: "PAS Leader Says Men Should Be Paid More," *Straits Times*, June 10, 2000, 46.

[175] Shaiffudin Saruwan, Registrar, Syriah Court, "Divorces Via SMS Discouraged," *Straits Times*, July 12, 2001.

[176] White paper, The Jemaah Islamiyah Arrests and the Threat of Terrorism (Cmd 2 of 2003). Newspaper reports presented the "weak minds" of the cell members as reasons explaining an increased susceptibility to extremist teachings: "How Their Weak Minds Got Twisted: Psychologists Say that Mind Control and Peer Pressure are Used to Snare Those Frustrated about Something," *Straits Times*, January 10, 2003. MUIS has also preached sermons along moderate lines: Friday Sermon, "Moderation in Islam," August 22, 2003, http://www.muis.gov.sg/rservices/oom_files/K1131.doc (visited 5 September 2003).

[177] "Challenge Every Extremist View ... Otherwise Such Ideas Will Take Root Here, Dr. Yaacob Warns Singaporeans: His Antidote for Extremism—Be Proactive," *Straits Times*, January 22, 2003. Prime Minister Goh warned that religious extremism marred inter-racial and religious interaction, and that "if religious communities refused to engage in mainstream secular society, this could fracture social cohesion": Speech on the Debate on the President's Address, Singapore Government Press Release, April 5, 2002. See Ahmad Osman, "Tolerant Form of Islam Best for Singapore," *Straits Times*, August 8, 2002.

[178] P. M. Goh, "Opening Remarks, Dialogue with Community Leaders on Impact of Arrest of Jemaah Islamiah Operatives," Singapore Government Press Release, January 28, 2002.

measure, in contrast with Malaysian politicians.[179] Muslim groups such as *Pergas* (Singapore Islamic Scholars and Religious Teachers Association) have also released a set of guidelines for moderate Muslims.[180]

On a more universal basis, religious communities do not present singular perspectives on internally contested issues. For example, the fervently debated practice of female genital mutilation (FGM) is, within Singapore, accepted largely as based on individual choice. Here, a mild symbolic version of FGM is practiced[181] and certain views hold that this custom lacks a religious basis and is not mandatory. Singapore Muslim women express views ranging from labeling the practice 'outdated and inhumane,' to likening it to a minor ear-piercing operation. A male MUIS spokesperson stated that this procedure "ennobled" women, ensuring they were not easily sexually aroused, which reflects a male attempt to control female sexuality.[182] This lack of consensus among Singapore Muslims indicates there is some room within this community for divergent views and practices, in matters left to communal self-regulation, falling within the 'private' sphere of religion.

Reserving Judgment

Domestic Exemptions from the General Law of the Land

The legal system accommodates some degree of legal pluralism in deference to Muslim sensitivities regarding dietary matters, prayer obligations and religious instruction through the AMLA, authorized by article 153. This regulates

---

[179] The PAS defended the Taliban's ban on women leaving home as constituting a protective measure, eliciting robust criticism: "PAS says Taliban's Treatment of Women was Right," *Straits Times*, March 7, 2002.

[180] Moderate Muslims have the self-confidence to stick to Islamic principles while coping with modern problems, and are willing to learn about other cultures and views not contrary to Islamic values. Pergas' expressed views are in line with those of the Islamic Religious Council of Singapore (MUIS): "Proposed Guide for Moderate Muslims," *Straits Times*, September 15, 2003.

[181] In Singapore, this involves nicking the prepuce: "Female Circumcision Alive and Well in S'pore," *Straits Times*, November 11, 2002. This may be contrasted with the more extreme versions practiced in parts of Africa and the Middle East: see generally Kay Boulware-Miller, "Female Circumcision: Challenges to the Practice as a Human Rights Violation," *Harvard Women's Law Journal*, 8 (1985): 155–178; Sabelle Gunning, "Arrogant Perception, World Traveling and Multicultural Feminism: The Case of Female Genital Surgeries" *Columbia Human Rights Law Review*, 23 (1991–92): 189–248; CEDAW General Recommendation 14, UN Doc A/45/38/1 (1990).

[182] Notably circumcision is also compulsory for Muslim men: "No Mutilation Here, Says Muis," *Straits Times*, March 21, 1994. The dangers of female sexuality also surfaced in MUIS sermons with respect to the need to constrain the free mingling between men and women, leading to loss of modesty and shame and "haram relationships": "Protecting One's Modesty," May 2, 2003, http://www.muis.gov.sg/rservices/oom_files/K1074.doc (visited 5 September 2003).

Muslim religious affairs and safeguards cultural particularities pertaining to personal laws. To some extent, the Muslim community is exempted from general laws; for example the Compulsory Education Act does not apply to *madrasahs* or Islamic religious education schools, although the state maintains an interest in ensuring minimal educational standards.[183]

Part III of the AMLA establishes the Syari'ah Court with jurisdiction over matrimonial and divorce related matters. Evidence may be taken through Muslim oaths and the decisions of the Court are generally immune from judicial review. Part IX lists Muslim-specific offences such as cohabitation outside marriage (section 134), and enticing an unmarried woman from the *wali* or lawful guardian (section 135). Testamentary disposition is to accord with Muslim law (sections 111–112).

Part II establishes the Majlis Ugama Islam or MUIS (Islamic Religious Council of Singapore) as a body corporate. This statutory body came into being in 1968 and advises the President on Islamic matters.[184] Conducting *in camera* meetings, its principal functions include collecting tithes (*zakat*), administering the Mosque Building Fund, *halal* certification and Mecca pilgrimages (*haj*). It oversees Islamic religious education and religious schools (*madrasahs*) and maintains a registry of converts. Muslim societies select Majlis members, but the state is involved as the Singapore President, advised by the Cabinet, issues these appointments and can terminate these in the public interest. The Singapore President must consult the Majlis before appointing the Singapore Mufti (highest religious leader). The Majlis Legal Committee is empowered to issue *fatwas* or rulings on Muslim law, presumptively based on the *Shafi'i* school of law, with acceptable sources listed in section 114.

Under the AMLA, Muslims enjoy a degree of cultural autonomy through the application of personal laws, entailing the 'privatization' of religion. State recognition of this degree of local autonomy actually buttresses patriarchal religious laws, for example those precluding women from certain public posts reserved for male Muslims, like the Registrar of Muslim Marriages and the post of Kadi.[185] In regulating marriage the AMLA also permits polygamous marriages, although statistics indicate that this is not the norm among Muslim men.[186]

---

183 Second Report, para. 6.10.

184 The website of MUIS is http://www.muis.gov.sg.

185 AMLA, ss 90(1), 91(1) and 146. Initial Report, para. 8.8.

186 Initial Report, para. 17.14. In 1997, less than one percent of Muslim marriages solemnised involved polygamy. A disapproving first wife may seek a divorce from the Syariah court if she is unhappy about her husband's second marriage. Polygamy is permitted by the Holy Quran at 4:3 which restricts the right of a man to only marry up to four women at one time:

The law does afford protection for Muslim women, as where section 119 provides that property acquired after marriage continues to belong to the wife, who may freely dispose of it without her husband's concurrence. At the same time, Islamic law privileges Muslim men by allowing them to divorce their wives upon pronouncement of the word '*talaq*'. Usually uttered before the Syari'ah court, the State regards this as a 'private' matter falling within the individual's sphere of autonomy.[187]

However, there are limits to religious expression, particularly in public spaces, as evident from the January 2002 '*tudung* controversy' when four female primary schoolgirls were suspended from school for breaching an educational policy directive mandating that only uniforms be worn in public school. This raised important issues as to whether the 'no *tudung*' rule violates religious liberty or, from a feminist perspective,[188] whether this liberates female Muslims from a repressive patriarchal practice—a view not publicly canvassed. The Mufti, Singapore's highest religious authority, considered that priority should be accorded education over *tudung*-wearing. The children's fathers rejected this view,[189] as did Pergas.[190] This range of views then clearly demonstrates dissent within the Muslim community.[191] The government's rationale was not to promote gender egalitarianism but to serve the instrumental purpose of preserving a common space to foster national solidarity. In this way, national goals limit the exercise of civil liberties, including religious liberties.[192]

Muhammad Sharif Chaudhry, "Woman and Polygamy," in *Women's Rights in Islam* (Delhi: S. Sajid Ali for Adam Publishers & Distributors, 1991), 83.

[187] Initial Report, para. 17.22: "the right to 'talaq' is entrusted to him by his Muslim faith which should be exercised with due care and after all efforts at reconciliation to save the marriage has failed."

[188] See Lama Abu-Odeh, "Post Colonial Feminism and the Veil: Considering the Differences," *New England Law Review*, 26 (1992): 1527–1537.

[189] Ahmad Osman, "Mufti Puts School First," *Straits Times*, February 6, 2002.

[190] Pergas is the Singapore Islamic Scholars and Religious Teachers Association. It stated that "No Muslim is allowed to remain complacent and feel satisfied with such hindrance towards fulfilling the religious obligation of the modest covering of aurat." Chua Lee Hoong, "Tudung Controversy a Test in Art of Negotiation," *Straits Times*, February 20, 2002. The English translation of the Pergas stand on the Hijab issue is available at http://www.pergas.org.sg/hijab-press2eng.html (visited 5 July 2003).

[191] Muslims also wrote letters to the press strongly supporting the government's stance and urging the fathers to send their daughters to madrasah (religious school) if he was insistent that his daughter wear the tudung. Norita Abdullah, "Send Daughter to Madarasah," *Straits Times*, January 8, 2003.

[192] See Thio "Recent Constitutional Developments," 355–66.

International Law and Reservations

To preserve this limited degree of Muslim communal autonomy,[193] Singapore appended reservations to CEDAW.[194] The effect of attaching reservations to articles 2 and 16 (modification or abolition of laws and customs that discriminate against women) "where compliance with these provisions would be contrary to their religious or personal laws" significantly limits CEDAW's potential reach in eliminating gender-biased stereotypes. The reservations allow the continued operation of inegalitarian Syari'ah-derived rules relating to marriage, divorce, citizenship and property disposition. For example, Islamic inheritance law stipulates that a male's share is double that of a female's.[195] While clearly discriminatory towards women, Singapore's initial CEDAW report explains that in Islam men and women bear differentiated responsibilities with the economic burden of family support falling solely on Muslim husbands.[196]

The CEDAW Committee considered that reservations to articles 2 and 16 constituted 'the very essence' of conventional obligations, impeding the CEDAW's full implementation.[197] It recommended that Singapore undertake comparative studies with a view to reforming personal laws and withdrawing the reservations.[198] While CEDAW subverts the public-private dichotomy in requiring government action to change public and private discriminatory

---

[193] On Singapore's reservations to CEDAW, see Thio Li-ann, "The Impact of Internationalisation on Domestic Governance: The Transformative Potential of CEDAW," *Singapore Journal of International and Comparative Law*, 1 (1997): 299–305.

[194] For Singapore's justifications of reservations to arts. 2 and 16 in aid of protecting minority rights, see Initial Report, paras. 2.2 and part II, para. 1.2. Other reservations relate to arts. 9, 11 and 29(2). Minister Jayakumar considered these reservations "not unusual," observing that Singapore took "international obligations seriously": 65 *SPR*, January 18, 1996, col. 443. When N.M.P. Kanwaljist Soin asked about national plans to comply with CEDAW, Minister Jayakumar stated that after studying existing laws, "we have already met the aims of the Convention", there being no "necessity" to amend the constitution, abolish discriminatory law or establish institutions to protect against discrimination: 65 *SPR*, January 18, 1996, cols. 444–6.

[195] Part VII of AMLA regulates property and s 114 lists a set of authoritative Islamic texts in relation to questions of succession and inheritance. Section 117(1) AMLA provides that when a wife dies intestate with her own property, preference is given first to her male children over 21, followed by her husband and then other relatives in this order: daughters, father, mother, brothers, sisters, uncles, aunts, nephews and nieces of the intestate. This shows a preference for male over female relationship in inheritance matters. On the Sunnite Law of Inheritance, see Asaf Iyzee, *Outlines of Muhammadan Law*, 4th ed., (Delhi: Oxford University Press, 1974), XIII, 390, 448.

[196] Initial Report, para. 17.33. Women under a man's responsibility include his wife, unmarried sisters, daughters, widowed mothers and grandmothers. Countries like Finland, Germany and Denmark criticized Singapore's reservations: Reservations and state objections available at http://66.36.242.93/html/singapore_t2_cedaw.php (http://www.bayefsky.com)

[197] 2001 CEDAW Report, para. 72.

[198] Ibid., para. 74. Singapore emphasised that Islamic views had been considered in formulating treaty reservations: CEDAW Press Release.

practices, its transformative potential has been blunted by appending extensive reservations to its most far-reaching clauses, in the name of preserving religious and/or cultural autonomy, thus placing religious or traditional values beyond law's reach. Insulating discriminatory practice from outside scrutiny has a regressive effect on women's rights. The often expressed countervailing point is that so called 'universal' human rights norms are actually culturally imperialistic impositions that impinge upon communal self-determination. However this culturally relative counter-argument masks the political fact that not all voices in the faith communities are accorded equal weight.

The Talaq Controversy: Censorship and Religious Patriarchy

Sense and Religious Sensibilities in Informing Censorship Rules

The administrative state, armed with licensing powers, regulates a great range of activities.[199] The exercise of such powers, such as those administrative rules governing censorship[200] may truncate the scope of constitutional liberties. Licences have been refused for plays, an aspect of constitutionally guaranteed expressive rights (article 14), which offend religious sensitivities.[201] Censorship has been protective of women by banning pornography.[202] As censor, the government acts cautiously,[203] reflected in the professed concern for racial and religious sensitivities in debates over state funding of the arts and the emphasis on prudent expenditure to avoid projecting 'wrong social values' or causing 'societal conflict'.[204]

---

[199] See, e.g., the Undesirable Publications Act (Cap 338) and Films Act (Cap. 107).

[200] There are a plethora of administrative rules governing censorship. Singapore's censorship model eschews liberal values and has in the past displayed sensitivity towards religious concerns. Notably, a Ministry of Information Communication and the Arts (MITA), September 2003 Press Release stressed that proponents for greater artistic freedom should be responsible and accountable and "be mindful not to offend the sensitivities of other members of society or undermine our racial and religious harmony": "Working Together Towards a Responsible and Vibrant Society," http://app.sprinter.gov.sg/data/pr/20030908-MITA.pdf (visited 5 September 2003).

[201] Pursuant to this, the government banned Salman Rushdie's *Satanic Verses*, and the movie The Last Temptation of Christ, which offended Muslims and Christians respectively: Ong Soh Fern, "Artistic Integrity vs Social Responsibility," *Straits Times*, November 1, 2000. See also "Three Scenes Cut from TNS' Play," *Straits Times*, December 4, 1999.

[202] One hundred internet porn sites were symbolically blocked out "as a statement of our values": MITA Minister Lee Yock Suan, 73 *SPR*, March 9, 2001, col. 557.

[203] Singapore Constitution mandates that freedom of expression may be restricted by concerns of public order or morality. For example, *Playboy* is banned, although the government in 2003 reversed the 1982 ban on *Cosmopolitan* magazine for its promiscuous values: "Singapore Really Is a Cosmopolitan City," *Straits Times*, September 10, 2003; "Censorship's Slow Reform," *Straits Times*, September 13, 2003.

[204] Nominated Member of Parliament Zulkifli, 73 *SPR*, March 9, 2001, cols. 532 at col. 541 and Minister Lee Yock Suan at col. 563.

The Talaq Controversy

It is instructive to examine the refusal to grant a licence to stage a play called *Talaq* in 2000 and the public debate that ensued. The play addressed marital violence within the Indian Muslim community, and questioned how a religious group may tolerate practices or attitudes deleterious to women.

In organizational terms, the granting of licences to arts groups is administered by the Public Entertainment Licensing Unit (Pelu), a division of the police, under the auspices of the Home Affairs Ministry, pursuant to the Public Entertainments Act (Cap 257). Pelu currently reviews all publicly held events, and incorporates law and order considerations like 'racial and religious sensitivities'[205] in deciding arts events licence applications.[206]

The term '*talaq,*' thrice uttered, enables a Muslim man to divorce his wife. This is an example of how Islam, run by a religious patriarchy, privileges men. The play *Talaq* questioned this practice in various respects, revolving round spousal abuse, marital violence and rape in the Indian Muslim community. It was autobiographical, based on the life of Nargis Banu who argued that the Qur'an conferred equal rights on both sexes: "I am trying to put across that some of these rights can be given back to women."[207] Through art, a Muslim woman was trying to present her views on the need to re-interpret the Qur'an, within the Islamic framework, to vindicate women's concerns.

Talaq Round One

Talaq was first staged in the Tamil language in 1998 and 1999. Even then, its controversial nature elicited death threats against the director Elangovan.[208] The script was cleared by the National Arts Council (NAC). Consequently Pelu granted it a licence over the protestations of Muslim groups like South Indian Jamiathul Ulama (SIJU), Tamil Muslim Jema'at,[209] the Federation of Indian Muslims and MUIS.[210] Jema'at President Mohd Ismail reportedly objected to the play's climax, a symbolic repudiation of Islam,[211] when Banu ends her marriage by throwing off her *hijab*, a long black Muslim robe

[205] In October 1998, in another play *Ikan Cantik* (*Beautiful Fish*) staged by Malay theatre company Teater Kami—6 actresses shaved their heads and used vulgar language: MUIS told *Life*! that going bald for a woman is haram (not permissible in Islam), even for art's sake. Clarissa Oon, "Muis shares the concern over Talaq play," *Straits Times*, March 12, 1999.

[206] Ho Peng Kee, 72 *SPR*, November 14, 2000, col. 1117.

[207] Braema Mathi, "Here Is My Story because I Want the Silence to Stop," *Straits Times*, December 13, 1998.

[208] Ong Soh Fern, "Artistic Integrity vs Social Responsibility," *Straits Times*, November 1, 2000.

[209] "A Story of Oppression, Not Just Sex," *Straits Times*, April 22, 1999.

[210] "Muis Shares the Concern over Talaq Play," *Straits Time*, March 12, 1999, L4.

[211] "You cannot discard clothes like that . . . It shows she is renouncing Islam": "A Story of Oppression, Not Just Sex," *Straits Times*, April 22, 1999.

designed to preserve female modesty. Elangovan explained that this disrobing, followed by Banu walking into a pool of green light, the color of Islam, was not blasphemous but symbolically represented "her discard of male oppression in her community."[212]

The 1998 staging was well-received, with two high ranking Muslim ministers being guests of honor.[213] The press reviews presented the play as an exploration into 'oppression, marital rape, arranged marriages, the duties of wives and husbands, and the culture of silence forced upon these women'.[214] It lamented the double standards extant in interpreting Muslim principles to favor males over females, whereby a Muslim wife with an adulterous husband was advised by her community to let the husband have fun with his mistress, as her dutifulness and attempts to please her husband would be rewarded in Paradise. It asked the Indian Muslim community why it was so easy to pronounce *talaq* over the wife, when Allah hates divorce, as in the play where the husband pronounced *talaq* when confronted with evidence of his adultery. Furthermore, the husband, in marrying a Hindu (i.e., outside the faith) received no community condemnation. The play thus exposes the patriarchal orientation of Muslim practice concerning marital relationships and how this buttressed female subordination within this faith community.

Talaq Round Two

Pelu refused to grant a licence to stage *Talaq* in English and Malay at the Drama Centre in 2000, deferring to expressed offended religious sensibilities; thus, "artistic experimentation ends where race and religious sensitivities begin."[215]

In attempting to mediate these competing perspectives, the NAC recommended allowing the play to proceed once certain references to Islam had been deleted, proposing that all publicity materials be accompanied by this disclaimer: "although the play is based on the experiences of an individual, it is not intended to reflect on or defame the Indian Muslim community at large." However, the MUIS considered this inadequate, and insisted that the play misrepresented Islam.[216] Indeed, certain members of the Indian Muslim Community considered it blasphemous and religious groups like SIJU called for a ban.[217]

---

212 Ibid.

213 These were Parliamentary Secretary for the Ministry of Communications Dr. Yaacob Ibrahim and Senior Minister of State for Education Sidek Saniff.

214 Braema Mathi, "Audience Cries over Double Standards," *Straits Times*, 28 December 28, 1998.

215 "No Child's Play," *Straits Times*, November 2, 2000.

216 Clarissa Oon, "Who Calls the Shots," *Straits Times*, November 18, 2000, 1, L6, L7.

217 The theatre company also refused to perform it before a specially arranged NAC panel as two members of a complainant group, the South Indian Jamiathul Ulama (SIJU) were members. The panel also included representatives from NAC, Pelu and MUIS. Teo Pau Lin, "No Go for Touchy Play," *Straits Times*, October 28, 2000.

SIJU Secretary Haji Ebrahim Marican said the play inaccurately depicted Islamic law which he interpreted as precluding marital rape charges: "In Islamic law, a husband cannot rape a wife as long as the marriage continues. He need not ask permission from his wife for sexual relations each time he wants to have it."[218] The play was "degrading to Muslim Indians" in suggesting that "Islamic law is not sufficient to solve Muslim problems."[219] This elicited two responses. Firstly, two female Muslims expressed views that a husband's conjugal rights could not be enforced by whim or force, but by the rule of law. Mumtaz Beum, a Muslim Indian marketing officer, watched the preview and considered that: "In Islam, a husband is not allowed to use force on his wife for sex. She must do it willingly. Mr Ebrahim got the religion wrong."[220] This was echoed by theatre group Agni Kootthus President Ms. S. Thenmoil, who opined that violation of conjugal rights should be addressed through marital counseling, terminating marriage or even polygamy, but not force.[221] Furthermore, both considered that the play did not exclusively deal with religion but with women's issues, being of interest to many women, irrespective of ethnicity.[222]

Evaluating the Decision not to Grant a Licence to Stage Talaq

Unsurprisingly, in deciding to refuse a licence for the performance in English and Malay, Pelu chose to attribute greater weight to MUIS's views, reflecting the premium placed by government on religious-racial harmony. However, this was not a tension *between* religious or ethnic groups, but rather *within* a single religious community whose membership includes those of Malay, Indian and Chinese ethnicity.

The Home Affairs Ministry made the final decision not to grant the licence, chiefly influenced by the play's "religious sensitivity."[223] Minister Ho explained that MUIS had "strongly objected" to the play as "it contained Qur'anic references and religious connotations that might give the audience

[218] Ibid., 3.

[219] Marican stated: "The drama distorted Islamic teaching by only quoting verses to suit the purpose of the organizer and excluding verses of the Holy Koran which protect women. Hence, the public will think that Islamic family law is lacking." Teo Pau Lin, "Plot Thickens over Talaq," *Straits Times*, October 20, 2000.

[220] Teo, "No Go for Touchy Play".

[221] Osman Sidek, "No Islamic Law Gives Licence for Marital Rape," *Straits Times*, November 7, 2000.

[222] Ms Mumtaz Begum was reported as saying: "The play has nothing to do with religion and it's not a disgrace to our religion. The character was just telling her story. Overall, there was no indecency, no vulgarities." Teo, "No Go for Touchy Play."

[223] Minister Lee Yock Suan, 73 *SPR*, March 9, 2001, col. 563.

a wrong impression of Islam." Thus, the relevant authorities had received "adverse feedback that the play was offensive and misrepresented the Indian Muslim community and Islam."[224] Furthermore, he admonished artistes to be "mindful of our social realities" and to "avoid creating racial or religious tensions."[225]

When asked by opposition Member of Parliament J. B. Jeyaretnam to make MUIS's objections public, the Minister merely indicated that MUIS had offered 11 reasons why the play was offensive, stating it was MUIS's prerogative whether to disclose its reasons and engage in public debate or to hold its peace.[226] Minister Ho further noted that since the proposal was to stage the play in English/Malay, this would reach a broader audience and might lead "people of other races" to have "an erroneous and lower impression of Islam," thus causing inter-racial misunderstandings.[227] When another Member of Parliament made the point that the licensed Tamil language performance had had English subtitles, Minister Ho maintained that the decision was justified since the "audience mix" and "impact" would be "vastly different."[228]

The play *Talaq* was not banned for reasons of obscenity or for substantive content, but because of its perceived impact, as it dealt with the politically explosive issue of whether Indian Muslim women were actually exploited. Indeed, the ban demonstrates the potency of religious sensitivity and the determinative weight it exerts in trumping competing claims of artistic freedom of expression. It also inhibits the ability of women, who are already in a weak position within a patriarchal religious order, to articulate their concerns. Although the play's author argued that it did not hit out at any race or religion but rather 'shows how some Indian-Muslim women live their lives and the ill-treatment they endure,'[229] the decision-makers gave this short shrift. This might contravene Singapore's CEDAW obligations to promote substantive and not merely formal equality and to modify socio-cultural patterns of conduct to remove prejudices about the inferiority of the female sex.[230] State action can in this case immunize a patriarchally controlled religious community from external human rights based critiques as well as from robust dialogue and debate from within that faith community.

---

224 Ho Peng Kee, 72 *SPR*, November 14, 2000, cols. 1117 at 1118.
225 Ibid., col. 1119.
226 72 *SPR*, November 14, 2000, col. 1120.
227 Ho Peng Kee, 72 *SPR*, November 14, 2000, cols. 1117 at 1118.
228 Jennifer Lee, 72 *SPR*, November 14, 2000, col. 1121.
229 Mathi, "Here Is My Story."
230 See articles. 2 and 5(a), CEDAW.

Concluding Observations

The CEDAW Committee's concluding observations expressed concern over Singapore's reservations which preserved Muslim personal law[231] and noted the potentially deleterious effects 'Asian values' about the family posed for women.[232] The Committee considered that the Singapore Government lacked a "clear understanding" of "gender mainstreaming" in relation to legislation and policies,[233] and manifested an insufficient awareness of how policies can buttress, rather than eradicate, culture-based gender stereotypes. It urged that policies be reviewed to prevent both direct and indirect discrimination.[234]

In an age of growing religiosity, the structural issues of how to delineate the spheres of religion and politics and to manage the co-existence of ethnic, religious and secularist groups within a multicultural nation remain pressing. In Singapore, there is no strict separation of religion and politics, but the neo-Confucianist national ideology is often proffered as an instrumental value to buttress economic development and sometimes to justify gender-biased policies. This entrenches the patriarchal mindset despite the fact that, as MP Irene Ng recently observed: "the last time I checked the Constitution . . . I did not see patriarchy being enshrined as one of its founding principles."[235] While article 12 constitutionally guarantees equality under the law, as do CEDAW norms, the extensive reservations to CEDAW and the lack of a dedicated institutionalized complaints mechanism has meant that certain gender discriminatory practices, inspired by 'Asian values,' go unchallenged.

In attaching reservations to CEDAW to allow the Muslim community some degree of communal autonomy, the legal tradition of deference to Religion allows law to buttress, rather than confront, authoritarian and patriarchal religious-based claims. Law strengthens such claims against competing women's concerns seeking to sift through patriarchal (as opposed to religious) dictate, in the hope of promoting women's rights within a religious framework.

In delegating the governance of private matters to religious communities, the state may be complicit in sanctioning oppressive and discriminatory religious practices, albeit in the name of communal self-determination or minority rights. The modern practice of separating law and religion into distinct

---

[231] CEDAW Committee, Concluding Observations: Singapore, CEDAW A/56/38 (2001), considering the Initial (CEDAW/C/SGP/1) and Second periodic report (CEDAW/C/SGP/2). Para. 74. ("Concluding Observations").

[232] Ibid., para. 79.

[233] Ibid., para. 83.

[234] "Discrimination against women" is defined in CEDAW article 1, which nullifies laws and policies with "the effect or purpose" of gender discrimination.

[235] Irene Ng, 75 *SPR*, April 2, 2002, col. 181.

jurisdictions does not merely restrict religion to a certain sphere; it also shores up a particular conception of religion.[236] The refusal of the state to intervene in deference to religion comes from accepting religion "as a sovereign, extralegal jurisdiction in which inequality is not only accepted but expected."[237] This flows from the public-private dichotomous ordering that rests on "the Enlightenment compromise that justified reason in the public sphere by allowing deference to religious despotism in the private."[238] The operation of constitutional equality provisions or human rights law within the 'private' religious sphere is thus precluded. Thus, law indirectly prefers the andro-centric claims of fundamentalists who discriminate in religion's name.

Law remains aloof from contested, plural views within religious communities, as the 'talismanic incantation of religion insulates the claims from critique.'[239] By preserving cultural stasis, hierarchical, patriarchal religions effectively enjoy legal protection against changes, pursuant to cultural exceptionalism or religious sovereignty, hindering internal reform towards more democratic and egalitarian practices.[240] Law consolidates and transfers power to religious elites in aspects of family, religion and culture, which are relegated to the 'private' sphere, beyond legal regulation. However, even this form of state non-intervention can entail state responsibility.[241] Indeed, conflict is inevitable as CEDAW purports to engage the private sphere by seeking alterations to religious or culturally influenced gender stereotypes, in defiance of claims of supreme religious authority, setting the stage for ideological conflict.

In deploying the legal technique of treaty reservations, invoking minority autonomy claims and refusing to institutionalize complaints procedures for gender discriminatory practices, the state privileges religious authority and immunises from scrutiny and effective redress its adopted neo-Confucianist ideology, insofar as this erodes women's rights. The state may have affirmed gender egalitarian norms in binding legal instruments, but it is hobbling slowly, feet still bound, in the direction of altering patriarchal mindsets, so integral to the project of vindicating gender equality.

---

[236] Madhavi Sunder, "Piercing the Veil," *Yale Law Journal* 112 (2003): 1421.
[237] Ibid., 1401.
[238] Ibid.
[239] Ibid., 1436.
[240] Ibid., 1408.
[241] In *Kitok v. Sweden* Communication No. 197/1985 of July 27, 1988, the Human Rights Committee refused the state's argument that it was not involved in the dispute between a Sami man and a Sami community. The state had enacted the 1971 Reindeer Husbandry Act delegating certain powers to the Sami community, including membership regulations. State responsibility was implicated by the Act's mere adoption.

INDEX